A THEOLOGY OF CHILDREN'S MINISTRY

BOOKS BY LAWRENCE O. RICHARDS

A New Face for the Church
Creative Bible Study
How I Can Be Real
How Far I Can Go
How I Can Experience God
How I Can Make Decisions
How I Can Fit In
69 Ways to Start a Study Group
Three Churches in Renewal
Reshaping Evangelical Higher Education
    (with Marvin K. Mayers)
A Theology of Christian Education
A Theology of Church Leadership
    (with Clyde Hoeldtke)
A Theology of Personal Ministry
    (with Gib Martin)
Discipling Resources Series
    (with Norman Wakefield)

A THEOLOGY OF CHILDREN'S MINISTRY

LAWRENCE O. RICHARDS

ZONDERVAN
PUBLISHING HOUSE
OF THE ZONDERVAN CORPORATION
GRAND RAPIDS, MICHIGAN 49506

A THEOLOGY OF CHILDREN'S MINISTRY
Copyright © 1983 by The Zondervan Corporation
Grand Rapids, Michigan

Library of Congress Cataloging in Publication Data

Richards, Larry, 1931–
   A theology of children's ministry.

   Includes bibliographical references and index.
   1. Christian education of children. 2. Church work with children. I. Title.

BV1475.2.R48   1983   259'.22   82-21975
ISBN 0-310-31990-0

Edited by Diane Zimmerman and Maureen W. LeLacheur
Designed by Paul M. Hillman

Printed in the United States of America

CONTENTS

FIGURES

PREFACE

How should we approach an exploration of ministry with children? One approach, a traditional one, has been to focus on methods to be used in the church. We've studied lists of characteristics to see how to arrange our classrooms and how many times the group should move around during the Sunday school hour. We've learned how to tell stories, and how to make sure that our curriculums are Bible based and Christ centered. And now and then we've stepped beyond Sunday school to look at children's clubs and choirs. This approach may have a place. But I believe it has not dealt realistically with issues we must face if we are to build meaningful patterns of ministry with children.

First of all, we need to realize that ministry with children, as all ministry, must be evaluated from the twin perspectives of theology and distinguishing characteristics of learner. The "how" of any effective ministry must grow out of a theological understanding of what it is we are trying to do and the nature of the persons with whom we are dealing. Part 1 of this book, chapters 1 through 9, turns first to Scripture to see what Old and New Testaments teach us about ministry with boys and girls. It then looks at critical areas in child development that help us further understand how we must shape ministry with children.

Second, with the foundations for children's ministry explored, we turn to the three primary settings in which ministry must be focused. When we understand how faith is communicated to children and how children learn, we see immediately that anyone concerned with helping boys and girls come to and grow in Christian faith must be concerned with three settings for ministry. These settings are the home, the church, and the school. Each of these settings is explored in part 2, chapters 10 through 19. In the unit on the home we explore ways that those responsible for ministry with children can move now to help parents nurture their boys and girls. In the unit on the church we explore what must be done in church agencies to bring patterns of present ministry into harmony with biblical ministry principles. In the unit on the school, we look at the suddenly explosive Christian school movement and sketch the issues that its leaders must deal with if the Christian school classroom is to become a location for effective ministry rather than simply a place for instruction.

11

Finally, we focus on how to use the Bible in ministry with children, looking at principles of teaching that can be used in any setting to help boys and girls respond to God's truth. Special attention is given in part 3, chapters 20 through 23, to principles for using Bible stories that take us beyond storytelling to more significant kinds of learning. The chapters also discuss and illustrate shaping the learning process for the total class or session to link Bible truths to the present experiences and needs of boys and girls.

Who is this textbook for? First of all, for the lay or professional person charged with guiding ministry to children. It is for Christian education boards, Christian school administrators, and college students. It is for anyone who is concerned with the spiritual development of boys and girls, anyone who wants to go beyond the superficial "how" to first grasp the foundational "why" and *then* go on to understand how.

I do not consider this, or any of my other textbooks, to provide "the answer." However, I hope this book will provide those who minister with children a theological framework within which to think about their ministry, and will suggest a number of practical approaches to better love and nurture the next generation of Jesus' people.

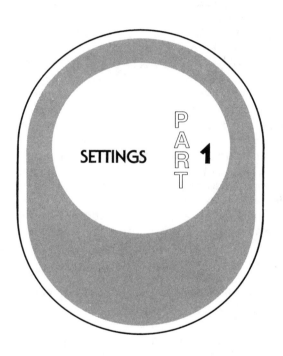

SETTINGS

PART 1

A *framework for ministry* is a theoretical base: a set of beliefs or assumptions concerning the nature of ministry and/or the nature of those being ministered to. Such frameworks are ministry-shaping; they determine the way we go about ministering whether or not we have stated our presuppositions.

Traditionally Christian ministry to children has developed within the structures of the congregations' agencies, and thinking about ministry has paralleled thinking about childhood education through the public schools. Courses in philosophy of Christian education have traced our nurture programs back to the same educational philosophers looked to for the roots of secular education.

Two things give focus to our exploration of frameworks. First, we are concerned with *theology*. We want to look back into Scripture and church history to see if there are theological imperatives that must be understood if we are to give healthy shape to our ministry with children. Second, we are concerned with *childhood*, and with understanding just what it is about these youngest of human beings that makes them something other than "little adults." Ministry with children must recognize their developing abilities to understand and to respond.

In this first section then we'll look at Scripture to attempt a theological formulation of essential elements in our nurture of children. We will also look at the data gathered by behavioral scientists about children's development that bears directly on how we minister to children in a faith-building way. Of particular concern, because of their direct revelance to our assumptions about children's ministry, are

1. Cognitive development—how children think
2. Social development—how children relate to and learn from others
3. Moral development—how children understand and integrate moral (and abstract religious) concepts

Some traditional areas (such as children's physical development) are not treated here because they lack direct relevance when our inquiry focuses on framework rather than on the size of chairs in the Sunday school or the number of times active and passive activities should alternate for the four-year-old.

These chapters may appear to some to be too "theoretical." Like the rest of the text, they are geared to those who have a serious interest in understanding the bases of ministry with children and developing practices that have clear theological and developmental roots. It is from our theology and our understanding of the nature of boys and girls that effective ministry on any level must grow.

PART 1

FRAMEWORK

A Theological Framework for Ministry

Nurture in the Old Testament
Nurture in the New Testament
The Role of Scripture in Nurture
The Nurture Process

A Developmental Framework for Ministry

The Developmental Perspective
Cognitive Potentials of Children
Social Relationships of Children
Moral Development in Children
An Integrated Perspective

What we search for in the Scriptures is insight into how to help children grow in faith. We seek to identify factors that encourage the free choice of good and openness to the supernatural working of the Spirit of God. We search and find nothing that

NURTURE IN THE OLD TESTAMENT

guarantees us success. But what we find does help us see a far wider meaning to "ministry with children" than is usually understood.

As we approach the Old Testament we need to remember it is not a simple document. It is complex. And it is a monument to failure.

The Old Testament story unfolds gradually, spanning centuries of sacred history. It carefully documents God's progressive revelation to man. And it gives us a series of pictures: images of the differing conditions under which human beings have been called to work out a faith relationship with God.

We're familiar with most of these Old Testament images.

- In Eden, a single command enables Adam and Eve to demonstrate daily their faith in the God who meets them at evening.
- For silent centuries, tradition enables men like Job to do right and honor the Lord.
- God speaks to Abraham; a promise is given and believed.
- Moses brings a detailed revelation of God's moral character, and law defines a lifestyle that will enflesh love.
- The theocracy is shattered by repeated sin during the era of the judges, after all too brief obedience in the days of Joshua.
- The monarchy that follows fails to bring the nation to godliness. Despite flickering revivals, the southern kingdom follows the northern into depravity and rushes headlong toward exile.
- The humbled few return to the promised land, to live subject to a series of Gentile overlords. New institutions are developed to refocus the life of the community on the Word of God: the synagogue, the scribe, and the school emerge.
- By Jesus' time, Israel flounders in turbulent unbelief. Jesus' message of the kingdom of God is trampled on by the tradition-bound crowds who rush to demand His crucifixion.

And so the Old Testament record stands. A record of life lived under many different conditions. And a monument to unbelief. At no time did Israel respond in faith to become that holy, loving community that alone could reflect God's character in our sin-darkened world.

As we search the Old Testament we must keep this image of shifting conditions and of failure in mind. It will help us to realize that there is no single, simple "Old Testament nurture system" to be found. At different times through the course of the centuries different approaches to nurture emerged. More importantly, at no time were these approaches successful in shaping a holy community. Individuals were touched. But the people as a whole continually fell short.

Why is this important to remember? Because the idealists of today still dream their dreams. If only human beings were brought up in a just moral community! If only children were enfolded in supportive love! Then, they believe, truly good persons and a just society might emerge. But human beings are not blank tablets on which environment writes. Neither children nor adults are passive. Each acts and is acted on. And the consistent testimony of the Old Testament reminds us that our active nature does not natively turn toward the good.

What we have to look for, then, is not some perfect nurture system that will guarantee success with individuals or groups. Our search in the Scriptures is both more narrow and more significant. We realize that God has designed the nature of man, and that God understands the way we come to faith and grow in faith. And so our exploration must be limited to discover how to help people grow in faith. Our exploration must be limited to understand those conditions that encourage openness to the Spirit of God and encourage the free choice of good.

Understanding the factors that facilitate growth in faith will not guarantee success in ministry with children. But it will provide vital insights into the way God calls us, in families and as the church, to live with our children. By searching the Scriptures we will have a much fuller grasp of what it means when we speak of "ministry to children."

THE SHINING IDEAL:
A JUST AND LOVING COMMUNITY

Of all the images cast in the Old Testament, perhaps the most important to us is the unrealized vision of the Mosaic ideal. When we look at the ideal community sketched in Exodus, Leviticus, and Deuteronomy, we find little explicit instruction on child rearing. But we do find a clear expression of the social context that God designed for the nurture of faith. That context can be simply defined. Children are intended to be brought up as participants in a loving, holy community.

The Community Shaped by Law

Whatever our attitude toward law in this age of grace, it's vital to keep law's intention in perspective. Law was never just a statement of impossible standards, designed to condemn. For the believer law was the window to a joyful vision. Law unveiled a loving lifestyle that God could and would bless.

We see the beauty of the lifestyle marked out by law when we glance at the community law describes. Drawn boldly in the words of the Old Testament is the blueprint for a society without poverty. Here is a community in which people are valued more than things. Here each Israelite is to be willing to lend to a brother without interest, whenever there is a need. Here land-owners leave part of their fruit on the trees and vines for the less fortunate to gather. Here, every seventh year, unpaid debts are freely forgiven.

Here is a community without a police force. Not that there is no crime. Instead, justice is the responsibility of all. A man's neighbors are obligated to give honest witness to what they know; local elders are called on to settle disputes and give judgments. Only in the exceptional case are disputes brought to the priests, and through them God will give His own judgment. In the closely knit community envisioned in law, mutual responsibility and mutual concern for righteousness blend in perfect harmony.

The principle of responsibility is carried over into laws on restitution. The damages of sin are to be repaired. One who steals is to repay, several times over. Even inadvertent harm calls for restitution. A fire out of control that burns another's property calls for the one who kindled it to repay. And restitution has a positive side. Members of the community are to guard what belongs to others. The straying ox of an enemy is to be returned to him. The donkey of one who hates you is to be helped if it falls beneath its load. In the interwoven society of the community shaped by law, everyone is neighbor.

The community has a model for tender forgiveness in the pictures of forgiveness so deeply embedded in Israel's worship. Every act of unintentional sin can be cleansed by an offering. Hidden sins are recognized as the community comes together for the great sacrifice of the Day of Atonement. Here the nation stands together, bowing before God, each aware of his own imperfection and the necessity of receiving, and extending, forgiveness.

Many of the laws governing the community speak of the family and relationships between the sexes. In this community, which affirms the value of all persons, women are not chattels to be used and discarded. There is a trust that can grow as a couple makes a lifetime commitment, sure their covenant will not be violated by sexual adventure and unfaithfulness.

While law calls the whole community to a mutually responsible lifestyle, many provisions reflect sensitivity to the needs of individuals. Careful distinction is made between premeditated murder and accidental homicide. The newly married or those

19

who have just improved their land are released from military service for a year. Any who are afraid or faint-hearted are also released. Even the enemy is treated with a respect surprising for the ancient world. Each besieged city is to be given an opportunity to surrender. No fruit trees are to be cut down to build siege works in a foreign land.

The community unveiled in the law is a community in which individuals are responsible not only for their own actions, but also to others for the quality of their lives. The community thus shaped steps beyond the ideal of justice as a ruling principle, and in its call to active caring for one's neighbor becomes a community shaped by love. This fact is behind Jesus' response to one expert in law who raised the issue of the greatest commandment. "Love the Lord your God with all your heart and with all your soul and with all your mind," Jesus replied. "This is the first and greatest commandment. And the second is like it: Love your neighbor as yourself. All the Law and the Prophets hang on these two commandments" (Matt. 22:37–40). And so law stands revealed as "holy, righteous and good" (Rom. 7:12), the blueprint of a beautiful ideal: a community ruled by enfleshed love.

Children's Participation in Community Life

The Old Testament description of the ideal community is striking for its lack of separate institutions for the nurture of children. No schools are established by the law. No individuals are set aside as teachers of the young. Instead the Old Testament assumes that children will grow up as participating members of the community. And it seems to be just this participation that is the central feature of Mosaic nurture.

This is particularly important, for the whole fabric of the divinely planned society is essentially educational!

1. *The calendar.* The cycle of weeks and year was a basic feature in the ongoing nurture of the whole community. Each cycle reaffirmed basic truths about God and Israel's relationship with Him.

Each week brought the Sabbath, with release from work and time to assemble for talk and worship. Thus the theme of creation, with its message of God's work and rest, reaffirming His identity as shaper of the universe, was constantly held before all Israel.

Recurring festivals recapitulated significant events in salvation history (see Figure 1). The participation of children is illustrated in the Passover and Tabernacles. At Passover, each family relived together the tense moments in Egypt before God worked deliverance. Each family sacrificed its lamb, sprinkling its blood on the doorpost just as the forefathers did. As the ancient rite was repeated, the ceremony stimulated fresh affirmation of Israel's faith.

"When you enter the land that the LORD will give you as he promised, observe this ceremony. And when your children ask you, 'What does this ceremony mean to you?' then tell them, 'It is the Passover sacrifice to the LORD, who passed over the houses of the Israelites in Egypt and spared our homes when he struck down the Egyptians'" (Exod. 12:25–27).

For Israel history is to be experienced and children are to participate as the community relives the past that has shaped its faith and identity.

The Feast of Tabernacles was another such occasion. During that joyous festival, which featured dancing and feasting and the waving of palm fronds, families lived outdoors. They slept through the mild nights in lean-to's made of branches, "so your descendants will know that I had the Israelites live in booths when I brought them out of Egypt" (Lev. 23:43).

How easily we can visualize the family, freed from work for seven full days, peering up at night to glimpse the stars through the woven branches above them. We can imagine them lying down, drifting off to sleep as mother and father tell again the stories of the patriarchs, of God's mighty acts in delivering Israel from slavery, or of wresting the land they now enjoy from a people more mighty and powerful than they.

And thus the endless, repeated cycle of week and year shaped the faith of the Mosaic community, affirming again and again the identity of the chosen people, and affirming again and again the identity of God as Creator and Redeemer.

FIGURE 1

THE ORIGINAL SACRED YEAR

Month	Festival	Theme	Key Passages
March/April	Passover	Redemption	Exod. 12, 13, 34; Lev. 23
May/June	Pentecost	Sustenance	Exod. 23, 34; Lev. 23; Num. 28; Deut.16
September/October	Rosh-Hashana	Civil New Year	Lev. 23, Num. 29
	Day of Atonement	Forgiveness	Lev. 23, Num. 29
	Tabernacles	The Exodus	Lev. 23; Num. 29; Deut. 16

2. *Institutions.* The Mosaic blueprint features only one set of institutions; they centered on worship. Later in history proph-

ets (other than Moses) appear. Later too the monarchy is established, bringing all the structures that central government implies. But at first there was only worship. The institutions of the ideal community are summed up in sacrifice, the central tabernacle, and the priesthood.

Each of these institutions is textured with rich symbolism. The crackling flames that consume the sacrifices on the altar are awesome reminders of sin and forgiveness. No matter how poor an individual, God is ready to meet with him at the altar. Two doves will be accepted if the price of a lamb is too dear. As families come, together, to worship at the single ordained location, they see humble and powerful, rich and poor, bring offerings for unintentional sins. The single location testifies to the fact that relationship with God is the basis of Israel's unity. The sacrifices offered are open confession of each person's failure and of God's overcoming grace. How clear the message is. We are one. For we belong to God.

Each feature of the tabernacle, as the writer of Hebrews points out, was a symbol of eternal realities. The priests who served there testified to the continuing need for mediators between God and man. The arrangement of the court, the design of the furniture, all elements held their message for the worshiping community. And as children participated with their families in the worship of Israel, they were introduced to those symbols that would be with them as they matured and grew old: symbols that would take on ever deeper meanings along with a growing understanding of the faith affirmed in worship.

3. *Memorials.* Memorials were another pervasive feature of the educational process woven by God into the fabric of ideal Israel. A mound of stones standing at the edge of Jordan below Jericho spoke of the miraculous crossing. An altar built by the tribes living across the Jordan bore mute witness to their unity with the people settled in Canaan. There was Jacob's well. Abraham's burial cave. The ruins of Jericho. Throughout Palestine were multiplied reminders of Israel's heritage in the Lord: reminders each new generation could see and touch and feel.

Each home had its memorials as well. There were no shrines or worship centers: these were forbidden. But there were phrases from God's Word written on doorframes and gates. There were name verses, folded small, tied to a wrist or forehead as a symbol. The psalms of Moses or Miriam might be chanted as parents worked in the house or at their trade.

To live as a member of the chosen people and participate in their life in the historic land was to live among constant reminders of God and His commitment to His covenant people.

The Role of the Family

Another component in the nurture system patterned for the Mosaic community is the home. This is the one component about which the Bible gives very explicit instructions. Two Old Testament passages repeat the same guidelines. Each is found in Deuteronomy, one of them framed by this striking statement: "It was not your children who saw what he [the Lord] did for you in the desert until you arrived at this place" (11:5). This statement captures the dilemma of nurture. What one generation has known through personal experience with God must somehow be communicated to a new generation that lacks those experiences. Yet faith must be communicated. The new generation must come to know, to love, and to obey the God of their parents.

How can adults communicate faith? The divine prescription is expressed in two parallel passages.

DEUTERONOMY 6	*DEUTERONOMY 11*
5Love the LORD your God with all your heart and with all your soul and with all your strength. 6These commandments that I give you today are to be upon your hearts. 7Impress them on your children. Talk about them when you sit at home and when you walk along the road, when you lie down and when you get up.	18Fix these words of mine in your hearts and minds; tie them as symbols on your hands and bind them on your foreheads. 19Teach them to your children, talking about them when you sit at home and when you walk along the road, when you lie down and when you get up.

These passages describe the *instructional component* in the ideal nurture system of the Old Testament. Each draws our attention to three factors.

1. *The teacher.* The personal spiritual life of the teacher is instruction's first consideration. Instruction in God's Word calls for a teacher who is himself or herself personally responsive to God. In context each of the Deuteronomy passages speaks of a love for God that finds expression by taking God's words into heart and mind and living them out in behavior. Thus the one who communicates the Word must be one who lives it. Communication of a living faith calls for living faith in the instructor.

2. *The family.* The family is consistently viewed in the Old Testament as the primary locus for instruction. Each parent is called by God to impress God's words on "your children." Par-

ents are not simply socializers of youth, but they are to instruct their own children in the Word of God.

3. *Daily life.* Instruction is to be woven into daily life, as life is shared by parents and their children. In the Old Testament ideal instruction is never isolated from life experience, either by time (to take place at a special hour) or by place (to take place in a special classroom). Instead, instruction is to be woven through the day, given as conversation about God's words as family members sit together at home, walk along a road, lie down at night, or rise in the morning. The underlying assumption seems to be that as life is lived together, godly parents will explain their actions by pointing out the words of God that are guiding their responses. Thus no school is found in the Mosaic ideal of community. Instead, instruction is to infuse all of life, as parents share those truths of Scripture that are needed by a child to interpret his or her experiences.

And so there does stand in the Old Testament an educational ideal. We can discern a nurture process woven through the life of the community. If we were to adopt a similar pattern today we would seek to develop a ministry with children that

- takes place in the context of a loving, holy community
- features participation by children in the life of the community
- calls for instruction by and within the family unit

The pattern and the principles are represented in Figure 2.

ACCOMMODATIONS TO FAILURE

The shining ideal expressed in law was soon tarnished, as the tragedy of human failure and sin warped Israel's history. The loving, holy community blueprinted in the Mosaic code was never realized. Jewish society turned aside as the beliefs, values, and behavior of the surrounding nations eroded the foundations of faith. The godly Israelite lived in a shattered world, with ungodliness competing for the commitment of each emerging generation. Without the supportive role intended for the community, the family was forced to carry a heavy nurturing load: a load it was never intended to carry alone.

Glimpses of two times, each much later than the Mosaic era, give us insight into the nurture patterns of Israel. One pattern is reflected in the sayings of the Proverbs. Another pattern comes from extrabiblical materials produced near the time of Christ.

Nurture in Proverbs

The Book of Proverbs is a unique Old Testament work. It contains a collection of pithy sayings, each understood to ex-

FIGURE 2

PRINCIPLES OF MINISTRY TO CHILDREN IN THE MOSAIC PORTRAIT OF THE IDEAL

Concept	Principle	Old Testament Expression
Modeling	The whole community is to live out and thus model faith's lifestyle.	Children are brought up within a community of adults who form a loving, holy community guided by the Mosaic ideal.
Participation	Children share with adults those experiences that give meaning to faith.	Children participate with adults in the worship, symbolism, and events that teach about God and faith relationship with Him.
Instruction	Teaching is woven into the daily experiences of adults and children.	Parents who love God and have taken His Word to heart teach that Word that has given their own lives shape and meaning.

press a general principle that is applicable to all humankind. This compendium of maxims is not to be interpreted in the same way as the didactic portions of Scripture. Each generalization in the Proverbs is understood to admit exceptions. Thus the nurture concepts found here are descriptive rather than prescriptive. They reflect the notions that were accepted in Israel as generally true, but not as having the same force as law.

When we sift through the Proverbs for nurture concepts, we find reflected the perception of godly Jews, nearly a millennium before Christ's birth.

The goal of nurture. This is perhaps the clearest message of Proverbs. Nurture has a specific goal: it is to guide the new generation to choose the way of wisdom. In Proverbs as in the rest of the Old Testament *wisdom* is a moral term. It is not related so much to intellect as to will as it implies a personal choice of the holy. This is seen in many Proverbs passages:

> Then you will understand what is right and just
> and fair—every good path.
> For wisdom will enter your heart,
> and knowledge will be pleasant to your soul.
> Discretion will protect you,
> and understanding will guard you (2:9–11).

> Thus you will walk in the ways of good men
> > and keep to the paths of the righteous (2:20).
>
> Do not withhold good from those who deserve it,
> > when it is in your power to act.
> Do not say to your neighbor,
> > "Come back later; I'll give it tomorrow"—
> when you now have it with you (3:27–28).

The holiness toward which Jewish education was directed was above all practical. It was the doing of good: it was following the pathway marked out so clearly in the law.

The nurture process. But how was a young person to be guided into the path of wisdom? The writers of the Proverbs clearly fix responsibility on the family and suggest the tools every family would use.

1. *Instruction.* Verbal instruction looms large in the thinking of the writers of Proverbs. "Listen, my son," echoes a repeated saying, "to your father's instruction and do not forsake your mother's teaching" (1:8). Another proverb repeats this idea and continues,

> For these commands are a lamp,
> > this teaching is a light,
> And the corrections of discipline
> > are the way to life (6:20, 23).

2. *Modeling.* Less clearly seen but still reflected in Proverbs is an awareness of the importance of adult modeling. "The righteous man leads a blameless life," Proverbs 20:7 points out, and adds "blessed are his children after him." Along with words of instruction a parent is to give his children an example. "My son, give me your heart and let your eyes keep to my ways" (23:26). Another observes that "he who walks with the wise grows wise, but a companion of fools [the morally evil] suffers harm" (13:20).

3. *Discipline.* The Proverbs lay great stress on discipline and do see it as including punishment. But discipline is to be modeled on that provided by the Lord for His people. The rod is wielded not with anger but with love.

> My son, do not despise the Lord's discipline
> > and do not resent his rebuke,
> Because the Lord disciplines those he loves,
> > as a father the son he delights in (3:11–12).

But punishment is not the only way to correct: natural consequences join instruction as part of the disciplinary armory (19:19). Yet there is no doubt that the "rod of correction must be used to "impart wisdom," for a "child left to itself disgraces his mother" (29:15).

Punishment is not a pleasure for parents. It is a duty and a responsibility linked with love. "Folly [moral evil] is bound up in the heart of a child," one proverb warns, "but the rod of discipline will drive it far from him" (22:15). Strikingly, little or nothing is said of praise as a way to encourage a child to choose wisdom, although the guidance of which punishment is only one part may imply warm and loving encouragement.

Responsibility for response. Proverbs clearly focuses on the responsibility of each child to respond to instruction. The parents are to instruct, to model, to discipline. The young are urged to accept, to heed, to remember, and to keep the parents' words.

> My son, do not forget my teaching,
> but keep my commands in your heart (3:1).

> Listen, my son, accept what I say,
> and the years of your life will be many (4:10).

The writers of Proverbs believe that "even a child is known by his actions, by whether his conduct is pure and right" (20:11). No wonder then there is constant urging of the young to exercise their freedom and to choose wisdom.

Influences encouraging positive response. The context of the nurture portrayed in Proverbs is the home. The primary influences on the child as seen above are the instruction, the example, and the discipline of parents. But there are other factors clearly recognized by those who framed the wisdom sayings of Israel.

Proverbs make it clear that *personal relationship with God* is critical if a young life is to take wisdom's path. "For the LORD gives wisdom," one proverb affirms, "and from his mouth come knowledge and understanding" (2:6). The following command is especially applicable:

> Trust in the LORD with all your heart
> and lean not on your own understanding;
> in all your ways acknowledge him,
> and he will make your paths straight (3:5–6).

But if the "fear of the LORD is the beginning of wisdom" (9:10), "folly [moral evil] is bound up in the heart of a child" (22:15). The sins that flow from the heart will ensnare one who follows evil impulses.

There is much stress in Proverbs on choice of one's friends. While good companions encourage a commitment to good, association with the hot tempered or the easily angered can lead a person astray. The wise comment points out that "you may learn

his ways, and get yourself ensnared" (22:25). So Proverbs warns
about the choice of companions.

> Listen, my son, and be wise,
>   and keep your heart on the right path.
> Do not join those who drink too much wine
>   or gorge themselves on meat,
> for drunkards and gluttons become poor,
>   and drowsiness clothes them in rags (23:19–21).

Proverbs does not speak specifically of the training of the very
young. But it does reflect clearly vital concepts of nurture. Nurture is intended to lead a child to a personal commitment to
practical holiness. Responsibility for nurture rests on the home.
Parents fulfill their responsibility when they provide instruction, example, and discipline. But Proverbs emphasizes individual responsibility. Each child growing toward adulthood will
make his or her own choices between the right and the wrong.
Each child will respond or fail to respond to external guidance.
Each will choose or reject godly companions. Each will reach out
trustingly for a faith relationship with God, the starting point
for all true wisdom, or will turn away. We can influence the
individual, but he or she must choose.

NURTURE IN JESUS' DAY

The nurture patterns common in the time of Jesus reflect
significant societal changes in Israel. During the captivity in
Babylon the people were cut off from the temple. There they
turned to the Scriptures. The synagogue took shape as a teaching institution, not a worship center. In Babylon the scribal
movement emerged. Men such as Ezra devoted themselves "to
the study and observance of the Law of the LORD, and to teaching
its decrees and laws in Israel" (Ezra 7:10). After the remnant
returned to Palestine and the temple was rebuilt, the synagogue
system persisted. Its intense concentration on Scripture led to
establishment of elementary schools. As the rabbinical tradition
developed it led to the legalistic interpretation of faith so graphically illustrated in the Gospels by the Pharisees.

By Jesus' day an approach to nurture different from both the
Mosaic approach and that reflected in Proverbs had emerged. We
see it described by a number of writers just after Jesus' time.

The Importance of Children

From Jesus' few remarks about children in the Gospels we
realize that in general children were highly valued. That impression is reinforced by Josephus, writing about A.D. 80. He speaks
several times about children and their nurture. In *Against*

Apion (1:12) Josephus says, "Our ground is good, and we work it to the utmost, but our chief ambition is for the education of our children." His explanation of the goal of nurture is solidly in the tradition of the Proverbs: "We take the most pains of all with the instruction of children, and esteem the observation of the laws, and the piety corresponding with them, the most important affair in our whole life."

Modes of Instruction

The home was still viewed in this later period as the center of Hebrew nurture. Philo says of the youngest children, "They are taught, so to speak, from their swaddling clothes by their parents, by their teachers, and by those who bring them up, even before instruction in the sacred laws and unwritten customs, to believe in God, the One Father and Creator of the world" *(Leg. ad Caium, 31)*. Many sources testify to the fact that as soon as children could speak, the father and mother began to teach them the law. But by Jesus' day, this duty was shared by the school.

Boys were expected to begin school between the ages of five and seven, with seven common. For several hours a day the boys studied under a teacher paid by taxes levied on all those who had children. The school program was one of memorization. Josephus describes its curriculum: it included learning "the most important laws, because this is the best knowledge, and the cause of prosperity" *(Antiquities, 4:8:12)*. In *Against Apion* (2:25) Josephus says the schools were to "instruct the children in the elements of knowledge, to teach them to walk according to the laws, and to know the deeds of their forefathers. The latter, that they might imitate them; the former, that, growing up with the laws, they might not transgress them, nor have the excuse of ignorance."

Of particular interest is the Talmud's insistence that the character of the teacher is of utmost importance. The teacher should use kindness, encouragement, and caring to motivate learning.[1]

The formal education given in school was oral. Learning was memorization. Promising youth might go on to advanced studies as did the apostle Paul. But all would know by heart the basic laws of the Book that gave meaning to the life of the people of God.

---

[1]For a significant list of teacher characteristics see A. Edersheim, *Sketches of Jewish Social Life in the Days of Christ,* (Grand Rapids: Eerdmans, 1957), pp. 135–36.

FIGURE 3

OLD TESTAMENT NURTURE SYSTEMS

	The Mosaic Ideal	The Time of Proverbs	The Time of Christ
Societal Setting	envisioned as a holy, loving community	a pluralistic, divided society	a pluralistic, divided society
Primary Modes of Nurture	community modeling participation in common life parental instruction	parental instruction	parental instruction schooling
Character of Nurture	socialization	instruction, discipline	instruction (memorization)
Primary Issue in Nurture	to know and love God as a member of His committed community	to make individual decisions to live out God's wisdom	to make individual decisions to live by God's Word
Goal of Nurture	holiness	holiness	holiness

The Community

Despite the fact that life in Israel was focused on the Scriptures, the society into which a child was born in Jesus' day was far from the harmonious, loving community envisioned in the Mosaic ideal. The rigorous Pharisees and the political, liberal Sadducees held far differing views of Scripture and conflicting visions of Judaism. Society was stratified into rich and poor. Hellenism had its adherents, and many made accommodations to the secular power of occupying Rome. Jerusalem alone was reputed to have over four hundred synagogues in Jesus' time, many emphasizing views that stimulated hot debate.

The divided and divisive religious community had a form of the biblical faith. But it failed to embody the kingdom lifestyle taught by Jesus and expressed in the Scriptures.

CONCLUSION

While there is no single "Old Testament nurture system," our survey of the Old Testament (summarized in Figure 3) has given us insight into many basic nurture issues. The most striking observation comes from the vision of life together as a committed community: a vision embedded in Mosaic law. Also striking is the fact that Scripture contains no evidence that the full educational approach envisioned in that ideal was ever practiced by historic Israel!

In later Judaism we see two prominent approaches to nurture. While each did produce godly individuals, neither produced a believing, whole community in which love was enfleshed. The first approach, reflected in Proverbs, rested full responsibility for nurture on the home. Without the supportive elements of community modeling and of participation by children in a common community faith/life, great stress was placed on verbal instruction by parents. Under these conditions the issue was in serious doubt. Father and mother might instruct faithfully and reinforce teaching with discipline. But always the individual would make his or her own choice of wisdom or folly.

By the time of Jesus the society had developed formal institutions designed to support the home. The school emerged, and focused on memorization of the law. The synagogue continued the process begun in childhood, providing lifelong instruction in the traditions and interpretations of law that encrusted the Scriptures.

But never was an educational system able to achieve its intended goal. The home alone was unable to keep the people of God on the path of righteousness. The home, supported by formal instruction in school and synagogue, produced the zealous but arid religion we know from the Gospels.

The experience of God's Old Testament people serves as a healthy example to us. The nurture of the next generation is both significant—and difficult. We must seek to learn all we can from the nurture principles stressed in Scripture. And we must avoid the trap of superficial approaches to nurture, which reduces our vision of what might be to the lowered standards of what seems "practical" under the circumstances.

In God's economy children *are* important. Ministry to children deserves the struggle nurturing requires.

PROBE

▶ *case histories*
▶ *discussion questions*
▶ *thought provokers*
▶ *resources*

1. Write a careful description of the nurture you received as a child. Then compare and contrast your upbringing with the features of the Mosaic ideal, summarized in Figure 2. Include an evaluation of the strengths and weaknesses in the Christian nurture you experienced.

2. There are a number of Scripture passages that might be profitably studied to flesh out impressions of the Old Testament nurture system.

   a. *Its concepts*

   Read through either Leviticus or Proverbs. Keep a running account of every feature that has nurture implications. After your study, write briefly on (1) which features should be included in contemporary ministry with children, and (2) how each feature you choose might affect current practices.

   b. *Case histories*

   Two Old Testament passages give fascinating insights into the family and what happened to the family when the nation as a whole turned away from the Mosaic ideal. Study one of these case histories, and summarize in writing its significance for us today. The two passages: Judges 19–21; 1 Samuel 2:12–3:21.

3. In the 1920s Eberhard Arnold founded the Hutterian Society of Brothers. One of the goals of the community, and still a goal of the four Bruderhof communities now in existence, was the nurture of children. The following are excerpts from Arnold's writings that explain the educational concepts of the movement. Read the excerpts and be prepared for discussion of the following questions.

a. Which of the three Old Testament nurture approaches is Bruderhof education most like?
b. What nurture principles does Bruderhof education seem to rely on?
c. What would be necessary if a local congregation were to attempt to structure its ministry to children on Bruderhof principles?
d. Which principles of Bruderhof education could be most easily integrated into church programs? Which would be most difficult? Why?

EBERHARD ARNOLD

A living education belongs in the midst of a living Church community. Therefore the children's community is part of the adult's community of faith, where people live in the spirit of true brotherhood and service (p. 15).

While the spiritual, emotional, and physical character of father and mother have a tremendous influence on unborn and newly born children, the educators and the whole community have just as great an influence on children. The strongest element in education is example. Children are led almost irresistibly by the examples they see and experience. They should experience examples filled with spirit and life. Therefore it is true that not only our teachers and educators help to mold the children's lives, but also the community as a whole (p. 16).

The teachers must work together as a team and meet frequently, at least once a week. Unless there is a regular sharing among the teachers they will have no discernment of the children's inner situation, no oversight of their progress in school, and no insight into the children's community as a whole. For the joy of the whole community, the school teachers should arrange often that the children sing to us, recite poetry, or report about a special experience; they should display the children's artwork or share other expressions of the school, preschool, or kindergarten activities. I do not think anyone will be bored. In this way everybody's interest in the children's community will be kept joyful and alive. The whole Brotherhood must be watchful that the activity of mind and spirit is not drowned by the practical work (p. 18).

In the community, the area of the child's activities as he grows up is the same as that of his future life. He helps in the community farm and workshops; he experiences the contact the Church has with the world, and its living, fighting participation in the needs and concerns of the whole world. So from his early years the child lives with all the problems and demands that the suffering of mankind raises.

FRAMEWORK

In a true Church life, with the children's community at its core, real freedom is given from the world-wide domination of economics over men's lives today. For here the children live in the community of the Spirit, which permeates all areas of life and work but is neither run by them nor violated by them. And yet in this life community—whose calling is not for its own sake but for the sake of the world, that its need may be overcome—the children get acquainted with the serious problems that arise from the spiritual destitution of the big cities (pp. 34–35).[2]

---

[2]Eberhard Arnold, *Children's Education in Community: The Basis of Bruderhof Education,* ed. Merrill Mow (Rifton, N.Y.: Plough, 1976).

PART 1

FRAMEWORK

A Theological Framework for Ministry

Nurture in the Old Testament
Nurture in the New Testament
The Role of Scripture in Nurture
The Nurture Process

A Developmental Framework for Ministry

The Developmental Perspective
Cognitive Potentials of Children
Social Relationships of Children
Moral Development in Children
An Integrated Perspective

The Gospels show, in Jesus' own sayings, a great concern for children. But the rest of the New Testament is strangely silent. Not only do the Epistles fail to outline a nurture program, but

NURTURE IN THE NEW TESTAMENT

the history of the early church contains no record of efforts to organize any training for the young!

Writings from New Testament times give us a clear picture of ministry to children in the Jewish community. But there are no parallel writings about nurture in the early church. Jesus often expressed concern for the littlest ones (see Figure 4). Surely Jesus' people shared that concern and were eager to see their own children grow up in the faith. Yet no written tradition exploring the "how" of early Christian nurture exists.

The New Testament itself tells us almost nothing about child rearing. Oh, children are to obey parents (Eph. 6:1; Col. 3:20). And parental discipline is to be distinctively Christian so children will not be provoked or discouraged (Eph. 6:4; Col. 3:21). But no definition of this "Christian discipline" is included in the Epistles.

The early church fathers also exhort parents to nurture their children. But they too fail to explain. Clement (ca. A.D. 110) says,

> Let our children partake of the training that is in Christ. Let them learn how humility avails with God, what pure love can do with Him, how the fear of Him is good and great and saves those who live therein in holiness and a pure mind *(To the Corinthians, 21:7–8).*

CHAPTER 2

Polycarp (ca. A.D. 150) adds only this:

> Let us teach, first of all, ourselves to walk in the commandments of the Lord. Next, teach your wives to walk in the faith given to them, and in love and in purity to love their own husbands in all truth, and to love all others equally in all chastity; and to train up their children in the knowledge and fear of God *(To the Philippians, 4:2).*

Beyond allusions such as these to nurture, nothing is written. While the early church carefully designed rigorous catechetical systems for adult converts and took care in planning training for ministry, it did nothing similar for its children. There were no agencies analogous to our Sunday schools. There were no Christian schools where believers' children might be educated.

In fact, we know that the children of Christians were normally sent to the pagan Greek or Roman schools that served children in that society. There the curriculum was the writings of pagan poets, and the subject matter the loves, hates, and sins of the gods. Even Tertullian (ca. A.D. 160–220), who insisted that no Christian could in good conscience be a school teacher, justified sending Christian children to such schools. After all, how else could they learn (see *On Idolatry,* 10)!

And so during its first dynamic centuries the church expanded throughout the Roman empire. It shaped generations of committed Christians who triumphantly withstood systematic persecution. And it transmitted its faith from generation to gen-

FIGURE 4
JESUS' TEACHINGS ON CHILDREN

"I tell you the truth, unless you change and become like little children, you will never enter the kingdom of heaven. Therefore, whoever humbles himself like this child is the greatest in the kingdom of heaven. And whoever welcomes a little child like this in my name welcomes me.

"But if anyone causes one of these little ones who believe in me to sin, it would be better for him to have a large millstone hung around his neck and to be drowned in the depths of the sea. . . . See that you do not look down on one of these little ones. For I tell you that their angels in heaven always see the face of my Father in heaven" (Matt. 18:2–5, 6, 10; cf. Mark 9:33–36, 42).

Jesus, knowing their thoughts, took a little child and had him stand beside him. Then he said to them, "Whoever welcomes this little child in my name welcomes me; and whoever welcomes me welcomes the one who sent me. For he who is least among you all—he is the greatest" (Luke 9:47–48; cf. Mark 9:36–37).

People were bringing little children to Jesus to have him touch them, but the disciples rebuked them. When Jesus saw this, he was indignant. He said to them, "Let the little children come to me, and do not hinder them, for the kingdom of God belongs to such as these. I tell you the truth, anyone who will not receive the kingdom of God like a little child will never enter it." And he took the children in his arms, put his hands on them and blessed them (Mark 10: 13–16).

eration with what appears to be no special ministry focused on children.

But "appears" is perhaps a necessary qualifier. It seems most likely that some powerful nurture process was in operation in the early church, a process that was so much a part of the life of the believing community that, until its dynamic was later lost, no special attention to children's ministry was required. So when we turn to the New Testament, we need to search out clues to such a "hidden" ministry to the child.

COMMUNITY WITHIN SOCIETY

It's wrong for us to idealize the New Testament church. Like churches today, the early church was formed of fallible human beings. The Epistles give ample insight into the divisions, the pettiness, and the sins that plagued the early Christian community. Then as now it was a struggle for congregations to live out the radical love to which they had been called in Christ Jesus.

So as we approach this study, we neither idealize the New Testament era nor assume that we can recreate its conditions or structures in our century. What we must do instead is discern what aspects of the church given in the New Testament are significant for ministry to children.

With this in mind, the first thing we must note is that the church immediately took form as a faith community existing within a hostile society. A picture of community life is found in Acts.

> They devoted themselves to the apostles' teaching and to the fellowship, to the breaking of bread and to prayer. Everyone was filled with awe, and many wonders and miraculous signs were done by the apostles. All the believers were together and had everything in common. Selling their possessions and goods, they gave to anyone as he had need. Every day they continued to meet together in the temple courts. They broke bread in their homes and ate together with glad and sincere hearts, praising God and enjoying the favor of all the people. And the Lord added to their number daily those who were being saved (2:42–47).

The community life pictured here was not fully maintained in the decades during which the faith flowed out beyond the Jewish homeland to flood the empire. Holding everything in common was not generally practiced (although generous sharing of funds to meet needs was a prominent feature of Christian lifestyle: see Gal. 2:10; 2 Cor. 8:1–3; 1 Tim. 6:17–19 with James 2:1–7, 14–17). There is no record of meetings that reproduced those early gatherings in the temple courts. But the most significant features of this faith lifestyle continued to characterize the expanding Christian movement.

Particularly significant are (1) the meetings of the church in home-sized groups, and (2) the pattern of mutual ministry in these groups.

Home-sized groups. There is general agreement that for at least two centuries the Christian church existed in small, home-sized groupings. There were no great meeting halls. In fact, archeology knows of no early church buildings at all. Ruins of small, synagogue-like structures where only a few could gather date from the third century. Paul's note to Priscilla and Aquila in Romans reflects the normal situation when it refers to "the church that meets at their house" (16:5). Never was the church a monolithic organization in those early days. It was instead a network of believers, formed of small, home-sized units that encouraged great intimacy.

Shared ministry. While the New Testament gives us no "order of service" for these home gatherings, we are given many glimpses of what happened when the believers met. We know that Christianity was essentially a lay movement during those early centuries. Paul placed great emphasis on the spiritual gifts given every believer, and he encouraged each to make his or her contribution to the growth of others. No clergy stood guard over home meetings. In fact, Paul wrote to the Romans, "I myself am convinced, my brothers, that you yourselves are full of goodness, complete in knowledge and competent to instruct one another" (15:14). And this is just what happened when the community assembled. Hebrews gives this brief picture of mutual teaching and encouragement:

> Let us hold unswervingly to the hope we profess, for he who promised is faithful. And let us consider how we may spur one another on toward love and good deeds. Let us not give up meeting together, as some are in the habit of doing, but let us encourage one another—and all the more as you see the Day approaching (10:23-25).

Paul adds another description in 1 Corinthians.

> When you come together, everyone has a hymn, or a word of instruction, a revelation, a tongue or an interpretation. All of these must be done for the strengthening of the church. . . . Two or three prophets should speak, and the others should weigh carefully what is said. And if a revelation comes to someone who is sitting down, the first speaker should stop. For you can all prophesy in turn so that everyone may be instructed and encouraged (14:26, 29-31).

Each member of the intimate groups that made up the early church was a full participant in the church's life, ministering to others and receiving ministry from them.

The Old Testament ideal of a community that shared the same beliefs, values, and commitments was now being realized, but in a radically different shape. Rather than a whole nation living out a faith relationship with God, now colonies of faith were established within hostile societies. Each colony met together in intimate fellowship. Each member shared responsibility for the encouragement and upbuilding of others. Each drew strength from the others to maintain his or her commitment to godliness as daily life thrust each out into the surrounding, twisted world.

THE NEW COVENANT

The Mosaic ideal was a call to life in community: a community where the expression of love for neighbor was guided by law. The New Testament agrees, affirming that whatever "commandments there may be, are summed up in this one rule: 'Love your neighbor as yourself.' Love does no harm to its neighbor. Therefore love is the fulfillment of the Law" (Rom. 13:9-10). But law failed to create a loving community. The fault was not in law. The fault was in what Paul calls the weakness of sinful flesh (Rom. 8:3).

Yet the older testament contains a promise. One day the ideal *will* be achieved! But not through the agency of some external law.

> "This is the covenant I will make with the house of Israel
> after that time," declares the LORD.

"I will put my law in their minds
and write it on their hearts.
I will be their God,
and they will be my people" (Jer. 31:33).

Only an inner transformation would enable realization of the ideal.

Thus when Jesus' death and resurrection ushered in the day of the New Covenant (Matt. 26:27–28; 2 Cor. 3:6–11; Heb. 8:7–10:18) there was no relaxation of God's standards. But there was the infusion of a power by which the ideal might at last be achieved. It would come through an inner transformation. And the life of the New Testament community was to be focused on those relationships, with God and with each other, through which transformation might come.

It's not surprising then to discover that relationships between believers within the new faith community are extensively explored in the New Testament Epistles. When we look at some of the major relational passages there, we build a striking image of what it means to be part of a transforming community.

The Relational Climate

Non-judgmental acceptance: Romans 14–15. Romans 14 and 15 speaks out against condemning or looking down on others for differences in personal convictions. This emphasis is important. Most groups find it necessary to insist on conformity of behavior, and in many associations deviation is seen as a threat to the existence of the group. The believing community is different. It extends broad freedoms to its members, for its existence rests on a relationship with God that demands recognition of fellow believers as brothers. Only when we freely "accept one another," just as Christ accepted us (15:7) can unity be experienced, and believers live together and follow Jesus "with one heart."

Equality: 1 Corinthians 1–4. The Corinthian church fell to quarreling and jealousy when its house-church units debated allegiance to various human leaders (such as Paul, Apollos, and Cephas). Paul called on the church to view these leaders simply as "servants of Christ," so that no one might "take pride in one man over against another" (4:6). The living center of the believing community is to be Jesus, for God alone is the source of transforming spiritual growth (3:6). Thus a unique equality is to exist in the new community. No individual is to be exalted over the others.

41

Spiritual significance: 1 Corinthians 12, 14. The doctrine of spiritual gifts is a doctrine of spiritual significance. Every person within the body is affirmed as an individual with a distinctive contribution to make to others. God Himself expresses His enriching influence through each individual! With this view of persons, no one can feel unneeded or be dismissed by the others.

In fact the gift passages specifically warn against our human tendency to relate to others in hierarchies and thus to assign some members of the community a greater significance than others. In contrast Paul insists that "there should be no division in the body, but . . . its parts should have equal concern for each other" (12:25). Each person in this community of gifted members not only merits the loving concern of others, but also is to be given honor by others.

Love: 1 Corinthians 13. Paul sees love as the supreme expression of spiritual maturity. Measured against love, the gifts a person may possess are relatively insignificant. Paul's simple definition of love in this passage (13:4–7) is one of the New Testament's clearest expressions of the lifestyle that makes community possible and of the kind of person the transforming community is intended to produce.

Transparency: 2 Corinthians 3. Paul compares the glory of the New Covenant to the splendors of the Old in this significant chapter. Under the New Covenant believers undergo a progressive personal transformation. God is writing His own character "not on tablets of stone but on tablets of human hearts" (3:3). This confidence in the working of God within its members gives the Christian community a unique freedom. Its members can remove the veils that mask their lives from one another. Yes, blemishes and faults will be revealed. But the presence of Jesus in the community will be sensed by all as time gives certain testimony to God's transforming work and the members of the community experience inner change.

Confidence: 2 Corinthians 4–5. Paul points out that in general human beings are forced to evaluate one another on the basis of what is seen (observed behavior), not what is unseen. Yet the Christian is convinced that the observed is transitory and change is sure (cf. 4:18 with 5:12). The certain conviction of the Christian community is that relationship with Jesus promises renewal; that Christ's love is life's one compelling, transforming force (5:17 with 5:14). This conviction shifts the focus of relationship in the Christian community away from behavior. The church can live with failure and lovingly affirm the individual who stumbled. We need no longer count "men's sins against them" (5:19), but instead can follow the reconciling path of Christ Himself. In the context of a loving fellowship, which believes in individuals against all the evidences of the senses, stumbling members of the church are supported until the promise is realized in them, and they become "the righteousness of God" (5:21).

Sharing: 2 Corinthians 8–9. The New Testament knows nothing of "giving." The biblical term is *koinonia:* a sharing that stretches beyond sharing of life to the sharing of material possessions. The goal of such sharing is clearly understood in the New Testament community. It is "not that others might be relieved while you are hard pressed, but that there might be equality. At the present time your plenty will supply what they need, so that in turn their plenty will supply what you need" (8:13–14). This kind of giving centers on both persons and needs. No giving was encouraged to build greater buildings or support institutionalized efforts. Giving, however, was an expression of love for brothers and sisters who were unable to meet their material needs. The Old Testament ideal of "no poor among them" is thus carried over into the experience of the New Covenant community.

It's possible to extend this study to many other passages. If we did we would read of forgiveness, of loving discipline, of humility, of mutual submission, and many other relational themes. But we have enough evidence now to establish one vital thing. *The New Testament does describe a relational climate that is normative for the Christian community.* Scripture gives consistent testimony to that community's attitude toward persons. In the body of Christ individuals are valued, and this value is acted out in many ways. We have freedom to differ, and yet be accepted. We are equal with others in an ultimate sense. Each of us is spiritually significant, with a contribution to make to others. In our fellowship love is more important than role. Material needs are the concern of all. In this community transparency is possible, and those who fall need never fear rejection. There is forgiveness for failure, discipline when needed, and the constant affirmation of the community, for all are confident that God will enable the stumbler to grow toward Christlike maturity.

This vision of the community's attitude toward people is important to us as we seek to understand the early church's approach to nurture. For this view of persons must have reached out to encompass children. The attitude toward persons expressed in the community must have shaped relationships between parent and child.

Family Relationships

There is no simple statement in Scripture that reveals the pattern of family life. But there is one New Testament passage that gives us many clues. That passage is found in the second chapter of 1 Thessalonians.

> [7]As apostles of Christ we could have been a burden to you, but we were gentle among you, like a mother caring for her little children. [8]We loved you so much that we were delighted to share with you not only the gospel of God but our lives as well, because you had become so dear to us. [9]Surely you remember, brothers, our toil and hardship; we worked night and day in order not to be a burden to anyone while we preached the gospel of God to you.
>
> [10]You are witnesses, and so is God, of how holy, righteous and blameless we were among you who believed. [11]For you know that we dealt with each of you as a father deals with his own children, [12]encouraging, comforting and urging you to live lives worthy of God, who calls you into his kingdom and glory (2:7–12).

In chapter 1 Paul makes it clear that his brief ministry among the Thessalonians (Acts 17:1–9) was a ministry of the Word of God (1 Thess. 1:5–6, 8). But in chapter 2 Paul also reminds the community of the relationship he had developed with them. To portray that relationship Paul is driven to the image of family. He speaks of a gentleness that mirrors a mother's care for a nursing infant (v. 7). He recalls the growing love that could only be expressed by sharing himself as well as the gospel. Clearly in Paul's mind being "dear to us" implies great intimacy, and Paul has no doubt that the Thessalonians have come to know him so well that they are sure he had never used flattery or acted from impure motives (vv. 7–8, cf. 3, 5).

The family image is expanded as Paul describes his way of life "among you who believed." He dealt with "each one of you" just as a father might deal with adolescent children (vv. 10–11). In that relationship each child is recognized as a unique individual: each is given just the encouragement, the comfort, or the urging he needs to help him live a life "worthy of God" (v. 12).

This description by Paul is doubly fascinating. On the one hand it tells us much about Paul as a person. On the other, it gives us a unique insight into family life. Through Paul's reminiscences we see the family as a nest of warm, loving relationships. We sense a touching tenderness and are given a vivid impression of unfolding familiarity: of a growth process in which parents share themselves with the young. In Paul's brief sentences we see the outline of a deep caring for individuals: a concern for every child as a unique person. There is recognition of individual differences and an effort by adults to adapt the guidance to each child's personality and needs.

In short, we see the same richly textured relational life and the same valuing of persons that marked the wider Christian community! We understand a little better why the New Testament church saw itself as an extended family (cf. Eph. 3:14–19), and so fastened on "brother" and "sister" as the most appropriate ways to think of and to speak to one another.

In the New Testament church, the Mosaic ideal of loving community began to be realized. Through the biblical description of those relationships and of the home, we can see a picture of the context in which Christian ministry to children first took place.

PARTICIPATION BY CHILDREN

It is one thing to understand the community that Christ's people formed. It's another to determine the role of children in community life. There is no question that participation by children was a basic feature of nurture in the Mosaic system. It is not so clear from the New Testament that participation had a parallel role in the early church.

Any argument that might be advanced to demonstrate children's participation in the life of the early church is weak. Perhaps the most compelling argument is simply the setting in which the community met: the home. We can hardly imagine children excluded from the shared meals. And we can easily visualize them joining in the times of singing and prayer. We know from a number of New Testament passages that men and women were together when the community met. Granted that the younger children probably slept, the fact that there was no teaching or other program developed for the young suggests that children were simply and naturally a part of the extended church family. It may even be such a participation in the church's common life that Clement is thinking of when he writes, "Let our children partake of the training which is in Christ" (*To the Corinthians*, 21:7).

This view cannot be proved. Yet the image is in fullest harmony with the Old Testament ideal. And there are infrequent hints that this theory may be correct. We know, for instance, that in choosing elders believers were to consider the behavior of a candidate's children. Surely all must have known and observed the boys and girls? How better than as participants in community life? We see another hint in Acts. Paul is traveling to Jerusalem and imprisonment and on the way lands at Tyre. He stays there only seven days. But when he leaves "all the disciples and their wives and children accompanied us out of the city, and there on the beach we knelt to pray. After saying good-by to each other, we went on board the ship, and they returned home" (Acts 21:5–6).

The New Testament is just as silent on family instruction. We can assume the pattern laid out in Deuteronomy 6 and 11. But all we *know* is found in such a reference as Paul's famous comment to Timothy: "From infancy you have known the holy Scriptures, which are able to make you wise for salvation through faith in Christ Jesus" (2 Tim. 3:15).

But there is a most compelling reason to believe that members of the early church did draw their children into the fellowship of local communities and did instruct them in the Word of God. That reason is deeply rooted in the nature of the new community itself. For this was a people devoted to Christ and to doing what is good. How could they fail to devote themselves equally to their children? How could those who at last found the meaning of life in their relationship with Jesus Christ fail to draw their families with them into that community that became the living center of their world?

CONCLUSION

There is abundant evidence that the early church did achieve a high degree of community. This community was different from that envisioned in the Old Testament. While the Mosaic ideal called for a whole society committed to love, the New Testament church took the form of mini-communities, whose members were welded together by intense love, planted in hostile, pagan society. (For a comparison of the points of similarity of the Mosaic ideal and the New Testament reality, see Figure 5.)

There is no doubt that children too experienced dual membership in community and society. The church provided no "Christian" schooling for its children. Instead children received their elementary education in secular institutions and were taught a curriculum that featured the exploits of the gods and goddesses enshrined in pagan pantheons.

It's clear there was no attempt by the early church to isolate the children from the surrounding world. Instead there was the conviction that children and youth who tasted the contrast between pagan society and Christian community would make their choice for Christ. And, in large part, history suggests that this confidence was well founded.

There is also no doubt that a distinctive relational climate marked the early faith communities and family units. Individuals were valued and affirmed. There was discipline, but in a context provided by unconditional love. There was freedom, and yet a sense of belonging that was rooted in Christ's acceptance of every believer. And with the wonder of belonging, there was the even greater wonder of being viewed as a spiritually significant individual. Not only was each human being precious to God, but in Christ each was enabled to make a contribution to the growth of others.

We can never overestimate the importance of this relational climate. As we'll see in later chapters, this climate is perhaps the most powerful single influence in child development. Wrapped in the love of parents and valued by other adults in the close-knit faith community, each child was gently guided to and nurtured in faith.

FIGURE 5
COMPARISON OF OLD TESTAMENT AND NEW TESTAMENT NURTURE

Mosaic Ideal	New Testament Reality
The whole society is envisioned as a loving community.	A loving community exists within the fabric of pagan society.
Children participate in the structured life and worship of the community.	Children participate in the spontaneous life and worship of the community.
Children are given daily instruction by parents in the context of shared family experiences.	Children are given daily instruction by parents in the context of shared family experiences.

Our study has not yet led us to any definitive statement of principles that must guide ministry to children in our own day. But the nurture systems we can discern in Scripture surely are suggestive. The patterns we see in the two Testaments must be given most serious consideration. For the roots of our educational ministries, like the roots of our faith, must be sunk deep in the reliable and relevant Word of God.

PROBE

▶ *case histories*
▶ *discussion questions*
▶ *thought provokers*
▶ *resources*

1. John Westerhoff III is a contemporary Christian educator who argues that the ministry to children practiced in most churches today is designed to teach religion, not to communicate faith. Church ministries are typically based on a schooling/instructional model. Westerhoff argues that only *community* provides a context for the birth and nurture of faith. Read the following excerpt from his *Will Our Children Have Faith?* How does his argument strike you? Do you see any alternative to the schooling/instructional approach suggested by our survey of the New Testament? If so, what?

JOHN WESTERHOFF III

We have too easily linked the ways of secular education with religion. . . . Recall the question asked in the Gospel according to St. Luke: "When the Son of Man comes will he find faith on earth?" (Luke 18:8). Surely he will find religion (institutions, creeds, documents, artifacts, and the like), but he may not find faith. Faith is deeply personal, dynamic, ultimate. Religion, however, is faith's expression. . . . Religion is important, but not ultimately important. Educationally, religion is a means to an end; faith is the only end. Faith, therefore, and not religion, must become the concern of Christian education.

The anomaly of the schooling-instructional paradigm is found in its natural and primary concern with religion. You can teach about religion, but you cannot teach people faith. Thus, this paradigm places Christian education in the strange position of making secondary matters primary. Teaching people about Christianity is not very important. Religion is at best an expression of someone's faith which, under proper conditions, can lead others to faith.

It appears that as Christian faith has diminished, the schooling-instructional paradigm has encouraged us to busy ourselves with teaching about Christian religion. As our personal commitment to Christ has lapsed, many church persons have turned for solace to teaching children what the Bible says, what happened in the history of the church, what we believe, and what is right and wrong. Sometimes, even when the school has succeeded, it has only produced educated atheists. For many today, Christian religion as taught in our church schools stands between them and God. The schooling-instructional paradigm easily leads us into thinking that we have done our jobs if we teach our children all about Christianity.

There is a great difference between learning about the Bible and living as a disciple of Jesus Christ. We are not saved by our knowledge, our beliefs, or our worship in the church, just as we are not saved by our actions or our religion. We are saved by the anguish and love of God, and to live according to that truth is to have faith.

Faith cannot be taught by any method of instruction; we can only teach religion. We can know about religion, but we can only expand in faith, act in faith, live in faith. Faith can be inspired within a community of faith, but it cannot be given to one person by another. Faith is expressed, transformed, and made meaningful by persons sharing their faith in an historical, tradition-bearing community of faith. An emphasis on schooling and instruction makes it too easy to forget this truth. Indeed, the schooling-instructional paradigm works against our necessary primary concern for the faith of persons. It encourages us to teach about Christian religion by turning our attention to Christianity as expressed in documents, doctrines, history, and moral codes. No matter what the rhetoric of our purposes, the schooling-instructional paradigm, modeled after modern psychology and pedagogy, leads us to focus on religion rather than faith. If for no other reason than this, the schooling-instructional paradigm needs to be questioned.

I have concluded, therefore, that the schooling-instructional paradigm is bankrupt. An alternative paradigm, not merely an alternative educational program, is needed (pp. 21–23).[1]

2. Complete the survey of the New Testament begun in this chapter. Locate major passages that seem to you to portray the relational climate of the church. Write a brief summary of the significance of each passage, patterned on the summaries in this text.

3. In the later days of the Roman empire significant change had come to the church. Many of the dynamics of community, so marked in the early centuries, were diluted or lost. In this later period (about A.D. 360), John Chrysostom penned *The Right Way for Parents to Bring Up Their Children.* His tract exists today, and it helps us sense shifts in the pattern seen in Old Testament ideal and New Testament reality. The following excerpts are taken from his discussion as translated in *Christianity and Pagan Culture in the Later Roman Empire.*

---

[1]From *Will Our Children Have Faith?* by John H. Westerhoff. Copyright © 1976 by The Seabury Press, Inc. Used by permission of the publisher.

FRAMEWORK

Read the excerpts quoted from Chrysostom and be prepared to discuss the following questions in class:

a. What is Chrysostom's apparent view of children? How does this compare with the view implied in the Old and New Testament?

b. What is Chrysostom's advice about the child's relationship to secular society? What is his rationale for this view? Does Chrysostom's view find expression today? How?

c. Would you characterize Chrysostom's approach to child rearing as "negative" or "positive"? Why?

d. The quotes provided below are typical of the whole tract. From them, how would you describe Chrysostom's apparent nurture system? What strengths and weaknesses do you see if you take the New Testament pattern as normative?

JOHN CHRYSOSTOM

Like the creators of statues do you give all your leisure to fashioning these wondrous statues for God. And, as you remove what is superfluous and add what is lacking, inspect them day by day, to see what good qualities nature has supplied so that you will increase them, and what faults so that you will eradicate them. And, first of all, take the greatest care to banish licentious speech; for love of this above all frets the souls of the young. Before he is of an age to try it, teach thy son to be sober and vigilant and to shorten sleep for the sake of prayer, and with every word and deed to set upon himself the seal of the faith (p. 96).

We must train the child to utter grave and reverent words. We must drive many strangers away, so that no corrupt men may also find their way in to mingle with these citizens. Words that are insolent and slanderous, foolish, shameful, common, and worldly, all these we must expel. . . . Let their words be giving thanks, solemn hymns; let their discourse ever be about God, about heavenly philosophy (p. 99).

Make a law straightway that he use no one in despite, that he speak ill of no man, that he swear not, that he be not contentious. If thou shouldst see him transgressing this law, punish him, now with a stern look, now with incisive, now with reproachful, words; at other times win him with gentleness and promises. Have not recourse to blows constantly and accustom him not to be trained by the rod; for if he feel it constantly as he is being trained, he will learn to despise it. And when he has learnt to despise it, he has reduced thy system to nought (p. 99).

Teach him to be fair and courteous. If thou dost see a servant ill-used by him, do not overlook it, but punish him who is free; for if he knows that he may not ill use even a slave, he will abstain all the more from insulting or slandering one who is free and of his class. Stop his mouth from speaking evil. If thou dost see him traducing another, curb him and direct his tongue toward his own faults (p. 100).

Tell him this [Bible] story one evening at supper. Let his mother repeat the same tale; then, when he has heard it often, ask him too, saying: "Tell me the story," so that he may be eager to imitate you. And when he has memorized it thou wilt also tell him how it profits him. The soul indeed, as it receives the story within itself before thou hast elaborated it, is aware that it will benefit. Nevertheless, do thou say hereafter: "Thou dost see how great a sin is greed, how great a sin it is to envy a brother. Thou dost see how great a sin it is to think that thou canst hide aught from God; for He sees all things (p. 104).[2]

---

[2]John Chrysostom, *The Right Way for Parents to Bring Up Their Children,* in *Christianity and Pagan Culture in the Later Roman Empire* by M. L. W. Laistner (Ithaca, N.Y.: Cornell University Press, 1951).

PART 1

FRAMEWORK

A Theological Framework for Ministry

Nurture in the Old Testament
Nurture in the New Testament
The Role of Scripture in Nurture
The Nurture Process

A Developmental Framework for Ministry

The Developmental Perspective
Cognitive Potentials of Children
Social Relationships of Children
Moral Development in Children
An Integrated Perspective

Two critical variables have shaped our ministry with children during the past one hundred years. One is our view of children. The other is our view of the Bible. And there is a long-

THE ROLE OF SCRIPTURE IN NURTURE

ranging debate over the nature of Scripture and thus over its role in the nurture process.

Most conservatives have been relatively unmoved by the debates about the nature of Scripture that have affected goals and practice of ministry with children. While the liberals studied and explored, conservatives held firmly to the simple conviction that the Bible is the Word of God. To the conservative the Bible shares revealed information: authoritative truth shared by God Himself. It is in the Bible that we learn about God and ourselves. In the Bible we find the meaning of life and how to live it. In the Bible we uncover the secrets of past, present, and future.

This view of Scriptures has produced a relatively plain approach to teaching children. Since the Bible shares revealed truths, teaching the Bible must mean to communicate what it says. And so, for ministry to adults or to children, clear priority has been given to the transmission of Bible truths. From the inception of the Sunday school movement in the 1780s, Bible stories and Christian moral principles have been the core of conservative curriculums. The methods of the public school, so effective in communicating information, have been adopted and applied to the teaching of the Bible in Sunday school and other church agencies.

CHAPTER 3

It's important for us to realize that in holding our traditional view of Scripture, we have quite possibly leaped to unwarranted conclusions about aims and methods of teaching the Bible. Certainly one's understanding of the nature of the Bible dramatically affects one's view of how it is to be used in nurture. Several recent approaches demonstrate a variety of points of view.

PERSPECTIVES ON SCRIPTURE

A number of ideas about the nurture of children have been suggested in this century. Each shaper of an approach that has had impact on ministry with children has relied heavily on his or her personal view of Scripture. Without going into their backgrounds here (see PROBE 2 at the end of the chapter), we can gain an idea of the systems of several significant theoreticians in the following sketches.

GEORGE ALBERT COE

Coe criticizes the traditional aims of Christian education, which he summarizes as the following: to instruct the child, or to prepare the child for membership in the church, or to save the child's soul, or to unfold religious capacities, or to produce Christian character. He argues that Jesus' teachings demand a commitment to what Coe calls the "democracy of God," using this terminology because he believes that "democracy" most fully expresses what Jesus meant by "kingdom of God." Christian nurture of children thus means "growth of the young toward and into mature and efficient devotion to the democracy of God, and happy self-realization therein" (p. 55).

For Coe, such growth requires a unique curriculum: the "present relations and interactions between persons." The Bible is a rich sourcebook, which will provide specific help for specific needs. But the starting point is always the present experience and the needs of learners. Thus the Bible is to be used by selecting passages and concepts that will give help in understanding and shaping our experiences. Coe says,

> We shall discover the true place of the Bible in the curriculum by applying to childhood the same principle of using the Scriptures in the interest of present living. If the curriculum is fundamentally a course in Christian living, the Bible will be used as each turn of the child's experience in such a way as to help with the particular problem that is then uppermost (p. 114).[1]

Extrabiblical materials will be used in the same way. For Coe, Scripture will provide help. But it is not in any traditional sense authoritative.

ERNEST M. LIGON

To Ligon, "our task is to build Christian character." Ligon's use of the Bible is particularly interesting. He focuses on the Gospels and the teachings of Jesus, and concludes that "Jesus believed character is developed in two major qualities, faith and love." He then looks further at the teaching of Jesus, where he believes he can discern eight general character traits, each of which is further broken down into a number of "attitudes."

While Ligon believes he has drawn his content and goals *from* Scripture, he does not see Christian education as the teaching *of* Scripture. Instead he turns to scientific research to determine the best ways to build character. Church and home must cooperate in this endeavor. And rating scales must be used to measure individual progress. "One must not underestimate the value of this," Ligon argues. "It is the very essence of obeying Jesus' command, 'By their fruits ye shall know them.'"

Ligon's curriculum is rigorous. It includes a statement of the attitude to be taught, an explanation of the psychological and educational principles involved in teaching "this attitude to the

---

[1]George Albert Coe, *A Social Theory of Religious Education* (New York: Arno Press and New York *Times*, 1969).

particular age level," a Church School Lesson and Project, and a Guide for the Parents. Along with topics for discussion, books to read, stories to tell, and projects to carry out are also "Biblical passages to study."

But for Ligon the task of character education is very different from training in biblical literature, church history, Christian doctrine, or any other subjects the church may wish to inculcate. Only in character education, carried out by application of the scientific method of applied research, "can we build the kind of personality of which Jesus dreamed" (p. 149).[2]

SOPHIA LYON FAHS

Fahs sees the goal of ministry with children as creative religious development and defines "religious" in the broadest terms. To Fahs, "all the specific beliefs one holds about many kinds of things in many areas of life," all drawn together in one emotional whole, constitute one's "faith" or philosophy of life. Religious education thus deals with the whole person and the whole fabric of beliefs and attitudes. It can no longer focus on specific beliefs that center around "such ideas as God, prayer, the Bible, Jesus, salvation, eternity, the supernatural and the moral law" (p. 177). Development of the whole person is the true concern of nurture.

Fahs comes directly at the nature of Scripture in her exploration of nurture. She speaks of an "old Bible" that was interpreted to tell a single story and give information about "God, his purposes, his commands for man, even to learn God's thoughts and feelings for man." She decisively rejects this "old Bible" view of Scripture as "God's Word." Instead she argues for a "new Bible."

The new Bible is something that has surfaced "as a result of our new knowledge" gained through biblical criticism. The new Bible is "a collection of records of human experiences. It is about people. It tells us what they were like and how they believed about God and their world and how these beliefs affected their living" (p. 76). Thus the new Bible is human. It is not the source for a system of beliefs, but rather the report of diverse beliefs and practices, with "no one message of truth pervading the entire collection of writings" (p. 77).

The result of Fah's thinking is a human development curriculum, which uses multiple sources and shared experiences to help a child grow as a healthy, happy personality. The Bible may

---

[2]Ernest M. Ligon, *A Greater Generation* (New York: Macmillan, 1948).

be used as one of the curriculum resources. But its use is not vital and may not even be important.[3]

JOHN H. WESTERHOFF III

Westerhoff insists that our task in ministry is not to teach Christianity, but to communicate Christian faith. He calls our schooling-instructional approach to nurture "bankrupt."

While Westerhoff has not yet developed an alternate paradigm, he is convinced that it must involve life lived in a faith community that affirms and experiences the shared meanings of Christian faith.

Westerhoff is convinced that the Bible must have a central role in the life of the community and individual. He argues that "the centrality of the Bible for Christian faith is derived from its record of God's activity. The Old and the New Testaments are important because they contain the story of God's actions in history and his people's attempt to understand and respond" (p. 34).

Westerhoff does not see the written words of the Bible as some final authority, any more than he sees the doctrines of the church or inner personal experiences as authoritative. "The Bible, however, remains the source and norm of Christian faith," for it is the source of the story that is the basis for our understanding, interpretation, and application of our own faith story (p. 34).

The enculturation paradigm that Westerhoff is developing does have a central role for the Bible, a role expressed to some extent in his list of aims that must be achieved if we are to communicate faith. He suggests that the first aim should be:

> To possess a personal knowledge and understanding of God's revelation as found in the Bible, and to be disposed and able to interpret its meaning for daily individual and social life.
> To achieve this aim we need: (a) To be introduced to the biblical story of God's action in history (as found in the stories of the Old and New Testament, as *our* story; (b) to be involved in an historical, critical interpretation of the biblical story; (c) to be engaged in reflection on current social issues in the light of the biblical story (p. 106).

While Westerhoff suggests that "a great deal more needs to be done on the paradigm itself as well as its application" (p. 126) it is likely that many will attempt to work out teaching/learning processes that will reflect the concepts of this influential contemporary thinker.[4]

---

[3]Sophia Lyon Fahs, *Today's Children and Yesterday's Heritage* (Boston: Beacon, 1952).

[4]From *Will Our Children Have Faith?* by John H. Westerhoff. Copyright © 1976 by The Seabury Press, Inc. Used by permission of the publisher.

The chart on page 60 (Figure 6) summarizes several of the significant elements in these typical shapers of ministry to children. One set of cells has been left blank. Fill them in with the views you believe are prevalent in your own church and tradition, as they are reflected in the curriculum you have most frequently used with children.

THE CURRENT CONCERN

The views described so far in this chapter have been influential. Various denominational curriculums have been designed to implement one or the other. But the educational experiments have generally proven unsuccessful. Often the "new" approaches have caused congregations to turn away from their denomination's "official" publications, and many have turned to one of the large independent or nondenominational publishers represented by Scripture Press, Gospel Light, and David C. Cook. These publishers have been marked by a consistent commitment to a conservative theology and to "Bible teaching" children's curriculums. And despite the impact of the thinkers on educators, the mass of teachers in church (Sunday) schools have somehow felt that their ministry to children must be one of teaching the Bible.

But one current movement strikes at the roots of conservative Bible teaching. This is the growing acceptance of the views of Jean Piaget and his followers. Piaget (whose views we'll describe thoroughly in the next section of this book) argues, and most would say has proven, that there is a distinct sequence to cognitive growth, and that at earlier stages many concepts simply cannot be grasped by young children.

Piaget's followers today are shaping much of the curriculum and teaching approaches used in the public schools. And Christian educators who understand Piaget are asking questions about our Bible teaching. How many of the concepts we try to teach through our Bible stories are beyond the ability of children to comprehend? How many of our applications demand ways of thinking that are simply beyond the young? Affirming, as the conservative does, that the Bible does share truth about God, which truths can be taught to children meaningfully? And which may not only be misunderstood but actually distorted by the way children think?

In *Living the Bible with Children*, Dorothy Jean Furnish sums up the dilemma of those who believe we must teach the Bible to children and yet recognize the validity of Piaget's understanding of children's thought. She describes the problem this way:

FIGURE 6
20th CENTURY CHRISTIAN EDUCATORS'
APPROACHES TO NURTURE

	Goal of Nurture	Curriculum	Nature of Scripture	Use of Scripture
Coe	build the democracy of God	present relations and interactions between people	history of human's religious experiences	"helps" with our present experiences
Ligon	build Christian character	projects that teach and build character traits	unstated	source of character description, of stories illustrating traits
Fahs	whole person (personal) development	experiences that help develop the whole person	record of man's conflicting beliefs	one of many resources for nurture
Westerhoff	enculturation of faith	the life and worship of the whole community of faith	the story of God's historic acts and man's responses to Him	to help us know, interpret, and apply "the story"
Your Church?				

1. The Bible is knowledge.
2. Children are minds.
3. Much of the knowledge of the Bible consists of abstract concepts.
4. Children's minds cannot grasp abstract concepts.
5. Therefore, we cannot teach the Bible to children.
6. But we want to teach the Bible to children.
7. Go back to 1.[5]

In setting up this dilemma, Furnish neatly isolates two assumptions that continue to underlie much conservative Christian educational practice: (1) the assumption that the Bible is knowledge, and (2) the assumption that persons are minds.

The Bible is knowledge. The theorists whose nurture approaches are described in this chapter have failed to influence conservatives. This is primarily because most of them abandoned a historic, traditional view of the nature and authority of Scripture. In contrast to seeing the Bible as a fallible record of humankind's religious experience, conservatives have insisted that the Bible is God's sure revelation of truth to humankind, given in words that have been divinely inspired. Thus the Scripture, to its very words, is reliable and relevant. More, by nature God's revelation is propositional. While God does communicate Himself in Scripture, that communication comes with and through information. Through the information revealed in Scripture we gain knowledge about God. When we respond with faith to His Word to us, we come to know Him in a personal way. Thus knowing about God and knowing God can never be divorced from one another . . . or substituted for each other.

This belief about the nature of the Bible and its role in Christian faith has seemed to conservatives to make one thing perfectly clear. We must teach the Bible. We must let children, youth, and adults, within and outside the community of faith, know what the Bible says. Since they must have the information provided in the Scriptures, it has seemed obvious that the mission of ministry is to communicate the necessary information.

In the best sense, conservatives have viewed teaching the Bible as a means to other ends. Conservatives have yearned for all to understand what the Bible says so they can come to personal relationship with God. Conservatives have wanted believers to understand so they can grow in faith relationship with God, mature in personal holiness, come to committed discipleship, and reach out with love to serve all human beings. But those of us who affirm a historic and traditional view of the Bible

---

[5]Dorothy Jean Furnish, *Living the Bible with Children* (Nashville: Abingdon, 1979), p. 20.

can be challenged. We can be challenged for one great unquestioned leap to a doubtful conclusion. We have said, "The Bible is revealed truth," and have jumped to the conclusion that our ministry goals will be achieved if we only teach that truth as something to _know_.

The assumption that an intellectual mastery of truth is that intermediate step between revelation and faith has shaped our approach to ministry. We have organized to convey what the Bible teaches, as information. We have locked into a schooling/instructional model for ministry, because this is an efficient way to communicate information. We have cast the teacher as a person who knows more (and thus is qualified to teach); we have seen the Bible as curriculum (and thus a source of information); we have made the people of God students (who know less, and thus must gain more information about the Bible if they are to be good Christians). We have taken the whole process of ministry into the classroom (which is set apart by time and space, and so is isolated from real life). In this often sterile context we have gone about the business of "teaching the Bible," treating it as information which all must come to know.

I've already explored the problems associated with schooling in A Theology of Christian Education.[6] It is not my intention to restate what I've written there. Here I simply want to point out that the leap, from our conviction that the Bible does communicate revealed truth, to the assumption that we should teach the Bible as information, has been made blindly. We need to go back to the Scripture, to see first of all the essential nature of truth, and then to see if the Bible itself gives us a pattern for its teaching.

Children are minds. This is the second assumption that Furnish pinpoints in setting up her dilemma. If we view teaching the Bible as communicating the information it contains, then we are going to focus our ministry on children's minds. It is the mind that grasps information. It is the mind that knows.

But there are a number of reasons to doubt that the mind is the key. If a person knows, will he or she believe? If a person has biblical information, will Christian attitudes and values be shaped? Certainly knowing is necessary. But it is hardly sufficient.

It is just because we have placed such a great stress on knowing, and have treated children as minds to be shaped by truth, that the findings of Piaget seem so threatening. If children _are_ minds and the Bible provides the information they

---

[6]Lawrence O. Richards, A Theology of Christian Education (Grand Rapids: Zondervan, 1975).

must know, to discover that children's minds cannot grasp many of Scripture's most vital teachings is devastating!

Furnish finds her way out of the Piagetan dilemma by stating a new set of assumptions. She suggests that

1. *The Bible is experiences.* It is a record of both accumulated experiences of the Judeo-Christian communities, and the personal experiences of individuals as they have encountered the Divine in their lives.
2. *Children are experiencers.* They have the ability to understand through their feelings, their curiosities, and their imagination. They find meaning in the experiences of the here and now.
3. *Therefore, we can teach the Bible to children.* With experience as the common denominator between the Bible and children, the barrier of intellectual limitations between the two is torn down, and a clear access is provided.

The task, then, is to help children enter into the world of the Bible and experience its content as their own. If we can accomplish this, the meanings of the Bible can be discovered.[7]

While conservatives would not agree with her concept of Scripture, we should appreciate her analysis of the issue facing us all. And we should appreciate her attempt at solution. The answer is to be found in clarifying our assumptions about the Bible—and in clarifying our assumptions about children.

THE BIBLE AS TRUTH

In a basic passage that defines the nature of revelation, Paul writes of words taught by the Spirit of God, unveiling what

> no eye has seen,
> no ear has heard,
> no mind has conceived (1 Cor. 2:9).

Human beings, limited to observation of the physical universe we inhabit, have no way to penetrate beyond the veil the material drops over our senses. And we have no imaginative capacity of mind to dream of hidden realities. "For who among men knows [even] the thoughts of a man, except the man's spirit within him," Paul continues. Surely, if we are unable to understand the thoughts and motives that underlie the human actions we observe, how could we ever deduce the intents and motives of God? We might see His mighty acts in history. But understand them or Him? Never! And so Paul continues, "In the same way no one knows the thoughts of God except the Spirit of God."

The Bible Reveals Reality

But that Spirit has touched us and has freely given us a stunning gift. In "words taught by the Spirit," God has bridged

---

[7]Furnish, *Living the Bible*, pp. 20–21.

the unbridgeable. In words reaching us through prophets and apostles, God Himself has spoken to us and made the unguessable our own.

The impact of this familiar passage (1 Cor. 2:9–13) is enhanced when we note the context from which the phrase "no eye has seen, no ear has heard, no mind has conceived" is taken. It is not, as is often supposed, a reference to Isaiah 64:4. It is taken from the Greek poet Empedocles who lived in the fifth century B.C. Speaking of the limitations of humankind, the poet writes,

> Weak and narrow are the powers implanted in the limbs of man; many the woes that fall on them and blunt the edges of thought; short is the measure of the life in death through which they toil. Then are they borne away; like smoke they vanish into the air; and what they dream they know is but the little that each has stumbled on in wandering about the world. Yet boast they all that they have learned the whole. Vain fools! For what that is, no eye has seen, no ear hath heard, nor can it be conceived by the mind of man.

The bits and pieces we stumble on in our wanderings, from which we try to construct our perception of reality, can never tell us about the whole. Our senses give us hints, and so we guess. But guessing wrong, humanity wanders, lost among its illusions, toiling on in a death-like life that apart from a word from God remains mystery.

But God has spoken! In His words the veils are stripped away, and through His eyes we at last can comprehend reality.

It is against this background that we need to understand the nature of Scripture and the meaning of truth—a term closely associated with the biblical *Word.* Many books and articles explore the use of this term in the Old and New Testaments. In each it is a significant term, with more than one shade of meaning. But there is a common meaning that links both Testaments. *Truth* is intimately linked with faithfulness and reliability. As truth, God's Word is reliable because it accords fully with reality.

We can trust the Scriptures, for they faithfully reveal the whole of which Empedocles despaired.

Biblical Reality Must Be Lived

In the New Testament both John and Paul often use the word *truth.* In using it they invite us to set aside surface appearances and reject the illusory perceptions of humankind. In the words of C. H. Dodd the Scriptures invite a wandering humankind to enter the "plane of reality."

With the affirmation in both Testaments that God's Word is truth comes a call to believers to walk in the truth. The plane of reality revealed in Scripture calls for a response. We are to live life guided by the vision of reality provided in the Word. For John the issue is clear. We can come to know the truth by living it, to be sanctified and set free, or we can continue to stumble, blinded by the dark.

To understand the Scriptures as God's revelation of reality is to realize that it is never sufficient to "know" the information in the Bible. Ideas can be known. Reality must be experienced. It may be appropriate to respond to a body of information by learning it. But the only appropriate response to the opening of a window, so we can at last see the furnishings of the room in which we live, is to let every step we take be guided by the light that floods in.

Two of many New Testament passages reinforce this fact. John 8 reports Jesus' words to some who believed in Him. "If you hold to my teaching," Jesus taught, "you are really my disciples. Then you will know the truth, and the truth will set you free" (8:31–32). The teachings or words of Jesus were not to be processed as information. The words of Jesus were to be lived. Only when Jesus' disciples live by His words will they come to "know" the truth. Only when we live our lives on the plane of revealed reality will we experience reality and find both freedom and release.

John shows us in his first letter a similar use of *truth*. There he couches his messages in terms of light and dark. "God is light," John writes. "In him there is no darkness at all. If we claim to have fellowship with him yet walk in the darkness, we lie and do not live by the truth. But if we walk in the light, as he is in the light, we have fellowship with one another and the blood of Jesus, his Son, purifies us from every sin" (1:5–7). This is no demand for sinlessness. It is a call to live by the truth. "If we claim to be without sin," John goes on, "we deceive ourselves and the truth is not in us." God is able to deal with the sins that cling to us. But only if we face reality. Only if we deal with God and ourselves honestly. "If we confess [admit] our sins, he is faithful and just and will forgive us our sins and [keep on] purify[ing] us from all unrighteousness" (1:7–9). Only a rejection of reality, and refusal to live on its plane, can cut us off from God. "If we claim we have not sinned, we make him out to be a liar and his word has no place in our lives" (1:10).

Implications of Scripture As Truth

Conservatives will continue to insist that the Bible is God's revelation, given in words taught by the Holy Spirit. But we must realize that the essential revelation they convey is not mere

FIGURE 7

IMPLICATIONS OF CONSERVATIVE UNDERSTANDING OF SCRIPTURE FOR TEACHING MODELS

	The Common Commitment	The Nature of Scripture	Therefore	Therefore	Therefore	Therefore
Track #1	biblical revelation is given in inspired words and is propositional in character	undefined	assume the Bible contains trustworthy information	assume that information can be known	assume that information must be taught	assume when the students know the true information they can apply or respond to it
Track #2	biblical revelation is given in inspired words and is propositional in character	in essence truth: an unveiling by God of reality	we can trust ourselves to live by the reality unveiled	assume that reality must be experienced as well as conceptualized to be truly known	we must lead others to a personal and experiential knowledge of reality	only when the learner experiences reality does he "know" God's truth in a biblical sense

When no questions are asked about the nature of Scripture's propositional revelation we simply assume that the information the Bible contains is to be transmitted to others. We are sure that information must be known, and so we structure ministry to transmit the contents of the Bible as information. It is this pattern of assumptions that has led to our present school-like approaches to the teaching of the Bible.

When we search the Bible we discover that its revelation is truth. As truth the Bible is an unveiling of a reality which Jesus' disciples are called to experience. *Immediately the issue in Bible teaching shifts!* Our First concern is no longer the best way to transmit information, but the best way to help learners experience (and thus come to "know") God's truth! Whatever we might say about the best way, there are many reasons why the school-like setting is *not* best. And these we will see.

information, but truth. As truth, Scripture has a unique function and must always be heard as invitation. God's Word must find its place in our lives, not just in our minds. To truly "know" this divine word we must experience the realities that it portrays.

The tragic inadequacy of the schooling/instructional model for teaching the Bible is that it does treat the Scriptures as information and children as minds. What is required is another model (see Figure 7 for a comparison) that will

- honor the Scriptures both as a revelation in words and as truth
- communicate the Scriptures in a way that is uniquely appropriate to a revelation of reality
- communicate the Scriptures to the whole person, so that heart and will are engaged as well as mind
- communicate the Scriptures in such a way that the learner is engaged in experiencing the truth as he or she hears its living message

SUMMING UP

While we have not yet sketched fully the instructional model that is appropriate to communicating Scripture as reality, we can see that this approach to the Bible provides an answer to the Piagetan dilemma. If the Bible were just a book of concepts and information, and if it were shown that children cannot grasp these concepts, the cognitive limitations of the young would prove an insurmountable obstacle to the use of the Bible with boys and girls. But the Bible is not just information. And children are not simply minds. We can and must begin our thinking about ministry of the Word on a different plane, with assumptions like these:

1. *The Bible is God's revelation of reality.* As an unveiling of reality, its truths can be and are to be experienced. We can experience reality without fully understanding it, though we cannot experience reality apart from faith.

2. *Children are persons.* As human beings children can respond in faith and can experience the realities which are unveiled in the Word, even when the concepts in which those realities are expressed are beyond their ability to grasp.

3. *Therefore, we can teach the Bible to children.* With a reality revealed in Scripture and experienceable by children providing common ground, the barrier of children's cognitive limitations is no longer insurmountable. We can find ways to communicate the Word of God meaningfully.

FRAMEWORK

PROBE

▶ *case histories*
▶ *discussion questions*
▶ *thought provokers*
▶ *resources*

1. One of the first researchers to explore the relationship of Piaget's findings about children's cognitive development to religious education of children was Ronald Goldman, a British educational psychologist. In England the Bible was a part of the school curriculum. So Goldman engaged in research to discover how children actually understood the Bible stories they were taught. Goldman was disturbed by what he perceived as great distortions in children's religious understanding.

   Goldman is no theorist of the stature of Coe, Ligon, Fahs, or Westerhoff. His concern is not nurture, but instruction. But he is interesting for several reasons. He was one of the first to challenge teaching the Bible to children on the basis of Piaget's insights about children's cognitive development. He was one of the first to suggest a solution. And his work demonstrates with striking clarity the determining role of our view of Scripture in *whatever* educational or nurture system we may hold!

   Goldman's concept of Scripture is expressed in the report of his research, *Religious Thinking from Childhood to Adolescence*. There he describes the Bible as "a library of inspired literature by many authors, tracing how a nation encountered God through revelation and experience" (p. 238). With this essentially neoorthodox perspective he believes that educators must "refine the theological world" of children, and says the "major task of religious education of the younger child is to feed the child's crude deity concepts and his physical anthropomorphisms in such a way that he refines his crudities of religious thinking as far as his limits of experience and ability allow" (p. 232).

   One fascinating aspect of Goldman's work is his attempt to define a curriculum with content that will avoid the dangers of teaching the Bible wrongly to children. His rather surprising recommendation: don't expose children to the Bible too early! From ages 5–9 one must seek to influence and not instruct, and children should not be allowed to acquire a religious vocabulary that "has no conceptual substance." Instead showing reverence for the world of nature, focusing on themes such as our homes and people who help us, will help create a (contentless) emotional frame of reference that will be the "basic religious experience" of this period of time.

   From ages 9–13 the Bible may be introduced. Poetical material can be used to help the child sense God as creator and heart of the

68

universe. Stories may be introduced to provide details of how people lived and their customs as a basis for later establishing the relevance of the Bible to our own lives. Narratives of Jesus' life may also be introduced here, with stress placed on His love, thoughtfulness, and influence without stress on miracle stories or, at this age, His death and resurrection. And at this age the Bible can be shown to be a library of books full of valuable ideas, but not the magical or holy book children typically think it.[8]

 a. How would each of the four writers (Coe, Ligon, Fahs, and Westerhoff) evaluate the position taken by Goldman?
 b. How would a traditional Christian educator tend to evaluate the position taken by Goldman?
 c. How would each seek to avoid the dilemma stated by Furnish?
 d. How do you think the author of this book would evaluate the position taken by Goldman?

2. Research into the nurture systems suggested by the writers quoted in this chapter is useful in exploring significant issues in ministry to children. A helpful project would be selecting and doing one of the following:

 a. Read one or more major texts by the individual.
 b. Discover what influence the individual has had in Christian education, and whom he or she influenced.
 c. Obtain and examine curriculum materials that have been developed from his or her theory base.
 d. Write a report that describes each salient element of the theory and that evaluates the attempts made to implement it.

You might begin with the following works of the men and women discussed in this chapter:

Coe, George Albert. *A Social Theory of Religious Education.* New York: Arno Press & the New York Times, 1969.

Fahs, Sophia Lyon. *Today's Children and Yesterday's Heritage.* Boston: Beacon, 1952.

Ligon, Ernest M. *A Greater Generation.* New York: Macmillan, 1948.

Westerhoff, John H. III. *Will Our Children Have Faith?* New York: Seabury, 1976.

3. There is a model for communicating the Scripture as reality provided in the Old Testament. You'll find that model on page 25. Study it and see if you can discern how it meets the requirements for an approach to communicating God's Word as truth.

---

[8]Ronald Goldman, *Religious Thinking from Childhood to Adolescence* (London: Routledge and Kegan Paul, 1964), see pp. 220–46.

4. Explore the Bible's use of the words *truth and know*. Use a concordance to locate critical passages for exegesis. Or use tools such as the three volume *New International Dictionary of New Testament Theology*.[9]

5. For further consideration of the implications of viewing the Scripture as a truth or reality system, you might want to study the following:

a. Richards, Lawrence O. *Creative Bible Study*. Grand Rapids: Zondervan, 1971. Chapters 1–12.
b. Richards, Lawrence O. "Experiencing Reality Together." In *Theology and Religious Education*, edited by Norma H. Thompson. New York: Religious Education Press, 1981.

---

[9]Ed. Colin Brown, 3 vols. (Grand Rapids: Zondervan, 1976, 1977, 1978).

PART 1

FRAMEWORK

A Theological Framework for Ministry

Nurture in the Old Testament
Nurture in the New Testament
The Role of Scripture in Nurture
The Nurture Process

A Developmental Framework for Ministry

The Developmental Perspective
Cognitive Potentials of Children
Social Relationships of Children
Moral Development in Children
An Integrated Perspective

Many of the questions we raise about children simply are not addressed in the Bible. But others are answered. Decisively. We need to distinguish between the two, and build our minis-

THE NURTURE PROCESS

try with children on the issues with which the Scriptures definitely deal. On the most significant issues, the testimony of both Testaments agrees.

Surprisingly, the questions that have divided theologians who pay some attention to children are not the issues dealt with in the Bible. The Bible makes little over such issues as: Are children to be baptized in infancy, or not? Do the offspring of believers have some special standing with God? If so, what is it? If not, what does Paul mean when he suggests to the Corinthians that the children of a believing parent are in some sense holy? Is there an age of accountability? If so, what is it? Can we say with Calvin that children of believers are "presumptively Christians"? Or argue, with Gaines S. Dobbins, that every child is "safe in his innocency until the realization of sin and its power dawns"?[1] If children are not somehow within the covenant, how should they be dealt with before conversion? Should they be treated differently after? Are infants, who have not sinned personally, saved? With or without baptism? How early may children be converted? What does a young child have to understand, or to do? Should communion be administered to young children?

These questions have been debated and discussed through church history. We find them pondered by church fathers and councils, argued by reformers and revivalists, and written on in catechisms and theologies. However important these issues may seem to the theologian, they are not the issues with which the Scriptures seem primarily concerned. When the Bible does talk about children it does not speak in these terms. Instead of supplying more fuel for our speculation, the Scripture seems to simply assume certain things about all human beings, and then go on to show us how to love children, to live with them, and to help them grow.

In a book on ministry with children, we have to adopt the focus of Scripture. We do need a general perspective on persons. But beyond that what we need is an understanding of the processes that help people grow. Like farmers, we are not primarily concerned with dissecting young plants. We want to work the soil in which they grow.

ASSUMPTIONS ABOUT PERSONS

The assumptions that are particularly important to us about persons are not the usual theological ones. We're familiar with those issues, and as Christians we too struggle to balance Scripture's exalted picture of human beings created in the image of

---

[1]Gaines S. Dobbins, *Winning of Children* (Nashville: Broadman, 1953), p. 120.

God with its brutal honesty about human debasement and sin. We know what it means to be members of a lost humanity yet remain objects of God's love. We have experienced the inner grip of death, traced it back to Adam, and felt the tug toward sin that warps society into a jumble of injustice and pain. We balance in our own experience awareness of our freedom and powerlessness, and the touch of a sovereign yet gentle grace. We know the delicacy of God's touch, as He comes to us with invitation, yet never crushes us with that sense of His power that would rob us of personal responsibility. All these things we know, for they are the great realities our faith affirms and our experience echoes. These are the givens: the convictions about the shape of reality unveiled in Scripture, held by the church through the ages.

These givens are not the assumptions we need to state as we look for a theological framework for ministry with children. Instead we need to state assumptions that help us understand human beings as learners. We can sum up the important testimony of Scripture about persons as learners simply, by saying that the Bible teaches us to view persons (including children!) as free, responsible individuals, whose growth can be influenced but never determined, and whose progress in faith is linked with personal relationship to God.

Human Beings Are Free, Responsible Individuals

Earlier we discovered that John Chrysostom spoke of children as statues to be fashioned for God by parents. The imagery is not unusual. Others have called children wax tablets, and still others have seen them as trainable organisms to be shaped by behavioral scientists who are learning what stimuli to provide to produce desired behavior. But never in Scripture do we catch a hint of adults or children dismissed with such disrespect!

In fact, the Bible seems to assume that each person has a wide-ranging freedom, which brings with it personal responsibility for every act.

From the Old Testament's many different terms for children we learn that limitations on personal responsibility exist. Isaiah speaks of an infant in arms who for some years will not know "enough to reject the wrong and choose the right" (7:15). And even up to age twenty, those who came out of Egypt with Moses were exempt from punishment for Israel's disobedience (Num. 14:29).

Yet, no person is without responsibility. No actions are excused as if determined by circumstances beyond an individual's control. Others will have an influence. In fact, that influence may reach down and affect three and four generations (cf. Num.

14:18). But as the prophet Ezekiel proclaims to a generation that shrugged off responsibility by saying that the fathers' sins made their own punishment inevitable, each individual's life or death hinges on his or her own choices (cf. Ezek. 18).

The Proverbs clearly reflect this conviction of freedom and responsibility. Bringing up a child in the way he or she should go will have a strong influence on the child's choices (22:6), but the young will make choices. "Even a child is known by his actions," one proverb observes (20:11). And never do the Proverbs suggest that the parent is known by the actions of the child. Sons are urged to accept their parents' words (e.g., 2:1; 4:2, 10; 13:1). But parents are not told to make their sons obey. At worst a child's behavior will reflect on the parent's suitability for leadership (cf. 1 Sam. 2:22–25 with 3:13; 1 Tim. 3:4). But never are offspring excused because of parental failings.

The freedom and the responsibility that the Bible ascribes to human beings remind us that nurture does not imply control. In fact, while we can enforce conformity, we can do nothing to require commitment. We cannot touch the heart and make another person freely choose to respond to God in faith and obedience.

From a Christian point of view, this is good. For only those actions that flow freely, by one's own choice, are either moral or pleasing to God. Even God's placement of the tree in Eden was not so much a test as an affirmation of Adam's freedom and an indication of the high value that God places on our free and willing response to Him.

This perception of persons has great significance for education and ministry. We will never treat adults or children as passive beings. We will never assume they can be patterned by knowledge. We will never expect to mold them by instruction, by patterning, or by behavioral modification. We will treat them with the respect due to individuals. We will expect them to be active, to select and to choose, to interact with us and the environment. We will realize that nurture is more intimately related to strengthening the will than to shaping the mind.

Human Beings Can Be Influenced

While each person is free and responsible, each of us will be influenced by others. When either Testament deals with nurture, this fact seems to be preeminent.

The Bible does not really touch on the issues raised by educational psychology. We are given no look inside to see what happens when persons "learn." There is no "biblical psychology of learning" to compete with the hypotheses of the behavioral sciences. Instead the Bible simply describes the personal and social environment that stimulates growth in faith.

We are guarded from looking at these factors from a humanistic point of view. Nothing we can do will *determine* the course of another's life. Instead we are reminded of the central role of the supernatural. The beginning of wisdom is rooted in that reverential awe of God that recognizes Him as Lord and responds with faith (Prov. 2:5–6; 9:10–12). Without the intimate presence of Jesus in the persons and in the processes, we can do exactly nothing (John 15:5). But in Scripture we do come to recognize that God is present in the process and that God has so designed humankind that His Spirit works most freely with rather than against the processes that are in accord with human nature.

What happens inside the heart is a secret. But *there is no secret about influence.* God has stripped away the mystery and shown us how to minister to others most effectively. This means that when we deal with ministry or with nurture from a theological point of view, *we are forced to deal with those processes through which we can best serve as God's agents of influence.* When we attempt to describe the theological framework for ministry with children, *we are forced to identify the processes by which we influence the growth of children in faith.* Children too are free. But they can be influenced. And the God who works within them and us has shown us the processes by which openness to Him and growth in faith are stimulated.

The critical processes have all been isolated in our first three chapters. It remains now to identify them and to describe them briefly. We must master them, for they provide the framework within which ministry with children can be designed.

The processes that influence the growth of faith are those that

- communicate *belonging* to a vital faith community
- involve *participation* in the life of a vital faith community
- facilitate *modeling* on members of the faith community
- provide biblical *instruction as interpretation-of-life*
- encourage growing *exercise of personal choice*

PROCESSES INFLUENCING SPIRITUAL GROWTH

Processes That Communicate Belonging to a Vital Faith Community

In both Old Testament ideal and New Testament reality, the dynamic provided by a vital faith community is essential. The linkage in each system is love: in the Old Testament a loving lifestyle patterned by law, and in the New Testament the enriching power of caring for those who "become so dear to us" (1 Thess. 2:8). Both Old and New Testament peoples are linked to God by covenant: both find their identity within community resting on their relationship with God. While the Old Testament utilized many visible symbols to affirm identity with the community, belonging in the New Testament community is communicated more directly, by the quality of personal relationships that exist.

Thus Jesus' new commandment, recorded in John 13: 34–35, is of supreme importance. "Love one another," Jesus said. "As I have loved you, so you must love one another. All men will know that you are my disciples if you love one another."

- Love is the prime commandment within a faith community.
- Jesus' kind of total love is the standard.
- Relationship with Jesus is testified to all—within and without the community—by the community's love.

We can understand then the emphasis in the New Testament on coming to know one another, on nonjudgmentalism, on acceptance, on honoring each other, on mutual ministry, and on valuing one another's contributions. For love is the wellspring of holiness as well as the mark of community: in fact, the Old Testament ideal finds fulfillment in the New Testament faith community, for "love is the fulfillment of the law" (Rom. 13:10).

It is utterly essential, then, to belong within the faith community. Within the network of relationships in the faith community, spiritual growth comes to the individual and to the congregation as a whole (cf. Eph. 3:14–21; 4:14–16). To influence spiritual growth in children and in adults, we need to be particularly sensitive to these personal relationships and to build the love between persons that community requires.

In ministry with children, then, we will pay close attention to the relational links of boys and girls to other children and to adults in the congregation. To belong—to be loved and to give love—is basic if our children are to have, and to grow in, faith.

Processes That Involve Participation in the Life of a Vital Faith Community

The Old Testament is rich in methods by which children were drawn into and participated in the life of the community envisioned in the Mosaic ideal. Festivals were family affairs, reliving historic moments in history when God acted for His people. A rich symbolism was woven through worship experiences, in which children and adults took part. The world around the growing child was filled with memorials and reminders of God's own involvement in the life/history of Israel.

Worship in the Old Testament was clearly formal, while New Testament assemblies in the house churches were much more spontaneous. It seems likely that children participated.

Many of the activities of the contemporary church in which children participate are social in nature. These do have a meaningful role in building a sense of belonging. But children also need to be participants on occasions when the whole community affirms its faith relationship with God. Such occasions might well involve worship, times of mutual ministry, and also times of mission and service when believers reach out to share Christ's love in the world.

In ministry with children, then, we will pay close attention to those occasions when the adults of the community meet to express their faith to God. To participate—to minister as well as be ministered to—is basic if our children are to have, and to grow in, faith.

Processes That Facilitate Modeling on Members of the Faith Community

Processes that build belonging and permit participation will result in children coming to know each other and adult Christians in significant ways. The influence of such adults through natural processes that involve identification and imitation is generally called modeling. Such modeling influences the person's whole development as well as overt behavior.

In an earlier book I summarized factors that enhance the impact of modeling:

1. There needs to be frequent, long-term contact with the model(s).
2. There needs to be a warm, loving relationship with the model(s).
3. There needs to be exposure to the inner states of the model(s).
4. The model(s) need to be observed in a variety of life settings and situations.
5. The model(s) need to exhibit consistency and clarity in behaviors, values, etc.
6. There needs to be a correspondence between the behavior of the model(s) and the beliefs (ideal standards) of the community.
7. There needs to be explanation of the lifestyle of the model(s) conceptually, with instruction accompanying shared experiences.[2]

Clearly every dimension of the shared life of the faith communities described in the Old Testament ideal and New Testament reality reveals a social context uniquely shaped for the

---

[2]Lawrence O. Richards, *A Theology of Christian Education* (Grand Rapids: Zondervan, 1975), pp. 84–85.

maximum impact of this natural process! In a vital faith community, where there is belonging and participation, and where the Scriptures are taught as an interpretation of the life lived by a people committed to obedient faith, the modeling impact on children will be extremely powerful.

In ministry with children, then, we will pay close attention to building relationships between adults and children, and among children, that will incorporate the factors enhancing modeling. To identify with others—to have persons on which to model—is basic if our children are to have, and to grow in, faith.

Processes That Provide Biblical Instruction as Interpretation-of-life

The Old Testament pictures instruction as something to be woven into daily life, taking place "when you sit at home and when you walk along the road, when you lie down and when you get up" (Deut. 6:7). This instructional model is never superseded in later Scriptures and is essentially the process used with adults as well as with children. This is clearly seen in the image of "teaching" provided in Titus 2, which views instruction as guidance in a life that is "in accord with sound doctrine" (2:1) and focuses on a range of daily life activities.[3]

The significance of this model of teaching-as-interpretation-of-life is seen when we focus on the Scriptures as truth: God's revelation in words of the shape of reality. It is clear from this understanding of Scripture's essential character that it is always to be used to provide perspective on the experiences of the individual and the church. Scripture is to be searched to show us how to live with God and with each other, in this world.

The theme is emphasized in a familiar exhortation: "Be transformed by the renewing of your mind" (Rom. 12:2). The Greek term for *mind* here does not identify an "organ of intellect." Instead it is a term that focuses on outlook, or perspective. And it links understanding with attitudes and motives. The "pattern of this world" is not to mold us, but is to be decisively rejected by God's people. Through Scripture we have a different vision of reality, a vision which shapes our understanding of events, captures our affections, and infuses us with new motivations. With our whole perspective on ourselves and our life in this world transformed, we act in faith, sure that what God has revealed is trustworthy. "Then," Paul goes on, "you will be able to test and approve what God's will is—his good, pleasing and perfect will" (Rom. 12:2).

---

[3]See also Lawrence O. Richards and Clyde Hoeldtke, *A Theology of Church Leadership* (Grand Rapids: Zondervan, 1981), chapter 9.

It is vitally important then that we examine our instructional models. How is the schooling/instructional model related to the communication of reality? What other options to this model do we have, and how do we develop them? What resources, training, experiences, will we need to bring to the faith community of which children are a part?

In ministry with children, then, we will pay close attention to instruction in the Word of God. To design instruction that fits a biblical model—that is instruction-as-interpretation-of-life—is basic if our children are to have, and to grow in, faith.

Processes That Encourage Growing Exercise
of Personal Choice

As free and responsible beings, persons must and will exercise choice. Faith itself is never mere intellectual assent. Faith always, if it is true faith, finds expression in an appropriate response to God. The rebellion of Israel in the wilderness was not rooted in a lack of knowledge of God's will, but rather in a "sinful, unbelieving heart" that turned away from God and toward disobedience (Heb. 3:7–12). Poised on the border of the promised land, the people saw the giants, rejected God's perception of the ease with which a supernaturally aided people could overcome them, and turned aside to perish in the wilderness.

We can never insulate our children from those situations in which they too must see clearly the gap between appearances and reality, and must choose to risk faith.

While the actions of the youngest children will be guided quite directly, nurture still must be designed to strengthen the growing child's ability to make responsible choices. Rather than engaging in a war to break the child's "sinful will," Christian nurture must seek to strengthen the will for obedience by building personal responsibility. This view is perhaps reflected in the early church's willingness to let its children participate in the schooling offered by a pagan society—and its success in shaping succeeding generations for Christ.

In ministry with children, then, we will provide opportunities for responsible choice. To choose—to be responsible for one's own faith response—is vital if our children are to have, and to grow in, faith.

SUMMING UP

These five critical processes, seen so clearly in the nurture concepts of the Old and New Testament and reflecting a conservative understanding of the nature of God's Word, provide our theological framework for ministry with children. Each of the five is a significant guideline for practices, and will provide guidance as we explore ministry to children in the church, the home, and the school.

PROBE

▶ *case histories*
▶ *discussion questions*
▶ *thought provokers*
▶ *resources*

1. Look carefully at Deuteronomy 6:1–9. Write a commentary on this passage, stressing its implications for ministry. Be careful to relate any of the five processes that provide our framework for children's ministry to this Old Testament instructional model.

2. It's always difficult to grasp concepts simply from explanations. Here are six case histories that are related to the framework processes described in this chapter. Each case describes something that actually happened. Each is related to one or more of the five processes . . . but may be a *negative* or a *positive* illustration. That is, the stress may be on how that process actually did take place in the situation, or it may illustrate the lack of that process. Your assignment:
   a. Read each of the six cases and identify the process that it illustrates most clearly.
   b. Identify any additional processes that may be illustrated.
   c. From your own experience, write a case history for each of the framework processes. You may provide either positive or negative illustrations for each process.*

CASE ONE

We did a simple sociogram with our primary Sunday school classes. We asked each child to write down the first name of three friends. Then we asked each about the friends named. What we found out was that all the names were of friends at school or in the home neighborhood. No one listed one of the kids in his Sunday school class unless they were also school chums or neighbors. Oh, yes, a couple of kids named each other. They were cousins.

So we got serious about relationships. We had some special Sunday school classes on listening to each other, and identifying

---

*NOTE TO TEACHERS: If possible, discuss in class the case histories students generate. Also it will be valuable to duplicate copies of case histories generated, to distribute to class members. These will be useful (1) for analysis of problems, (2) as a resource for ministry planning, and (3) for clarification of the processes themselves.

feelings, and sharing feelings, and things like that. And we changed curriculums too: we got one that taught the Bible and used learning activities that helped the kids come to know each other too. Six months later when we did the sociogram again, nearly all the kids wrote down the first name of at least one child in the same class. And about half wrote down the first name of the teacher!

CASE TWO

The whole church has a great time on our annual retreat. We go to a camp where there's a swimming pool . . . boy, the kids love that. We have a good speaker, and we always have special stuff for the kids. This year we rented a video player, and got three movies free . . . a couple of Disney films and that new one about the boy and the horse.

It's really good for our kids to get together and play, and we have softball and volleyball for the adults. I guess you can say it's the one time we're together as a church family.

CASE THREE

We always did something special at home on holidays. One of the neatest things about them was dad always planned for them late at night, long after our regular bedtime. I remember one Easter vacation we were talking about how important it was to early Christians to know that Jesus was alive. Dad found a book about Christians in the catacombs . . . I think it was fiction, I don't remember . . . and all Easter week we had a family meeting at midnight in our own catacomb. We didn't have furniture in the living room then, so every midnight we'd slip in there, and dad would light a single candle, and we'd huddle close together with the dark all around while dad read a chapter of the book, and then we'd pretend we were Christians living then and talk about it just like it was our story. I guess things like that were some of the best parts of our childhood. At least, I remember them when Christmas and Easter come now.

CASE FOUR

We meet in houses today, just as the early church did. Our little group has grown . . . there are three homes now, pretty full, where we had only one. But what I like best I guess is what happens with our kids.

They're really a part of everything, you know. We get together Thursday evenings and Sundays, and we always have a meal together. Our meetings take about two hours. Officially, anyway. Usually a bunch of us stay late. But, anyway, for the first forty-five minutes or so when we have our meetings we're all together, kids and grownups. We sing together, and there's always some kind of feature we and the kids do. It's really good to see kids talking, and listening. And I really like it when we talk one on one—Jack has us do that a lot. Usually kids talk with an adult, someone who's not their own mom or dad. And it's just great to get to know them, and see how they learn. And I know it means a lot for someone like my Ginny, she's eight, to have everybody take her problems seriously and pray for her. Why, when I grew up, I didn't even know any adults in our church, except my Sunday school teachers, and I only saw them Sundays. My kids know everyone, and everyone knows them.

Of course, the kids do not stay all the time. We have a time just for adults after the time with the kids, and one of the couples takes them off in another room for a time of their own.

I think it's good for the grownups too. I know one of our older ladies really likes my two kids. Every couple weeks or so they go off for a penny trip. That's what they call it, anyway, because whenever they come to a corner as they drive they flip a coin to see which direction to take. You should hear them tell about some of the places they've ended up! Laugh? Well I guess!

I know I'd never take my kids back to a regular church. I guess they might miss some things. But they just love church now, and I can almost see them grow.

CASE FIVE

When Paul was in third grade, he used to be afraid of the dark. Of course, he never admitted it. But you could tell. At bedtime he'd come and find some excuse to get me to go to his room with him. Or he'd say, "Dad, I'm busy. Will you get my PJ's for me?" He wasn't about to walk down that hall and into his dark room alone!

Well, one evening I told him I thought we ought to write a book together. He looked real funny at the idea, but you could see he was intrigued. So we talked about how his little sister and brother were growing older, and soon would be at an age when they might be afraid of different things. Our book might help them not be afraid.

That night we got out a concordance and I read the snatches of verses under "fear," and "afraid," and "trust." Whatever Paul thought sounded good I underlined in red.

Then next evening we went back into my study and looked up the underlined verses. Paul read them from his Bible and underlined them, and I typed them off on 3 x 5 cards. That night we went up to the drugstore and got a composition book and some construction paper, and Paul wrote the name of the book on the outside. He called it Paul's Not Being Afraid Book.

We started the book the next evening. Paul chose the verse in Genesis where God says to Abraham, "Fear not, Abram, for I am your shield and exceeding great reward." He cut out a construction paper shield, and cut out arrows and spears. He pasted them onto the first page of the book, with the spears breaking on the shield. And I wrote the verse under it.

Another night we looked at the verse in one of David's psalms that says "What time I am afraid I will trust in thee." Paul drew a picture of Daniel being thrown to the lions to illustrate that verse. And on the next page we wrote down some times when kids like the kids in his school might be afraid. He listed fear of being kidnapped, and of the Russians bombing Chicago, and tornados (his mom's terrified of tornados), and of course we had fear of the dark on that list.

I guess we never did really finish the book, though we worked on it a dozen nights or so. And I never did accuse Paul of being afraid of the dark, or tell him to go on down to his room and be a man. Actually, I never had to. Somehow as we were working on the book, the fear just seemed to go away, and Paul started going on down at bedtime without needing one of us to go with him.

CASE SIX

I suppose no kids like bedtime. But we got around the problem pretty well. By the time the kids got to be in first grade we had a conference with them when the school year started. We got out some books for them on how much sleep children need at different ages, and showed them why their bodies and minds need sleep. And we talked about how they felt when they were tired, and how it made them feel grumpy at times.

Then we figured what time they wanted to get up to be sure to make the bus. Then we figured back, and let them decide when they needed to be getting to sleep to get enough rest.

Of course, every kid likes and needs some bedtime routine, so we figured that in. Our kids liked to be read to at bedtime, and to sing a while. So if they had to be ready for sleep at 9, say, we agreed on when to start getting ready for bed to have the story or the singing or the talk they wanted at bedtime.

It wasn't perfect, of course. And sometimes there was a special TV show they wanted to stay up late and watch, and usually—if it was really special—we'd let them. But they understood why they needed to be in bed, and they'd figured out their own bedtime. If they started right away they'd get the most possi-

ble story and singing time. If they fooled around they got less. So usually they went off pretty cheerfully.

Of course, it meant we didn't get TV time ourselves. But I never saw a program yet that was as important as my kids, and actually I suppose I liked our evening times together as much as they did.

3. The final PROBE suggestion might well be a major project or a single item midterm essay. It's simply this:

You have been called to a large church as Minister to Children. You have exactly one hour and thirty minutes to write a paper that (a) states your goals for children's ministry in your church, and (b) sets up a three-year plan showing what you will do to work toward achieving those goals.

PART 1

FRAMEWORK

A Theological Framework for Ministry

Nurture in the Old Testament
Nurture in the New Testament
The Role of Scripture in Nurture
The Nurture Process

A Developmental Framework for Ministry

The Developmental Perspective
Cognitive Potentials of Children
Social Relationships of Children
Moral Development in Children
An Integrated Perspective

The first concern of the ancients was what children should be taught. In Scripture, the emphasis is on several processes (explored in the first four chapters) that facilitate the growth of

THE DEVELOPMENTAL PERSPECTIVE

faith. In our day the focus of attention is the children themselves, and the questions raised concern how children change and grow.

Every now and then the thinkers who shaped western culture commented on the training and education of children. It's not too surprising to find a common emphasis in the writings of early Christian and secular thinkers. Both were concerned with the kind of adult who would be produced. And both assumed that a desirable person could be shaped if one could only control what a child might learn. In a real sense it was assumed that children were simply raw material, that human beings, like statues, could be carved. It was similarly assumed that this shaping would follow if one could only manage the information fed to the mind. We see these assumptions reflected in the following passages from Plato, Aristotle, and St. Jerome.

PLATO

You know also that the beginning is the most important part of any work, especially in the case of a young and tender thing: for that is the time at which character is being formed and the desired impression is more readily taken.

And shall we just carelessly allow children to hear any casual tales which may be devised by casual persons, and to receive into their minds ideas for the most part the very opposite of those which we shall wish them to have when they are grown up? (*The Republic*, 7:221).

C
H
A
P   **5**
T
E
R

ARISTOTLE

When children have been born, the particular mode of rearing adopted must be deemed an important determining influence. . . . All amusements should prepare the way for their later pursuits; hence, most children's games should be imitations of the occupations of later life. . . . For children of this age, and up to seven years of age, must necessarily be reared at home; so it is reasonable to suppose that even at this age they may acquire a taint of illiberality from what they see and hear. The lawgiver ought, therefore, to banish indecent talk, as much as anything else, out of the state altogether (*Politics*, Book VII, section xv).

ST. JEROME

Thus must a soul be educated which is to be the temple of God. It must learn to hear nothing and say nothing but what belongs to the fear of God. It must have no understanding of unclean words, and no knowledge of the world's songs. Its tongue must be steeped while still tender in the sweetness of the psalms. Boys with their wanton thoughts must be kept from Paula: even her maids and female attendants must be separated from worldly associates. . . . The very words which she tries bit by bit to put together and to pronounce ought not to be chance ones, but names specifically fixed upon and heaped together for the purpose, those, for example, of the prophets or apostles or the list of patriarchs from Adam downwards as it is given by Matthew and Luke. . . . (*Letter to Laerta*, 17:164).

These and other writings at the roots of western culture show an appreciation for the importance of children that was lost during the Middle Ages and restored only with Luther and the Reformation. But it's clear from these excerpts that the concept of nurture assumed what one writer has called the Mechanical Mirror Theory: the notion that man grows to be what he is made to be by his environment.[1] What nurture requires, then, is simply censorship. Like Plato, each would desire that the young be exposed only to the good and not the bad; that only authorized information be made available to the young. "Let them fashion the mind with such tales," Plato insists, confident that whatever the young are exposed to will form the next generation. "Anything that [a young person] receives into his mind at that age is likely to become indelible and unalterable; and therefore it is most important that the tales which the young first hears should be models of virtuous thoughts" (Republic, 7:223).

The first educator to seriously challenge this assumption was John Comenius (ca. A.D. 1650). He wrote from a broad perspective that was striking in the seventeenth century: a perspective that integrates concern for the individual, for the society, and for communication of the gospel. He argued for universal education of children within every community of any Christian state and insisted that a fitting education must consider the developing capabilities of the child. Like Plato, Aristotle, and Jerome, Comenius believed that childhood is important. But unlike them, he rejected the notion that nurture is merely mechanical patterning. Looking at nature as a whole, he saw growth processes that led him to a unique theory of nurture, a theory that teaching and learning must be adapted to the characteristics of the child.

These quotes from the Great Didactic help us sense the unique contribution of Comenius and his rediscovered sense of the importance of childhood.

COMENIUS

Soft wax can be molded and remolded, hard wax will crumble. The young tree can be planted, replanted, trimmed, and bent to any shape; not so the grown. So also the hands and limbs of man can be trained for art and craft only during his childhood, as long as the sinues [sic] are soft. . . . In the same way piety must be implanted into the hearts during infancy lest it not root. If we want to educate a person in virtue, we must polish him at a tender age (chapter 7).

---

[1]See Jonas Langer, Theories of Development (New York: Holt, Rinehart and Winston, 1969).

The images Comenius uses to explain his concern for the young seem like those of earlier writers. But Comenius departs from them when he explores *how* the child is to be trained. In General Postulates of Teaching and Learning (chapter 16 of the *Great Didactic*) he says, "Nature follows a well ordered time plan." It follows then that "all material of learning must be divided according to age levels so that only what is within the compass of his capacity may be assigned to the child." This statement lies at the heart of the developmental concern of today. *We must understand the child, so that our teaching may be designed to match his capacity.*

Comenius goes on to identify the "steps of nature" that he believes must be followed if education of children is to be fitted to their nature and patterns of growth. To summarize his words, this means that:

> (1) Instruction must begin early and before the mind is corrupted. (2) The minds must be made ready for it. (3) It must proceed from the general to the particular, and (4) from the easier to the more difficult. (5) Progress must not be rushed. (6) The minds must not be forced to do anything but that to which they aspire according to their age and motivation. (7) Everything must be related through some sense impression, if possible. (8) Everything must be applied immediately, and (9) everything must be taught consistently according to one and the same method (chapter 17).

Comenius introduces us to the issue that has taken on a dominant role in contemporary education. What, Comenius asks, in the nature of the children themselves, will shape our efforts to educate them? How do we fit our teaching to children's motivations and abilities? How does the mind of a child of six years grasp and perceive concepts? Is it different from the mode of thought of a child of nine? How do we order the sequence of learning to fit the ways children think at varying stages of life? With the emergence in the past fifty years of concerns like these, our approach to the education of children has shifted from one that concentrates on subject matter and views the child as an object, to approaches that treat children as developing, growing persons.

Most of the discoveries about the development of children have been directly applied to teaching in schooling-instructional settings. But those discoveries have a direct relevance to our exploration of a wider ministry to children. In particular, they help us develop a sensitivity to children's capacities and help us understand what we can expect of boys and girls as we minister. Perhaps most importantly they provide insights into those processes identified in the first four chapters as the keys to any ministry in which we seek to encourage growth in faith.

THEORIES OF CHILD DEVELOPMENT

One essential element of the scientific method is the development of theories. As bits of information are gathered in both physical and behavioral sciences, thinkers struggle to fit them into a coherent whole. A theory attempts to explain how the bits of information gathered relate to each other. But a theory does far more than this. A theory also suggests a number of hypotheses and predictions. Does one theory suggest that interpersonal relationships are critical in motivating learning? Then it should follow that those who learn in a programmed-learning situation or a computer-assisted setting might not learn as well as those in a classroom. This can be tested, and the prediction either confirmed or proven wrong.

In the process of testing, the theory itself will be refined. What *kinds* of relationships facilitate learning? Relationships between teachers and children? The praise or affection a teacher communicates? Or the quality of relationships between the children in the class? Perhaps the key is the place the individual child has in the classroom social system: Is he or she chosen as friend by others, or is he or she an isolate? And what *kinds* of learning do relationships facilitate? If there is no demonstrable increase in cognitive learning as relationships are improved, may there be a change in values or attitudes?

It's clear that the development of theory opens the door to a world of excitement. Any significant theory will suggest hypotheses that can be experimentally tested. Every experiment will add more information. Every bit of information will allow us to refine, redefine, add to, or disprove elements of the basic theory. And each experiment produces information that can be applied to improve teaching and learning, fitting the whole process more closely to the kinds of persons that we discover children are.

Today much knowledge has been gained about children through this process of theory construction, hypothesis generation, and experiment. Nearly always the theories being tested in this process are subtheories: that is, they are smaller elements of a larger perspective, or theoretical frame of reference. Many of the schools of thought of which we read (such as role theory and behaviorism) are actually subschools existing within a theoretical framework that encompasses them and others. At this point, rather than examining each subschool and its differences, we need to understand the basic theories—the broad perspectives on children—that dominate contemporary understanding of children and their development. After looking at these basic theories, we'll go on and look at some of the insights that have emerged and are generally recognized by all schools of thought.

Psychoanalytic Theory

The historic roots of this theory are Freudian; they reflect Freud's view that human beings are raging seas of passions and aggression. Freud saw the goal of nurture as socialization of the child: that is, as developing controls that will keep the adult from expressing native destructive impulses and will channel passions into acceptable patterns of behavior. Freud assumed that the process of growth toward control took place in stages that are directly linked to human sexual nature. Freud identified five psychosexual stages, which he linked in progressive sequence to chronological age. Freud's concepts, however, grew out of his work with those suffering from varying degrees of mental illness. His work hardly provided a basis for the definition of normal development.

The most significant name within the psychoanalytical tradition is that of Erik Erikson. While accepting some of Freud's basic concepts about personality, Erikson modified Freud's dark view of human nature. Erikson viewed children as seekers, who eagerly explore and try to master their environment. His emphasis was not on illness but on health. And Erikson's concern was to identify the stages through which a child must pass on the way to a healthy maturity.

Erikson has made a number of contributions to thinking about childhood, including the significant concept of developmental tasks. This theme, that certain tasks must be successfully accomplished if healthy personality development is to occur, has been very influential. Erikson himself has focused attention on those relationships with significant others that enable or inhibit growth through the developmental stages.

While Erikson is best known for, and most interested in, his work with adolescents and their "identity crisis," his notions about the other stages of childhood have stimulated much exploration and research (see Figure 8). Erikson's basic notion can be quickly summarized.

Trust versus mistrust. Erikson sees the first developmental issue as one faced by the infant. The child is born, helpless, in a hostile environment over which he or she has no control. Somehow he or she must develop enough sense of trust during this stage to grow in a healthy way through the next stages. Erikson holds that the mother is the key to resolving this stage's crisis. It is through the warmth of social contacts with the mother—the touching, the smiles, the affectionate tone of voice—that the necessary trust develops.

FRAMEWORK

FIGURE 8
ERIKSON'S DEVELOPMENTAL THEORY[2]

Age in Years	Psychosocial Crisis (State)	Significant Person(s)
Birth-1	Trust vs. Mistrust	Mother
1-3 Years	Autonomy vs. Shame/Doubt	Parents
3-6 Years	Initiative vs. Guilt	Family
6-12 Years	Industry vs. Inferiority	Neighborhood, Teacher, School
12-17 Years	Identity vs. Role Confusion	Peer Groups, Heroes
Young Adulthood	Intimacy vs. Isolation	Friends, Opposite Sex
Adulthood	Generativity vs. Stagnation	Spouse, Children
Old Age	Ego Integrity vs. Despair	Relationships with others

Autonomy versus shame/doubt. Erikson observes that during the years between one and three the child gains physical mobility and exercises native curiosity in an autonomous way. During this time the parents find some restriction necessary. Erikson sees the way parents restrict as the critical element in whether a child will develop into a self-reliant rather than overly dependent person. If the parents restrict too much, or punish too harshly, Erikson believes that an overly strong sense of shame will grow and hurt the child's later efforts to become an independent person.

Initiative versus guilt. Erikson views the span between three and six as the time when a crisis develops over the conflict of initiating activities and the disapproval of others. Children are active, with inquiring minds, and they may very well initiate activities that are potentially destructive or harmful. Parents during this time show disapproval and use various means of discipline that will inhibit some activities and in the process will produce guilt.

The process of channeling exploration into constructive activities is necessary for the child and for society. But the problem is that parents may again be too restricting. They may cut off all

---

[2]Adapted from David R. Shaffer, *Social and Personality Development* (Monterey, Calif.: Brooks-Cole Publishing, 1979), p. 40.

94

initiating behavior, overcontrol the child, and build a pervading sense of undifferentiated guilt that will hold the child back from achieving his or her full potential in later life.

Industry versus inferiority. Erikson places the child's self-evaluations that occur between six and twelve at the center of this stage's developmental crisis. In school and neighborhood children begin to evaluate themselves against others in many different ways. They evaluate in terms of competency the skills needed for achievement in school. They evaluate in terms of acceptance by others who value them for their social skills. To Erikson, failure to develop competency in such areas leads to a sense of inferiority and inhibits the acquiring of a sense of self-worth and value that is necessary for growth toward self-assured adulthood.

The familiarity of the ideas sketched here gives some insight into the influence of Erikson. Many of the concepts suggested by him have led to various kinds of research. Yet the influence of Erikson and of the psychoanalytic school is no longer strong. The vitality of the other two theoretical perspectives dominates current thought and research.

There are several reasons for the waning of the psychoanalytic school. The basic notions on which the theory rests (of ego, id, personality strength, etc.) are difficult to test or to even demonstrate. And other schools have developed a mass of evidence to support their theoretical constructs. In addition, the other schools have generated more productive hypotheses for testing and have suggested more clearly ways that instruction might be redesigned or parenting strengthened.

Social Learning Theory

Social learning theory provides the dominant contemporary view of social and personality development. There are many different schools included within this broad framework theory. The key element that links them together is the common belief that the significant aspects of human personality are learned.

Early social learning theorists took a radical position. They discounted any abilities or predispositions with which children might be born and essentially viewed the newborn as blank tablets. Humans are active organisms, moved to relate to the environment, but the personality that any individual develops is shaped by what happens to him or her.

Today behaviorists in the school of B. F. Skinner continue in this tradition, seeing persons simply as trainable organisms. They believe that the young can and should be acted on by others and should be shaped to create a better society.

But this view is not held by all. Theorists in the school of Albert Bandura, for instance, see children as active participants in the learning process. It is believed that what we call "personality" is actually a set of responses that have been learned by observing social models and interacting with them. But children do exercise choice in the process, instructing and reinforcing themselves, and in that sense shaping their own personalities.

Social learning theorists are avid practitioners of the experimental method. They have used this approach to develop and to refine their theories. While the early theorists used a simple S–R (stimulus–response) model to explain learning, contemporary theory is quite sophisticated, and the processes envisioned are complex. In the drive to identify and to understand the social processes that are believed to shape persons, a whole language has been developed. This language is used to explain the various forces believed to operate in social settings, and to identify the processes by which beliefs, attitudes, values, and behavior are acquired. A survey of terms helps us see what social learning theorists believe is important, and also gives us some insight into the contributions of the movement.

Socialization. This is the process by which a growing child is shaped, through interaction with the persons in his or her environment. It is through social interaction that a human being learns language, gains the skills necessary to relate to others in society, and adopts the beliefs and values of the culture. Interaction with others exerts a life-long influence. But socialization is particularly significant in the case of the young.

While all persons with whom a child comes in contact will have some influence, certain persons will be more important than others. A child might be influenced by what is seen on television, but it is persons with whom a child has long-term, close relationships who will be most influential. This means that the family will have the greatest impact on the growing personality and that play groups and school experiences will also exert powerful and shaping influence during childhood.

Modeling. How does socialization take place? What is the nature of the learning process? Social learning theorists believe that learning takes place by observation and imitation of the behavior of social models. Any person an individual observes may serve as a model. But a child does select or reject modeled behavior. Much research has been focused on exploring the factors that encourage a child to model on another person.

While many experiments in modeling fix on observation of a specific action by a person who may be a stranger, social learning theorists are generally agreed that a long-term, close relationship marked by warmth and affection enhances the impact of modeling. Other factors that stimulate an individual to model on another person include opportunities to observe the model in a variety of life situations, having the model explain his or her behavior and having the model reveal the beliefs, values, and feelings associated with that behavior.

Role-taking. A vital element in social learning is the ability to see things from the perspective of other persons. This capacity to mentally put oneself in the place of another is called role-taking. It is particularly important if the child is to adequately model on another: he or she needs to be able to understand what is observed, from the model's point of view.

Recently a separation has been made between a child's ability to understand through role-taking and the capacity to empathize. Young children seem able to understand another's point of view better than had been supposed, but often seem to lack the capacity to care.

Much experimentation by social learning theorists focuses on how soon a child can develop social role-taking skills, and on how to help children develop this ability. One reason for the concern is the belief that role-taking is directly linked to moral development.

Recently too a distinction has been made between social role-taking, an inner activity, and role-enactment. Enactment involves one person acting out another's behavior, as might a child playing "mother" with dolls.

Identification, imitation, and internalization. As a child observes the behavior of a model, he or she mimics it. Several terms relate to this mimicking activity. "Identification" involves a learner fixing on the individual whose behavior is then "imitated." As behaviors are imitated and thus learned, they may become "internalized": that is, they may become a part of the child's own pattern of behavior and personality. Internalization is a vital concept in social learning theory, and researchers are particularly interested in factors that enhance identification and subsequent internalization.

Reinforcement. The behaviors that a child adopts and internalizes will stimulate reactions by other persons. Reactions by others to any behavior are considered reinforcement.

97

Positive reinforcement is considered to be any response that is pleasant to the child and thus tends to strengthen the particular response. Positive reinforcement may come in the form of praise, reward, or even nonverbal expressions of approval such as a smile or a nod or warm hug.

Negative reinforcement is considered to be any response that is unpleasant to the child and thus tends to suppress or extinguish the particular response. Negative reinforcement is often equated with punishments, although simple lack of any response may be a negative reinforcer.

Thus social learning theory suggests that while behavior is learned socially from models, the continuation or abandonment of particular behaviors will be influenced by how others react when a child tries out the behavior himself or herself.

Much research in social learning focuses on the kinds of reinforcements that are most effective in encouraging desirable behavior and reducing the undesirable. In particular much work has been done on the effects of punishment.

Social learning theory has drawn criticism. The primary accusation is that all social learning theorists ignore the nature of the child and fail to take seriously internal changes that occur as a person matures. Social learning theory alone certainly cannot explain the differences between a three year old and an eight year old, or explain the apparent sequence of change through which all persons seem to pass. Yet the criticism is not valid for all theorists, many of whom do seek to take into account the capacities of children at different ages.

The field of *social cognition* is one clear attempt to bridge the theoretical gap. This field assumes that the way a child perceives and responds to social influences is related to cognitive abilities, which themselves change as a child grows. The research in this field focuses on understanding the cognitive abilities of children at different ages and relating that understanding to social influences.

Overall, the research stimulated by social learning theorists has proven extremely productive. It has not only contributed helpful theoretical concepts, but has also defined a number of specific parenting and teaching techniques that have direct application to the nurture of children.

Structural Theory

When we think of the physical development of children, we have an image of a well-defined sequence of changes that normal boys and girls all over the world experience. There are sequential increases in size and weight; changes in bone and muscle;

development of the teeth and other structures; inner hormonal changes most clearly seen in the onset of puberty. And all these follow a genetically predetermined sequence.

Not only are we aware of these patterns of growth and change, we also recognize the impact of them on a child's abilities. We do not expect, for instance, that a three year old will be able to color within the lines, because we know that small muscle groups have not yet developed sufficiently to permit control of the crayons. We would never expect a five year old to play basketball like a high schooler, no matter how surrounded he or she might be by models or how the efforts might be positively reinforced. While the environment might have an influence, the child's efforts would be limited by the demands of the human genetic code that ability develop only when the appropriate physical structures are in place.

Structural theorists stress the notion that learning, social activities, morality, and personality develop in a way that is analogous to physical development. The environment of the growing child is important. But the kinds of interaction that can take place with the environment are controlled by the imprint of the genetic code, which decrees a predetermined sequence in the development of cognitive structures (abilities).

The focus of structural theorists on cognition is important. The founder of this school is Jean Piaget, a European psychologist who has studied children's cognitive growth and abilities. He views persons as active and adaptive. By "adaptive" Piaget means to say that each individual constantly seeks to understand the environment so he or she can live effectively within it. As cognitive structures develop the child is better and better able to understand the environment, and is thus better and better able to live effectively in a social and physical world. What is important here is the insistence that a child is not *shaped* by parents or others through social interactions. Instead children, rather than mirroring experience, actively process all data and *construct* the explanations or understandings that then guide their actions and responses. Personality and behavior can best be understood in terms of the cognitions of children, through which they not only interpret experiences but also shape themselves.

Much of Piaget's work involved definition of the sequence of cognitive growth and description of the cognitive processes of which children are capable at various ages (see Figure 9). Whether or not children *will* think and respond in certain ways will be related to the richness of their environment. Whether they *can* think and respond in certain ways will be determined by the development of cognitive structures. These will be further discussed in chapter 6.

The most influential development from structural theory comes from the work of Lawrence J. Kohlberg, who links moral thinking to Piaget's stage theory of development. According to Kohlberg moral thought, like any other, is determined by the development of cognitive structures. His theory has stimulated much research and many attempts to define instructional proc-

FIGURE 9

PIAGET'S STRUCTURAL STAGES

Age	Stage	Description of Child's Thinking
1½-4	Preconceptual	• imitative language, only partially understood • objects seem stable, not able to grasp changing shapes due to perspective • lacks abstracting ability to perceive space apart from perspective • beginning to distinguish between past, present, and future • reasoning is by analogy to experiences
4-7	Intuitive	• language and thought still tied to phenomenal experience: words represent child's own experiences and perceptions (a bottle is "where you put water") • comprehends and can respond to complex adult language, but does not understand such processes as conservation (the transfer of a principle or characteristic across situations) • objects now maintain identity despite changes in position perspective • number sense develops with ability to measure quantity • can compensate fully for perspective changes caused by change in position • time sense is still personalized, and interactions between time, distance, speed, etc. not grasped • great interest in explaining causes of what is observed, understanding of causes still highly intuitive
7-10	Concrete	• can trace change in states through complex series rather than rely on impression of a particular observed state • can take others' points of view and integrate their perspective with his own • can begin to distinguish variables that cause change and mentally predict changes • capacities to perceive objects, numbers, time, space all significantly developed • mechanical explanations of cause are given priority (clouds move because the winds push)
10-15	Formal Operations	• only now does the ability to think about thought—to explore relations between the real and the possible develop, "adult" kinds of thinking become possible

esses that will encourage development of moral thinking in children.

Kohlberg's work (which will be explored in chapter 8) tends to link somewhat with social learning theory in that he emphasizes the influence of parents, peers, social models, and all kinds of interpersonal interactions. The child's perception of social experiences will be shaped by his or her cognitive structures, and thus there will be a fundamental unity between social and intellectual development.

Several concepts are particularly important in structural theories. These need to be understood, as they are fundamental in current moral as well as cognitive theories.

Invariant sequence. Physical growth follows a specific and unchanging pattern, printed in humanity's genetic code. Growth toward one's potential takes place in stages that can be clearly defined, and one stage always follows another. Stages are never found out of order, nor do persons skip stages. Followers of Piaget and Kohlberg insist that cognitive growth takes place in just this way in an ordered sequence, whose stages can be defined. The full mental or moral potential of humanity may not be reached by individuals, or even in cultures, if certain environmental elements are absent. But clear stages of growth can be defined, and the sequence from one stage to the next is related in a general way to chronological age. While a child may reach a particular stage earlier than his or her age mates, or earlier than children in another culture, no child will ever "skip" a stage. Each human being will pass through the defined stages *in order.*

Egocentrism. This is a term coined by Piaget. It expresses the conviction that young children simply cannot see things from the perspective of others. The inability to see others as independent persons with their own feelings, wants, and experiences is far different from selfishness. It is instead related directly to a particular stage of cognitive development. Young children do not apply the Golden Rule simply because they cannot!

Thus studies of social role-taking are important to structural theorists as well as to social learning theorists. And this issue is also important to Christian educators, who ask questions about the validity of trying to teach young children moral and ethical behaviors (such as "sharing" in preschool curriculums) that they simply are unable to comprehend.

Equilibration. Structural theorists see children as actively involved in a struggle to understand and adapt to their environment. Persons are not blank tablets, shaped by social influences. Instead persons are the shapers, constructing from their experiences a picture of reality, and then shaping themselves to live in the world they construct.

Piaget and other structural theorists believe that the way children will perceive their world is determined by the cognitive structures that develop sequentially as they grow. Structuralists postulate a state of harmony or equilibrium, which is achieved as a particular cognitive structure develops and is used to shape adjustment to the environment. But cognitive growth continues. The things and people in the environment are seen in new perspective. This introduces disequilibration (sometimes called cognitive dissonance). Elements of the child's mental picture of the world no longer "fit," so the child actively works at reconstructing his or her picture of the universe, reordering the elements present to provide a more consistent view of reality.

This process of seeking equilibrium at a different level cannot be "taught." It must await the development of internal structures of mind permitting the new ways of thinking. However, *when the structures exist,* social and other experiences can introduce disequilibrium by focusing attention on the inadequacies of present ways of perceiving reality, and thus encouraging new learning and ways of thought.

One of the contributions of the structural theorists is to make us more sensitive to the limitations of children. Another is to suggest teaching methodologies that, through the use of disequilibration, stimulate the inner mental processes of children to achieve the new levels of understanding of which they become capable.

INSIGHTS FROM THE BEHAVIORAL SCIENCES

In the past several decades psychologists and sociologists and educators have taken very seriously questions about the nature of children and how they learn. The emphasis has shifted from a millennium's focus on *what we should teach children* to questions about *how we should help children learn and grow.* What are children like? How do they think and conceptualize? What does each age of childhood contribute to the development of personality? What is the impact of social relationships? How do we motivate learning? These and a host of other significant questions about children have been asked, and many experiments have been designed and conducted to find answers.

Most of the experiments have been rooted in one of three broad theoretical orientations (summarized in Figure 10). Each theory system makes certain assumptions about human beings

FIGURE 10

COMPARISON OF THEORIES OF DEVELOPMENT

Feature	Psychoanalytic	Social Learning	Structural
Assumptions	growth involves a series of personal adjustments by human beings to their social environment	the growing person is shaped by relationships with others through learning from social models	growth is prepatterned by cognitive abilities that develop in invariant sequence
Concept of personality development	crisis resolutions shaping the human organism	learning a pattern of responses that make up personality	growth of cognitive structures enabling new adaptations to social and physical environments
Primary factors in development	passage through a series of developmental tasks	relationships with others	maturing of cognitive structures
Mechanisms in development	interactions with significant persons	socialization modeling identification imitation reinforcement	interaction with the physical and social environment
Impact of personal relationships	support or inhibit successful completion of developmental tasks necessary for healthy maturity	the critical factor, as development is essentially learning through social relationships how to be a human being	vital factor stimulating growth from a lower stage of cognition to a higher stage when mental structures make such progress possible

and how they learn. Each theory then generates a number of hypotheses that are tested experimentally. These provide data to further refine the theory and suggest more issues for exploration.

Everyone realizes that no theory adequately describes reality. At best theory approximates reality and comes close to explanation. The value of theory is not found in arguing for one and against another, but is found rather in the experiments that theories generate and the information they help us gain about how to help children grow and develop in healthy ways. Another value is found in the way theories force exploration and make us challenge popular ideas that are often proved wrong. In the next chapter we'll look at research results that have direct impact on our understanding of ministry with children. For now, let's simply look at two examples of relevant research reported in recent texts. These will form the basis of a PROBE question to help us apply these ideas to particular areas of ministry.

Self-esteem

What are the effects of viewing yourself as a worthwhile and valuable person? And how is higher self-esteem developed in children? Janice Gibson, in an excellent 1978 text, summarizes research findings:

> Coopersmith (1967) found that he could predict the self-esteem of school-age boys more accurately by the behaviors and attributes of their parents than by factors more commonly assumed to be related to self-esteem in school children, such as physical attractiveness, intelligence, or motor ability.
>
> Boys rated high in self-esteem described themselves as "worthy human beings." These boys tended to be more inquisitive, more interested in activities around them, less afraid to question the teacher, and more creative than lower self-esteem boys. They also tended to be less aggressive toward their peers. Lower self-esteem boys either reported they were unsure of their self-worth or, more sadly, that they were unworthy.
>
> What distinguished parents of the high self-esteem children? They tended to be more strict than were the parents of lower self-esteem boys. They were at the same time less punitive—that is, they established clear-cut rules of behavior for themselves and their children and administered these rules consistently. High self-esteem boys disobeyed infrequently. Parents rarely administered punishment; when administered, punishment was consistent and not harsh. Parents of high self-esteem boys tended also to use reasoning in their disciplinary methods, an approach consistent with nonauthoritarian methods of upbringing.[3]

Verbal Modeling and Altruism

What is the relationship between preaching goodness or

---

[3]Janice Gibson, *Growing Up* (Reading, Mass.: Addison-Wesley, 1978), p. 356.

kindness and providing a living example? David R. Shaffer reports the results of some research on this subject:

> Parents generally instruct their children that it is good to share and help others, and they assume that these words will not fall on deaf ears. But is this a valid assumption?
>
> Joan Grusec and Sandra Skubiski (1970) sought an answer for this important question by comparing the effectiveness of verbal and behavioral models on children's sharing behavior. Elementary school children were each assigned to one of three experimental conditions. In the *behavioral-modeling* condition, children watched an adult play a game and donate half his winnings to charity. Children in the *verbal-modeling* condition were exposed to an adult who did not play the game but who strongly endorsed the idea that players should donate half their winnings to charity. Children assigned to the control situation did not observe a model. Each child was given an opportunity to then play the game and donate a portion of his or her winnings to a charitable cause.
>
> Grusec and Skubiski found that behavioral modeling elicited larger donations from the children than did verbal exhortations. In fact, verbal models prompted no larger donations than no model at all.
>
> Bryan and Walbek (1970a, 1970b) exposed children to models who behaved either charitably or selfishly *and* who preached either charity or greed. When children were given an opportunity to donate their own valuable resources to charity, *the size of their donations was determined by the model's behavior rather than his exhortations.* In other words, children faced with a model who practiced greed and exhorted charity (or greed) showed a low level of altruism themselves, while those who observed a charitable model who exhorted greed (or charity) gave sizeable amounts to charity. These findings appear to have important implications for child rearing: parents would be well advised to back up their verbal exhortations with altruistic deeds if they hope to instill a strong sense of altruistic concern in their children.[4]

PROBE

▶ *case histories*
▶ *discussion questions*
▶ *thought provokers*
▶ *resources*

1. The overview of developmental thought here is necessarily sketchy. Recommend books for collateral reading are:

    Garrison, K. and A Kingston with H. Bernard. *The Psychology of Childhood.* London: Staples Press, 1968.
    Shaffer, David R. *Social and Personality Development.* Monterey, Calif.: Brooks-Cole Publishing, 1979.

2. There is a fascinating relationship among the three approaches to childhood sketched so far in this book. The three in question are:

---

[4]Shaffer, *Social and Personality Development.* p. 391.

    a. Focus on *what* is to be taught (represented by Plato as well as by Jerome and other early church fathers).

    b. Focus on *processes* that promote the birth and growth of faith (represented in the Old and New Testaments).

    c. Focus on *how* the child learns and develops (represented by the theories of child development sketched in this chapter).

    How would you compare and contrast these three approaches? How are they related to each other? Write a three-page paper relating these approaches to one another and evaluating the contribution of each to shaping an effective ministry with children.

3. This chapter closes with two illustrations from the literature on child development, one sketching a study on self-esteem and the other sketching a study on the relationship between preaching kindness and modeling it. Select one of these two reports and *thoroughly* explore its possible implications for ministry to children in three settings: the home, the Sunday school, and the Christian school. By "thoroughly explain" I mean spell out as completely as possible what it may suggest about the effectiveness of common practices in each setting, and define any practices that might be followed in each setting to make nurture more effective.

4. Carefully relate each of the five processes that facilitate the communication of faith (see chapter 4) to each of the two illustrations of research findings. Are the research findings in harmony with the processes, and if so, how? If they are not in harmony, how and why not? Be thorough, and think carefully.

PART 1

FRAMEWORK

A Theological Framework for Ministry

Nurture in the Old Testament
Nurture in the New Testament
The Role of Scripture in Nurture
The Nurture Process

A Developmental Framework for Ministry

The Developmental Perspective
Cognitive Potentials of Children
Social Relationships of Children
Moral Development in Children
An Integrated Perspective

Cognitive development deals with changes that take place from birth to maturity in a child's ability to think, in the way he or she thinks, and in how that thinking is expressed in behavior. This is an extremely complex field of study, with dozens of books and hundreds of articles devoted to each issue.

COGNITIVE POTENTIALS OF CHILDREN

So we can only summarize a few of the findings about children's cognitive potentials. But those few have great significance for us as we seek better ways to communicate faith in our ministry with boys and girls.

One of the first questions we need to ask about children as we consider teaching them is, What can children understand? The next question is, What can we expect them to *do* with what they have been taught? While this issue of concept formation and use is not our only concern in exploring children's cognitive potentials, it is surely the place we must begin.

CONCEPT FORMATION

In an excellent work Herbert J. Klausmeier and Patricia S. Allen summarize what is involved in concept learning. They distinguish four levels of concept attainment: the concrete, the identity, the classificatory, and the formal. Each level is attained in sequence, and each requires ability to perform specific mental operations.

The Concrete Level simply requires that a young child be able to discriminate a particular object in the environment from other objects, and that he or she remember and recognize it.

If the object is a bottle or a favorite toy, concrete concept formation does not require that the child understand "bottle" or "toy," but simply that he or she come to know this particular toy as an object with permanence.

The Identity Level requires the ability to pick out a particular object or quality when it is observed in a setting different from normal. This can be illustrated by recognizing a plant in the living room as the plant that used to be in the kitchen.

The Classificatory Level requires generalizing. It involves realizing that two or more things are equivalent. Thus "my highchair" can now be understood to belong to the class of highchairs. To function on this level demands more than recognition. It demands that the child be able to explain the generally accepted defining elements of the class as well as to recognize examples and nonexamples. As this capacity develops further, children will be able to point out less obvious attributes of concepts and will generalize to many different examples, even when examples are very similar to nonexamples.

The Formal Level of concept formation requires a still higher order of cognitive ability. This level involves identifying objects or qualities, being able to define the objects or qualities, and telling how they differ from nonexamples.[1]

Klausmeier and Allen have summarized the mental opera-

---

[1]Herbert J. Klausmeier and Patricia S. Allen, *Cognitive Development of Children and Youth* (New York: Academic Press, 1978), pp. 16–24. Used by permission.

tions involved in concept formation on these two levels in chart form (see Figures 11 and 12).

In their study of concept formation Klausmeier and Allen selected four concepts. They developed a battery of tests to measure mastery of that concept on the concrete, identity, classification, and formal levels. And they developed tests to measure understanding of principles incorporated in the concept as well as ability to use that principle to solve problems.

The method of the study was longitudinal: the experimenters selected a group of children and followed them through their school years, testing regularly for attainment, mastery, and

FIGURE 11

MENTAL OPERATIONS IN CONCEPT ATTAINMENT: CONCRETE, IDENTITY, AND CLASSIFICATORY LEVELS[2]

Classificatory Level

Attending to the less obvious attributes of at least two examples of the class of objects

Discriminating each example from nonexamples

Remembering the discriminated examples

Generalizing that each example when experienced in different contexts or modalities is the same example

Generalizing that the two examples are equivalent (belong to the same class)

Remembering the generalization (internally representing, storing, and retrieving the classificatory-level representation)

Identity Level

Attending to perceptible features of an object

Discriminating the object from other objects

Remembering the discriminated object

Generalizing that the object when experienced in different contexts or modalities is the same object

Remembering the generalization (internally representing, storing, and retrieving the identity-level representation)

Concrete Level

Attending to perceptible features of an object

Discriminating the object from other objects

Remembering the discriminated object (internally representing, storing, and retrieving the concrete-level representation)

[2]Ibid., p. 18.

FIGURE 12
MENTAL OPERATIONS IN CONCEPT ATTAINMENT: FORMAL LEVEL[3]

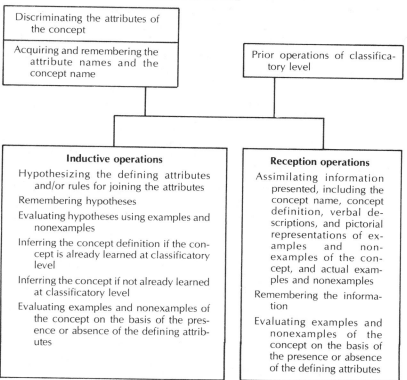

ability to use the selected concepts. The four concepts chosen for the study were *cutting tool, tree, equilateral triangle,* and *noun.*

The results of the study are significant. The children did move from level to level in the sequence predicted by Piaget. But there was a great difference in the ages/grades at which individuals attained and mastered concepts. The fact that very large individual differences exist is important for us to realize. We simply cannot describe "the characteristics of the nine year old" as though all nine year olds attain a common stage of growth.

Another important finding was that there were great differences in the ages/grades at which the different concepts themselves were mastered. For instance, the researchers report that "of the Grade 1 students 45% mastered the formal level of *cut-*

----

[3]Ibid., p. 20.

ting tool, but only 35% of the Grade 9 students mastered the formal level of *noun.*"[4] The evidence was clear that concepts such as tree and cutting tool, which have many concrete, physical examples existing in the child's environment, are mastered early. However, those concepts that are represented symbolically and are abstract in nature are much more difficult to master, so that mastery of such concepts comes at a much later age! Klausmeier and Allen point out an even more significant fact:

> Analysis of the cross-sectional and longitudinal data showed that many students in the primary and intermediate grades mastered the concrete or identity level of the different concepts *as their highest achievements,* but that they *rarely* mastered understanding principles . . . or problem solving. . . . Few students during the primary school years fully attained the formal level of any concepts except cutting tool, and in Grade 6 only one had fully attained the formal level of noun [emphasis mine].[5]

We can see how significant these findings are when we reflect on the fact that much Christian education of children attempts to communicate symbolic and abstract concepts and expects children to be able to apply principles of Christian morality in making choices in their daily life! Yet these are the very concepts and use of concepts that children are least able to master!

PIAGET'S FRAMEWORK

The study of Klausmeier and Allen helps us sense the significance of the work of Jean Piaget, mentioned in chapter 5. He has shown that there is a definite sequence in the growth of cognitive abilities (structures) through childhood. He has also demonstrated that younger boys and girls simply are not able to think in certain ways or to grasp some of the concepts that adults assume they should be taught.

We can summarize Piaget's picture of how children think and how their ability to think develops (see also Figure 9, in chapter 5). While we can accept the stages of growth and the sequences he describes, it is important to remember that the ages associated with each stage are broad generalizations. As all research has shown, there are great and often dramatic differences in how early or how late given individuals may reach the defined levels.

Preoperational Period (2–7 Years)

Preconceptual phase (2–4 years). The child is egocentric, unable to take the physical/spatial or the social viewpoint of others. The child categorizes by a single characteristic of objects

---

[4]Ibid., p. 272.
[5]Ibid., p. 273.

(such as big or red) and not by multiple characteristics (big, red, and round). Objects are grouped perceptually (by being physically together) and not logically.

Intuitive phase (4–7 years). The child is still egocentric, and judges subjectively by his or her own perceptions. But he or she is now able to think in terms of classes (to group on the basis of some characteristic such as color or triangularity). The child can also see relationships and can begin to use numbers. However these capacities are said to be intuitive, because the child cannot verbally explain or show awareness of classification principles.

The major achievement of this period is movement from sensorimotor (visual, tactile, aural, etc.) interactions to representational experience (interactions tied to inner mental images rather than objects themselves).

A key to learning and to understanding children's behavior at this stage is imitation. This concept includes deferred imitation: the ability to repeat what was seen when the model being imitated is no longer present. A preschooler playing "mommy" with dolls is engaged in deferred limitation. Yet studies of this kind of play indicate that children do not copy exactly what they see. Instead they actively reconstruct and interpret the behavior in their imitations.

Often problem solving (making choices of how to behave in a particular situation) will be attempted through deferred imitative activity, rather than through representational thought.

Egocentrism is a key concept for our understanding of young children. This term simply indicates that preoperational children see from their own perspective only. Much research has demonstrated that preoperational children cannot visualize objects from a different viewpoint in space (for instance, they cannot describe how a person *behind* a television set would be unable to see the picture), and that children's use of language typically assumes that the listener already knows what the child knows. One of the most significant kinds of cognitive growth, which begins in this period, is away from egocentrism (which Piaget calls *decentering)* toward ability to represent objects or events from other viewpoints.

Piaget notes that it is important to realize that children will often *appear* to understand certain things intuitively as they grow older. However, he insists that this is not the case until they explain the reasons for their conclusions. This is one key to understanding Piaget's ideas and some of his limitations. For Piaget, the test of true understanding is awareness of how a particular conclusion was reached. A child may intuitively grasp the right answer, or make a valid response, but for Piaget "real understanding" requires explaining.

Concrete Period (7–11 Years)

The growth and change during this period is more complex than that marking the preoperational stage. Thus the cognitive processes are more difficult to define precisely. Yet we can generalize and note that cognitive growth here focuses on a child's increasing ability to deal with *concepts*. This is one reason why research on concept acquisition is so significant for ministry during these childhood years. And it is a reason why we need to pay particular attention to three salient aspects of Piaget's explanation of children's thought.

Conservation. The concept of conservation is the first of these three issues. Conservation speaks of a child's ability to understand that an attribute remains constant across changing situations. For instance, the number of objects in a row will not change even if they are rearranged in a circle. When a child sees and can explain this phenomenon, identifying "ten" objects however they might be arranged on a field, he or she has been able to conserve the attribute of number.

Most of Piaget's work has been done with concrete items, and with materials that children can physically manipulate. As the work of Klausmeier and Allen shows, we might expect ability to conserve such an attribute as number to develop relatively early. The reason conservation is important is that much of ministry with children has assumed that children will be able to acquire an abstract, symbolic concept such as "forgive" or "share" or "trust" and to actually conserve that concept across situations and apply it appropriately in their own daily experiences! Such an approach to teaching children, relying on teaching concepts or principles that children are expected to be able to apply on their own, is, to say the least, unrealistic.

Sociocentrism. The growth of ability to link, to see cause and effect, and to understand series of events in the objective world, requires a change in the egocentric viewpoint of young children. Children must discover that others have different views, that other persons also think and experience even as does the child. This whole shift calls for many significant mental changes.

Piaget and other structuralists point out that changes in a child's cognitive structures (inner "mental muscles" if you will) cannot account *alone* for mental growth. The shift to sociocentrism requires in addition relationships with adults and other children. These relationships will force the child to use new mental abilities and adjust reasoning and communication in order to function effectively in a social environment filled with other autonomous beings.

As the new capacities to reason, to distinguish between motives and actions, and to see causal links develop, various forms of cooperative activity and reciprocal behavior become possible.

Moral reasoning. This concept of moral reasoning is a third issue raised here by Piaget, but it will be discussed at length in chapter 8.

We can summarize by noting that the critical feature of this extended stage is a gradual decentering of the child's world, matched with a growing ability to think representationally, using concepts that conserve particular attributes across situations.

Formal Period (11–15 Years)

It is only during these later years that children seem able to begin to think abstractly and logically, creating hypotheses and deducing logical conclusions. The ability to plan, to predict, to isolate key factors, and to manipulate several variables—all emerge here and introduce for the first time true "adult" thought.

This very sketchy overview of Piaget helps us sense his contributions to education. First, the framework of description Piaget has provided does help us to understand children better. He helps us hear more accurately what children are really saying and thinking, without reading adult perceptions into their words. Second, many have found Piaget's framework significant for development of curriculum. Third, and most important, the framework gives us many specific directions for developing teaching strategies.

Before leaving this section, let's look at one example of Piaget's influence on developing such strategies. Piaget stresses the need for children to develop their budding abilities for representational thinking. This is basic to cognitive growth during the concrete (7–11 years) period. Appropriate strategies would stress active thinking, learning by discovery, and stretching to perceive from a sociocentric viewpoint. In an excellent book, *Cognitive Development from Childhood to Adolescence,* Irving E. Sigel and Rodney R. Cocking suggest an exciting variety of teaching strategies designed to develop representational thought and thus more significant learning. That list of what they call "distancing strategies" is suggestive for ministry with children as well as for their education in the schools (see Figure 13).

FRAMEWORK

FIGURE 13
DISTANCING STRATEGIES[6]

STRATEGY	DESCRIPTION
Observing	"Watch . . . This is how"; examining or asking the child to examine; teacher demonstrating also: "Look at what I'm doing"
Labeling	*Naming* a singular object or event. (To be distinguished from concept labeling); identifying, for example, "What do you call what she is doing?"
Describing	Provide elaborated information of a single instance; defining. Static; no dynamic relationships among elements, no use, not functional. "Appears like, looks like"; also describing inner states of self such as feelings (an action can be described—"What are you doing?")
interpretation	To attribute or explain meaning such as "What do you mean?" "What does it mean to be something?"
Demonstrating	Showing primarily through action or gestures that something is to be done: "Show me how . . ."
Sequencing	*Temporal ordering* of events, as in a story or carrying out a task. Steps articulated, next, afterwards, start, begin, last
Reproducing	Construct previous experiences; the dynamic interaction of events; interdependence; functional understanding "How was it done?"
Comparing	
describing similarities	Noting ostensive common characteristics (perceptual analysis), "Are those the same?"
describing differences	Noting ostensive differences among instances (perceptual analysis)
inferring similarities	Noting nonobservational commonalities (conceptual)
inferring differences	Nonobservable differences (conceptual)
Proposing alternatives	Key words: other, another, something different from before
Combining	
symmetrical classifying (counting)	Recognition of the commonalities of a class of equivalent instances "How are these alike?" Counting like objects; estimating
asymmetrical classifying (counting)	Organizing instances in some sequences comparative to the previous and the subsequent instances; seriation; relative (big to small). Enumeration of number of things
synthesizing	To reconstruct components into a unified whole; explicit pulling together
Evaluating	
consequence	Assess *quality* to outcome, feasibility, or own competence; right-wrong, good-bad
affect	Assess quality of personal liking, opinion "How do you like the way it looks?" Evaluate the quality of a feeling state; "How do you feel about feeling sad?"

[6]Irving E. Sigel and Rodney R. Cocking, *Cognitive Development from Childhood to Adolescence* (New York: Holt, Rinehart, and Winston, 1977), pp. 179–85.

Inferring	Nonapparent, unseen properties or relationships
cause-effect	Prediction of causal relationships of instances, "How" "Why"; teacher may state cause and effect as well as infer
feelings	Prediction of how persons will feel; having to do with affect, not descriptive feelings of things
effects	Predictions of what will happen without articulation of causality; effects of a cause
Resolving conflict	Presentation of contradictory or conflicting information and resolution; problem solving
Generalizing	Application of knowledge to other settings or objects
Transforming	Changing the nature, function, appearance of instances
Planning	Arranging conditions to carry out a set of actions in an orderly way; actual carrying out of a task in which the child is involved; acting out a rule of the task (nonverbal)
Concluding	Relating actions, objects, or events in a summative way; summarizing

CONCEPT UTILIZATION

Intelligence Versus Creativity

One of Piaget's great contributions is helping us realize that children are *constructive* in their approach to life in our world. That is, they do not passively receive information and build a knowledge system. Instead they actively interact with the social and physical environment, and they build from the experience and information gained a picture of the world that is limited by the ability to develop and use concepts.

The structuralist sees four factors in cognitive development:

Heredity and maturation. All human beings share a common genetic code that patterns the process and sequence of their abilities. Some individuals will have more potential cognitively than others. But in the mental realm the abilities will be of the same *kind* for all, as both potential and limitations are inherent in the nature of humanity.

Experience. A person's knowledge and world view are rooted in individual experiences. It is through active involvement in the social as well as physical environment that a person's perception of reality is shaped.

Social interactions. A person's interactions with others have a special impact on the development of outlook and personality. The concepts, feelings, and behaviors that are modeled affect one's perceptions and are reinforced during interaction with other people. These affect the capacity to understand and the perception of reality.

Equilibration. This final factor is the "fit" or the "balance" of each of the others. Relationships and experiences force people to deal with new ideas or to learn how to act in new situations. Inner capacities for conceptualizing develop and individuals begin to see things in new ways and comprehend new relationships. Each jolt that throws people off balance causes them to seek new balance: a new way to fit things together so they may live comfortably and effectively in the world.

This process of balancing and rebalancing is stimulated by each of the other factors, and the impetus to find new balance is a major cause of growth.

"Learning" then can be seen as an interaction between maturation, active experiences, and social interactions. Any model of teaching/learning must take each of these factors seriously. By providing experiences and concepts and by interacting with children in ways that help them use their maturation-related potentials, we help them construct their own understanding of the world and how to live successfully in it.

This constructivist understanding of learning is, as I said, one great contribution of Piaget and his followers. However, there is another assumption embedded in Piagetan thought that is not a positive contribution! It is the assumption that thinking *ought* to be logical and must always be characterized by *understanding,* in the technical sense of being able to explain the process by which conclusions were reached. The problem is that this focus has led to the disregard of what has been called "creativity."

The writers of much of the literature on children's cognitive development are concerned with what has been called "intelligence." There has been much discussion of intelligence, but no agreed upon definitions have emerged. There are, however, some distinguishing characteristics. Intelligence is linked to logical thinking. It is related to the expanding knowledge and to the academic skills needed to pass the kinds of tests used in schooling/instructional settings to measure learning. It is concerned with those kinds of things that Piaget identifies as "true reasoning."

However, other lines of research have identified a different kind of thinking, related to what we call "creativity." The evidence of this research does suggest that creativity involves a different mode of thinking. Strikingly, research has also shown that creativity is not necessarily linked with intelligence. A creative person may be of higher or lower intelligence. An intelligent person may be of higher or lower creativity.

Various terms have been chosen to contrast the intelligent and creative modes of thinking. Edward de Bono calls intelligence-related thinking *vertical thinking* and the creativity-related pattern *lateral thinking.* Others speak of convergent and divergent modes of thought. De Bono's description of the differences between the two patterns is reflected in Figure 14.

FIGURE 14

CONTRASTS BETWEEN TWO MODES OF THOUGHT
VERTICAL (INTELLIGENCE) AND LATERAL (CREATIVITY)[7]

Vertical Thinking	Lateral Thinking
Selective rightness matters selects by excluding seeks "best way"	Generative richness matters seeks added paths searches for many ways
Movement goal-oriented moves when a goal is established and a definite technique available to reach it	Movement experimental explores for the joy of discovery
Analytical reaches conclusion and stops	Provocative uses conclusions to go on
Sequential moves a step at a time each step connected to preceding step each step must be sound and correct	Intuitive may jump ahead, fill in gaps later rightness required only in conclusion, not in each step
Exclusive works in given framework excludes what does not belong in framework uses fixed categories, labels, classifications	Expansive welcomes new and even apparently irrelevant ways to alter frame of reference established categories not pigeonholes but aids to fresh thinking.
Self-limiting follows most likely paths	Explorative traces unlikely paths

It is important to recognize that these two modes of thinking are fundamentally different, adopting quite distinct thought processes. Yet the two modes of thinking are not mutually exclusive. In fact they are complementary. Creativity will generate

---

[7]Summarized from Edward de Bono, *Lateral Thinking: A Textbook of Creativity* (London: Ward Lock Educational, Ltd., 1970).

new ideas and insights. Intelligence will allow the new insights to be developed and evaluated. Each type of thinking is important and has great value.

This affirmation of the value of both kinds of thinking helps us put one assumption of Piaget in perspective. He insists that logical thought is the measure of cognitive development. Independent thinking and the unique insights that mark creativity are likely to be dismissed by Piaget as mere intuitions. In a schooling approach that takes Piaget with too much seriousness, the training will not encourage development of creativity and the intuitive leap to the unique is likely to be simply marked "wrong" on the answer sheet in what one writer has called the "tyranny of misplaced emphasis"!

Research by Michael A. Wallach and Nathan Kogan suggests that two things encourage creative thinking. One is an emphasis on producing abundant and unique associations (a stress on many answers and appreciation for unique answers rather than insistence on giving the one "right" answer). The other is the creation of a "playful, gamelike context rather than one implying that the person is under a test."[8] A pressured, task-centered environment is not conducive to creativity and lateral thinking.

It is important for us to understand the creative potential of children and to balance the Piagetan stress on an "understanding" that is defined not only as providing an adaptive solution but also as being aware of the thought processes by which the solution was arrived at. It seems clear that the living faith to which the Christian community is called demands the ability to apply biblical truth in a constantly changing world, where many varied associations of biblical principles with changing situations is vital. It also seems clear that children are able to generate spiritual insights that they arrive at intuitively, which can be expressed in true faith responses. How tragic if we were to dismiss the intuitive insights of children and their acts of faith as somehow irrelevant to nurture because the theological concepts they express are not "really" understood.

It seems important then to keep an open mind to nurture approaches that encourage lateral thinking as well as to those ways of teaching that develop vertical modes of thought.

Associative Emotional Content

One factor on concept utilization that has not been well researched is the affective "loading" of concepts. Typically how

---

[8]Michael A. Wallach and Nathan Kogan, *Modes of Thinking in Young Children: A Study of the Creativity-Intelligence Distinction* (New York: Holt, Rinehart and Winston, 1965), p. 290.

children acquire and master concepts and how they use them have been the focus of exploration. Yet it is clear that human beings are not simply rational: that the emotions and attitudes associated with concepts are vital in determining appropriate response to them.

It is easy to understand why emphasis has been given to intelligence-linked knowledge and skills. For one thing, these learnings can be easily measured. But it is difficult to measure the affective weighting of newly gained concepts and skills. Still "I can add numbers, but I hate math" must be significantly different in human terms and impact from "I can add numbers, and I just love math."

When we think of ministry with children, it's clear that the communication of faith must be vitally concerned with affect. This is obvious when we consider a common dilemma. "God is a Heavenly Father" will have one import to a child who has a loving father and another to a child whose father beats and mistreats him or her.

While this is an obvious observation, it is also an important one. In ministry with children, we should be concerned with the concepts from which children will build their picture of their world. But we also should be concerned with the way these concepts are communicated, to be sure that they are as heavily laden with positive affect as possible. Thus the relational/emotional context of communication of faith becomes vitally important to what happens in the cognitive domain.

IMPLICATIONS FOR MINISTRY

An understanding of cognitive development has many implications for ministry with children. We can look only at a few that are influential in shaping our approach to ministry in home, church, or school settings.

Implication One: The Necessity of Biblical Data

Some followers of Piaget have argued that many biblical concepts should not be introduced to children until preadolescence (see chapter 3, PROBE 1). The assumption is that the abstract concepts central to Christian faith will be misunderstood and will thus lead to a distorted faith. There are several factors that determine our rejection of this view.

Constructivism. Cognitive theory understands the human being to actively integrate experiences and concepts by building a picture of the world (environment) in which he or she lives. This is understood to be an adaptive process: that is, it is on the basis of

121

how a child perceives reality that he or she will make a choice of responses to things and to other persons.

No cognitive theorist imagines a child will have a formal (adult) understanding of the world around him. But the concepts a child has are functional. They do guide actions and choices. It seems clear then that biblical concepts (the content of faith) should be available to children if they are to build a truly appropriate picture of the world in which they live, and have necessary data to make faith responses to various situations.

The issue is well illustrated in the four-year-old boy in a New York City preschool. After observing construction machines gouging out a foundation for a new office building, he turned to his teacher and asked, "What kind of machine made the world?" Like other preschoolers, he was actively constructing a picture of his world from the data available to him. How foolish we would be to withhold information needed to help children build a biblical picture of reality.

Revelation. In chapter 3 we saw that Scripture must be viewed as truth: as a revelation of reality. Thus Scripture is to be used to build our picture of the world and to guide our responses to the life situations we face. In this sense "faith" becomes adaptive behavior (choices to act) based on perspectives gained from Scripture's unveiling of reality. We saw in this context that the true use of Scripture within the community of faith is to shape our view of reality and thus guide our daily choices. We saw too that an implication of this understanding of Scripture is to realize that the reality that Scripture unveils can be experienced, and that to "know the truth" demands experiencing it.

What our view of Scripture does then is to show us that *the issue in teaching children is not the communication of biblical concepts and their mastery on the formal (adult thinking) level. Instead the issue in teaching children is to translate the great truths of faith into thought units that can be experienced by boys and girls!* Because Scripture is a propositional revelation, its concepts *can* be dealt with on a formal level. But because Scripture is a reality revelation, the great realities it portrays can be experienced on every level.

For instance, the theological concept of *omnipresence* is a concept that can be mastered on the level of formal thought. In Piagetan terms only then would it be "understood." But that same concept can be dealt with on a much different level as it is translated into terms and experiences appropriate for three year olds.

An illustration comes from an Illinois three-year-old girl

taught such a lesson I designed on "Jesus Always Sees Me." Later that week she came in from her yard and said petulantly to her mom, "He won't leave me alone!" Going outside, mom looked for the neighborhood child teasing her daughter, but found no one. A few minutes later the child returned with the same complaint. "He won't leave me alone." Again mom went outside and found no one. Only later did she discover that her daughter had wanted to pick some forbidden flowers from the garden. When she reached out to grab them, she remembered that "Jesus always sees me." Frustrated, she drew back, and her complaint to mom expressed her wish that Jesus would go away so she could do what she knew was wrong without being observed! I had not really expected this particular response. But clearly the abstract concept of omnipresence had been communicated to a three year old as experienceable reality.

The challenge this raises for ministry with children is significant. We are not to try to force children into adult modes of learning or into modes that demand cognitive processes beyond their abilities. Instead it is our task to translate the great truths of Christian faith into terms that can be both understood and experienced by boys and girls as they grow up in the Christian community.

Growth. One last point must be made here. A constructivist understanding of cognitive growth points out that children are constantly reinterpreting and reordering the information they have as new cognitive structures develop. This is important for those who fear that children's "distorted" notions about Christianity will dominate later life. In fact *every* concept that finds a place in a child's picture of reality will be modified and changed as growth progresses.

Earlier we saw that even on a ninth grade level almost no children had mastered the formal level use of the concept "noun." Yet no one ever suggests that the concept "noun" should not be introduced until high school because it will be misunderstood! How foolish then to argue that ideas like "God" should be withheld until preadolescence for fear of childish misunderstandings. We cannot expect a formal mastery of God from children. But we can expect that as children grow up in a vital faith community their concept of God will grow too, and be constantly reshaped into a more and more appropriate view.

Again, what is important is that children *have* faith concepts that they can use at every stage of development to guide them in their exercise of faith responses in life. It is our task in ministry with children to teach them what they need to know, in ways they can understand and experience, and guide them lovingly to live out that simple faith that Jesus chose to commend.

In Christian education we must not be deceived by the Piagetan assumption of the superiority of logical thought, *and must in fact specifically teach for intuitions!*

We have many evidences that even curriculums designed for logical thought processes do provoke faith responses from children. What is important to realize is that these responses are intuitive (in the sense that the child does not really understand the principle), and that they are yet valid as true responses of faith.

The intuitive nature of children's faith responses enables us to appreciate the active working of the Holy Spirit in children's lives. And the intuitive nature of children's faith responses also guards us against expecting a child who responds appropriately in one situation to respond the same way in another situation *that we see* as parallel. We must always remember that children must not be expected to read situations correctly on the basis of abstract symbolic concepts they have been taught.

Implication Two: Curriculum Design

From its origins, the American Sunday school has been concerned with moral training. Doctrine has been downplayed, and Sunday school curriculums have focused on the teaching of Bible stories and their application to moral behavior.

The moral emphasis continues to dominate curriculum today, and with that emphasis has come a common design or pathway that has been followed in an attempt to generate moral behavior. This design pathway can be traced quite simply:

1. A Bible story that illustrates a particular faith principle (e.g., trust) or moral principle (e.g., honesty) is taught.
2. One or more illustrations of application of the principle to life are provided.
3. Children are encouraged to apply the principle in appropriate situations in their own daily living.

The schooling/instructional model then has tended to rely on a logical process of thought moving from principle → illustration → application.

The difficulty with this curriculum design is that it requires an ability to conserve a symbolic, abstract attribute. Conservation is the ability to see an attribute across changing situations. The attribute may be something like "number" that is conserved no matter how we may rearrange ten items on a field. Or the attribute may be a quality that is not directly linked to concrete objects, such as "trustfulness." However, the ability to conserve the symbolic and abstract is undeveloped even in later childhood.

It follows then that the best way to help children grasp the concepts of Christian faith in usable form is *not* to teach them in a way that relies on cognitive abilities that children do not have! Two questions must be answered by those involved in a ministry to children. When we *do* have a formal learning setting to use in our overall ministry with boys and girls, what processes should curriculums rely on to communicate the content of faith in usable form? If the lesson plan that flows from concept → illustration → application in logical order is not appropriate, what process *is* appropriate?

There is one particularly important point to make here, which is a critique of Piaget's system. For Piaget, to "really understand" requires that not only an appropriate response be made but that the logical processes that led to that response must be explained by the individual. Responses that are appropriate but cannot be explained are dismissed as "intuitive" and not involving "real thought."

Implication Three: Use of the Bible With Children

As we noted in discussing the implications for curriculum above, curriculums have tended to use the Bible in the teaching setting *as a source from which to derive abstract principles.* We tell the Bible story—and then *apply* it.

While much more needs to be said in definition of how to use the Bible in teaching children, we can simply note that as a revelation of reality Scripture has at least three easily definable functions. It serves us as a

1. source of concepts about God, man, the world, and relationships between them
2. report of how the people of God have lived in harmony with or out of harmony with revealed reality
3. standard against which to measure the appropriateness of our responses to revealed reality

In teaching children we note that *what we choose to teach* is derived from propositional expressions of concepts that children cannot understand, but *we are responsible to translate these concepts into units of experienceable thought.* It seems wise in designing curriculum to focus on the basic theological realities as the content to be taught and not to build our curriculum base on attempts to teach moral principles.

The function of Scripture as a report of the experiences of

God's people as they lived in harmony with revealed reality seems to suggest several exciting ways to use the Bible in teaching children. These are summarized below.

Enactive uses. Children play the Bible story, participating imaginatively in the events, experiencing what happened as real to them (reliving Exodus in booths).

Associative uses. Children are introduced to a biblical concept translated to be meaningful and experienceable (such as "Jesus always sees me"). The Bible story chosen (in this case that of Nathanaiel, John 1:43–51) is not the *source* of the concept, but illustrates it, and can be associated by the child with the concept to link his or her understanding with the Bible.

Imitative uses. Children act out the Bible story or see it acted out by others (or even with flannelgraph figures) as a way of providing models of how to respond in particular situations. While we cannot expect logical processes to conserve to the children's own life situations whatever principles the story may illustrate, we *can* expect intuitive responses to be made, *especially when the rest of the class process focuses on modeling the appropriate response in a variety of relevant situations.*

The point, then, is that an understanding of children's cognitive abilities and limitations enables us to recognize the weakness of our typical use of Scripture with boys and girls as a source from which we derive abstract principles. Instead our actual in-class use should focus more on enactive, associative, and imitative uses of the Bible. All these should be guided by responsible selection of truths that are basic to Christian faith. They must be further translated by adults into units of experienceable thought appropriate to children's abilities.

Implication Four: Instruction-as-Interpretation-of-Life

We noted in chapter 4 that one of the processes that we see in Scripture as basic in the communication of faith involves instruction-as-interpretation-of-life. It is in the lying downs, the risings up, and the walking along the way that parents interpret situations by reference to the words of God.

Understanding the process of cognitive growth we sense the genius of this approach. For cognitive research has shown that children do not think in terms of abstract verbal concepts that are learned as concepts and then applied to situations. Instead children interact with their environment and *from situations* construct an understanding that then guides their responses. This response to situations is intuitive in nature: that is, the rational processes by which responses have been arrived at cannot be explained by children. But the responses of children *are* adaptive. Despite the fact that they cannot deal with cause and effect, that they do not think in terms of series of events linked through past and present into the future, children still do get along. And their understanding of life and how to respond does develop.

In children's thinking both learning and response patterns are situation specific: they cannot be explained in terms of logical processes such as conservation, but instead they include imitative and other kinds of learning intuitively recognized as appropriate by the children.

The unique thing about teaching children with instruction that comes as interpretation of life is that it is *situation-specific instruction.* It brings the words of God (the biblical truths) into the child's world to interpret a specific situation or event, and it does not attempt to communicate an abstract concept that children are expected to apply across situations!

For instance, I noted earlier that a three-year-old girl had responded intuitively to a flower-picking impulse, remembering from her Sunday school class that "Jesus always sees me." The design of that class featured a variety of situations and a repetition of the concept phrase, which the child was able to carry over into a unique situation of her own. But how easily this could be taught in the home. "Jesus sees Sue when she's eating." "Jesus sees Sue when she's helping." "Jesus sees Sue when she's napping." How easy to weave this thought into the life pattern of the child, and how easy to associate it with praise and positive statements. How simple to enact the Nathanaiel Bible story, with the mother or father and the child exchanging the roles of Philip. "I couldn't see you Nathanaiel. But Jesus could see you when you were hiding behind the sofa. How glad we are that Jesus always sees us."

At every progressive stage of children's growth there will be truths that are particularly appropriate to teach: particularly significant to the child's life experiences. And there will be different ways to build that teaching into the situations of daily life. But the biblical pattern of instruction-as-interpretation-of-life is a unique and vital one, fitted perfectly to the way children learn!

A situational approach to teaching that does not seek to communicate concepts that must be formally understood or require mental operations beyond children's abilities is exactly fitted to the child's way of learning. And it is just this pattern that the Old Testament describes . . . and the schooling/instructional model of teaching so drastically distorts.

FRAMEWORK

PROBE

▶ *case histories*
▶ *discussion questions*
▶ *thought provokers*
▶ *resources*

1. *Read.* A vast number of books and articles discuss cognitive development. Many guidelines, warnings, and exciting implications for work with boys and girls may be gleaned in a study of the behavioral science literature. The following are suggested as "best books" on the basis of the clarity of their presentations and their value as a source book to stimulate application to children's ministries.

   De Bono, Edward. *Lateral Thinking: A Textbook of Creativity.* London: Ward Lock Educational, 1970.

   Klausmeier, Herbert J. and Patricia S. Allen *Cognitive Development of Children and Youth: A Longitudinal Study.* New York: Academic Press, 1978.

   Sigel, Irving E. and Rodney R. Cocking. *Cognitive Development from Childhood to Adolescence: A Constructionist Perspective.* New York: Holt, Rinehart and Winston, 1977.

2. *Examine curriculum.* Select three commonly used curriculums and select at random (say, the fifth lesson in each) for second or third grade levels. Study the lessons carefully and analyze the following.
   a. Does the lesson seek to communicate a biblical concept translated into a thought unit understandable to and experienceable by the children to be taught?
   b. Does the lesson seek to communicate an abstract, symbolic concept that the children are expected to conserve and be able to apply? That is, is there a "moral" generalized from the story, with application attempted in the traditional generalization → illustration → application flow?
   c. How is the Bible story used in the lesson? As the source of the moral or concept to be taught? Or is it used enactively? Associatively? Imitatively?
   d. After analyzing select a "best" and "worst" lesson from the three, and carefully defend your choice in writing with specific analyses and illustration of your points from the lessons you chose.

3. *Reshape curriculum.* Take your "worst" lesson from #2 above, and rewrite it. You must use the same passage of Scripture, but need not take anything else (aims, objectives, etc.) from the lesson. Your goal is to design a lesson that will "fit" the cognitive characteristics of the age group in the fullest sense. You have *no other* restrictions or concerns.

4. *Interview children.* If one wants to gain insight into children's thinking one must actually talk with and listen to children. A good project for a class would be to develop a "standard interview" and then have each person interview two or three children of different ages (five, eight, eleven), record the responses, and then compare the responses gained by others in the class. The following steps might be used in setting up this kind of project.

   a. Select two concepts to discuss with children. One concept might relate to an attribute or quality of God. One concept might relate to an aspect of moral behavior related to Sunday school teaching. Select either by surveying Sunday school literature for the age groups, or by interviewing Sunday school teachers and determining what they feel they have "taught" the children in the last three months.

   b. Work out as a class several "stimulator" questions about each concept. These stimulator questions should not be designed to obtain definition, but to encourage the boys and girls to talk about the subject chosen.

   c. Have each class member "interview" three children. Each may find his or her own subjects, possibly in the individual's own church or Sunday school. The students should be asked to interview either three five year olds, three eight year olds, or three eleven year olds. Each child's answers to the questions should be written down after each interview as nearly verbatim as possible.

   d. Collate the responses of all fives, all eights, and all elevens and duplicate for all class members. Then as a class discuss the responses, and explore any implications they may have for ministry with children.

PART 1

FRAMEWORK

A Theological Framework for Ministry

Nurture in the Old Testament
Nurture in the New Testament
The Role of Scripture in Nurture
The Nurture Process

A Developmental Framework for Ministry

The Developmental Perspective
Cognitive Potentials of Children
Social Relationships of Children
Moral Development in Children
An Integrated Perspective

In our introductory overview in chapter 5, we looked briefly at social learning theory. Now, instead of further examining the mechanisms that theorists propose, we want to ask a simple question. What kinds of relationships are important in the

SOCIAL RELATIONSHIPS OF CHILDREN

healthy development of boys and girls? We need to understand the function of various types of relationships, and their role in the communication of faith, if we are to minister effectively to boys and girls.

Give the normal child the food and shelter he or she needs and the child will develop physically, in a manner appropriate to our common human genetic code. But there seems to be no "normal" parallel for the growth of personality. The genetic coding reflected in the maturing of mental structures, which we explored in the last chapter, certainly is *necessary* for personality growth. But it is not *sufficient* for true human development. To become a person a child must mature within a social environment. The kind of social environment (e.g., culture, language, and the warmth or hostility of parental relationships) will have a shaping impact on personality.

It's not surprising then that in our concern to encourage growth in faith we must pay close attention to children's relationships, with family and peers, in church and school and to how these relationships are perceived.

NURTURANT RELATIONSHIPS

In an interesting discussion Mia Kellmer Pringle explores four basic needs of children. Few would argue against the inclusion of each need as essential. They fit so well the common sense conclusions that, every now and again, are actually shown by research to be extremely wise. What is significant is that each need clearly depends on intimate relationships if it is to be met. Pringle lists a need for love and security, a need for new experiences, a need for praise and recognition, and a need for responsibility.[1] Often this list includes other elements described as *nurturant* relationships that form a context of generous love.

CHAPTER 7

Because we are so aware of the need for children to be loved, and loved wisely, we'll not dwell on this point in detail, except to point out that the impact of nurturant relationships on children cannot be overestimated. More and more research is tracing trait after trait of healthy personality back to the experience of nurturant love. David R. Shaffer comments on such research when he says:

> The results of several child-rearing studies indicate that warm, nurturant parents tend to raise altruistic children. . . . Perhaps we should not be surprised to learn that warm, nurturant relationships with socializing agents facilitate altruism in children, for parental nurture has a special relevance for the child's acquisition of altruistic responses when one considers that nurturance given to the child is itself an example or model of altruism.[2]

[1]Mia Kellmer Pringle, *The Needs of Children* (London: Hutchinson, 1974).
[2]David R. Shaffer, *Social and Personality Development* (Monterey, Calif.: Brooks-Cole Publishing, 1979), p. 391.

Positive self-concepts are also encouraged by nurturant relationships. Shirley C. Samuels has pointed out the significance of the early years in this process:

> The early childhood years are significant ones in the development of "core" self-concepts. The influence of healthy or unhealthy parent-child relationships are reflected in children's attitudes about themselves and are developed from birth onward. During the first year, consistent, loving care leads to a sense of trust, which is the foundation for the development of identity. . . . Positive self-concept in all its dimensions will result if trust, autonomy, and initiative are appropriately encouraged.[3]

Samuels continues this emphasis by stating

> Studies suggest that parental love manifested by warmth, supportive encouragement, consistency, realistic expectations, and a balance between protectiveness and reward rather than punishment is more likely to result in positive child self-concept.[4]

On the other hand cross-cultural studies show that "the less the opportunity in a culture for a son to get to know, love, and identify with his father, the higher the crime rate of that culture will be."[5]

These few quotes could easily be multiplied. Over and over again research has traced positive traits, from adventurousness to altruism and sociability to healthy self-concept, back to a context of nurturant relationships in childhood, and, contrariwise, has found the lack of such nurture to be detrimental.

And over and over as we explore the Old and New Testaments, we find just such nurturant relationships are to mark the loving lifestyle of the faith community.

SOCIALIZING RELATIONSHIPS

Social learning theory describes several mechanisms by which children and adults grow as persons. But the underlying assumption is very simple. That assumption is that persons become who they are through their interaction with other human beings.

Most studies of social influence do not touch on this underlying assumption. Instead they focus on specific, simple actions (such as giving half one's winnings in a game to charity), and try to isolate factors that lead young children to mimic the behavior of an (often unfamiliar) adult, who performs some action in their sight. Such studies are weak in that they only measure be-

---

[3]Shirley C. Samuels, *Enhancing Self-Concept in Early Childhood* (New York: Human Sciences Press, 1977), p. 73.

[4]Ibid., p. 91.

[5]Ronald C. Johnson and Gene R. Medinnus, *Child Psychology* (New York: John Wiley & Sons, 1974), p. 199.

havior, not the internalization of attitudes and beliefs and behaviors. But still the studies have demonstrated beyond question that one source of children's learning, as measured by their actions, is imitation of models.

What is important to remember is that this concept of *modeling* is global (referring to the total person) as well as related to specific, simple acts. Social learning theory assumes, and many studies illustrate, that the quality and kind of long-term relationships affect everything about children, from their self-concept to their altruistic impulses; from their values and attitudes to creativity and freedom from excess anxiety and undifferentiated guilt. Far more than language is learned by living with others. The whole perspective a person has of himself, and life, and others, develops within and from that network of interpersonal relationships that a child knows first with his family, and then wideningly with playmates, schoolmates and teachers, and others.

Two broad concepts have been suggested to explain global development. One concept is *enculturation,* and the other is *socialization.* The difference has been described clearly by Stewart Cohen. He describes enculturation as follows:

> Cultural membership plays a crucial role in establishing personal identity. This occurs largely through the existence of a person's unique cultural heritage. In general, the young child partakes of specific experiences that help him establish a continuing legacy with other human beings of comparable cultural tradition. Enculturation refers to the learning of one's culture by an assimilation of the distinct living patterns characteristic of that culture. In general, as a learning mechanism, enculturation provides reference to the operation of broad categories of experience that serve to characterize one's cultural heritage (e.g., special religious rites, distinct cooking arts, traditional forms of dress, etc.). The ordering of social arrangements, in turn, is assumed to be responsible for the child's learning less formalized but related attitudes and behaviors that define the operation and quality of interaction surrounding one's cultural membership. In brief, through cultural experiences the child learns the behavior of his culture.[6]

Socialization, on the other hand, is the view

> . . . that growth occurs through the establishment of direct personal relationships. This view is founded upon the idea that socialization occurs primarily within those immediate face-to-face social units where an individual shares intimate affiliations or associations. Under this principle socialization is usually achieved through family ties, established school bonds, and peer group relationships.[7]

---

[6]Stewart Cohen, *Social and Personality Development in Childhood* (New York: Macmillan, 1976), p. 8.

[7]Ibid., p. 10.

It's clear that the Old Testament nurture system reviewed in chapter 1 may use both processes, but that the Mosaic ideal stresses enculturation. The image there is of a unitary culture: a society in which every social agent with whom a growing child might interact, and every institution, would support a common system of belief, values, and behavior.

Looking back to the New Testament pattern, however, we find no unitary culture. In fact, the church that exploded into the first-century world was a countercultural movement! In the most significant of areas—those linked with personal identity, with the most critical values and beliefs about the meaning of human life—Christianity was at odds with Roman, Greek, and even Hebrew cultures! And yet from that early church emerged a dynamic faith that has continued through the centuries to capture the allegiance and transform the lives of men, women, and children as well.

The New Testament emphasizes those close, face-to-face relationships on which socialization rests, and it helps us to realize that socialization does provide a model for the communication of faith. Socialization takes place through "direct personal relationships," with those with whom an individual "shares intimate affiliations." It is in this intimate context of loving community, where individuals are known and loved as individuals by individuals, that Christian faith is discovered by adults as well as by children.

We can appreciate the specific mechanisms that theorists suggest: the presence of others who serve as models; the reinforcement that comes through praise and correction; the learning that takes place as imitation leads to experience and experience to fresh learning that shapes the inner person. Each of these mechanisms will continue to be open to debate and to additional definition. But one thing is beyond debate: the fact of the vital significance of close and loving personal relationships in a socialization-linked communication of faith.

So we see again the importance of the kinds of relationships that facilitate this type of learning: frequent, long-term contact with those loving persons who will serve as models for children; warm, loving relationships with those persons who are models; exposure to the inner states—the feelings, thoughts, and values—that lie behind the actions of children's models; opportunity for boys and girls to be with and to observe those who will serve as models; and, of course, the commitment of models to faith's lifestyle, so that beliefs and behavior blend and produce the beauty that Christ came to reintroduce into the world of lost humanity.

PEER RELATIONSHIPS

Most researchers have assumed that adults are the primary socializing influences in children's lives. But recently increasing attention has been paid to children's relationships with each other.

Peer Modeling

It is obvious that between the ages of three and twelve children spend many thousands of hours with other children, in a variety of settings. Research conducted since the late 1960s has shown results that seem obvious when they are pointed out. Shaffer comments that

> peers are important sources of social reinforcement. . . . that social behaviors are often strengthened, maintained, or in some cases virtually eliminated depending on the reactions they elicit from peers. Furthermore, young boys and girls respond selectively to their playmates, and exchange rewards in a reciprocal fashion. We may conclude that, when children interact in their peer groups they are not merely passing the time until adults come on the scene. Perhaps it is more accurate to say that they are engaged in a series of affective exchanges that clearly influence the course of their social and personality development.[8]

One study also reported by Shaffer illustrates the impact of peer modeling.

> O'Connor (1972) compared the effectiveness of contingent reinforcement and peer modeling as methods of improving the social skills of withdrawn preschool children. Half of the children watched a 23-minute film in which an initially withdrawn child engaged in a series of increasingly complex peer interactions, and was reinforced for her participation (peer model condition). The remaining children watched a nature film that contained no peer interaction (control condition). In addition, half of the children who had watched each film were later reinforced by an adult when they interacted with peers (social reinforcement condition). The remaining children received no such reinforcement (no reinforcement condition). O'Connor reported that modeling and contingent reinforcement produced a comparable short term increase in the social interactions of withdrawn children. But follow-up observations made three and six weeks later revealed that only those children who had seen the peer-modeling film had actually *maintained* a high level of positive social interactions with their peers.[9]

Replications of this and similar experiments, some with live peer models, showed that "modeling strategies can produce reasonably stable changes in a child's social skills that benefit the child and those peers with whom the child interacts."[10]

---

[8]Shaffer, *Social and Personality Development*, p. 531.
[9]Ibid., p. 582.
[10]Ibid., p. 583.

The influence of peers does seem to vary with children's ages. It seems less during early childhood and preadolescence, but during the primary years it's clear that other children have a very significant socializing impact on each other. Certainly in our ministry with children we must pay close attention to children's relationships with each other as well as their relationships with adults.

Friendships

We've seen that the intimacy of relationships is significant in encouraging children to model on adults. It seems important to ask if close relationships between children might also be significant. Many studies have shown that even watching strangers perform certain actions has its effect on children's behavior. What is the impact of longer term affectional relationships?

Before we can explore that issue, we need to be aware that "friendship" has different meanings at different ages. In the primary grades children describe their friendships in terms of kind actions: being nice rather than being mean or hostile. A person who is friendly and smiles is often identified as a friend within a particular situational frame. It is the actions of persons toward the individual that distinguish them as friends.

From about age nine on friendships begin to be linked with personality as well as behaviors. A sense of cooperation and mutual willingness to adjust, which permits failures and has room for forgiveness, begins to develop. Later still children tend to seek out as friends those who have similar personalities and whose values match. And during all of childhood, friendships are linked with gender, so that boys build friendships with boys and girls build friendships with girls.

The evidence is mounting increasingly that the ability and the opportunity to develop real friendships during childhood meets a vital need and is a significant factor in healthy personality development. For instance, one study suggests that childhood friendships may have life-long impact. In it adults who were classified as "warm" were found to have had more mutually satisfying chumship relationships during childhood than other adults who were "aloof." Figure 15 is a "Chumship Checklist" from a boy's point of view.

Distinctives of Peer Relationships

Growing awareness of the importance of children's relationships with each other has stimulated much exploration of friendships. With this exploration has come a pair of very interesting questions. What really is the difference between child/

FIGURE 15

CHUMSHIP CHECKLIST[11]

1. Play games in which you take turns being the leader.
2. Walk to school together.
3. Help out when one of you gets behind in his work.
4. Talk about girls.
5. Share each other's games, bat and ball, etc.
6. Tell each other things you wouldn't tell anyone else.
7. Stick up for each other if an older boy is picking on one of you.
8. Sit together on school bus.
9. Try to be on the same side when choosing teams, even if he is not the best player.
10. Do fun things together, like going to movies or ball game.
11. Tell each other if one of you has done something wrong.
12. Phone each other about school assignments.
13. Talk about what you want to be when you grow up.
14. Sleep over at each other's house.
15. Talk about your parents.
16. Find it hard to disagree with him on important things.
17. Go on vacation or short trip with him and his family.

child relationships and child/adult relationships? And, what are the distinctive contributions of each kind of relationship in the development of children?

The first question seems relatively simple to answer. The difference is not so much in maturity level or way of thinking as it is in differences in social power. Different writers speak of this factor in different ways. William Damon calls it the right of *social imposition.* Piaget speaks of it as a power of *unilateral restraint.* Others simply call it *authority.* Whatever the name, the meaning is clear. In most adult/child relationships the adult is likely to relate to the child as a power figure, with the right to impose his or her structure on the social situation. On the other hand, peers are those who *do not claim the right of unilateral imposition* but who instead operate as coequals. In a coequal relationship children build friendships in which reciprocal behaviors are a vital part of the process.

It is not yet clear what the impact of these two types of social relationships is. It's clear that children do learn many things from adults who relate from an authority position. It is tempting to theorize that the relationship marked by such power is more likely to lead to conformity than to inner commitments. But that is not certain. It does seem clear, however, that the true peer relationship encourages kinds of learning in which free, autonomous choices and insights are paramount. Beyond this

[11]A. P. Mannario, "Friendship Patterns and Altruistic Behavior in Preadolescent Males," *Developmental Psychology* 12 (1976): 555–56. Copyright 1976 by the American Psychological Association. Reprinted by permission.

there is little that can be said at this time. But the whole area is clearly significant, particularly in view of the findings of several studies that modeling influence is closely linked with reciprocity: one is more likely to model on a person who has modeled in some way on him or her.

One area that deserves study is the extent to which adults can build true friendships with children, in which the patterns of relationships tend to the coequal rather than the imposition style.

In especially interesting research, James Youniss has isolated particular procedures that children describe in speaking of friendship (see Figure 16). It seems likely that true reciprocal relationships between adults and children can and should be developed, and that friendship processes may have great potential for the communication of faith—perhaps even greater potential than those relationships in which adults freely exercise their overwhelming power of social imposition.

ROLE-TAKING

One last area needs to be reviewed. It is an area closely linked with what is commonly called *social cognition.* William Damon

FIGURE 16
CHILDREN'S DESCRIPTION OF FRIENDSHIP BEHAVIORS[12]

1. *Taking turns.* The one who has a bike will take turns. You let them take turns on a swing. They won't always be the boss; sometimes they'll let you decide. They'll take turns deciding.

2. *Conceding.* Like if I wanted to play baseball and they wanted to play tennis . . . go along with them. You're playing and one of them cheats. The other one says, "OK," he lets it go. He's always interested in what you are interested in and vice versa.

3. *Supporting the other.* Take up for him if someone's picking on him. I sort of got in trouble and sort of blamed my friend. He would let it stay. If you did something wrong, they'll share the responsibility. If you get in trouble, he won't say you did it but stays with you. Won't leave you if you get in trouble.

4. *Explaining.* If the person is stuck, show them the answer but tell them why it's the answer. If someone's being mean to that person, you can tell them not to and ask why. Talk over assignments. She gets in trouble with her parents; Jill gives her advice.

5. *Discussion.* You know each other good and talk things out; talk problems out with you. You can talk to him and he'll talk to you. Ask questions of each other. A friend wants to come and talk about your problem. A person you can talk to who will listen and tell you their problems.

6. *Reflecting values.* When you have a problem, you can tell that friend and talk it over with him and he'll understand. She'll help you understand how you feel and give advice. Someone you can talk to. . . . They can tell you what's wrong and what's right in a way. Then you can go to your friend and he would know what to say.

---

[12]James Youniss, *Parents and Peers in Social Development* (Chicago: University of Chicago, 1980), pp. 243–44.

describes the field as one that seeks to "free the child from being a mere reflection of social input from others." Damon describes the central issue this way: "When social influences determine thought, the child is reduced to a composite of results from external, determining sources. When cognition is understood to be a structural, self-propelling developmental process, the child remains relatively uninfluenced by society."[13] Social cognition thinkers seek to develop a theory that accounts for both positions.

Of particular concern in social cognition theory is the interaction between others and the child's own abilities to perceive relationships. One of the most important areas of investigation focuses on the social role-taking ability of children.

We saw in the last chapter that Piaget demonstrated the difficulty children have in conceiving of an object's shape as it might be viewed from a position other than their own. This egocentrism is significant in Piagetan thought.

Piaget's early research led to a number of assertions about children's ability to role-take, described in terms of the following stages.

Stage IIA (4–6). The child is unable to free himself from the egocentric illusion and sees all things from his own viewpoint.

Stage IIB (6–7). Minimal movement toward role-taking and awareness that others somehow have a different point of view.

Stage IIIA (7–9). The child realizes perspectives are different, but is unable to coordinate the relationships successfully.

Stage IIIB (9–10). The child is able to understand and to represent with considerable accuracy the perspective of others.

This particular point of view is quite pessimistic about children's abilities to see and feel with others, and might thus have a significant impact on the limits of the learning children might be expected to experience in social settings that require role-taking. However, a number of experiments have been devised to test the stages described by Piaget and his earliest disciples.

- Children are given the task of telling a continuing story, represented visually on a series of cards. When several of the cards are taken away, will the story-telling child realize he must "fill in the gaps"?
- Children are asked to select a "favorite" picture and then are asked to place it "so I can see it as you see it."
- Children are shown matched cards, on which different animals are on reverse sides. For instance, one card might

[13]William Damon, *Social Cognition* (San Francisco: Jossey-Bass, 1978), p. 4.

show a dog on one side and a cat on the other. Children are shown one picture and asked to select the card like theirs from several with the opposite side showing.

- Children are shown pictures of children with different expressions on their faces and told a story. After hearing the story they are asked to select the face that shows how the child in the story feels.

Experiments like these have modified the early, limited view of children's ability to take others' roles in social situations, but they still indicate that "many children of the early preschool period are simply unaware of perspective variation as one of life's possibilities."[14]

Flavell and his collaborators suggest several processes involved in role-taking ability. (1) *Existence* speaks of the fact that children must become aware that such a thing as "perspective" exists. Older preschoolers do show this awareness. (2) *Need* speaks of the necessity to see, in a given situation, that it is important to take the perspective of others into account. First graders may show this awareness. (3) *Prediction* speaks of the ability to analyze the other's perspective appropriately, while (4) *maintenance* is the ability to adjust their thinking continuously during the experience. (5) *Application* is the ability of children to modify their own behavior to fit the needs of the other in the situation.[15]

Children's ability to social role-take is apparently not as limited as was earlier thought. (See Shaffer's summary in Figure 17.) The extent of this ability remains a factor we must always be aware of when we seek to understand the ways of boys and girls.

But there is a parallel issue that is important in our ministry with children. We not only want boys and girls to be able to see things from others' perspectives, but we also want them to develop empathy. Larry C. Jensen and M. Gawain Wells appropriately define empathy as "the human capacity to perceive another's emotional reactions and to share in these reactions."[16] The authors describe passage through several stages in the development of empathy. Summarizing such growth the authors point out that

> The child must learn to develop a sense of his own thinking and feeling as being different from others. A child may recognize other children as physi-

[14]John H. Flavell, et al., *The Development of Role-Taking and Communication Skills in Children* (New York: John Wiley & Sons, 1968), p. 64.

[15]Ibid.

[16]Larry C. Jensen and M. Gawain Wells, *Feelings: Helping Children Understand Emotions* (Ogden, Utah: Brigham Young University Press, 1979), p. 15. Used by permission.

cally different, but may still assume that his needs and his internal world are the primary world.

In a study by Borke (1971), children from three to eight years of age were told stories in which the main character experienced emotions of happiness, sadness, fright, or anger. Borke then gave the children blank

FIGURE 17
SOCIAL COGNITION IN CHILDREN[17]

1. THE SOCIAL COGNITION OF PRESCHOOL CHILDREN (YOUNGER THAN AGE 5)

Shantz concluded that preschool children are rather egocentric, but perhaps not so profoundly egocentric as Piaget had thought. These youngsters are capable of a primitive form of role-taking, for they do recognize that another person may have a perspective that differs from their own. But they are clearly unable to specify what that perspective is. Preschool children can identify a few of the simple emotions that another child may be experiencing in situations that are familiar to them, such as sadness, when someone has broken the child's toy, but they are not likely to empathize with the child (that is, feel the same way in response to the child's misfortune). Preschoolers do not anticipate the thoughts of others, as shown in guessing games in which the child must infer another player's strategy in order to win. Finally, when preschool children are asked to give their impressions of others, the resulting descriptions are highly egocentric: "He hits me," "She plays with me," and so on.

2. THE SOCIAL COGNITION OF TRANSITIONAL CHILDREN (AGES 5 TO 7)

Social cognition becomes much more sophisticated from ages 5 to 7, or about the time children are beginning to move from preoperational thinking to the stage of concrete operations. At this age, children are much more aware that other people may have perspectives (on visual tasks) that differ from their own. Likewise, in making social inferences, the 5- to 7-year-old realizes that other people have thoughts that do not match his or her own, but the child is not yet proficient at inferring what these thoughts might be. Children at this level of social cognition are better able to recognize the emotions of others and are more likely than preschool children to use facial rather than situational cues to infer emotions. When asked to judge the "goodness" or "naughtiness" of an act, 5- to 7-year-olds are able to discriminate accidents from intentional responses. They can also distinguish between good and bad intentions when allocating blame for an act—but only if the consequences of the act are not too negative. If the consequences of another person's behavior are extremely negative, the 5- to 7-year-old will blame the person regardless of the person's intentions. Finally, the child's verbal impressions of others (given in response to open-ended items such as "a girl that I know very well and like . . .") are less egocentric than those of a preschooler, but rather concrete. For example, other people are often described in terms of their appearance or possessions. When a description does include personal attributes, rather diffuse and simplistic labels are used: "He's good," "He's horrible," and so on.

3. THE SOCIAL COGNITION OF MIDDLE CHILDHOOD (AGES 7 TO 11)

Dramatic advances in social cognition occur during middle childhood. Children's role-taking abilities are rapidly maturing, so that they are able to infer the thoughts of other people. In fact, many 8- to 10-year-olds recognize that their own thoughts, feelings, and intentions can be the object of another person's thinking. When making judgments about harmful acts, children now consider the actor's intentions (good versus bad) to a greater extent than the amount of harm done. The 7- to 11-year-old can infer the emotions of others who are in situations that are not at all familiar to him or her. The child's impressions of others now contain attributes that are much more subtle or precise in their meaning, such as "shy," "considerate," "helpful," "affectionate." When observing social interactions, 7- to 11-year-olds attend less to the overt responses of others than to the underlying motives that may have prompted these actions.

[17]Shaffer, *Social and Personality Development*, pp. 122–23.

faces on which to fill in the emotional expression they thought the main character was feeling. Young children were able to correctly differentiate between happy and afraid stories. The majority of the five-to- six-year-olds were able to correctly identify a sad story, but the angry stories were not correctly interpreted by a majority of even the oldest children.

Three- to six-year-olds were asked to describe how an individual felt when they were shown pictures in which the facial expression of the individual differed from the circumstances (frowning at his birthday party, for example). Five- and six-year-olds were able to respond appropriately to the pictured expression. Three-and four-year-olds, however, judged the pictures more in terms of how they would feel in the situation, and apparently did not perceive the incongruity.[18]

Recognizing the importance of social role-taking and empathy, we should ask whether these skills come automatically or if we can help children develop them. While it is necessary to have a certain level of mental development, again research shows that social sensitivity does not come automatically. Jensen and Wells suggest we help children develop perspective and empathy.

First, allow the child to have the normal run of distress experiences; the child will develop a greater sensitivity to the needs and feelings of others. Shielding a child from distress experiences may narrow his base for empathic understanding in later years. Second, provide the child with opportunities to take the role of others and to give help. This care should foster empathic awareness of the others' perspective. Third, encourage the child to put himself in the others' place—talking it through with him, including differences as well as similarities between himself and others. Also, of course, the opportunity to observe his parents and other persons behaving in altruistic manners will be important to the development of altruistic motives. Models facilitate the process by communicating their thoughts and feelings as they help. Using stories to help the child understand others' feelings is an effective method for learning about individual emotions.[19]

SUMMING UP

In brief, then, social relationships are important to children in every way. Nurturant relationships provide a context in which children find the freedom and support they need for healthy development. Socializing relationships provide models and reinforcements, which guide learning and which have a shaping impact on the whole personality. Peer relationships, especially those that are friendships with coequals, are particularly significant. In addition, a wide range of experience with other persons is important to help children learn, as they become able, to empathize and to grow into the kind of caring adults who reflect, in the deepest way, the impact of personal relationship with God on the human personality.

[18]Jensen and Wells, *Feelings,* pp. 16–17.
[19]Ibid., p. 19.

PROBE

▶ case histories
▶ discussion questions
▶ thought provokers
▶ resources

1. Early ideas about children and how they learn are reflected in the following "Rules for Sunday Schools," which were printed in 1824 to be taught to boys and girls. What do these rules suggest about the role perceived for relationships by those concerned with ministry to children at that time? How would you rewrite these rules to provide a valid set of guidelines for the Sunday school today?

> I must always mind the Superintendent and all the teachers of this School.
> I must come every Sunday, and be here when School goes in.
> I must go to my seat as soon as I come in.
> I MUST ALWAYS BE STILL.
> I must not leave my seat till School goes out.
> I must take good care of my book.
> I must not lean on the next boy.
> I must walk softly in the School.
> I must not make a noise by the Church door or School door, but must go in as soon as I come.
> I must always go to Church.
> I must behave well in the street when I am going to Church.
> I must walk softly in Church.
> I must sit still in my place till Church goes out.
> I must go away from the Church as soon as I go out.
> I must always mind the Superintendents and all the Teachers of this School.

2. Many excellent books explore the impact of relationships on children. For further reading and research these are recommended as among the best.

   Cohen, Stewart. *Social and Personality Development in Childhood.* New York: Macmillan, 1976.

   Damon, William, ed. *Social Cognition.* San Francisco: Jossey-Bass, 1978.

   Foot, Hugh C. with Anthony J. Chapman and Jean R. Smith. *Friendships and Social Relations in Children,* New York: John Wiley & Sons, 1980.

3. The first case history on page 81 describes a simple research project carried out in several Sunday schools. It was designed to check the perception of the children of their relationships with Sunday school classmates, and led to changing the pattern of teaching to encourage the growth of friendships. One result of measurements later was discovery that many children listed their teachers as friends.

Go back over the case history carefully. In view of the information provided in this chapter, be prepared to discuss the following questions:

a. What were the probable reasons for the initial findings?

b. What kinds of changes were probably introduced into the class process to produce the results obtained?

c. What is the significance of the teacher being identified by the children as a friend? How do you think this result was probably obtained?

4. After the discussion (3b, above), work out your own study of friendship relationships of boys and girls in a local Sunday school. First, work together to develop predictions of what you think you will find. Then develop ways to check your predictions. Third, conduct your research, using either the technique described in the case history, or some other method. Finally, analyze and discuss your results, and consider what the results might imply concerning a congregation's ministry with children.

5. Figure 16 identifies six processes that seem to children to mark out relationships as "friendships" between coequals. Select a series of three consecutive Sunday school lessons, from any curriculum publisher you choose, on either primary or junior level. Analyze the instructions given to the teachers, focusing on what they are to say or do with the children. Identify each teacher instruction, and then classify it by placing it in one of two categories: actions characterized by *unilateral imposition,* or by *coequality.*

When you have cataloged the teacher actions, write a brief summary of your findings, and also a paragraph or two giving your own personal evaluation of the curriculum.

PART 1

FRAMEWORK

A Theological Framework for Ministry

Nurture in the Old Testament
Nurture in the New Testament
The Role of Scripture in Nurture
The Nurture Process

A Developmental Framework for Ministry

The Developmental Perspective
Cognitive Potentials of Children
Social Relationships of Children
Moral Development in Children
An Integrated Perspective

For some years "moral development" issues have been captured by the structuralists. The current movement has grown out of the work of Lawrence J. Kohlberg, Princeton psychologist, who has added much to our understanding of how chil-

MORAL DEVELOPMENT IN CHILDREN

dren think about moral issues. But at the same time Kohlberg's work may have obscured other issues that may be even more vital when we seek to understand ministry to boys and girls.

It's difficult to define morality, especially when we're thinking of morality in children. Do we take a dictionary definition of morality as "conformity to ideals of right human conduct"? Or does morality have more to do with values and behavior and conscience? Or is morality perhaps linked most closely with how we think about issues of right and wrong?

MORAL THINKING

To many today the critical issue in children's moral development is their ability to think about moral issues. Those who take this point of view are structuralists, holding that moral development is integrally linked with cognitive development. Structuralists believe that the ability to reason morally develops like cognitive development through a series of stages, each linked with higher levels of cognitive ability that become possible as children mature into adulthood. These structures, and thus the progress of moral thinking, are thought to grow through a series of stages that always appear in invariant sequence. Thus children's moral capacities, like their capacities to think, are rooted in the genetic heritage of humanity. To be human—and to grow into all that being human promises—means necessarily to grow in morality.

Structuralists do not discount the role of personal relationships in moral growth, realizing that like cognitive abilities moral abilities grow through interaction with the environment. As new experiences bring children into new moral situations, and as the necessary changes take place within their growing minds, children's moral assumptions will be challenged and disequilibration will force a new interpretation of moral reality.

Lawrence J. Kohlberg developed the dominant structuralist theory of moral development. He reasoned from the work of Jean Piaget that children's thinking about moral issues must be determined by their cognitive abilities, as is their thinking about the physical universe. He set about trying to discover the way children think about moral issues in an effort to define stages of moral thought through which children, youth, and adults might pass.

Kohlberg interviewed children and youth, and he attempted to classify their moral thought. It is important to understand that Kohlberg was not concerned with the *content* of their moral thought. That is, he did not measure morality by the actions they approved or disapproved. Instead Kohlberg was interested in the *reasoning* his subjects used to explain their choices.

149

FRAMEWORK

FIGURE 18
KOHLBERG'S MORAL STAGES[1]

I. Preconventional level

At this level, the child is responsive to cultural rules and labels of good and bad, right or wrong, but interprets these labels either in terms of the physical or the hedonistic consequences of action (punishment, reward, exchange of favors) or in terms of the physical power of those who enunciate the rules and labels. The level is divided into the following two stages:

Stage 1: *The punishment-and-obedience orientation.* The physical consequences of action determine its goodness or badness, regardless of the human meaning or value of these consequences. Avoidance of punishment and unquestioning deference to power are valued in their own right, not in terms of respect for an underlying moral order supported by punishment and authority (the latter being Stage 4).

Stage 2: *The instrumental-relativist orientation.* Right action consists of that which instrumentally satisfies one's own needs and occasionally the needs of others. Human relations are viewed in terms like those of the marketplace. Elements of fairness, of reciprocity, and of equal sharing are present, but they are always interpreted in a physical, pragmatic way. Reciprocity is a matter of "you scratch my back and I'll scratch yours," not of loyalty, gratitude, or justice.

II. Conventional level

At this level, maintaining the expectations of the individual's family, group, or nation is perceived as valuable in its own right, regardless of immediate and obvious consequences. The attitude is not only one of *conformity* to personal expectations and social order, but of loyalty to it, of actively *maintaining,* supporting, and justifying the order, and of identifying with the persons or group involved in it. At this level, there are the following two stages:

Stage 3: *The interpersonal concordance or "good boy–nice girl" orientation.* Good behavior is that which pleases or helps others and is approved by them. There is much conformity to stereotypical images of what is majority or "natural" behavior. Behavior is frequently judged by intention—"he means well" becomes important for the first time. One earns approval by being "nice."

Stage 4: *The "law and order" orientation.* There is orientation toward authority, fixed rules, and the maintenance of the social order. Right behavior consists of doing one's duty, showing respect for authority, and maintaining the given social order for its own sake.

III. Postconventional, autonomous, or principled level

At this level, there is a clear effort to define moral values and principles that have validity and application apart from the authority of the groups of persons holding these principles and apart from the individual's own identification with these groups. This level also has two stages:

Stage 5: *The social-contract, legalistic orientation,* generally with utilitarian overtones. Right action tends to be defined in terms of general individual rights and standards which have been critically examined and agreed upon by the whole society. There is a clear awareness of the relativism of personal values and opinions and a corresponding emphasis upon procedural rules for reaching consensus. Aside from what is constitutionally and democratically agreed upon, the right is a matter of personal "values" and "opinion." The result is an emphasis upon the "legal point of view," but with an emphasis upon the possibility of changing law in terms of rational considerations of social utility (rather than freezing it in terms of Stage 4 "law and order"). Outside the legal realm, free agreement and contract is the binding element of obligation. This is the "official" morality of the American government and constitution.

Stage 6. *The universal-ethical-principle orientation.* Right is defined by the decision of conscience in accordance with self-chosen *ethical principles* appealing to logical comprehensiveness, universality, and consistency. These principles are abstract and ethical (the Golden Rule, the categorical imperative); they are not concrete moral rules like the Ten Commandments. At heart, these are universal principles of *justice,* of the *reciprocity* and *equality* of human *rights,* and of respect for the dignity of human beings as *individual* persons ("From Is to Ought," pp. 164–165).

---

[1]Excerpted from Lawrence Kohlberg. "The Claim to Moral Adequacy of a Highest Stage of Moral Judgment," *Journal of Philosophy.* 25 October 1973, pp. 631–32. *Used with permission.*

From this early work, Kohlberg felt he could distinguish three levels of moral thought, which could be further broken down into six stages.

While Kohlberg does not chart his stages by age, he believes that children up to age nine seldom pass his Preconventional (stages 1 and 2) level (see Figure 18). This means that children essentially lack an understanding of society's rules, and simply defer to the superior power of adult authorities, who are able to reward or punish behavior.

Kohlberg further suggests that most adolescents and adults in all societies remain at a Conventional level of moral thinking. This level is characterized by identifying with law and upholding it simply because it *is* the law. At this level the underlying concern is loyalty to the group and to its rules.

Finally Kohlberg believes in a Postconventional level of morality. At this level individuals make judgments on the basis of self-defined moral values or principles. Kohlberg says that moral thinking of this level is not achieved before age twenty, and that few adults in any society function on this level.

It is very important in understanding the structuralists' approach to moral development to realize that they assume that, while many factors may influence behavior, the only distinctively *moral* element in behavior is moral judgment. One who does the "right thing" (does not cheat, for instance) simply from an impulse to please the teacher is, in this framework, not making a moral judgment or engaged in moral action. It is only when a situation demands a choice, made on the basis of a reasoned moral judgment, that morality is involved. Thus what the structuralist is primarily concerned about is the way children reason.

We can illustrate this with a chart (see Figure 19) that shows how persons *might* reason about a specific moral choice. Should you cheat to help a friend who could not study for the big test because he had to work late to earn money for his sick mother? What is interesting here is that the product of the reasoning might lead one either to cheat *or* not to cheat. The specific moral content is not at issue, but the way persons reason at each stage is.

Remember when looking at the chart that Kohlberg believes children up to age nine will not be able to reason beyond stages 1 or 2.

Implications of Kohlberg's Approach

There is no doubt that Kohlberg's findings are both significant and helpful and that the implications of the structuralist system reach into a variety of areas.

151

FIGURE 19
MORAL REASONING DILEMMA

Should you cheat to help a friend who couldn't study for the big test because he had to work late to earn money for his sick mother?

YES	Stage 6	NO
There are times when the special needs of an individual come first, and this is such a time.	Concern for self-evaluation based on maintaining personal moral principles.	Good does not come from doing wrong so it would not really "help" the friend to cheat.
YES	**Stage 5**	**NO**
None of your friends would respect you if you were afraid to help. How could you be a friend and not help?	Concern about maintaining the respect of others and of one's self.	Most adults trust you and expect you to be honest. You can't cheat and keep the respect of other people.
YES	**Stage 4**	**NO**
You won't want to let your friend down, because you are supposed to help friends. You'll feel real guilty if you don't help.	Action motivated by expected dishonor, failure to do duty, and guilt over harm to others.	You may want to help, but when they send you home from school with a note to your dad, you'll feel guilty for breaking the rules.
YES	**Stage 3**	**NO**
People will think you're mean if you don't help your friend. If you don't help and he fails, you'll always feel it was your fault.	Action motivated by expected disapproval of others, real or imagined.	Your teacher and your parents will think you cheat on your own tests if you help. If people think you're a cheater you'll never want to go to school again.
YES	**Stage 2**	**NO**
If you get caught the worst that would probably happen is staying after school. And your friend will like you better.	Action motivated by a desire for benefits. Guilt/punishment implications likely to be discounted.	Even if your friend doesn't pass the test they won't hold him back. He shouldn't feel bad if he doesn't get a good grade.
YES	**Stage 1**	**NO**
If you don't help he might beat you up.	Action motivated by punishment/reward implications.	You get kept after school for cheating and if your folks find out you get spanked.

One area for which Kohlberg has significance is philosophy. His theory is extremely attractive to the humanist for a very simple reason. One of the basic problems in ethics for those who do not accept the notion of divinely ordained truth is how to establish a basis for morality. One can't simply say that a particular value system (say, the democratic) is something we can *like* better than another (say, the Nazi system). Morality is supposedly a matter of ordering ethical concerns, and involves justifying the claim that some actions are morally better than others. But how, if there are no external moral absolutes, could any claim of moral superiority be defended?

What Kohlberg's theory has done for ethics is to introduce an objective standard by which "lower" and "higher" moral systems can be evaluated. That objective standard does not come from without, but instead comes from within the very nature of human beings.

At this point it is important to note that Kohlberg finds the common element in each of his stages of moral thought to be that each is concerned with *justice*. Morality, as reflected in the thinking at each stage distinguished by Kohlberg, is linked to fairness and is rooted in the rightness of liberty, equality, and reciprocity. At every stage justice is the issue, but at *each level the concept of justice is reorganized.* Thus it follows that the moral reasoning that takes place at each succeeding stage is of a *higher order* than that of the stage below it, and thus is morally superior. It follows then that we can apply the principles implicit in the highest order of moral reasoning, and have an objective basis for arguing that a particular ethical system, concept, or society is "better" than another.

Kohlberg himself describes the understanding of justice at each level:

> At Stage 1, justice is punishing the bad in terms of "an eye for an eye and a tooth for a tooth." At Stage 2, it is exchanging favors and goods in an equal manner. At Stages 3 and 4, it is treating people as they desire in terms of the conventional rules. At Stage 5, it is recognized that all rules and laws flow from justice, from a social contract between the governors and the governed, designed to protect the equal rights of all. At Stage 6, personally chosen moral principles are also principles of justice, the principles any member of a society would choose for that society if he did not know what his position would be in the society and in which he might be the least advantaged.[2]

While Kohlberg's formulation has been criticized on the basis that only stages 1 through 4 are psychological and stages 5 and 6 belong in the realm of philosophy, this criticism only points up the implications of the Kohlberg formulation for humanistic ethics.

Another set of implications developed from Kohlberg's work affects education. If morality is really an issue of how we think

---

[2]Lawrence J. Kohlberg, "The Cognitive-Developmental Approach to Moral Education," in *Values Concepts and Techniques* (Washington, D.C.: National Education Association, 1976), p. 20.

about moral choices, then it follows that moral education must focus on helping children and others think about moral issues up to their potential developmental stage.

As a result, a number of classroom strategies have been developed and tested. While of course such strategies cannot lift boys and girls to levels of moral reasoning of which they are not capable, studies have shown that increases of a half-stage or so in moral reasoning can be obtained in children's classrooms.

It should also be noted that Kohlberg insists that social settings, whether schools or prisons or others, incorporate justice principles. He sees the existence of a "just moral community" as vital if children are to grow toward their moral potential.

A final implication is important for us to note. It is obvious, but must be stated. Kohlberg has shown that *the moral reasoning of children is not like the moral reasoning of adults.* Just as children can not conserve abstract verbal concepts across situations (see chapter 6), so they are not able to approach moral choices by reasoning from principle. This is particularly important for us in our thinking about ministry with children. Whatever we may try to do with boys and girls morally, we simply cannot rely on "teaching" moral concepts and then expect children to analyze their life situations and apply the moral concepts we have tried to communicate. Whatever "morality" may mean for children, it does not mean the same thing that morality means to the mature.

Critiques of Kohlberg

Kohlberg's work is so significant that it has gathered a crowd of detractors as well as of supporters. Just as we have not looked at nearly all the implications of Kohlberg's system, we cannot look at the host of criticisms. But we can identify two issues that may be of particular concern.

One assumption that needs to be challenged is the assumption that *justice* is the supreme value on which morality hinges. The Christian, sensitive to the reality of grace and experiencing a love that far surpasses justice in its concern for others, finds the identification of justice as the moral keystone inadequate.

Even more, there is need to challenge the assumption that if justice is accepted as the key moral value, we are helped in our search for true morality. Why? Because Kohlberg's system deals with moral reasoning and not moral content . . . and there is no clear bridge between the two. For instance, in one interview Kohlberg referred to statistics that suggest that each execution of a murderer saves two innocent lives. Yet he clearly states that anyone operating on level 6 principled morality must surely reject capital punishment! Yet a reading of the debate concerning capital punishment makes it clear that some arguments in favor of it *reason in a level 6 way*!

It seems clear from the possibility of disagreement about *most* moral questions that *how we reason* has little in itself to do with the rightness or wrongness of the conclusions we reach! Thus it is doubtful that a theory about reasoning processes can ever be used to establish or to evaluate the content of moral thought.

There is another area open to criticism that is of far greater concern to us than the philosophical issue raised above. It is an issue often raised these days, and surely a valid one. It is one thing, many observe, to be able to tell the difference between right and wrong. It's something else to care enough to actually do right.

And here the research of the structuralists is very weak. They have not demonstrated that operating on progressively higher levels of moral thought has a causal relationship to progressively acting on moral convictions! One can teach to raise the level of children's moral thinking. But one cannot expect this kind of training to actually affect an individual's behavior.

There are a few studies that indicate that adolescents who can reason more effectively about moral dilemmas are more likely to make positive moral choices. But the same studies show that even those with the most highly developed reasoning capacity do not necessarily choose the moral actions they intellectually approve.

The question that this line of criticism raises is very basic. What are we really talking about when we speak of "morality" or of "moral development" in boys and girls? Are we talking, when we use this kind of language, of the narrow issue of how children reason about morality? Or when we use the language of morality are we talking about content: about what is actually right and wrong? Or perhaps we are really talking about the choices we see children make in their daily lives, so that with children "morality" focuses on behavior? As soon as we ask such questions, we move away from the ground that so intrigues the structuralist, and we seem to suggest that our concern for moral development in children should lead to something more than research into the process of reasoning about morality that children use.

SOCIAL ROLE-TAKING

The later work of Kohlberg takes increasing account of factors typically associated with social learning. In general, however, the structuralist continues to display a rather awed belief in reasoning as generator of morality.

FRAMEWORK

FIGURE 20

RELATIONS BETWEEN SOCIAL ROLE-TAKING AND MORAL JUDGMENT STAGES[3]

SOCIAL ROLE-TAKING STAGE	MORAL JUDGMENT STAGE
Stage 0—Egocentric Viewpoint (Age Range 3–6) Child has a sense of differentiation of self and other but fails to distinguish between the social perspective (thoughts, feelings) of other and self. Child can label other's overt feelings but does not see the cause and effect relation of reasons to social actions.	**Stage 0—Premoral Stage** Judgments of right and wrong are based on good or bad consequences and not on intentions. Moral choices derive from the subjects wishes that good things happen to self. Child's reasons for his choices simply assert the choices, rather than attempting to justify them.
Stage 1—Social-Informational Role Taking (Age Range 6-8) Child is aware that other has a social perspective based on other's own reasoning, which may or may not be similar to child's. However, child tends to focus on one perspective rather than coordinating viewpoints.	**Stage 1—Punishment and Obedience Orientation** Child focuses on one perspective, that of the authority or the powerful. However, child understands that good actions are based on good intentions. Beginning sense of fairness as equality of acts.
Stage 2—Self-Reflective Role Taking (Age Range 8-10) Child is conscious that each individual is aware of the other's perspective and that this awareness influences self and other's view of each other. Putting self in other's place is a way of judging his intentions, purposes, and actions. Child can form a coordinated chain of perspectives, but cannot yet abstract from this process to the level of simultaneous mutuality.	**Stage 2—Instrumental Orientation** Moral reciprocity is conceived as the equal exchange of the intent of two persons in relation to one another. If someone has a mean intention toward self, it is right for self to act in kind. Right defined as what is valued by self.
Stage 3—Mutual Role Taking (Age Range 10-12) Child realizes that both self and other can view each other mutually and simultaneously as subjects. Child can step outside the two-person dyad and view the interaction from a third-person perspective.	**Stage 3—Orientation to Maintaining Mutual Expectations** Right is defined as the Golden Rule: Do unto others as you would have others do unto you. Child considers all points of view and reflects on each person's motives in an effort to reach agreement among all participants.
Stage 4—Social and Conventional System Role-Taking (Age Range 12-15 +) Person realizes mutual perspective taking does not always lead to complete understanding. Social conventions are seen as necessary because they are understood by all members of the group (the generalized other) regardless of their position, role, or experience.	**Stage 4—Orientation to Society's Perspective** Right is defined in terms of the perspective of the generalized other or the majority. Person considers consequences of actions for the group or society. Orientation to maintenance of social morality and social order.

[3]Source unknown.

156

To others, the link between cognitive growth and morality seems more likely to be the ability to see, and to take, another person's point of view. That relationship is well defined in Figure 20, a chart developed by the premier theorist in this school.

If social role-taking, including empathy for others, is a source of morality, it would seem important to identify the factors that encourage the development and exercise of this capacity. The process most suggest is relatively simple. Give the child opportunities to be exposed to a number of other people. Help him become aware that they are different from him and that they have views and feelings that differ from his own. Then in a variety of ways, e.g., adult and peer modeling or reinforcement, help the child learn to take these views into account.

Sheila Stanley stresses the contribution of family experiences in building children's sensitivity to others.

> The family is a crucial source of such role-taking opportunities for the growing child. But, as yet, there has been little research on strategies for moral education in the family. Research on learning theory provides some tentative support for the notion that parental styles influence the child's moral development (Hoffman 1963; Bandura and Walters 1963). To be more specific, the use of inductive discipline by parents appears to be correlated with more advanced moral reasoning and behavior than either the use of coercive power or threats of withdrawing love (Hoffman and Salzstein 1967; Schoffeitt 1971). Inductive discipline refers to techniques that appeal to the child's rationality and responsibility, to his sense of right and wrong. By encouraging the child to consider carefully his obligations and the rights of others as well as his own, inductive discipline may furnish the child with important role-taking opportunities. In a similar vein, Holstein (1969) and Peck and Havighurst (1960) found that moral maturity in children is related to active participation in family discussions and decision making.[4]

To experience fair treatment and to talk about the needs and feelings of others seem important not only to develop awareness of others but also to learn to care.

SOCIAL LEARNING

Social role-taking, linked as we noted in chapter 7 with social cognition, seems to merit special attention. It not only may stimulate moral reasoning, but also may motivate moral behavior. And social role-taking serves as a bridge between the structuralist approach and social learning theory. Myra Windmiller sums up this school's view of morality in her introduction to *Moral Development and Socialization:*

---

[4]Sheila Stanley, "The Family and Moral Education," in *Moral Education, A First Generation of Research and Development,* ed. Ralph L. Mosher (New York: Praeger, 1980), p. 343.

Social learning theorists, because they see morality as being taught through modeling and imitation, agree that exposure to more mature others helps stimulate maturity in our own value processes. They think values are relative and a reflection of the culture in which they are found. In fact, part of the responsibility of parents and teachers is transmitting cultural values. They do not agree with the structuralists that values come from inside, but rather they maintain values originate from outside. Once internalized, however, the values are a part of the individual. Social learning theorists would not necessarily see the process of learning values as significant, so much as the manifestation of specific values. This is because the behavior that follows from holding certain values is considered to be preeminent (p. 10).

In social learning theory, there is the presumption that morals are first acquired from one's parents through modeling and imitation. These are then gradually internalized in early childhood, probably between the ages of five and eight. Reinforcement, whether positive or negative, and punishment help determine which of the learned social behaviors will be internalized. If the child considers violating a parental prohibition, he or she will experience feelings of guilt. The anxiety that accompanies the guilt, or the anticipation that guilt will follow from a violation, deters the child and later the adult, from committing an act contrary to that sanctioned by the parent, and later, by society.

Much of the social learning literature reporting parental influence on moral understanding emphasizes three categories of parental contributions to their children's moral learning: (1) the direct modeling role filled by the parent. (2) The administration of simple rewards and punishments and the effect of discipline on children's behavior, and (3) the general impact of child-rearing practices on moral behavior (p. 22).[5]

A social learning perspective on morality, then, suggests that both the content of morality and the motivation to internalize and act on moral values are learned through personal relationships.

Implications of Social Learning Theory

A philosophical issue raised by social learning theory challenges the very notion that children can be spoken of as "moral." Structuralists argue that, for an action to be considered moral, there must be reasoning about the right or wrong of available choices. If children's responses to situations involving moral choice are simply imitative behavior, some mimicking of the actions of adult models for which they have been rewarded, perhaps we should speak of children following a social convention rather than taking a moral stance.

This question is more than philosophical. Much research has indicated that children's judgments are situational. That is, a child's actions at one time and place do not permit us to pre-

---

[5]Myra Windmiller, *Moral Development and Socialization* (Boston: Allyn and Bacon, 1980).

dict how he will act in another similar situation. One reason for this is that children are not able to conceptualize and to conserve abstract symbolic concepts. Whatever the source of a child's good action in a given situation, it is unlikely to be his "honest character" or his "commitment to altruism." Simply put, we have to admit that generally children will respond to recognized cues in ways that have been modeled and reinforced by others, *without necessarily being aware of the moral nature of their actions!*

It follows then that in a social learning framework the real issue is learning to behave morally. It follows also that this kind of learning will later coordinate with growing cognitive abilities and will together provide the foundation of adult morality. Summing up, Sieber says, "Thus, moral, nurturant adults who establish and discuss clear and understandable rules which they enforce firmly and consistently provide the most effective environment for learning to behave morally."[6]

IMPLICATIONS FOR MINISTRY

Many aspects of the long search to understand moral development have not been presented in this chapter. Two major fields of study, values development and conscience development, have not even been discussed. Yet we have identified the most critical issues. And we have enough information to suggest several implications for our ministry with children.

Implication One: Moral Content Is Significant

Structuralists concentrate on describing children's reasoning. And social learning theorists are interested in the mechanisms by which behavior and personality are influenced. In all our appreciation for these schools of thought, we need to be sure not to lose sight of the fact that moral content (ideas about what actually constitutes right and wrong) is important too.

The concept of structural moral development is theologically significant. The Book of Romans asserts that "when Gentiles [here, those living without the light provided by divine revelation], who do not have the law, do by nature things required by the law, . . . they show that the requirements of the law are written on their hearts, their consciences also bearing witness, and their thoughts now accusing, now even defending them" (Rom. 2:14–15). Paul's point is that humanity does have a moral nature: that there is within humankind's physio-psychological makeup structures that are distinctively moral.

---

[6]J. Sieber, in Windmiller, *Moral Development and Socialization,* p. 155.

But man's moral structures are inadequate. Fallen humanity may have an innate capacity for moral thought. Yet the existence of that capacity fails to move us to *do* what we approve. All cultures show remarkable similarity in what they identify as moral issues. Each establishes rules concerning such issues (sexual behavior, personal property, etc.). But cultures differ concerning the specific *content* of morality (for instance, it is moral in one culture to have four wives, while another demands one wife). The human capacity to recognize moral issues and reason about morality neither *produces* moral behavior, nor establishes standards on which all can agree.

Christianity affirms a moral content that is external not only to individuals but also to cultures. God has spoken, and the picture of reality that He has unveiled includes within it definitions of the moral, by principle and by example.

It's clear then that in exploring moral development in children we can't dismiss moral content, and deal only with rational processes or inculcating of values. Instead we must be concerned with moral behavior. We must help our children actually *do* right. We must help our children turn from what is wrong—whether or not they can understand *why* their actions are right or wrong.

Implication Two: Moral Conduct Is Significant

I've just suggested that because moral content is important, we need to be concerned that children do what is right and avoid what is wrong. But there is another important reason why moral conduct is important in the development of boys and girls.

The moral content of Christianity comes to us, as do its theological truths, in the form of abstract symbolic concepts. As we've seen, children's cognitive development does not permit them to deal with such concepts effectively. They cannot grasp, and cannot conserve, such concepts across changing situations. Thus it is extremely difficult to even consider "teaching" moral principles to children.

What we need to do then is to adopt a strategy for encouraging moral growth and comprehension that is quite different from the schooling/instructional approach to teaching, a strategy that fits completely with what we know of how children actively construct their own perception of reality. That way is to take a *situational approach* to teaching moral behavior. Rather than attempt to present and explain a moral abstraction in a classroom setting, and hope children will be able to apply the concept, we need to *use moral terms when giving children guidance as to how to respond in a number of life situations.*

Providing children with multiplied examples of "honesty" is more likely to help them build a picture of what honesty means and intuitively sense right actions to take when we are not present.

If we take this approach to moral development, and stress the situational aspect along with the need for adult guidance, we're forced to a position that raises questions about the "morality" or lack of "morality" of children's actions. As adults we commonly insist that morality cannot be separated from motive. We might see a person regularly helping an older neighbor. But we would have completely different reactions to the morality of such actions if we discovered that rather than expressing concern, the helping actions were intended to win a place in the older neighbor's will.

Morality, as we understand it in adults, combines the content of actions (whether they are objectively right and wrong), the character of the actors (implying that actions are not isolated but part of a consistent pattern of behavior), and their motivation. We would hardly call an action "moral" if these factors were not taken into account.

But with children only the behavioral component seems to be essential. We know that children often act as they do, not because of some commitment to right or wrong, but to please others or avoid their displeasure. We know that it's too early to speak of character, as children lack the capacity to grasp and apply the abstract moral principles that may mark out the content of their behavior as right or wrong. We realize that specific actions taken by children may simply reflect intuitive recognition that imitation of a particular adult behavior is appropriate.

What this seems to indicate is that we should not expect *developed morality* from boys and girls. Instead we should place stress on encouraging moral conduct through many means. Children will be more likely to build moral awareness through many specific experiences in which we model and encourage and explain a moral act, than in any other way.

Implication Three: Trust Relationships Are Important

One of the fascinating comments in Scripture is one that identifies the commandment to "honor your father and your mother" (Deut. 5:16) as the "first commandment with a promise" (Eph. 6:2). It is true that this is the first commandment with which a promise is associated ("that you may live long and that it may go well with you in the land the LORD your God is giving you"). But it is also the *only* commandment of the Decalogue that adds a promise.

It is also fascinating that, while the commandment is ranked fifth in order, it is undoubtedly the first commandment to be experienced by a growing child! The others speak in terms of relatively abstract concepts—stealing, coveting, etc. This one focuses on a simple issue: respond to your parents.

What is so fascinating about this is the suggestion that the critical moral issue for children is responding to the judgment of parents concerning right and wrong! We've seen that children's capacity for moral reasoning is limited. We've seen that children are unlikely to conserve an abstract moral concept across situations, or apply it to identify right and wrong acts. Simply put, children *must* rely on others to define right and wrong for them!

Two things are again emphasized. First, building a trust relationship with children is important, for they must be willing to respond to adult guidance when they themselves are unable to evaluate, and even when some things they are encouraged to do will not seem "right" to them.

Second, we see in this again the importance of the Old Testament pattern of instruction-as-interpretation-of-life. Moral instruction and guidance need to be provided in a recurring way in the various situations of a child's life. The introduction of teaching in the lying downs and getting ups and the walkings along the way recognizes children's need for adults to identify moral issues for them and to point the way to doing the good.

In this kind of a process, children are not expected to do something they are as yet unable to do. Instead, children are simply called on to trust the judgment of their parents, to do what is pointed out to them as right, and not to do the wrong.

Implication Four: A Loving Community Is Vital

No single factor accounts for the development of morality through childhood and into adolescence. But it does seem clear that the relational context as a whole—not just situational guidance—makes a vital contribution.

Children need to live within a community where they can experience moral behavior directed toward them. Children need to live in a community where they have as models adults and peers who display moral behavior. Children need to live in a community so that in many different relationships they can be reinforced for doing what is right and can come to appreciate the feelings of others. And children need to live in a community that provides many who will share, in situation upon situation, the reasons and the motives they have for commitment to doing right.

This kind of community is exactly that loving community

that we see shining through the New Testament description of Christian interpersonal relationships. The first experience of loving community will come in the family. But soon, as the child's world expands, the loving community needs to be of the neighborhood, the church, the school. Life lived in loving Christian community will make a significant contribution to growth toward moral maturity.

PROBE

▶ *case histories*
▶ *discussion questions*
▶ *thought provokers*
▶ *resources*

1. There are again many books exploring the moral development issues we have touched on in this chapter. However the following are especially recommended for additional reading and research.

   Mosher, Ralph L., ed. *Moral Education*. New York: Praeger, 1980.
   Rosen, Hugh. *The Development of Sociomoral Knowledge*. New York: Columbia University Press, 1980.
   Windmiller, Myra, et al. *Moral Development and Socialization,* Boston: Allyn and Bacon, 1980.

2. In an interesting book for Christian parents, Ted Ward identifies the strongest influences on children at various levels of moral judgment. The following chart (Figure 21) is taken from this book, and suggests several interesting possibilities. Study the chart, and then think through these questions:
   a. What ages would you assign to each of these levels?
   b. If you were a teacher, what might you do to reduce cheating? Develop a strategy for each level.
   c. Who would be most likely to influence children at each level? That is, what settings would these children be found in, who there would influence, etc.?

3. Ronald E. Galbraith and Thomas M. Jones suggest teaching strategies to adapt Kohlberg's theories to classroom use in the public schools. The following material is adapted from the introduction to their book, *Moral Reasoning*. Read it carefully, and then respond in writing to *one* of the project suggestions following.

FRAMEWORK

FIGURE 21

THE STRONG
MORAL INFLUENCES
AT EACH
LEVEL OF MORAL JUDGMENT[7]

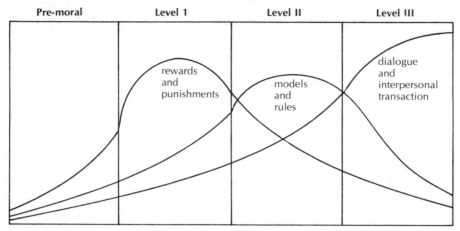

| Pre-moral | Level 1 | Level II | Level III |

rewards and punishments

models and rules

dialogue and interpersonal transaction

GALBRAITH & JONES
Some Generalizations About Kohlberg's Theory

1. *The stages are cross-cultural.*
2. *Movement through the stages progresses through an invariant sequence, and stages cannot be skipped.*
3. *Development occurs because of an attraction to the next higher stage of reasoning.*
4. *There are individual differences in the rate of moral development and in the highest level of moral maturity attained.*
5. *The stages are not a set of cultural beliefs taught to children.*
6. *Moral maturity increases with a person's ability to resolve moral conflicts.*
7. *Moral reasoning is related to behavior.*
8. *Moral development can be stimulated in the classroom.*

These generalizations provide a direction for a new, nonindoctrinating form of moral education. Moral growth is determined by an individual's awareness of perspectives beyond the immediate self. Moral growth represents an ability to see the other side and to focus on the great issues. In order to grow morally, individuals need to opportunity to role-take the parts of

---

[7]Reprinted by permission from *Values Begin at Home* by Ted Ward, published by Victor Books, Wheaton, IL, p. 79. Copyright 1979 by Ted Ward.

others in dilemma situations. Individuals, especially students, need the opportunity to engage in discussions of social and moral problems. Participants in these discussions need to have an opportunity to present their own reasoning and to listen to the opinions of others.

This understanding of the Kohlberg theory of moral reasoning implies a specific teaching strategy for stimulating moral development. A discussion of a moral dilemma should provide students with the following opportunities:

a. To consider genuine moral problems.

b. To experience genuine social and cognitive conflict during discussion of a moral problem.

c. To apply their current level of thought to problematic situations.

d. To be exposed to the next higher level of thought.

e. To confront their own inconsistencies in reasoning over a variety of moral issues without someone stressing a right or wrong answer.

Curriculum materials featuring dilemma stories are designed to confront students with genuine moral problems. Creating a situation where students disagree over the appropriate action for a central character promotes genuine social and cognitive conflict. The class discussion that focuses on reasons for recommending a particular course of action provides students with the opportunity to apply their current level of thinking. An active discussion among students also creates the setting for exposure to higher levels of moral reasoning. Finally, asking students to work through a number of social and moral problems throughout their educational experience provides an opportunity for them to confront some of their inconsistencies in reasoning.[8]

Projects

a. Evaluate thoroughly the position taken by Galbraith and Jones.

b. Develop a Sunday school lesson, for an appropriate age group, that uses the design advanced by Galbraith and Jones.

c. Beginning from the standpoint of social role-taking, write a parallel paper that, like the above, defines its assumptions and spells out an appropriate teaching strategy that might be used in curriculum materials.

---

[8]Ronald E. Galbraith and Thomas M. Jones, *Moral Reasoning* (Minneapolis: Greenhaven Press, 1976), pp. 35–36.

PART 1

FRAMEWORK

A Theological Framework for Ministry

Nurture in the Old Testament
Nurture in the New Testament
The Role of Scripture in Nurture
The Nurture Process

A Developmental Framework for Ministry

The Developmental Perspective
Cognitive Potentials of Children
Social Relationships of Children
Moral Development in Children
An Integrated Perspective

We have explored two broad areas—the theological and the developmental—that provide frameworks for thinking about ministry with children. But how do these frameworks fit together? What do they say about the shape our ministry will

AN INTEGRATED PERSPECTIVE

take? Before we move on to look at specific settings for ministry with boys and girls, let's pause to describe our integrated perspective.

In another book, *A Theology of Christian Education*,[1] I've described theories that lie behind various educational approaches, in terms of the factors that the theorists assume must be taken into account. A review of this material is helpful for delineating the factors with which Christian educators must be concerned.

REVIEW OF EDUCATIONAL THEORIES

Single-factor Theory

Behaviorism provides a contemporary example of a single-factored approach to education, as to some extent does the classic approach of such thinkers as Plato. In behaviorism human beings are not really differentiated from their environment. Humans and the world are seen as products of a common evolution, and both are determined in the sense of being shaped by antecedent causes. This leads to the conviction that if we can only control the environment, we can shape the person. To Plato and some early Christian writers on education this meant that growing children should hear only the "right" things, and they

would be shaped by that content. To a behaviorist like Skinner, who insists we must move beyond the old notions of freedom and dignity, the key to transforming the individual and the race is behavioral modification. Human beings are to be acted on—trained—and when we learn just how to reinforce the behavior we want and to extinguish the behavior we do not want, a new day will dawn.

Two-factor Theory

Enculturation theory is a good representative of two-factor theory. In this approach human beings are differentiated from the environment, in the sense that they are dynamically involved with environment. There is a transactional relationship between humans and the world, and in the transaction the environment is shaped by human beings. Through processes associated with social learning theory humans grow into their culture and learn the culture's view of the world.

In two-factor theory the individual's perception of the world is shaped by participation in a society, through which the heritage of the culture is transmitted. For instance, Western music is based on a seven-tone system; much of Eastern music is based on a twelve-tone system. A wide range of sounds exists in

---

[1]Lawrence O. Richards, *A Theology of Christian Education* (Grand Rapids: Zondervan, 1975).

nature, and there is no set of seven "ideal tones" that exist as "music" to be discovered by humans. Instead it is the culture that defines the one as "music" and the other as "noise." Human beings thus structure their own environment as they interact with the universe, and that way of structuring or perceiving the universe is transmitted through the culture into which a human being is born.

Three-factor Theory

The work of Piaget, and its reflection in Kohlberg, introduces a third factor. Human beings are still viewed as active and constructivist in their relationship with environment. But human perceptions are not merely cultural: they are rooted not only in the society but in the very nature of the individual. We know now that the way human beings perceive and organize environment is limited by cognitive capacities that develop in invariant sequence and are rooted in humanity's genetic makeup. Thus it's clear that our approach to teaching or to encouraging any kind of development must take this factor also into account.

Four-factor Theory

Humanistic approaches stop with three-factor theories. They accept the world as we find it as a given. They accept the influence of culture in shaping perspective. They accept the revolutionary notion that human beings are structured by cognitive capacities. But the Christian wants to take another step and affirm that the social environment as well as the material world is also structured. Only the Christian insists that nurture take into account an objective interpersonal "reality" that exists apart from cultures, to stand above and to judge objectively every society's construct of moral reality.

It has always been obvious that there is a structure to the material universe that exists apart from human constructs. For instance, one cannot shape a culture in which a person steps out a window and falls *up* or one in which there are three sexes. The structure of the material universe exists objectively and imposes its own limits through physical laws of operation. But humanistic theories, despite Kohlberg's venture into philosophy with his "justice" concept, are forced to assume a cultural relativism. Moral and religious ideas are understood to originate within cultures as mere constructs of humanity, and thus "right" and "wrong" can only validly be measured by criteria *within* a specific culture, and never across cultures. But the Christian affirms a structure to faith and to morals that is objec-

170

tive: a structure that is just as real as the structure of the material universe.

There are obvious differences between material and theological/moral structures. If you step out of a window, you fall down *now*. If you practice sin, evidence of the disastrous results may be long delayed. There is no immediate feedback in the moral world as there is in the material. In addition, the structure of the material universe is learned *directly,* through the senses that all possess. The structure of the theological/moral universe is learned indirectly through revelation and is not verified by direct experience but is accepted by faith. We can touch and see and handle the material, but it is only "by faith we understand that the universe was formed at God's command, so that what is seen was not made out of what was visible" (Heb. 11:3).

In ministry with children, then, the Christian takes a number of factors into account: we deal with children, who are active, interacting with their environment in search of understanding and ways to live successfully with others. We deal with children who are limited in their capacity to understand and to respond, whose perceptions are necessarily different from those of adults. We deal with a physical universe that is structured, not by us, but by physical laws designed by God. And we deal with a spiritual/moral universe that is also structured, not by us, but by God's decree, known only to Him but revealed to us in the words of Scripture.

And the task we have in ministry with children is to communicate to boys and girls (with their nature) the spiritual realities that they can know by experience, and thus grow in faith.

NURTURING FAITH

The critical question for us is, on the surface, a very complex one. How do we work with children so that each of these factors is taken into account? How do we adjust to the human active, constructivist nature? How do we adjust to children's limited capacity? How do we work with a physical universe that gives immediate sensory feedback of its structure, and with a spiritual/moral universe that does not give such feedback but requires instead the development of faith based on a perception of spiritual/moral reality that comes to us in words of revelation?

The best answer to this complex question is surprisingly simple. *We are to focus on those processes seen in Scripture that influence the development of faith and that are in fullest harmony with what we know of how children learn!* We may not understand all the mechanisms of learning that are involved. But there is enough evidence for Scripture *and* the behavioral sciences to indicate that these processes are critical in ministry with children. Let's review them briefly.

Processes That Communicate Belonging

Both Scripture and the research on learning stress the importance of affectional relationships and the development of a sense of security that comes with trust in others. This has been shown to be vital in the earliest stages of a child's life and during growth toward maturity.

The child's first experiences of belonging are with the family. As children grow their social world expands to include neighbors, school, and church. When the worlds to which the growing child belongs are vital faith communities, the context for growth toward faith has been provided.

Processes That Involve Participation

Children learn and grow through active involvement with their environment. Experience gained through participation is important in many ways. On the one hand it permits observation of others, with consequent learning through identification and imitation. On the other, repeated experiences provide the raw material from which children actively construct—and reconstruct—their perceptions of the world. And participation provides opportunities for children to try out different behaviors for which they will be positively or negatively reinforced by others. We know that children will not understand what they are experiencing as an adult understands and interprets the same experiences. But we also know that the opportunity to participate is a vital element in children's growth toward maturity.

As members of the Christian community of faith, children need to be involved—at home, as well as at church—in experiences through which that faith is expressed. And they need to be involved as participants, not merely as observers.

Processes That Facilitate Modeling

We know that whatever learning theory we may hold, a child's experiences with other people are understood to be critical. In all systems modeling—the process of imitating and identification that leads a child to develop attitudes and values as well as behavior—has a significant role. We know too that the

New Testament constantly stresses the role of example in communication of faith.[2]

It is important then to build relationships with children that will facilitate the modeling process. The long-term relationships, the warmth and affection, the opportunity to observe in many life situations, the talking about feelings and beliefs and actions, and the other factors identified on page 78 must be critical elements in our ministry strategies, as we seek to guide children's growth in faith.

Processes That Provide Instruction-as-Interpretation-of-Life

The instructional model for communicating a written revelation found in the Old Testament, and reflected in such New Testament passages as 1 Thessalonians 2 and Titus 2, finds striking explanation in the work of modern structuralists. We understand now why the schooling/instructional model, which relies on talk about concepts to communicate them, is ineffective for the transmission of the theological and moral concepts of faith. Our understanding of children's egocentrism, inability to conserve qualities across situations, and other cognitive limitations combine with the constructivist nature of humans to make *situational* teaching, with multiplied repetitions in multiplied situations, the key to helping children develop their own understanding of the realities that are our heritage in Christ. And we understand why we need to translate theological abstractions to fit not only the understanding but also the experience of boys and girls, at each stage of their development.

To affirm the importance of instruction-as-interpretation-of-life is not to deny any place to the Sunday school, but it is to insist that other settings for ministry are more important, and that our use of the Sunday hour, our use of the Scripture in that hour, and the design of teaching require serious evaluation.

Processes That Encourage Exercise of Choice

This dimension is more difficult to define either in terms of the behavioral sciences or biblical patterns. Yet it seems to be significant in both frameworks. We've seen that "morality" for a child seems to be an issue of "doing right," while much more is involved in moral acts by adults. We have also seen, however, that encouraging children to talk about situations helps to develop their skill both in social role-taking and in moral reasoning. Perhaps even more suggestive are studies that show a correlation between adolescent and adult altruism and a consis-

---

[2]See Richards, *A Theology of Christian Education*, chapters 3, 4, 8, 9.

tent, mild childhood discipline that involved talking over correction. What all this seems to indicate is a context in which a child experiences consistent love and has freedom to make mistakes without experiencing rejection.

We see the same atmosphere reflected in the New Testament portrait of relationships in the faith community. There is a commitment to holiness, but at the same time a freedom that permits a wide range of differences in matters of personal conviction (cf. Rom. 14–15). Nonjudgmentalism is stressed, as is the building of a reconciled community by "not counting men's sins against" the members (cf. 2 Cor. 5:19). The love and modeling of the Christian community, with its forgiving instruction, creates a context in which freedom to explore and test exists, while gentle persuasion encourages the regular choice of that which is good.

LOOKING AHEAD: MINISTRY SETTINGS

What remains for us to do now is to look at the settings in which faith development may take place. We can distinguish these settings easily: Where do children spend most of their time? And, where do we attempt to minister to them? The answer to these questions is clear. Children spend most of their time in the home, the church, and the school. And our efforts to minister to children also are linked to the home, the church, and the school. If we look at each of these settings and use the processes linked with the communication of faith as guidelines, we should be able to both (a) evaluate our present efforts, and (b) see practical ways to build the most effective ministry to children possible.

It is to this task we must now turn in the second major section of this book: settings for ministry.

PROBE

▶ *case histories*
▶ *discussion questions*
▶ *thought provokers*
▶ *resources*

1. I have suggested that processes linked with the communication of faith can guide us as we plan for ministry with children in several settings. Respond to the following by ranking as number 1, 2, or 3 the phrase that you believe *best completes* each:

a. It is most important for children to feel belonging in
    _____ their home
    _____ their church
    _____ their school

b. It is easiest to permit children significant participation in
    _____ their home
    _____ their church
    _____ their school

c. Children are most likely to model on adults in
    _____ their home
    _____ their church
    _____ their school

d. Instruction-as-interpretation-of-life is done most naturally in
    _____ the home
    _____ the church
    _____ the school

e. The child has most opportunities to exercise choice in
    _____ the home
    _____ the church
    _____ the school

f. Most ministry with children is expected to take place in
    _____ the home
    _____ the church
    _____ the school

g. Most efforts to train adults prepare for ministry in
    _____ the home
    _____ the church
    _____ the school

h. Most money for materials to use with children is spent to use for ministry in
    _____ the home
    _____ the church
    _____ the school

i. Children spend most of their time in
    _____ the home
    _____ the church
    _____ the school·

On the basis of your own check marks, write a one-page paper defining "my personal strategy for children's ministry."

2. Thoroughly review the first nine chapters of this book and write out in your own words a series of twenty-five "guidelines for ministry with children." Each of the first eight chapters should contribute at least *two* guidelines. Be prepared to explain and to defend your guideline statements.

FRAMEWORK PART **2**

A *setting for ministry* is a relational setting, a context in which children spend a major amount of time. Such settings are life-shaping; in them children come to know others with whom they have long-term relationships.

Traditionally we've thought of "ministry to children" as what happens when children come to church or join one of a congregation's educational agencies. Certainly the church is one ministry setting. But it is not the only setting or even the most important. The home is far more significant. And the rapidly growing Christian school movement reminds us that, today, we must be sensitive to the potential of the day school as a ministry setting.

Two things give focus to our exploration of ministry settings. First, we are concerned with *building faith*. It is valid to ask how to best conduct a catechism class or tell Bible stories to first graders. But that is not the focus of this book, except as such things may relate to building faith. Second, we've already seen that encouraging five processes does seem to be related to building faith. What we need to do, then, is to look at each ministry setting to see how we can build children into a vital faith community where they can be nurtured through processes that

1. communicate belonging
2. involve participation
3. facilitate modeling
4. provide instruction-as-interpretation-of-life
5. encourage exercise of choice

So we will look at three faith community settings—the home, the church, and the Christian school. In each section, an initial chapter defines the critical issues. The following chapters explore how those who are responsible to minister to children can enrich each setting as a context for the communication and development of faith.

These chapters, like the book as a whole, are geared primarily to the professional or lay leaders in local congregations who have responsibility for children's ministries. The intended hearers are the minister of education, the minister to families, the administrator of a Christian school, a Sunday school or department superintendent, members of councils or committees, rather than parents. As a helping book, the goal is not simply to state theory, but to suggest how ministry with children can be practically carried out, and how we can actually encourage the free flow of those vital processes linked with the communication of faith.

In designing ministry with children, a number of factors must be considered. These were touched on and explored in the first part of this book. The most significant are summarized in Figure 22. They represent the factors I have kept in mind as I described how to develop ministry to children in each setting.

PART 2

SETTINGS

The Home

The Impact of Family
Intergenerational Models
Information Models
Intervention Models
Patterns in the Home

The Church

The Church as Organism and Institution
Sunday School as Faith Community
Sunday School Curriculums

The Christian School

The Christian School Ideal
Faith Community in the Classroom

All developmental theories hold that the family is critical for healthy child development. The Bible also holds up the family as critical in faith development. It is here that faith is first sensed, is born, and is nurtured.

THE IMPACT OF FAMILY

But is today's family able to carry this kind of burden? What is the present shape of the family, and how do patterns of twentieth century life affect our ministry with boys and girls?

Very few in our churches would argue that the family is no longer important in faith formation. But most church leaders feel helpless. And most leaders responsible for ministries to children feel helpless. So they devote their energies to improving the Sunday school or establishing a local Christian day school. The frustration is understandable. And it is not new. Martin Luther too spoke disparagingly of parents "who are so lacking in piety and uprightness that they would not do it [educate their children] if they could, but like the ostrich, harden themselves against their own offspring and do nothing for them" *(Letter to the Mayors and Aldermen)*. Whatever one tries to do for parents—hold training classes and PTA sessions, or even provide subscriptions to Christian family magazines—parents seem unresponsive. Mom and dad appear satisfied to send children to Sunday school or confirmation classes and later insist the church hire a youth director to "do something" when they feel their teens slipping away.

But possibly the problem with the family is not simply a lack of parental piety. Could it be that the family, a significant institution in Bible days and at the turn of the century, simply isn't as important as it once was? Is it possible that ministry with children needs to be channeled through other institutions, which have taken on the traditional functions of the home?

CHAPTER 10

THE CURRENT SITUATION

Family Life Has Changed

Everywhere we look there is evidence that significant changes have taken place in the family in the last few decades . . . and that changes continue to overwhelm us. Mario Fantini and René Cardenas review a number of significant changes still in process.[1] The size of families is changing. The role of parents is changing. Between 1970 and 1973 there was an 18 percent increase in female heads of family, compared to a 24 percent increase the previous decade. As of the late 1970s some 12.4 percent of American families were headed by females, and 60 percent of these homes have children under eighteen, with 24 percent having children under six. Some believe that as we enter the 1980s half the families rearing children under six are single-parent families, due to the steady rise in divorces in families with children. Some considerations for the implications of this change are presented in Figure 23.

---

[1]Mario Fantini and René Cardenas, *Parenting in a Multicultural Society* (New York: Longman, 1980).

FIGURE 22

GUIDELINES FOR MINISTRY WITH CHILDREN

THOUGHT

Children's ability to conceptualize is limited. Be aware and adapt by keeping in mind . . .

- egocentrism
- inability to conserve abstract concepts across situations
- intuitive nature of children's thought
- value of creative (lateral) thought as well as intelligence (vertical)
- constructivist character of children's learning

RELATIONSHIPS

are essential and meet several needs

- Need for nurturant relationships, (warmth, love, acceptance)
- Need for socializing relationships— long-term, warm, close—with adult and peer models
- Need for both *authority* (where others have power of unilateral imposition) and *friendship* relationships.
- Need to develop social role-taking skills and sensitivity

THE CONTEXT FOR MINISTRY IS

Processes to enrich
- Belonging
- Participation
- Modeling
- Instruction-as Interpretation-of-Life
- Choosing

Settings
- Home
- Church
- School

A VITAL FAITH COMMUNITY

SCRIPTURE

is God's revelation of a reality that can be experienced

- Use Bible terms, linked with children's experiences
- Use the Bible itself
  enactively
  associatively
  imitatively
- Shape the lifestyle of the faith community in each setting to live out the reality Scripture reveals

MORALITY

- Moral reasoning is severely limited
- Children need guidance on how to *act* morally
- Moral content (concepts) should be introduced in situations rather than as abstract principles
- Children need to be treated, and to see models treat others, according to the moral concepts they are taught

FIGURE 23
HELPING SINGLE-PARENT FAMILIES

A 1971 Canadian report to governmental agencies included the following recommendations, designed to help meet the needs of single-parent families. What special ministries or actions do they suggest for those concerned with Christian family life?

- Because the greatest common problem of one-parent families is financial need, more adequate public support is recommended.

- Single parents tend frequently to be subject to social isolation because of their status. It is recommended the public be educated to recognize the importance of keeping single-parent families in the mainstream of social life.

- Subsidized day-care services are needed by more one-parent families with small children if they are to become self-supporting.

- Counseling services and additional volunteer programs are important, and are recommended to help prevent further family breakdown.

- Rehabilitation services to assist single parents who wish to become self-supporting should be more realistic and helpful.

Many social scientists have pointed to other factors that, they suggest, tend to make today's American family a place of alienation and isolation. Children today have little contact with adults other than their parents. Families flit from one community to the next, constantly tearing up all too shallow roots. The automobile has made the neighborhood obsolete. Children are segregated by age in large impersonal schools and even in churches. Examining the "Family and Moral Education," Sheila Stanley points up the effect of these changes.

> The lack of emotional support formerly provided by an extended family and a neighborhood places added stress upon the already overburdened nuclear family. When the family fails at the impossible task of meeting all our needs for belonging, we condemn it as a "faultily constructed piece of social engineering." We do not recognize that conditions of life have changed and that the actual responsibility for child-rearing has shifted away from the family to other sectors of society.[2]

A number of studies clearly show that a definite trend has developed over the last three decades and that children today are paid less attention by their parents. Parallel studies show that school-age children not only are more dependent on attention from friends, but that more children in all age groups prefer to spend time with friends rather than family. Even the time that is spent at home has changed in character, largely through the influence of television. Surprisingly, the main impact of television does not seem to stem from the violence it models, but rather is related to declining development of communications

---

[2]Sheila Stanley, "The Family and Moral Education," in *Moral Education, A First Generation of Research and Development*, ed. Ralph L. Mosher (New York: Praeger, 1980), p. 342.

skills. About eighty percent of families who watch television report that they do not speak at all when the set is on!

All of these changes—in work patterns, in fragmentation of families, in segregation of children by age, in mobility, in the decrease of the amount of time spent by parents with children, and many other changes as well—force us to realize that the modern American family is not the family of the Bible. It is not even the family of those decades prior to the 1940s. And so questions about the validity of the family as a viable contemporary institution are important to ask. Specifically, perhaps we should question whether those who minister with children should concern themselves with the home, or focus efforts on some other ministry setting.

The Family Continues to Be Significant

Despite all the changes taking place in the American family, evidence continues to mount that family experiences are critical in children's development. The evidence for the continuing significance of the family comes from many sources. All schools of developmental psychology continue to find family experiences central. Joan Sieber writes that

> there is much evidence indicating that internalization is affected by the nurturance the child receives in his or her early years. In this sense, there is a critical period in moral development. If a satisfactory emotional attachment is not formed with an adult during the first year, and if that attachment is not continued through the first few years of life, the internalization of moral values is unlikely to occur at all.[3]

Other studies find similar importance in family relationships during the school years. While most studies have concentrated on mother-child relationships, studies reported by Michael E. Lamb suggest that "fathers play an important role in determining children's moral development. Father's attitudes and behaviors, along with children's perceptions of their fathers, seem to affect moral development."[4]

But more than moral development is linked with the family. Shirley C. Samuels is concerned with the relationship of children's self-concepts to the self-concepts of other family members:

> The first "significant others" in the lives of children are their parents. In the review of theory and empirical research, it was found that a child's self-concept is related to how she is treated (the looking-glass theory) and

---

[3]Joan Sieber, in Myra Windmiller et al., *Moral Development and Socialization* (Boston: Allyn and Bacon, 1980), p. 140.

[4]Michael E. Lamb, *The Role of the Father in Child Development* (New York: John Wiley & Sons, 1978), p. 232.

to how the mother sees herself. . . . Both the "looking glass" and "modeling" theories must operate at the same time, since theory and research has supported the premise that "significant others'" behavior and attitude toward a child are affected by his or her self-acceptance and self-feelings very early in life. Those children who feel negatively about themselves are most likely to have parents who also feel negatively about themselves.[5]

Even the common notion that we shift nurture functions from the home to preschools or grade schools has been shown invalid. Burton L. White of the Harvard Graduate School of Education, reports,

We do not mean to say there is now a general belief that going to school is of no use, but rather that if a family does not do a minimally adequate job of rearing and educating a child in the first years of life, professional educators, given our current capabilities, are not often able to overcome the resultant educational weakness. To put the issue more directly, the results of Projects Head Start and Follow Through seem to indicate that if a child of three years is six months behind his peers in the development of language and problem solving ability, the chance that he will ever become an average or superior student is rather small. The widespread ineffectiveness of all but a handful of remedial programs focuses attention on the prevention of the buildup of educational deficits.[6]

Yes, the family situation has changed, and is changing. Yet the family remains significant, and its impact on the development of children is still critical. Family experiences are still intimately linked with the healthy development of boys and girls as whole persons. The family still performs its ancient functions. The issue is, How can we help it perform them well?

The Christian Family Faces Stress

It's important at the outset to admit that the Christian family is first of all a family in our society. That is, the same forces that have altered the shape of the American family have had a parallel impact on the Christian family. Faith is no buffer against social change.

All families have been changed by mobility. All have been affected by increasing numbers of mothers in the work force. All churches have adults who have suffered through divorce, and others who are trying to raise children in single-parent units. Studies show that, like their secular neighbors, Christian parents of this generation spend less and less time with their boys and girls. The family as an institution is far more subject to

---

[5]Shirley C. Samuels, *Enhancing Self-Concept in Early Childhood* (New York: Human Sciences Press, 1976), p. 250.

[6]Burton L. White et al., *Experience and Environment: Major Influences on the Development of the Young Child* (Englewood Cliffs, N.J.: Prentice-Hall, 1978), 2:4.

societal changes than it is shaped by the presence or absence of some form of Christian faith.

With this said, we need to add that Christian faith does seem to add its own special strain on parents. In fact, the more committed parents are to their faith, the greater these strains may be. For instance, in one of my own research projects, 98 percent of parents from strongly conservative, evangelical churches reported, when asked "How important is it to you personally that you successfully give your children a Christian upbringing?" that it was "very important." (In comparison, 81 percent of parents in "more liberal" churches indicated this is "very important" to them.) At the same time, only 4 percent of the conservative, evangelical group report being "very satisfied" with their "progress in providing a Christian upbringing." For both populations, a significant gap exists between their report of the level of importance of providing Christian upbringing and of satisfaction with their progress in providing it. This gap between ideal and perceived performance often leads to a diffused sense of guilt and of failure, which seems most intense in those to whom faith is most significant.

My research provides some insights into what Christian parents believe to be important in the home, and their perception of nurture itself. Figures 24 through 27 record results of questionnaires filled out by some five hundred parents of children between the ages of four and twelve. Approximately half the reports came from adults in churches that were identified as "conservative, evangelical." The other half came from churches identified by their members as "more liberal." Each chart shows the percentage of parents in each group who checked each item. No effort was made to survey families without church affiliation.

From my research, which has extended over the past eight years, we can make some generalizations that help to define the nature of special pressures on Christian families.

- Most parents assume that "progress in providing a Christian upbringing" requires a daily form of "devotions," or some kind of formal teaching of children by parents.
- Most parents who consider Christian nurture important have made repeated attempts to provide some form of teaching or devotions.
- Nearly all parents have failed to be consistent in their efforts at teaching and nurture as they understand it. As a consequence most feel both guilty and inadequate. This sense of inadequacy is typically brewed as resulting from a lack of sufficient understanding of their faith, and from a lack of "know how."

186

FIGURE 24

ELEMENTS OF A CHRISTIAN UPBRINGING
CONSIDERED IMPORTANT IN
THE HOME

Conservative evangelical	Liberal	Elements
84%	69%	prayer
74	73	family together
42	24	Bible stories
38	35	parental sharing
38	21	Scripture memorization
34	29	worship
22	19	music
14	18	bedtime activities
8	20	holiday celebration
6	8	mealtime activities
2	7	projects

FIGURE 25

CONTENT OF TEACHING CONSIDERED NECESSARY
FOR A CHRISTIAN UPBRINGING

Conservative evangelical	Liberal	Content of Teaching
88%	81%	who God is
82	59	salvation
76	76	Christian living
75	78	Christian values
62	39	making godly choices
50	32	Bible doctrines
36	47	right and wrong
22	27	Bible stories
16	16	Bible characters
16	13	missions
10	12	Bible events
6	11	church history

The impact of this diffused sense of guilt is very significant. For many, repeated failure to meet their own idealized expectations has made it too costly to make any fresh effort. Offers of training that promise new skills also carry the expectation of performance. And the price of additional failures—fresh guilt—has become so high that many are unwilling to try again.

Much research, and many publications, document the first two points made in this chapter. Yes, significant social changes *have* affected our family life. Yet despite these changes and attempts to shift functions of the family to other institutions, research shows that what happens in the home continues to have

FIGURE 26
THE HELP A VALUABLE CHRISTIAN UPBRINGING IS EXPECTED TO PROVIDE

Conservative evangelical	Liberal	Help Desired for Children
86	85	to love others
82	79	to develop self-discipline
80	80	to develop a good self-image
65	63	to develop responsibility
62	59	to make right choices
54	34	to be obedient
44	46	to resist temptation
41	49	to resist peer pressures
40	38	to overcome fears
30	45	to be respectful
28	32	to choose good friends
22	27	to overcome anger

FIGURE 27
SERIOUS DIFFICULTIES IN PROVIDING A CHRISTIAN UPBRINGING

Conservative evangelical	Liberal	Difficulties
78%	63%	finding a regular time
46	34	doing advance preparation
46	48	keeping the kids interested
38	35	having everyone participate
28	25	finding good resource material
24	33	knowing how
22	18	spouse does not cooperate

the greatest impact on the developing personalities of children. There is no reason to doubt that those same factors that influence personality development continue to have an impact on the growth of faith.

There is little published research on special pressures on the Christian family. Yet what little research has been done does give us insights into some of the unique challenges faced by those who seek to minister through Christian parents to children. Three factors in particular must be considered. (1) We need to be aware of the perception of most parents of the character of Christian nurture. (2) We need to be aware of the complex motivations that lead many Christian parents, who actually are deeply concerned with the Christian nurture of their children, to draw back from programs that purport to offer them help. And (3) we need to deal with the great uncertainty that exists among

Christian educators who work in the local church as to how the family can be strengthened and how better parenting can be enabled.

MEETING THE NEED

Is Training the Answer?

In an excellent discussion of attempts to train parents, Robert D. Hess distinguishes two approaches to training.[7] One has been knowledge-based, attempting to provide useful information. The other is competency-based, attempting to provide specific skills or techniques. Examples of knowledge-based approaches in the Christian context would include many seminars, books, and the Dobson film series on parenting. Examples of competency-based training would be Christian adaptations of P.E.T. (Parent Effectiveness Training), and several books and training manuals, such as those by Bruce Narramore. Hess criticizes both approaches, and makes a number of telling points.

He points out that the advice provided by the experts has shifted radically over the years. Those who use knowledge-based and competency-based approaches often build their theories on experiments that Uri Bronfenbrenner has characterized all too well: "Much of American developmental psychology is the science of the behavior of children in strange situations with adults for the briefest possible periods of time."[8] Not only have the theories derived from such approaches changed, but also we have no reason to generalize from behavior modification techniques (for example) that are effective in a brief encounter to suggest long-term use in the family. Even if desired behavior is achieved, we have no guarantee that the long-term impact of manipulation will be healthy.

Hess also criticizes parent training efforts on pragmatic grounds. Such training programs just don't work. A report to the Advisory Committee on Child Development of the National Academy of Sciences (1972) states that "the research literature provides little in the way of information for policies regarding parent education. If anything, the evidence seems to indicate that parent education is ineffective in altering child rearing practices."[9] Hess comments,

---

[7]Robert D. Hess, "Experts and Amateurs: Some Unintended Consequences of Parent Education," in Fantini and Cardenas, *Parenting in a Multicultural Society* (New York: Longman, 1980), pp. 153–61.

[8]Uri Bronfenbrenner, "The Future of the American Family," address to the American Association of Advertising in Peuto Rico, 1976, p. 11.

[9]Hess, "Experts and Amateurs," p. 150.

There are several reasons why parent education is not likely to be effective if pursued in its present form. The efforts of the past have not taken into account the processes through which parents learn to be effective parents. We know very little at the present time about how this kind of competence is acquired. Conventional wisdom is that teachers learn to teach in the classroom; I suspect that parents learn to be parents in their encounters with their children. . . . Parents do not usually store up information to be applied in a future occasion; it is difficult to anticipate the problems and demands of developmental stages their children have not yet encountered. Parent training programs designed for large audiences cannot provide information when it is needed and most likely to be utilized.[10]

Hess further points out that, implicit both in the advice of experts and in training materials provided, is a "mistrust of the family as an institution for raising children." In fact, parent education approaches appear to convey three messages to parents:

First, they probably do not have the competence needed for child-rearing; second, knowledge and techniques for dealing with children are available; third, if they wish, they can acquire these skills. A fourth message is implicit but unavoidable—if parents are not successful, it is their own fault.[11]

What does Hess suggest should be done? He sets out several characteristics of parent support approaches that he feels will help. For one thing, he suggests we keep away from training techniques and emphases that increase self-doubt and uncertainty. Many of the competency approaches focus on a technological approach that robs the parent of spontaneity and focuses attention on "Am I doing it right?" rather than on the child. Hess also suggests that we stress the complexity of the child-raising task. He notes that "a sense of effectiveness is a function of the perceived difficulty of the task. If the task is difficult, failure can be accepted; if it is perceived as easy, failure is a serious threat to confidence and self-esteem."[12] The program that promises three easy steps to success is bound to be destructive in the end!

Finally Hess makes his major suggestion, which is "based on a concept of self-help and mutual support among parents from different families and with varying levels of experience." He expands,

The wisdom and experience of other parents may be the major resource available for developing competence. Groups of participating parents might themselves identify, through discussion of their own personal experience, the problems that they face, and their techniques for dealing with

---

[10]Ibid.
[11]Ibid., p. 155.
[12]Ibid., p. 156.

them. There is an authenticity that comes from having shared an experience; to realize that another parent has been through the problem gives a sense of confidence in their judgment and advice.

Mutual support groups assist parents in another way. The realization that other parents have problems they find difficult to solve carries a unique reassurance. Parents who are unable to deal with a particular problem of find they have feelings of guilt of anger about their role or about their child often experience a great sense of relief when they discover that these feelings are shared by other parents. The fear that one is uniquely incompetent is dissipated by the knowledge that others have similar struggles.[4]

Hess's point of view is interesting for several reasons. His suggestion that we put less emphasis on providing information about parental competency is given support by studies that indicate little relationship between techniques parents use and their impact on their children's development. Instead, the quality of relationships between parents and children is the critical factor. Johnson and Medinnus survey studies that suggest that "what a mother *is* bears more on child adjustment than what she *does*"; that "the essence of parent-child relations, it must be emphasized, is more in how a parent *feels* than what a parent *does.*"[14] Perhaps our focus, then, should be less on the methodologies we want parents to use and more on the parent as a person! Perhaps much of parent-training has assumed that adults have arrived, and all they need is skill. Hess's approach is different because it insists we view parents as persons who are themselves growing and developing, and who need to be nurtured!

Another important implication of Hess's criticism and his suggestion needs to be thought through carefully. We have in our culture and in our faith *idealized* the nuclear family. *We have assumed that, for marriage, and for the rearing of children, the nuclear family is an adequate support system, even when isolated from other relational networks!* We are concerned about single-parent families because we believe that somehow the lack of one parent threatens the development of children. But we have not been concerned that today's isolated and alienated "normal" family unit may *also* have needs that threaten the development of both its adults and children!

Training approaches that attempt to provide parents in isolated nuclear units with techniques for raising their children suggest that parents are capable, alone, of meeting all family unit needs. These will always tend to create a sense of guilt and

---

[13]Ibid., p. 157.

[14]Ronald C. Johnson and Gene R. Medinnus, *Child Psychology*, 3rd ed. (New York: John Wiley & Sons, 1974), pp. 308–10.

failure for the simple reason that, with or without techniques, the family cannot go it alone!

If we take the view of parents as persons who themselves continue to require nurture, the model Hess suggests for training is fascinating. It is fascinating because it utilizes *and depends on* nurture processes that we have discovered in Old and New Testaments! Hess's description of the support group, the sharing taking place in it, the free expression of feelings, and the sharing of experiences, are all encompassed in the concepts of belonging, participation, modeling, and instruction-as-interpretation-of-life. In the whole process of support group experience, the focus is on helping the adult grow as a person who is a parent, not on the management of children.

The Faith Community

The discussion by Hess leads us back to the theological framework established at the beginning of this text. Recalling that framework, we can begin by stating clearly two convictions. First, the nurture of adults has priority in the church. And second, nurture of adults requires their participation in faith community.

The Deuteronomy prescription points to parents as the starting point in ministry with children. "These commandments . . ." Moses writes, ". . . are to be upon your hearts." The basic issue has always been, not the skills a parent has or techniques he or she has mastered, but rather the type of person the parent is and is becoming.

The reason this remains true was beautifully stated long ago by Horace Bushnell, in a work whose value was unfortunately clouded by debate between revivalist and covenant theologians. Bushnell's argument ascribes an organic relationship to the family, through which faith is communicated. He writes in *Views of Christian Nurture and Subjects Adjacent Thereto* (1847),

> It seems to be clearly held that grace shall travel by the same conveyance with sin, that the organic unity, which I have spoken of chiefly as an instrument of corruption, is to be occupied and sanctified by Christ and become an instrument also of mercy and life. And thus it follows that the seal of faith, applied to households, is to be no absurdity; for it is the privilege and duty of every Christian parent that his children shall come forth into responsible action, as a regenerated stock. The organic unity is to be a power of life. . . . The church life, that is the life of Christ, collects families into a common organism, and then, by sanctifying the laws of organic unity in families, extends its quickening power to the generation following, so as to include the future and make it one with the past. And so the church, in all ages, becomes a body under Christ the head, as the race

is a body under Adam the head—a living body quickened by him who hath life in himself, fitly joined together and compacted by that which every joint supplieth. . . . In the great and momentous truth now set forth, you perceive it is not what you intend for your children, so much as what you are, that is to have its effect. They are connected, by an organic unity, not with your instructions, but with your *life.*[15]

If the critical issue in communicating faith is the *life* of the parents, then it is clear that we must concentrate our efforts on nurturing them and stimulating their growth in Christ, just as the early church appears to have done!

Such nurture, as we have seen, requires participation in a faith community. Neither Old nor New Testament describes a Lone Ranger faith, a Christianity engaged in by individuals who flit from crisis to crisis without ever setting down roots or depending on others. Instead both Testaments give consistent witness to the fact that growth in faith, and the transformation of individuals, takes place in community.

We must distinguish participation in a faith community from membership in an organization (even in a church). Community is relational, and demands belonging and participation in a fellowship where personal relationships deepen and loving mutual ministry takes place. Adult members of families— whether of two-parent, one-parent, or reconstituted families (the product of divorce and remarriage)—must have roots sunk deep in supportive faith community relationships.

There are two reasons why it is vital, if we are serious about ministry to children in a family setting, to give priority to parental participation in faith community relationships. The first is that this context is vital for their own growth in faith. The second is that, as Hess suggests, this kind of group can give specific support and help in dealing with specific child-rearing problems as the problems emerge. Faith community groups become in fact strategic means through which to work in cases when it *is* important to introduce parenting information or encourage the development of skills.

Figure 28 diagrams the nuclear family (within a nurturant faith community) and the points of reference it already has in our society. It shows that the family exists within the context of a broad culture, with material and social characteristics. The culture is represented by the locality (city, country, suburb, slum, country-club, etc.) and in a pervasive way by the media. The family is linked physically to specific places, which may or may not be institutions, where time is spent and specific activ-

---

[15]Horace Bushnell, *Views of Christian Nurture* (1847; New York: Scholarly Facsimiles, 1975), pp. 201, 206.

FIGURE 28
POINTS OF REFERENCE FOR FAMILIES

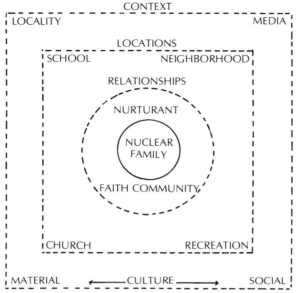

ities are engaged in. These include the neighborhood (the block, the back yards, homes, etc.), the school, the church, and places used for recreation (parks, movies, etc.).

In the last century these places commonly provided a network of personal relationships. Neighbors spent time together. Church was an all-day affair, with picnics and conversation between morning services and a late afternoon Sunday school just before people returned home to milk the cows. Today these places are commonly locations where services are provided, rather than where relationships are developed. Even in many churches the occasion for gathering is a service—a class, a choir, a club activity—rather than an opportunity to build relationships with fellow believers.

I do not want to suggest that such services are irrelevant or unimportant. But I do want to suggest that these points of reference are not adequate for ministry to families, or as avenues through which to provide support for families.

What is needed by parents is participation in a faith community group that will provide them with nurturance for their own growth in faith and will also serve to support them in parenting.

For anyone serious about enriching ministry to children by working through families, the establishment of faith community groups in which parents participate is a necessary precondition.

Necessary, But Not Necessarily Sufficient

Participation by parents in faith community relationships is necessary for effective ministry to children in the family setting. It need not be considered sufficient. There are many ways those engaged in children's ministry can enrich the family setting and can encourage those processes critical in faith development (belonging, participation, modeling, instruction-as-interpretation-of-life, and exercising choice). In the rest of this section we'll look at a variety of models through which the building of faith-transmission processes can be encouraged.

PROBE

▶ *case histories*
▶ *discussion questions*
▶ *thought provokers*
▶ *resources*

1. One tradition in research on the family and its influence on children focuses on two major psychological dimensions in the home: that of acceptance/rejection, and autonomy/control. The theory suggests that a family's psychological climate may be described as falling into one of four quadrants identified by laying out the factors on opposing axes (see Figure 29).

FIGURE 29
PSYCHOLOGICAL CLIMATE

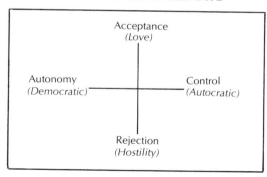

This tradition has also concluded that the acceptance/rejection axis is the single most important, and it has identified the following behaviors by parents as evidence for acceptance or for rejection (see Figure 30).

FIGURE 30
ACCEPTANCE/REJECTION BEHAVIORS

Evidence for Parent's Acceptance of Child	Evidence for Parent's Rejection of Child
Participates in games, sports, hobbies with child, takes trips together, special vacations	Takes no interest in child
Makes rearing child a main job, with high priority	Has no time for child—often neglects him or her
Shows interest in child's plans	Makes unfavorable comparisons with others
Gives loving care and protection	Punishes verbally, with nagging and scolding
Shows interest in school achievements	Does not express support or praise
Expresses and demonstrates affection	Often criticizes and blames the child
Speaks well of the child	Uses strong physical punishments
Wanted the birth of the child	Ridicules
Encourages child to bring friends home	Does not speak well of child
Worries when child is ill	Opposed the child's birth
Accepts child as individual, not just as a "child"	Acts and feels suspicious of child's behavior
Talks over plans and requests with child	Gives too much supervision
Does not expect too much of child	Neglects health, clothes, etc.
Expresses encouragement and praise	

In this chapter I have suggested that the key to ministry to children through the family setting is not the *training* of parents, but involvement of parents in vital faith community relationships with other adults. The reasons for this can be seen if we consider the particular training taken by four families, described below. Read the description of the families and of the training, and, using Figure 31, predict the outcome of the training within each family.

The Smiths and the Joneses are *rejecting* parents. The Johnsons and the Robinsons are *accepting* parents. The Smiths and Robinsons have recently become members of a neighborhood group, from their church, that functions as a faith community. The Joneses and the Johnsons attend church services but have developed no close relationships with other Christians. All four families are enrolled in a four-week course at church on "How to listen actively to our children." Predict what will actually happen to listening patterns in each home, at the given points in time. Can you explain the basis on which your predictions are made, and justify them theoretically?

2. A description of findings in a particular research program is given below, without interpretation. *How would you explain what the researchers discovered?*

> *Our goal was to form Sunday school classes for parents, to study the same themes on an adult level their children were learning in*

their primary and junior classes. Even those churches where this approach was fully supported by the leadership seldom had over 15 percent of the parents who chose to participate. In most of the 430 churches the average was closer to 8 percent. In addition, we noted that in some churches the parents' groups grew quite steadily, but in other churches the class groups lost participants rapidly. Checking on churches that experienced either significant growth or loss of adults in these classes, a single factor seemed to account for adult response. In classes where growth took place, the adult leaders concentrated on helping class members explore the meaning of the Bible truths studied for their own lives. In classes where participants were lost, the adult leaders focused on sections in the parent materials that suggested ways to carry over the teaching from Sunday into the week. It seemed the more the leader concentrated on the specifics of what parents could do in their homes, the more quickly class attendance dropped.

3. This chapter contains several charts that report the response of parents to questions about Christian nurture. Study these charts (Figures 24 through 27). (1) Write down at least five observations or conclusions you might draw from each. (2) Write a paragraph describing what you think most parents in the conservative, evangelical group perceive "Christian upbringing" to require.

FIGURE 31
LISTENING PATTERNS

Family	two weeks after course	one year after course
Smiths		
Joneses		
Johnsons		
Robinsons		

PART 2

SETTINGS

The Home

The Impact of Family
Intergenerational Models
Information Models
Intervention Models
Patterns in the Home

The Church

The Church as Organism and Institution
Sunday School as Faith Community
Sunday School Curriculums

The Christian School

The Christian School Ideal
Faith Community in the Classroom

One of the most promising ways to touch the lives of children is to let them become part of the support group of which their parents are members. But even when this is not always possible, intergenerational learning and growing experiences can

INTERGENERATIONAL MODELS

have great value. Each of the models explored in this chapter illustrates the fact that we need not continue to segregate our children by age or isolate them from others from whom they can learn faith.

Both Old and New Testament nurture systems rely on involving children with adults in the life of the faith community. Even today, some local fellowships follow this model of life together as God's people.

One significant impact of adopting the schooling/instructional approach in our churches has been a resultant segregation of children into narrow, graded groups. The intergenerational experience has been swallowed up by multiplied agencies dominated by the principle of segregation of children and even of adults by age. But the segregated approach is not the only one available. In a variety of ways we can, and some *do*, restore children to significant participation with adults in nurturant groups. In this chapter we look at three approaches that have potential for those seriously concerned about ministering to children through families.

THE HOUSE-CHURCH MODEL

For several years Shared Life Fellowship has met in homes in Phoenix, Arizona. The gatherings of this growing congregation, on Thursday evenings and on Sundays, feature building adult members into a supportive faith community, including a special role for children. The meetings of the church provide many intergenerational experiences. And the leaders model, in their own homes, sensitive parenting.

Dr. Norm Wakefield, who pastors this multi-house congregation, explains the ways that children participate in congregational life.

CHAPTER **11**

We meet together twice a week, Sundays and Thursdays. On Sunday the first half hour or forty minutes is spent together. During this time children and adults sing together, and are free to share. Often during this time we have a feature where children talk one-on-one with adults, or share in small groups. We have each person tell his favorite Bible story, or describe a favorite teacher, or tell about one time each felt loved.

Also, we periodically have all-age Bible studies on Thursday nights. These are designed to involve first graders through adults. We include puzzles, games, and other activities. Everything is done in small, mixed groups of adults and children. Each group is guided by a work sheet, designed so that no one in a study team is perceived as a teacher. Both adults and children follow the work sheets. To keep anyone from taking over the leader role, we'll have instructions like, "Let the person closest to age 12 . . ." and "The person whose birthday is closest to November will now. . . ." We try to get everyone involved in all these studies on the same level, whatever their age. [Note: Figures 32 and 33 are two of the all-age studies used by this congregation.]

It's exciting to see the results in our fellowship, how children and adults come to know each other. For instance, this summer some of our singles decided they wanted to take the children in our fellowship on a week-end back-packing expedition. We often have things like this happening. It's common now for children to stay overnight at others' homes, including homes of older couples without children.

We also found it exciting that when we had a couples retreat single adults in our fellowship volunteered to care for the children. And one couple that have never had children have "adopted" a single parent's children, and spend a lot of time with them.

We do have separate teaching times for youth and adults, of course. And when we do, the children have something planned just for them. But the boys and girls are a real part of our fellowship. Parents who have learned to share and build close relationships within our fellowship are eager for their kids to have the same kind of relationship. I'm excited, because the children in our fellowship really are learning to share, to build close relationships with many adults, and to care about the other adults and children. It really is shared life.[1]

FIGURE 32

A SHARED LIFE FELLOWSHIP
ALL-AGE BIBLE STUDY
My Heavenly Father Watches Over Me

1. Write down one reason you love God. Afterwards share this with the others in your group.

2. Unscramble the message. Each number stands for a letter of the alphabet: 1=a, 2=b, 3=c, etc.

   9-14 16-19-1-12-13 *18* 4-1-22-9-4 19-1-9-4 20-8-1-20 8-5

   12-15-22-5-4 7-15-4 2-5-3-1-21-19-5 ?-15-4 23-1-19 20-8-5

   15-14-5- 23-8-15 16-18-15-20-5-3-20-5-4- 8-9-13

3. Read Psalm 18:1–2. List all the words that David uses to tell how God is his protector.

   my   my   my
   my   my   my
   my   my

   What do the different words say about how God protects us?

4. List several ways that people try to protect themselves.

5. Beside each verse below tell what it says about God protecting you:

   1 John 4:4 (leader explain)
   Matthew 6:31–32
   Romans 8:37–39
   Psalm 23:4
   Psalm 27:1–3

6. Share one thing that you tend to be afraid of (adults go first).

   Which of the above verses says that God will protect you from the thing you fear?

   Write out the verse on the name tag. Then (1) fasten it to the inside of your Bible, or (2) wear it for the rest of the night, or (3) put it on the mirror in your bedroom or bathroom to remind you that your heavenly Father will protect you.

---

[1]Letter from Dr. Norm Wakefield.

FIGURE 33

A SHARED LIFE FELLOWSHIP
ALL-AGE BIBLE STUDY

WHO IS MOST IMPORTANT?

FIND the following words in this puzzle. They may be written up, down, across, diagonally, or backwards.

leprosy
Naaman
Elisha
Jordan
Pharpar
gift
king
girl
seven

```
X  R  T  E  B  E  T  E  G  A
P  R  I  N  C  E  Y  G  K  H
S  H  O  A  N  S  O  I  L  S
G  E  A  D  O  A  N  R  I  I
A  O  U  R  N  G  M  L  N  L
S  F  P  O  P  Q  T  A  D  E
S  E  G  J  N  A  M  O  A  N
L  L  G  I  F  T  R  N  L  N
S  E  N  E  V  E  S  O  U  P
```

TAKE TURNS telling what each of the words had to do with the story. Tell as much as you can about each word.

LOOK at the chain below. It leads from Naaman's leprosy to his healing. In each link put the name of a person that had a part in Naaman's healing.

Naaman's leprosy

Naaman's healing

TALK about this: who was most important in Naaman getting healed? Explain your answer.

THINK about this. God used many people to help Naaman find healing from leprosy. God uses many people in our lives to help us grow. Sometimes we forget or overlook people who do important things. Now, READ 1 Cor. 14:21–27 and answer this question: What important lesson does this passage teach us?

LIST the names of all the people you can think of who have helped you grow as a Christian. Circle the names of those who are helping you now. Don't overlook "hidden" people. (List the names on the back of this sheet.) Then pray together THANKING God for others who help you grow.

What is so significant about the pattern of life Norm describes is that Shared Life Fellowship intergenerational experiences have, over time, patterned the lifestyle of the members of this faith community. Intergenerational sharing is not just a "program," or something for a few of the members. Instead intimate relationships that stretch across the generations to enfold infant and ancient have become the natural way in which these believers live together as a faith community.

INTERGENERATIONAL SUNDAY SCHOOL

Few feel ready to totally reshape the lifestyle of a local congregation to the pattern established at Shared Life Fellowship. But there are ways that agencies long established in the traditional congregation can be adapted to intergenerational learning. Intergenerational Sunday school is one of the easiest to adapt, although churches with midweek services might use the same intergenerational plan. Most churches that offer an intergenerational Sunday school offer such groups as electives, letting others continue to meet in age-graded classes.

Intergenerational Sunday school classes usually work best with groups of some twelve to fifteen persons. Groups are established as extended family units. They include children from first through sixth grades, with adults. Two or three families may serve as the core of an intergenerational family unit. One or more is often a single-parent family. At times singles or older adults may be blended in, as are children whose parents do not come to Sunday school or church.

FIGURE 34
AN INTERGENERATIONAL STUDY GUIDE

JESUS IS WITH US
Mark 4:35–41

MASTER TEACHER: filmstrip of "Jesus Stills the Storm"

"FAMILY" UNITS (to be read by the boy nearest third grade)

1. Let each person use the crayons and paper at our table to draw a picture of what he or she likes best about this Bible story.

2. Let's tell each other about our pictures. What did we like best about this Bible story?

3. I will read the Bible story. Then we will talk over two questions.

    The disciples were in a boat with Jesus. A furious storm came up, and waves broke over the boat, so it was nearly swamped. Jesus was in the stern, sleeping on a cushion. The disciples woke him up and said to him, "Teacher, don't you care if we drown?"

    Jesus go up, and spoke to the wind and waves. "Quiet!" Jesus said. "Be still!" Then the wind dies down and it was completely calm.

    Jesus said to his disciples, "Why are you so afraid? Do you still have no faith?"

    FIRST QUESTION (go around the circle, and everyone answer)

    "Can you think of a time when you were afraid like the disciples? Tell us about it."

    SECOND QUESTION (talk about this in groups of five or six)

    "Jesus is with us today like he was the disciples. When are you happiest that Jesus is with you?"

4. Let's each pray a sentence prayer, Pray for someone else in our circle. Thank God that Jesus will be with that person this week, to care for him or her.

Several safeguards are critical when working with intergenerational units in Sunday school. First, the units should be maintained as stable units over extended periods of time. Because one goal is to help children build relationships with adults who can serve as models, and with other children who can also model, it's important not to reshuffle group membership or add new persons every few weeks.

Second, it's important not to have anyone in the group take on the role of "teacher." This role in our culture is a managerial role, and shifts relationships from the "friend" mode described in Figure 16, to a controlling mode. If significant interpersonal relationships are to grow between the adults and the children in intergenerational study groups, it's important to protect parents and other adults from being cast in a managerial role that will inhibit free flow of "friend" behaviors.

This is typically done by establishing a Master Teacher to provide input and overall guidance (such as time keeping) for several intergenerational study groups, and by using a printed sheet of step-by-step instructions for each group to follow. An outline for one intergenerational study that used the guide sheet and Master Teacher approach is provided as Figure 34.

Intergenerational classes fit well in a variety of facilities. A single large room can be used for four or five extended family units, with a single Master Teacher guiding the process. Or individual "family" groups can meet in smaller classrooms, without a teacher, with the process guided solely by a study outline.

While intergenerational Sunday school is not as powerful an approach as that represented by Shared Life Fellowship, where the whole life of the membership is built around intergenerational relationships, the Sunday school model can make significant contributions. The intergenerational approach will help children come to know several adults not their parents in significant ways. By guiding the learning activities, the week's study sheet can encourage the kind of sharing that helps children be sensitive to others (building social role-taking and empathy), and that lets others model faith on the levels of emotions and values.

SHORT-TERM INTERGENERATIONAL EVENTS

Each of the two models we've looked at so far have advantages over short-term approaches. Each is a continuing, long-term structure, which has the capacity to build increasingly intimate relationships over time. In addition, each approach has the capacity to train parents unobtrusively in ways to teach, to listen to, and to communicate with their children. Each model in effect provides continuous though unobtrusive training in parenting.

Short-term intergenerational experiences have different purposes and advantages. Parents who are not ready to commit themselves to a long-term structure can get a taste of intergenerational learning through retreats, intergenerational Vacation Bible Schools held on summer evenings, or family camps. These short-term experiences help moms and dads understand how to relate to children and communicate the Bible in modeling rather than instructional modes. They also may encourage some parents to participate in longer term intergenerational structures.

Intergenerational Retreat

How might an intergenerational retreat be designed? Dr. Norm Wakefield, who leads Shared Life Fellowship, often conducts family camps and retreats. Below is the plan of a family retreat that he led recently for a Colorado congregation (see Figures 35–41).[2]

Vacation Bible School

Vacation Bible School sessions also provide opportunity for family adventures that cross the generations. Typically an approach will utilize five consecutive nights, of about two to two and a half hours each. One such course has been developed through Sunday School PLUS, an experimental curriculum tested by Dynamic Church Ministries.[3] This particular unit, titled *Exit to Freedom,* uses an enactive Bible study. It also features take home materials (not reproduced here) that involve nuclear family units in follow-up projects and discussions.

The first of five sessions is included here to illustrate what might be done in a more flexible setting with intergenerational learning (see Figure 42). The same kind of approach might well be taken during the "Family Night" features that some churches inject periodically as midweek services.

Family Camp

Neither retreat nor VBS intergenerational experiences are typically linked with adult participation in small, regular faith community groupings. Where such groups exist, a camping experience shared by all the families of the support group could adopt such approaches for intergenerational times at camp.

---

[2]Anyone wishing to contact Norm about leading a retreat or camp, or for consultation in the area of family ministries, can reach him at 330 E. Sharon, Phoenix, AZ 85022; Tel. (602) 993-9949.

[3]For more information, contact Dynamic Church Ministries, 1266 Woodingham Drive, E. Lansing, MI 48823.

FIGURE 35
INTERGENERATIONAL RETREAT OUTLINE

This retreat is developed around the theme of communication.

Session 1

A. Hand out the "Tic Tac Toe" sheet (see Figure 36) to each person. Allow about fifteen minutes for each individual to get names and information from others. Encourage information from individuals not well known and from all age groups.

Place each person's name on slips of paper and place them in a container. Ask an individual to draw out a name. All the people who have that individual's name on their sheet are to stand and share the information that they have written down about that person. Then, draw a second name, find out about that person and so on. If an individual gets all names across, down, or on a diagonal he receives a prize.

If you like, continue the "Tic Tac Toe" exercise at the beginning of each session as a means to continue getting to know individuals.

B. Form groups of 6–7 in the following manner.
1. Count the number of individuals to know how many groups you will need.
2. Choose a "father" for each group. The individual does not need to be an actual father to qualify.
3. The "father" now chooses a lady to be a "mother" (NOT HIS WIFE).
4. The "couple" choose a "son."
5. The "family" now chooses a "daughter."
6. The "family" now chooses a "grandfather." Anyone can be chosen but he becomes a "grandfather."
7. The "family" now chooses a "grandmother."

Allow the group fifteen minutes to get to know each other. If it is helpful suggest questions that can be answered to give direction.

Each group is now to develop their own group name and cheer. Allow about fifteen to twenty minutes for preparation, then allow each group to share its name and cheer with the other groups.

(This group will work together for Sessions 2 and 3 when group exercises are called for.)

C. Pass out a sheet of paper and pencil to each individual. Then ask for a volunteer who is sixteen or older. The individual is given "Communication Data Sheet A" (see Figure 37) and instructed as follows: "You are to tell the group how to reproduce the diagram that you have, but you cannot look at the group. You will have three minutes to tell them how to copy your diagram on their sheet."

The group is instructed to make no sounds, ask no questions during the three minute period. Each individual works alone.

Locate the "instructor" where he cannot be seen so that he gives no nonverbal clues and receives no nonverbal clues from the group.

At the end of the three minutes ask group members to express their feelings during the three minute exercise. Do NOT have them see the diagram the volunteer worked from.

Ask for another volunteer. He is given "Communication Data Sheet B" (see Figure 38). Then, he is instructed to tell the participants to reproduce his diagram on their paper. He cannot show them the diagram, but he can be visible to them and two-way communication is allowed—questions can be asked, etc. Again, allow three minutes for the exercise.

At the end of the exercise talk about how individuals felt during the first and second exercise. Compare the accuracy of drawings with the original. Discuss: What does this exercise teach us about communication? The leader should take a brief time to talk about the importance of communication to family life, especially two-way communication.

Close the session with prayer.

Session 2

A. Ask each individual to gather with his group members and again share the group cheer.

B. Distribute "Helpful Words" Bible study sheet (see Figure 39) to each person. Give groups about thirty minutes to complete the study.

C. Plan a Leader's Input to help individuals discover basic principles of communication. Keep the information clear, simple, and illustrated. It is helpful to allow demonstrations of the principles using group members.

D. Ask family groups to form. Then distribute the "Communication Effectiveness Inventory" (see Figure 40) to each person and have each one complete it. When it is completed have it exchanged with a family member and ask him or her to complete it as he or she sees the other family member. Emphasize that it is important to be positive and constructive.

Ask each family to discuss together how they could improve communication within the family. Again emphasize the importance of being positive and not attacking individuals.

Session 3

A. Plan an "Emmaus Walk" for the entire group. Individuals go for a 30 minute walk with another individual. During the first fifteen minutes person A talks, sharing information about himself to person B. Person B listens. Then reverse the process, giving person B the opportunity to share for fifteen minutes while Person A listens. Team people who are of different age levels and sex.

B. When all individuals have returned have the original groups assemble. If it is appropriate ask each group to share its group cheer with the entire group.

C. Distribute a copy of "Learning to Listen" Bible study (see Figure 41) to each person. Allow thirty minutes for each group to complete the study together.

D. Using Norman Wakefield's *Listening: A Christian's Guide to Loving Relations* (Waco, Texas: Word, 1981) prepare a brief input time giving several helpful principles of listening that can enrich family relations. Try to allow group members to practice the principle if possible.

This retreat is designed to include a "Skit/Talent Night" that will involve the entire group and encourage interage skits and talent.

FIGURE 36
"TIC TAC TOE"

Instructions: Talk to nine different people that you do not know well. Find out several facts about them that other people might not know. Be sure to write down the information in the space by their names.

P.S. You might win a prize!

Name:	Name:	Name:
Name:	Name:	Name:
Name:	Name:	Name:

FIGURE 37
COMMUNICATION DATA SHEET A

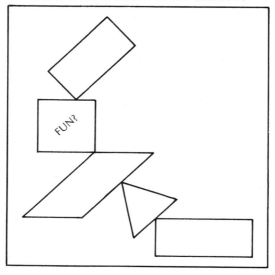

FIGURE 38
COMMUNICATION DATA SHEET B

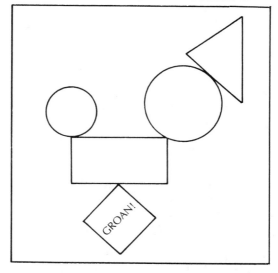

FIGURE 39
HELPFUL WORDS

DECIPHER: Work together as a group and unscramble the verse written below. Remember, do it together, but give *everyone* a chance to help.

od ont sue fularmh sword ni ginkalt use lony pulfelh sword,

het kidn atht lidbu pu dan videorp wtah si eeeddn os ttah

twah uyo asy ilwl od odgo ot setho how earh oyu.   Hepesanis 4:29

DISCUSS: What is the difference between harmful words and helpful words? What do harmful words do to people? What do helpful words do to people? Write your answers on the back of this paper.

DECIDE: Take turns reading the situations below (Start with the person closest to 44-years-old. Decide what a person would say in a harmful way. Then, let another person share how it could be said in a helpful way. Let everyone have a chance.

1. It is time to leave for church. Everyone is in the car except mother who is putting on her make up. Dad turns to the children and says—
2. Ray comes in the house with mud on his feet. Mother says to him—
3. Sue and Ramona get in an argument. Sue says to Ramona, "You're stupid! I don't want you around anymore!" Ramona replies—
4. Jeff shows his report card to Dad. He has a B, three C's, and a D. Dad says—
5. Sixteen-year-old Alicia normally vacuums the living room. Today she says to her younger sister, Terry, "I have a headache. Will you vacuum the living room for me?" Terry answers—

DISCOVER: Look up the following verses in the Bible. Write down what the verse is saying about how we talk to each other. Be sure that everyone in the group understands what the verse is saying.

1. Prov. 12:18
2. Prov. 15:1
3. Prov. 18:2
4. James 3:2

DECIDE: Think of one person (perhaps a family member) whom you can encourage by helpful words. Share the person's name and suggest what you would like to tell the person to encourage him/her.

FIGURE 40

COMMUNICATION EFFECTIVENESS INVENTORY

Instructions: Insert the name of the person being evaluated in blank space.

	Usually	Sometimes	Seldom	Never	Usually	Sometimes	Seldom	Never

1. _____ will sit down with someone and encourage him/her to talk informally.

2. _____ is sensitive to another who is discouraged, restless, troubled, or silent.

3. _____ interrupts others when they are talking.

4. _____ compliments other individuals about things they do.

5. _____ enjoys talking conversationally with other persons.

6. _____ frequently criticizes others.

7. _____ acts as though he/she is listening to a person when he/she really is not.

8. _____ asks others' opinion about things they would like to do, receive, etc.

9. _____ is sarcastic to individuals.

10. _____ tries to see another's point of view.

11. _____ enjoys listening to other people.

12. _____ monopolizes conversation.

13. _____ encourages others to share their thoughts, feelings, convictions.

14. _____ is able to speak the truth in a loving manner.

15. _____ gets upset or defensive when others disagree with him/her.

16. _____ tends to be too detailed or complex when sharing ideas or opinions.

17. _____ asks questions or makes statements that are irrelevant.

18. _____ shares so little of himself/herself that others cannot get to know him/her.

FIGURE 41
LEARNING TO LISTEN

1. In the space below jot down everything you remember that the person told you himself/herself on the Emmaus Walk.

2. Share with your group members what you learned about the person.

3. Everyone close his/her eyes: (1) Listen quietly for any sounds you hear. Try to decide what the sound is. Tell others what you hear. (2) Keep your eyes closed. Try to make sounds that others must guess. (example: jingle car keys).

4. Make a list of times of places when it is hard to listen to others. Start with the youngest person and let each person share an idea.

   a. (Example:) when I am tired.

   b.

   c.

   d.

   e.

   f.

   g.

   h.

5. Remember a time when you misunderstood what another person said and it caused a problem or embarrassment.

6. Take turns reading the verses below. Talk about what the writer wanted us to know about listening.

   a.   "A fool thinks he needs no advice, but a wise man listens to others" (Proverbs 12:15).

   b.   "Any story sounds true until someone tells the other side and sets the record straight" (Proverbs 18:17).

   c.   "The wise man learns by listening; the simpleton can learn only by seeing scorners punished" (Proverbs 21:11).

   d.   "My dear brothers take note of this: Everyone should be quick to listen, slow to speak and slow to become angry" (James 1:19 NIV).

FIGURE 42
AN INTERGENERATIONAL TEACHING PLAN[4]

LESSON 1

FOCUS "SLAVES!"

Exodus 1-4, Acts 7, Hebrews 11

Although God promises Abraham that his descendants will be a great nation and one day possess their own land, He permits them to suffer slavery under the hand of Egypt's Pharaoh . . . for a time.

"Lord! What are you doing to me!" I remember feeling beaten by God and man that hot, hot week in August. Monday I found out that I didn't have enough money to pay off a car wreck that I didn't 'cause. I'd be losing $500 out of my own pocket and I was innocent! Tuesday I received a pleasant letter from my own insurance company advising me that my insurance had been cancelled. "Please reapply," it said. Wednesday my bank card was no longer valid. "Please reapply in October," was the only salve provided. "They're going to take back my social security card next," I groused, jokingly. But underneath I was beaten.

Try to do right, obey the law, pay my debts, give up good-paying jobs in the past for "the Lord's work" and what happens? No one trusts me. I have no credit. I have no car. Things just go from bad to worse!

Then in a flash it hit me. "So this is how it feels. No matter how good you try to be, you always lose. This is what it feels like to be oppressed, eh? Wow. What a lesson, God."

Slavery. Some of your children may be from poor or deprived families. But 99 chances out of 100, they have never been slaves. In fact, they have probably never seen a slave. So how can we help them know what it feels like to be a slave? Think back to my experience with the car, and all the concurrent financial disappointments. It wasn't till then that I realized what it felt like to be poor and not trusted. Even though my problems lasted only for a few months, they were certainly real! And I'll never be quite the same again. I can begin to understand when someone says to me, "Dorothy, I just can't get credit anywhere. Do you know how that makes me feel about myself? Like I'm nobody!" Do I know how that feels? Yes. I've been there.

So what does this have to do with your class? Well, this month is "You Are There" month for you and them. Since so many of the Exodus story facts are familiar, but so many of the experiences and feelings from the story are not, this unit your whole

6

Sunday School—including Sunday School Plus parents—will *live* through the Exodus experience!

For one whole month, you, your children and their parents will be actors. You will stay in your roles for at least the first three weeks (during class time, that is). Week 4 is a special activity you'll all enjoy. Now to work.

Cast. First, all teachers, parents and children are slaves. (How do you like that pronouncement? Already getting slave feelings?) One teacher keeps the action going. Another acts as a grandparent. OPTION: invite an older couple from your church to act as grandparents throughout the unit.

Support cast: recruit two teens to act as (1) an Egyptian taskmaster, and (2) a Hebrew teenager. OPTION: teachers can play those roles. Please do not have parents play the role of oppressor!

"**Costumes.**" The symbol for slavery this unit is bare feet. Only Egyptians may wear shoes or sandals. See DISCOVER TOGETHER 1 for more sophisticated costume ideas.

Tribal names: Name each class in your department an Israelite tribal name. During or after today's Bible story explain that each tribe was named for one of Jacob's 12 sons.

Tribal banners. You might want to make tribal banners ahead of time, or let children make them between weeks 1 and 2, or, if yours is a long-session Sunday School, make banners in class this week.

Banners can be made by cutting out the English or Hebrew letters from cloth and gluing them onto a burlap background. Decorate banners with cut-outs of symbols of slavery or Jehovah, or elements in prophecies by Jacob about each of

his sons (Gen. 49).

Hebrew first names. Prepare nametags before class for each child, parent and teacher, to be worn all four sessions this month. OR, let parents and children make their own nametags during lesson 1. If you choose this option, post the following names and meanings using a chart or chalkboard.

These names were probably common at the time of the Exodus.

boys

Joshua	god saves
Abraham	Father of a multitude
Jacob	Taking another's place by trickery
Joseph	He shall add
Reuben	Look, a son!
Simeon	Hearing
Judah	Praise
Ephraim	Doubly fruitful
Benjamin	Son of the right hand
Dan	Judge
Naaman	Pleasant
Asher	Happy
Isaac	Laughter

girls

Sarah	Princess
Rebekah	Flattering
Leah	Weary
Rachel	Lamb
Mahlah	Mildness
Tirzah	Delight
Judith	Jewess
Elisheba (Elizabeth)	God is Promiser

(Save out Moses, Miriam, and Aaron—for obvious reasons.)

Setting. All chairs are removed from your classroom for one month. One area of the room is designated as Pharaoh's palace. If you're really ambitious, you could arrange Pharaoh's quarters on a platform, to give the impression of impor-

7

[4]*Exit to Freedom*, Teacher's Guide, Unit 9, pp. 6–13. © 1976, Sunday School PLUS.

tance—superiority. When Pharaoh appears (week 2), no one should ever be as tall as him. All must stoop, bow, etc., before him.

Other areas of the room are for the Hebrews. If you wish, you can decorate with rough lean-to's or shacks painted on kraft paper. A campfire or home-like area could be created for the nighttime story telling. If possible, rig covers for windows if there are none, to darken the room for nightime scenes.

ADVANCE PREPARATION WEEK 1. A Sunday in advance, or during the week, tell your children to wear play clothes to class this week.

Also, bring out any liturgies, songs, dances, banners, projects or art work you saved from the *God is All-Powerful* unit. Decide what will go with each week of this unit.

Scene 1

Slaves!

As parents and children enter the room, play records or tapes of Hebrew music—preferably plaintive sounding, or music from soundtracks of "Exodus" or the TV special series "Moses the Lawgiver." OR, have someone sing or play minor melodies "live."

Put on nametags (unless you plan to have parents and children make theirs later). Whenever you put them on, that is your in-class name for the rest of the month. All teachers, parents and children must remove their shoes.

Action! Egyptian taskmaster puts you and your children and their parents right to work. Taskmaster divides children and parents into work crews. You, "grandparent" and any other teaching staff are told to be

crew leaders.

Work projects might be like those listed in SERENDIPITY: gathering rocks, moving furniture, scrubbing floors, etc. Taskmaster gives a time limit on the project, oversees closely and critically does not permit slaves to ask questions or complain. Work project lasts about 20 minutes.

Scene ends when someone closes blinds, curtains, etc. and turns off lights. Taskmaster abusively tells Hebrews to return to hovels in Goshen, then exits toward palace area.

Scene 2

Getting Organized
Day's End:

Scene two is a fun catch-all for working out the organization of this unit with your parents and children, as well as for developing 'tribe' spirit.

Scene two is also a bit like an accordian. It can be expanded or contracted according to the amount of time you have. Choose number and length of activities not only with time allotment in mind, however, but also considering which activities your parents and children would enjoy and the children are capable of doing.

ACTIVITIES

1. If not done already, let class choose Hebrew first names and make their own nametags.

2. Let each class choose a Hebrew tribal name and find a spot in the "Goshen District" for their home.

3. Let each tribe make a tribal banner to be hung in their home area and carried during future celebrations, parades, etc., this month.

Scene 3

The Bible Story

Now gather everyone around a family campfire kind of setting. One teacher, with the help of a few children serves 'supper'—a chunk of unsliced crusty bread, perhaps figs or dates and a small drink of water.

After the meal, spend 15 minutes learning and talking about the meaning of verse 1 of "O Come, O Come, Emmanuel." Once learned, it can be sung spontaneously as a slave song during future work scenes.

Picking up on the song's phrase "ransom captive Israel," you raise the question How *did* we get to be slaves, anyway?

Grandpa (or grandma) answers by telling the following account of Israel's history—"From Abraham to Egypt." As he (or she) talks, teachers make sure children are comfortable, perhaps holding younger ones on their laps, etc.

From Abraham to Egypt

Well, children, here's how we came to be slaves. My grandfather told me about it when I was just about your age.

Long, long ago, about 400 years to be exact, a wonderful man named Abraham, heard the voice of Yahweh—the God who made all heaven and earth. He told Abraham to leave the big rich city where he lived and to go to a new land—a land without big cities, a land of strangers to Abraham and his family. So Abraham obeyed God. And God loved Abraham very much.

(As the story is told, grandfather can illustrate roughly the geographic locations of where the story's events happen. Stones can be used as markers on the floor.)

One day, when Abraham was in this new land, God told him. "Abraham, some day I'm going to make a great big nation from your family." Abraham was very happy to hear this, but he had no children. Where was this great big family going to come from? He didn't even have one son!

Abraham's God was a powerful God, and he never forgot this promise to Abraham. Years later, He gave Abraham the son he wanted. And Abraham named him Isaac.

But there was a sad part to God's promise. God told Abraham that one day, all the land Abraham walked on would belong to this great promised nation, but before that, Abraham's great-great-great-great grandchildren —this great nation to grow from his family, would be slaves in another country for 400 years!

Well . . . Abraham grew old and died a peaceful death. His son Isaac also spoke with God. And so did Isaac's son Jacob. Abraham's grandson Jacob. Now there's a man. Quite different from Abraham, but he knew this great God, just the same. God told Jacob also about this wonderful promise that a great nation would come from their family.

But Jacob had hard times, too, just like us. He must have wondered how God could ever keep His promise sometimes.

(*Teacher: What were some of the hard times that Jacob went through?*

(*Teacher: you can chime in here and there with leading comments, like: "What happened, Grandfather? We sure aren't free now!"*)

Once we were a proud people! And we were rich! And we didn't have any masters. We were free! Never forget that, children, free.

Grandfather?)

Well, children, first, his favorite son disappeared. Jacob was led to believe that this good boy—Joseph was his name—had been killed by a wild animal. How Jacob's heart was broken by this news!

Then another hard thing happened some years later. This time all Jacob's sons and their families faced death—starving to death! There had been no rain in their country for a long time, and soon there was no food. Jacob was desperate! How would his large family of 11 living sons and their wives and children be fed? His family would never become that big nation God promised if they all starved!

Then Jacob heard good news. Down in Egypt—yes!—where we're living right now—there was lots of food. And people from other countries were coming here to buy Egypt's extra food. So Jacob sent his sons to Egypt to buy grain, too. And guess who was in charge of selling grain to people from all over the world? Yes! None other than his long lost son Joseph! Have any of you children heard any of this part of our story before?

(Let children briefly tell Joseph's story and how God worked out his situation from slavery to saving his family's life (Gen., chapters 37, 39 - 45).)

When Joseph let his brothers know who he was, he told them all to go back to their father and bring him and their wives and children and all their sheep and cattle to come live in Egypt. Because there were still going to be five more years of famine!

When Pharaoh heard this exciting story, he too wanted Joseph's whole family to come down to Egypt. He

10

said, "Take wagons for your wives and children and father Jacob. The best of all the land of Egypt is yours."

So that's how Abraham's grandson Jacob and all his sons and daughters and their sons and daughters and sheep and cattle—everything—came to Egypt.

Yes, sir. Abraham's great family—70 in all—sure was important in those days. Pharaoh couldn't do enough for them.

(Teacher: Well, what does this story of Abraham and Isaac and Jacob have to do with us?)

Ah ... you see child, you are part of that great big family of Abraham! And so are you and you and you (he nods to one child or parent after another)—all of us Hebrews are part of Abraham's big family. And it's been just about 400 years since Abraham's grandson Jacob and all his children moved here to Egypt.

(Teacher: Oh, yes. God's promise to Abraham that his family would live in another land for 400 years came true! But what happened? Pharaoh was kind to Jacob and Joseph and their families. He gave them food and a nice place to live. But look at us! Our clothes, What happened?

(Grandparent answers angrily.) Those Egyptians soon forgot how helpful Joseph had been. They forgot that Pharaoh had *invited* us to Egypt to be honored guests!

Long after Joseph died, a new Pharaoh came along. He was mean. He was afraid of us. Remember that, children. We're slaves because the Egyptians are afraid of us and because they're greedy—not because there's something wrong with us! You see, Pharaoh was afraid that if one of his enemies invaded his (scornfully) beloved Egypt, that we'd

help the invaders—that we'd turn on him.

(Teacher: I would! I'd fight him if I had the chance!)

(Another teacher: Well, why doesn't he just let us go away? Why doesn't he just set us free? We wouldn't fight him. We don't have any chariots or army anyway.)

It's simple, child. Where would Pharaoh get free workers if we left? Who would build all his cities for no pay, if he didn't have us slaves?

(Teacher: Well, Grandfather, what are we going to do? Isn't there any hope? If we've been here almost 400 years, isn't it time for this great God of Father Abraham and Isaac and Jacob to deliver us? I'm sick of being a slave! I'd like to beat that ugly taskmaster we have. Do I hate him!)

Peace, child. Peace. Someone tried that about 40 years ago. One of our most promising young Hebrew men tried helping us out that way. He did just what you want to do, (teacher's Hebrew name). He killed an Egyptian taskmaster who had been beating one of us. But your parents and grandparents couldn't trust this young man—who did he think he was—trying to take over things? That's how they felt.

Now I was pretty excited about him. I was young then, too. I thought, "There's a man with spunk!" Besides, he was raised right in the Pharaoh's palace. He was raised by Pharaoh's very own daughter! He'd be the perfect leader—had lots of courage, was loyal to us Hebrews, and knew what it was like to be a leader since he had lived with the king of this whole land for so many years. Yep, I thought he was our man, all right ... but, between our people not liking or not trusting him,

and Pharaoh finding out that he had killed an Egyptian, he had to flee for his life! Last we heard of him he was heading east—out into the desert of Midian.

(Teacher: What was his name, Grandfather?)

His name, (teacher's Hebrew name) Why, (awed) his name was Moses.

Well, it's getting late, children. It's time for bed. We have to be up before sunrise to get back to work. I just wonder how and when this God of Father Abraham is going to deliver us from this wretched place!

Teachers and grandparent help everyone find their sleeping mats and places. (Mats can be woven mats, thin towels or blankets; or people can just sleep on the floor.) Play plaintive Hebrew music again as transition (tape, record, or "live").

SCENE 4   Back to Work

Before sunrise, taskmaster wakes everyone abruptly, yelling "It's time for work, you lazy Hebrews!"

As you and your children work, you sing "O Come, O Come, Emmanuel."

Taskmaster grumbles about your singing so early. Then it begins to dawn. (Rooster sound effects, lights on, shades or blinds opened, etc.) Teachers grumble about having to work even before sunrise.

After about 20 minutes of hard work, the taskmaster moves towards the palace for a drink of water. Just then a Hebrew teen comes running in all excited. He has this week's DISCOVER TOGETHER in his hand. In a garbled fashion, he blurts out

11

freedom.

Verbal clues: Your goal that your class experience the lifestyle and feelings of the Hebrew slaves was met if you heard your parents and children probing for more information as the grandparent told their story, if the class chimed in on the griping, if they volunteered information and suggestions on their own. Another verbal clue would be if they were talking about what went on in class as they left the room.

AFTER CLASS CHECK

Did your class enter into their roles?

Body language clues: They entered into their roles if they participated in the work scenes without inhibition, if they "knew what to do with their hands" as they listened to the story and helped around the "campfire," if they showed sign of anger when the Egyptian taskmaster pushed them around or if they cheered and smiled at the news of coming

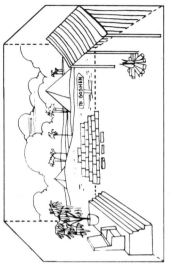

**Suggested arrangements of classroom
for this unit's classes**

13

---

that freedom is coming! All cheer in response.

By this time everyone has stopped working and has huddled around the fire to hear the news. He says that somebody named Moses has just come to Goshen and is talking about everyones 'leaving Egypt! Grandfather rejoices, "I knew it! I knew it!"

Just then the taskmaster notices that work has stopped. He rushes over, whip in hand. "What's going on here?" he yells.

"Here, take these," whispers the teen. "They're written by Egyptians, but they'll give you an idea of what's happening." He shoves the DISCOVER TOGETHER into your hand and sneaks off just in time. You put them away just as the taskmaster arrives.

END OF CLASS

Have everyone work until dismissal time. The taskmaster is more abusive than ever. But you and the grandparent encourage: "Don't give up, (person's Hebrew name), we'll be free one of these days."

When it's time for class to end, the taskmaster announces: "All right, you slaves. You'd better be back here at (9:00 a.m.) sharp next (Sunday)!" You hand out DISCOVER TOGETHERS as class leaves encouraging them to read about this Moses who's going to lead them to freedom. Be sure to collect nametags before everyone goes.

EXTRA IDEAS FOR LONGER SESSIONS:

These ideas would all fit in the evening times around the fire.

- Music: playing simple flutes, tambourines, and drums; singing minor melodies, doing a very simple circle dance; thinking up a song or chant to help in memorizing the names of the twelve tribes.
- Games:

  outside: tag; something like huckle-buckle-beanstalk, hiding a leather thong or piece of pottery; archery, tug-of-war; juggling.

  indoors: rough forms of checkers or chess; dolls; asking riddles.
- Chores: filling pails with water from another part of the building; straightening bedrolls; gathering wood for the fire.
- "School": having demonstrations by folks from your church who can do leather work, simple weaving, making pottery; giving a talk on how irrigation works (in its simplest form); demonstrating how to skin a fish "fresh from the Nile!"
- Food preparation: mixing bread dough together and baking it in the kitchen or outside and then eating it!
- Shopping: visiting a simulated market place or having a door-to-door vender come by selling bread, sandals, herbs or garments. (Some form of money or "tradable" goods would have to be given the parents and children in advance.)
- Discussion: talking about feelings toward the taskmaster—if he showed favoritism, was he fair in his treatment of slaves, what does God think about him, etc.

12

(After class check on following page)

PROBE

▶ case histories
▶ discussion questions
▶ thought provokers
▶ resources

1. We've said in many places that in working with children we need to be sensitive to five critical processes that are at the root of faith development. On Figure 43 below, evaluate each of the three models of intergenerational learning experiences described in this chapter (the house church, the intergenerational Sunday school, and the short-term intergenerational event). How would you rate each in terms of its potential to provide for free flow of the critical processes?

2. Using the teaching outline in Figure 34 as a guide, develop at least two similar plans for an intergenerational Sunday school class. Be sure that the activities you plan facilitate as much as possible the critical processes linked with faith development.

   If you are part of a class using this book as a text, why not duplicate the plans of all class members and distribute them as a resource for future use?

3. There are several sources you can use for additional help on intergenerational learning and events. Here are three.

   Duckert, Mary. *Intergenerational Experiences in Church Education.* Geneva, Ill.: Geneva Press, 1976.

   Griggs, Don and Patricia Griggs. *Generations Learning Together.* Nashville: Abingdon, 1980.

   Koehler, George E. *Learning Together: A Guide for Intergenerational Education in the Church.* Nashville: United Methodist Church Discipleship Resources, 1974.

FIGURE 43
INTERGENERATIONAL LEARNING EXPERIENCES: AN EVALUATION

	Great	Process Potential To . . .	Little
communicate belonging			
involve participation			
facilitate modeling			
provide Instruction-as-Interpretation-of-Life			
encourage choice			

PART 2

SETTINGS

The Home

The Impact of Family
Intergenerational Models
Information Models
Intervention Models
Patterns in the Home

The Church

The Church as Organism and Institution
Sunday School as Faith Community
Sunday School Curriculums

The Christian School

The Christian School Ideal
Faith Community in the Classroom

Earlier we noted that parent training approaches, whether providing information or seeking to train in skills, have proven ineffective in changing the way adults parent. This isn't surprising. As we've argued, a necessary condition for significant

INFORMATION MODELS

ministry to children through the family is parent participation in a nurturing faith community. But participation in a faith community need not rule out providing parents with information that can help.

Today most churches exist as both institution and organism. As institution, a congregation provides services to its members and others through a variety of agencies, committees, and other structures. As an organism, a congregation provides that network of close nurturing interpersonal relationships that constitutes faith community. Some churches exist only as an institution, with faith community relationships ignored or lost in the rush to provide services. Other churches exist only as organism, with the emphasis on relationships, and with service to others done not as part of a "church program."[1]

It's possible for a church to exist as both institution and organism. But it is vital for members of any local body to experience the church as organism. Both the Old and New Testaments portray faith community relationships as the necessary context for nurturing the faith of adults as well as of children. A larger church can, through a variety of small group or neighborhood structures, provide faith community experiences, although these will seldom be as dominant as the faith community experiences in forms like Shared Life Fellowship. But a larger church does have an advantage when it comes to providing services. Certainly the information services, through which parents learn how to better understand their children and how to help them, can be more easily provided in a large congregation with many resources. We can find information-providing models in both institutional and faith community settings.

CHAPTER 12

AN INSTITUTIONAL MODEL

The Broadway Church of Christ, in Lubbock, Texas, recently hired Ron Rose as Minister of Family Care. His vision, and the resources of this 2,200 member congregation, have made possible a variety of ministries directed to families.

Ron's first step in approaching family ministry was to profile the congregation. He identified the existing groups and how many persons were in each: singles, engaged, young married, new parents, parents with school-age children, dual-earner families, divorced, single parents, stepparents, grandparents, widows, widowers, and shut-ins. Following identification, Ron spent time to find out the needs that a family-oriented ministry might meet for each group. The result was a program designed

---

[1]See further discussion of this subject in Lawrence O. Richards and Clyde Hoeldtke, *A Theology of Church Leadership* (Grand Rapids: Zondervan, 1980) and Lawrence O. Richards and Gib Martin, *A Theology of Personal Ministry* (Grand Rapids: Zondervan, 1981).

FIGURE 44

FAMILY CARE PACKET²
Broadway Church of Christ

THE PROMISE OF LIFE

FAMILY CARE

SPECIAL EVENTS FOR 1980

* Marriage Encounter

(A communication weekend for good marriages)

Dates for 1980

June 6 - 8	October 3 - 5
August 1 - 3	December 5 - 7

For information call 793-2130/799-0166

* Family Strengths Seminar

(A series with Ken Dye and Tom Cunningham)

July 20	August 3
July 27	August 10

All sessions are on Sunday evenings at 6:00 p.m.

* Focus On the Family Film Series

(James Dobson, M.D.)

Sept. 3	Strong Willed Child
Sept. 10	Shaping The Will Without Breaking The Spirit
Sept. 17	Christian Fathering
Sept. 24	Preparing for Adolescence, Part I
Oct. 1	Preparing For Adolescence, Part II
Oct. 8	What Wives Wished Their Husbands Knew About Women, Part I
Oct. 15	What Wives Wished Their Husbands Knew About Women, Part II

All sessions will begin at 7:30 p.m.

L.I.F.E. SEMINARS

The Lubbock Institute of Family Enrichment (L.I.F.E.) is actually a catalogue of seminars. Each seminar, taught by qualified Broadway members, is designed to be insightful and encouraging. The seminars will be from one hour to six hours in length; some will meet over several weeks, some will be scheduled as an all day affair (Saturdays).

Several L.I.F.E. seminars may be offered during a given week. Once the schedule is announced you may enroll for these opportunities by calling the church office 763-0464.

The following list of seminar topics are set to be offered during the last half of 1980:

THE PROMISE OF LIFE

SPECIAL EVENTS FOR 1980
L.I.F.E. SEMINARS
SUPPORT GROUPS
LIBRARY & RESOURCE CENTER
COUNSELING SERVICE
PEOPLE HELPERS

FAMILY CARE

In a society of broken promises and fading dreams, we claim a promise of life that is for sure. Built on this promise the Broadway Family Life Ministry, is called **Family Care.** This **Family Care** ministry has two focuses: 1. Support - People helping people in a spirit of warmth and acceptance is at the heart of this ministry. Every person of every age has a place in **Family Care.** 2. Strength - To build strength we need exercise. Training sessions, seminars, resource materials, and other opportunities are provided to exercise our minds and build our strengths.

WHAT'S HAPPENING NOW.

Each page provided above describes a currently available dimension of our **Family Care** Ministry. As other dimensions are developed new pages will be added. Thus, we will always have a current description of what's happening in the **Family Care** Ministry.

²Ron Rose, *The Promise of Life* (Lubbock, Tex.: Broadway Church of Christ, n.d.).

- Engaged Couples Seminar
- TV: Making The Most Of It
- Stress and Life
- The Middle Years
- Relationship Development
- Finding Your Talent/Building the Skill
- Treating Depression
- Understanding The Elderly

Other seminars and repeats of these will be offered in 1981.

- Engaged Couples Seminar
- TV: Making The Most Of It
- Stress and Life
- The Middle Years
- Relationship Development
- Finding Your Talent/Building the Skill
- Treating Depression
- Understanding The Elderly

Other seminars and repeats of these will be offered in 1981.

LIBRARY & RESOURCE CENTER

Family books are among the priority selections in our church library. Dozens of informative and helpful family books are available through the church's growing library. These books may be checked out for a two week period.

Audio cassette tapes are being added to our collection of books. (Available in July, 80)

Video cassettes and a video cassette player are scheduled to be installed as soon as possible. (Available September, 80)

COUNSELING SERVICE

A Christian counseling service is provided at the Broadway building in the Family Care office. Ron Rose is coordinating this service.

Several highly trained people are involved in the operation, providing personal counseling and relationship development counseling as the need arises.

Couple counseling and parent/child counseling are available by setting up an appointment through the church office. Call 763-0464.

This service is free except for testing fees.

SUPPORT GROUPS

When the Bible speaks about loving, caring for, and encouraging one another, it's speaking of action, not words. When a crisis comes into our lives we need more than words—we need the warmth and presence of a person. This program of person-to-person support meets that need.

On an as needed basis special care groups will be formed to provide support for those going through crisis times, such as death, divorce, children leaving home, recent relocation, retirement, old age, terminal illness, etc. The leaders of these groups are especially trained in helping these people share their concerns by feeling supported by others in the group. These support groups will last six to eight weeks and will have no more than ten persons per group.

Call the church office for scheduling and enrollment 763-0464.

PEOPLE HELPERS

This program is not designed to train professional counselors, but it is designed to offer on going training in aspects of becoming a more effective listener and people helper.

Those interested will sign up through the church office - 763-0464.

This training is available for adolescents and adults, men and women.

to support persons at each stage of adult experience: a program described in the little packet shown as Figure 44.

The family care approach described in the booklet includes special events, seminars, support groups, a library and resource center, counseling services, and people-helper training designed to enable others to be more effective in listening and ministering.

Making helpful information available is one of the emphases at Broadway. One of Ron's first steps was to study books that might be helpful and to order several copies of each for the church library. (See Figure 45 for a list of these books.) The

FIGURE 45

RECOMMENDED READING ON FAMILY

Ahlem, Lloyd H.; *How to Cope*; Regal Books; 1978; $3.25

Allred, G. Hugh; *How to Strengthen Your Marriage and Family*; Brigham Young University Press; 1979; $7.95

Atlas, Stephen L; *Single Parenting: A Practical Resource Guide*; Prentice-Hall, Inc.; 1981; $5.95

Brecheen, Carl; *Whatever Happened to Mom, Dad, and the Kids*; Sweet; 1979

Bock, Lois; *Happiness is a Family Walk with God*; Revell; 1977; $4.95

Deen, Edith; *The Family in the Bible*; Harper & Row; 1978; $6.95

Dillow, Joseph C.; *Solomon on Sex*; Thomas Nelson, Inc.; 1977

Dobson, James; *The Strong Willed Child*; Tyndale House Publishers, Inc.; 1978; $7.95

Dobson, James; *What Wives Wish Their Husbands Knew About Women*; Tyndale House Publishers, Inc.; 1980; $6.95

Drescher, John M.; *If I Were Starting My Family Again*; Abingdon; 1979; $4.95

Duska, Ronald; *Moral Development*; Paulist Press; 1975; $3.95

Dyer, William G.; *Creating Closer Families*; Brigham Young University Press; 1980; $5.95

Evans, Gloria Jay; *The Wall: A Parable*; Word, Inc.; 1977; $3.50

Garrett, Yvonne; *The Newlywed Handbook*; Word, Inc.; 1981; $5.95

Gaulke, Earl H.; *You Can Have a Family Where Everybody Wins*; Concordia Publishing House; 1975

Grollman, Earl A.; *Living When A Loved One Has Died*; Beacon Press; 1977; $7.95

Grollman, Earl A.; *Talking About Death*; Beacon Press; 1976; $3.95

Hamachek, Don E.; *Encounters with the Self*: Holt, Rinehart, Winston; 1978

Hansel, Tim; *When I Relax I Feel Guilty*; David C. Cook Publishing Co.; 1979; $3.95

Hunt, Gladys; *Honey for a Child's Heart*; Zondervan Publishing House; 1974

Jensen, Larry C.; *Responsibility and Morality*; Brigham Younger University Press; 1979

Johnson, Spencer; *The Value of Curiosity*: Value Communications, Inc.; 1977; $5.95

LaHaye, Tim and Beverly; *The Act of Marriage*; Zondervan Publishing House; 1977; $3.95

Livingston, Carole; *Why Was I Adopted?*; Lyle Stuart, Inc.; 1978; $8.95

Logan, Ben; Television Awareness Training; Abingdon; 1979

McGinnis, Alan Loy; *The Friendship Factor*; Augsburg Publishing House; 1979; $2.95

Meier, Paul D.; *Christian Child-Rearing and Personality Development*; Baker Book House; 1977; $3.95

Narramore, Bruce; *Adolescence Is Not An Illness*; Fleming H. Revell Company; 1980; $8.95

Navigators, The; *Husbands and Wives—God's Design for the Family*; Navpress; 1980; $2.50

Nutt, Grady; *Family Time*; Million Dollar Round Table; 1977

Powell, John; *The Secret of Staying in Love*; Argus; 1974; $2.95

Segal, Julius; *A Child's Journey*; McGraw-Hill; 1979; $3.95

Shedd, Charlie W.; *Then God Created Grandparents and it Was Very Good*; Doubleday & Company, Inc.; 1976; $7.95

Stinnett, Nick; *Family Strengths*; University of Nebraska Press; 1980

Swindoll, Charles R.; *Home—Where Life Makes Up Its Mind*; Multnomah Press; 1979; $8.95

Taylor, Barbara J.; *Dear Mom and Dad*; Brigham Young University Press; 1978; $5.95

Thornburg, Hershel D.; *You and Your Adolescent*; H.E.L.P. Books, Inc.; 1977; $3.95

Ward, Ted; *Values Begin at Home*; Victor Books; 1979; $3.50

Welter, Paul; *How to Help a Friend;* Victor Books; 1979; $3.50

Wheat, Ed; *Intended for Pleasure;* Fleming H. Revell Company; 1977; $8.95

White, Jerry; *The Christian in Mid-Life;* Navpress; 1980; $5.95

White, John; *Eros Defiled;* Inter-Varsity Press; 1979; $4.95

White, John; *Parents in Pain;* Inter-Varsity Press; 1979; $4.95

Wright, H. Norman; *The Pillars of Marriage;* Regal Books; 1980; $3.95

Wright, H. Norman; *Preparing for Parenthood;* Regal Books; 1980; $4.95

library is not tucked away in some dusty corner at Broadway. Instead portable shelves are moved into most meeting settings, and books signed out and in before and after services. Because of the high visibility of this ministry through print, most of the books in the library are in circulation at any given time.

When a church has the resources and institutional structures to provide this kind of information and training to its members, such services can be a significant way to minister to children through the home. But, again, such services can never be a substitute for that necessary precondition: participation by parents in a truly vital faith community.

AN ORGANIC MODEL

The problem in providing parents with information is not whether or not the information is received. The problem is whether the information is used. The studies quoted in chapter 10 indicate that information-providing models—whether they use printed materials or seminars, and whether they stress facts or competency—seldom lead to a change in family lifestyle.

Facing this fact, we are forced back to the primacy of the faith community and the Deuteronomic principle that the prerequisite for reaching children is to reach the parent. You shall "love the LORD your God," Moses says to adults, so "these commandments that I give you today" will be "upon your hearts" (Deut. 6:5–6). It is *then* the parent is enabled to nurture the child.

Two illustrations highlight the significance of ministry to adults if we are to affect children. The first comes through a report by Myrna B. Shure and George Spivack. They note the failure of Parent Effectiveness Training to actually change communication patterns in the homes, but add that even in dealing with clinically disturbed children, verbal interaction patterns in homes *were* changed, "strikingly," in a completely different way.

By helping mothers of these youngsters understand and articulate their own problems and those they experienced in childbearing, Heinike (1976, 1977) found they became more available, more communicative, and more affectionate, and their children's school behavior and peer relationships significantly improved. Baldwin and Baldwin (1976, and in personal communication) found that similar counseling techniques decreased the amount of coercion imposed, increased the positive affect shown, and enhanced the quality and frequency of parent-child interaction.[3]

In other words, meeting the needs of the parents changed the way parents related to their children!

The same phenomenon is illustrated in the case of Joan, a young mother of two- and four-year-old boys. Joan took part in one of my classes for parents. These were conducted during the Sunday school hour with groups that had already built faith community relationships. The approach involved teaching to adults, on an adult level, the themes being studied at the same time by their children in the Sunday school. The expectation? That parents who began to experience the truths their children were taught would be enabled to better relate that truth in daily life to their own boys and girls.

The first sessions, held with a group of some twenty adults, were on the theme of *imago dei* . . . that we are made in the image of God. This concept was translated for children into the simple phrase, "I'm Special." This phrase was also used with adults.

The first activity in the first session was to go around the circle and have each person in the class share one thing he or she liked about himself. When we came to Joan there was a painful pause. Finally she blurted out, "I don't know anything I like about myself." The whole group shared her embarrassment for a few moments. Then someone commented, "Well, I like your smile," and we moved on around the circle. During the next four weeks together we looked into the first chapters of Genesis and, through a variety of simple activities, explored something of what it means for us to see ourselves as God sees us: special, made in His own image.

The final session of the four-week study involved going around the circle again, to share which of the key concepts studied was "most important to me," and why. When Joan's turn came, she told us that that very first session, stressing that God made us in His image, was most important. "I remember," she said quietly, "when I was ten years old. My folks were old fashioned, and didn't want any of their children to grow up like the frivolous teens they were so critical of. So whenever I'd glance in a mirror, my dad would say, 'You don't have to look in a mirror to see if you're pretty. I'll tell you when you're pretty.' And

---

[3]Myrna B. Shure and George Spivack, *Problem-Solving Techniques in Childrearing* (San Francisco: Jossey-Bass, 1978), p. 5.

he never did. That was thirty years ago. And when you asked me that question four weeks ago, I realized that there wasn't one single thing I really liked about myself."

Joan went on to tell how much it meant to her, to realize that she is special to God. She shared that in three special ways that first week God had told her that she truly was special to Him. "And you know," she concluded, "for the first time in my life, I actually like myself!"

After the session, I chatted with Joan outside the YWCA where we were meeting. She volunteered how her discovery had affected her relationship with her two boys. "I used to get so upset when they wouldn't pick up their toys, and I yelled at them a lot. My youngest was real nervous, and would never settle down for his nap. Then this month I realized I was treating my boys just like my father treated me. So I've been taking time every day to just hold each one on my lap, and tell him how special he is to God and to me. And I try not to yell. In fact, we're making a game now out of picking up toys. And you know, my youngest isn't nearly as nervous as he was, and he's actually sleeping at nap time."

Joan's story, like the research reported by Shure and Spivack, points up the critical issue. The primary need of parents is not for information about how to parent. It is for that which meets their own personal needs. We can have a greater impact on children by ministering to their parents than in any other way. But Joan's experience and the research focuses on a second issue. A supportive group setting, like that provided by a faith community, *is the most effective context through which to introduce needed information.* When information is introduced in and through the faith community setting, where that information can be discussed and personalized, that information is most likely to be *used.*

I've noted that the faith community context is one in which we can introduce information that will help parents understand and articulate their own problems. This is what happened with Joan as she discovered the great reality that she is special to God—discovered that truth as something more than an item of belief. But other kinds of information can also be introduced through faith community groups.

Look for instance at the material below, which summarizes guidelines for rearing children (see Figure 46). Material of this kind is readily available from a number of sources, on a number of vital parenting topics. Simply handed out, there is little likelihood the guidelines will be used. How then will we introduce such material through a faith community group? By asking

227

FIGURE 46
GENERAL GUIDELINES FOR EFFECTIVE
CHILD-REARING PRACTICES[4]

1. *Provide access to as much of the house as possible so that the child has the maximum opportunity to exercise his curiosity and explore his world.* The hypothesis involved is that the opportunity to explore the world around the child is basic to the nourishment of his curiosity and instrumental to the development of social relationships as a natural outcome.

2. *Provide a wide range of materials for the child to explore.* Common household objects such as plastic jars with covers, large containers filled with smaller interesting objects, a baby-proofed kitchen cabinet with pots, pans, and canned goods, are all perfectly suitable for a child between 7 and 18 months of age. The hypothesis involved is that the newly crawling child will, for several months, have a very special interest in the physical properties of small objects and the characteristics of motion they display when pushed, dropped, rolled, etc.

3. *Be available to your child for at least half of his waking hours.* Do not hover over him constantly but be available to provide attention, support, or assistance as it is needed. The hypothesis involved is that a child needs the direction provided by a more experienced person to support his curiosity, to instruct in the area of language, and to encourage the development of using and interacting with other people.

4. *Utilize the following pattern of response to the degree it is possible when your child begins to make overtures to you from age 9 or 10 months on:*
   a. Respond promptly as often as possible.
   b. Respond favorably as often as possible.
   c. Make some effort to understand what the child is trying to do.
   d. Set limits; do not give in to unreasonable requests.
   e. Provide encouragement as often as possible.
   f. Provide enthusiasm as often as possible.
   g. Provide assistance as often as possible.
   h. Use words as often as possible.
   i. Use words the child understands or words that are a little too hard for him.
   j. Provide a related idea or two.
   k. Do not prolong the episodes if a child wants to leave; the interchange will usually last less than one minute.
   l. Encourage make-believe or pretend activities.

5. *If the child seems bored, and if it is convenient, provide things for him to do.* The hypothesis involved is that substantial periods of time spent doing little of anything in the way of organized activities is, on balance, a poor sign with respect to the development of the young child.

6. *If a child is misbehaving, discipline him firmly and consistently.* The hypothesis involved is that children require that limits be set to their behavior in order to develop into socially acceptable individuals who feel comfortable with other people.

7. *Allow a child to try to do something that seems somewhat unsafe but would not be unsafe if he were closely supervised.* Give the child the chance to try the activity, under supervision, rather than stop him completely. The hypothesis involved is that if the child wants to try a new activity, it probably is a naturally interesting and a potentially beneficial one. Such activities, when encouraged, lead to better development.

In addition to the positive guidelines and related hypotheses, the following list of practices to be discouraged tends to round out our picture of an effective set of child-rearing circumstances.

1. Do not cage the child or confine him regularly for long periods during the day.

---

[4]Burton L. White with Kaban/Attanucci/Shapiro, *Experience and Environment: Major Influences on the Development of the Young Child*, Vol. 2, © 1978, pp. 157–59. Reprinted by permission of Prentice-Hall, Inc., Englewood Cliffs, N.J.

2. Do not allow him to concentrate his energies on the primary caretaker to the point where he spends most of his time following that person around or standing nearby, especially during the second year of life.

3. Do not allow tantrums.

4. Do not worry that he will not love the primary caretaker if the primary caretaker says *no* from time to time.

5. Do not try to win all the fights with him, especially from the middle of the second year on, when the baby may start becoming negative.

6. Do not try to prevent the baby from cluttering the house. It is an inevitable sign of a healthy, curious creature.

7. Do not be overprotective. Babies are more careful than people think.

8. Do not overpower the child. Let him do what he wants to do as often as possible.

9. Do not take a full-time job or otherwise make yourself unavailable. A caretaker should not take a full-time job or otherwise be largely unavailable to the baby during this period of life.

10. Do not bore the baby if it can be avoided.

11. Do not worry about when the baby learns to read, count numbers, or say the alphabet, or even if he is slow to talk as he seems to understand more and more language as he grows.

12. Do not try to force toilet training. By the time he is two or two and a half, it will happen rather easily.

13. Do not let the baby think the whole world was made just for him.

each person in a gathering of the group to read the guidelines and (1) mark the guideline that is most difficult to follow, and (2) mark the guideline that contains an idea that is helpful. Then the group members share, stimulated by the response of each to these questions. Rather than attempt to design a class and set up specific objectives that describe behavioral outcomes, we expect that needs will be different in each group. We also believe that persons present are the resources through whom ministry and help will come. Differences in attitudes, perceptions, and feelings affected in such a group process will change the way parents live with and relate to their children.

SUMMING UP

In summary, then, several kinds of information can be provided to families, in a variety of ways. The institutional programs available through a larger church can be used. And the simple, organic setting can also be utilized. In addition, we can distinguish information types. The first type of information bears directly on who the parent is as a person and seeks to affect the children by meeting the needs and touching the personality of mom and dad. The second type of information bears on how the parent acts in the home or relates to children. This second type of information, like the first, should be introduced in such a way that it will be *processed interpersonally.* The

229

question "What guideline is most difficult to follow" and subsequent sharing with others in a faith community are basic to bringing any kind of information to families in a useable way, so that it may actually be translated into family lifestyle.

PROBE

▶ *case histories*
▶ *discussion questions*
▶ *thought provokers*
▶ *resources*

1. I have suggested in this chapter several factors that need to be considered if we are to minister to children through information provided to their parents. These factors are:
   a. Mode of communication (institutional, organic)
   b. Type of information (meet parental personal needs, help to solve child-rearing problems)
   c. Processing of information (individual intellectual, or relational, processes within faith community)
   Suppose you were invited to be a consultant in the church served by Ron Rose as Minister of Family Care. Examine the ministry pattern described in Figure 44. Then prepare a written report. In your report identify the most effective elements of the church's program and least effective elements, and then suggest specific steps that might be taken to make the family care ministry even more effective next year.

2. What is a good book on family ministry? Try

   Sell, Charles. *Family Ministry: Enrichment of Family Life Through the Church.* Grand Rapids: Zondervan, 1980.

3. *Family Life Today* is an attractive magazine published by Gospel Light Publications, Inc., 2300 Knoll Drive, Ventura, CA 93003. It contains a number of family-oriented articles and special features designed to enrich parenting.

   When the magazine was first published in 1974, a highlight featured extensive plans for weekly "family night" experiences. Each family night plan was for two or two and a half hours, with study and project suggestions. The goal was to help parents train their own children, in their own homes.

   Initially the magazine was sold through bulk orders to churches. It was marketed with a special emphasis on the family night feature, which was expected to meet an often verbalized and recognized need. Initial bulk orders from churches were encouraging. A Continental Congress on the Family and heavy promotion of a variety of family-oriented books and seminars at that time made Christian leaders particularly sensitive to family issues.

But the size of the bulk orders from churches quickly dropped off. The expected impact on family life did not seem to occur. Even churches that actually shifted midweek services to homes and tried to get groups of families together to follow the family night plans in the magazine found that parents would or could not!

The family night feature was continued for some years, but was eventually dropped. And the marketing approach shifted too. The magazine is no longer sold in bulk to churches, but sold on individual subscription. The October 1981 issue, with a cover price of $1.75, contains only 44 pages.

From what we have seen in this chapter and in chapter 10, write a paper which: (a) explains why the family night material was not used, and (b) why the magazine did not fulfill the expectations of churches which purchased it in bulk. Also (c) suggest in your paper the kinds of articles and features that should be included in such a magazine. Finally, (d) predict what will happen to this magazine in the next five years.

4. This chapter mentions an *I'm Special* study involving a group of adults who have established faith community relationships. Below is on overview of the four studies (see Figures 47–50). Each features a personal Bible study (which might be completed before the class meets or during class time) and a simple discussion outline.

If a well-established group with faith community relationships exists in your congregation, why not teach this unit over a four-week period? Two weeks after completing the unit, interview parents in the group to see if their relationships with their children have been affected in any way.

FIGURE 47

I'M SPECIAL STUDY 1[5]

WEEK 1 **PERSONAL STUDY**	

Which have you tended to think of as the most "Christian" attitude:

_____ 1. As a sinner, I should be ashamed of myself.

_____ 2. I should dwell more on my weaknesses than my strengths.

_____ 3. I should love and appreciate myself.

_____ 4. I should take real joy in my strengths and good qualities.

Think about this. Jesus said, "You must love your neighbor as yourself" (Mark 12:31). Write down how much you think this means you are to love your neighbor.

_____

_____

_____

_____

_____

Look back over what you've written. Does Jesus' gentle command mean you are to view *yourself* this same way? Can you read what you've written and honestly say, "this is how I am to care for myself"?

Here are descriptions of negative feelings people often have about themselves. Check any which describe how you *often* feel about yourself.

_____ I find it hard to accept my weaknesses.

_____ I get angry with myself easily.

_____ I'm afraid to take on difficult tasks.

_____ I don't really think other people could be interested in me.

_____ I worry that God is disappointed in me.

_____ I honestly don't like myself very well.

_____ I have a hard time believing anyone who tells me about my "strengths" or good points.

If you checked several of these items, you may have a poor self-image, as did Sue of the opening story. To get rid of a poor self-image we need first to admit such negative feelings. But then we need to go on and affirm *God's* view of us as the reality.

To help you soak in this Divine viewpoint, spend some time now meditating on Ps. 139:13–18, and write down your thoughts.

_____

_____

_____

_____

_____

LESSON 1

GOD MADE ME
IN HIS OWN IMAGE

Genesis 1:26–27; 2:4–25

Discussion Guide

This week help parents share and explore their specialness as preparation for helping their children experience theirs:

1. Seat parents in a circle. Have each tell his name, and one thing he likes about himself.
2. Put study questions on the chalkboard, and divide the class into threes (separating husbands and wives) to study Gen. 2 for answers.
   a. How did God show He loved Adam?
   b. What in the passage helps us see that Adam is special?

   After 10-15 minutes, discuss discoveries.
3. Encourage discussion of the following:
   a. As Adam, you are made in God's image. How does awareness of your specialness make you feel? Why?
   b. Why do we feel about ourselves as we do?
   c. How can we help our children sense their specialness?

---

[5]*I'm Special,* Unit 1, Personal Study and Discussion Guides. © 1977, Sunday School PLUS.

FIGURE 48
I'M SPECIAL STUDY 2

WEEK 2   **PERSONAL STUDY**

Write down one thing you really like about yourself. _____

_____

_____

_____

Now, before going on, thank God that the thing you just wrote is part of you and that He, too, is pleased with you in this regard.

Gen. 2 showed how special Adam was to God in the careful preparation of Eden for him. Jesus affirms that we are *still* special to God. Read His Words in Matt. 6:25–33, and underline in your Bible any phrases which help you realize your specialness to Him.

Part of your specialness and mine is found in God's gift to us of dominion (Gen. 1:26). The psalmist grasped the wonder of his destiny and expressed it in Psalm 8.

Read this psalm now, several times, and when its meaning has soaked in, read it aloud to God as your own prayer.

Often early failures keep us from sensing our destiny of dominion. Our inadequacies may keep us from realizing that in making us for Himself, God *enables* us to serve and

please Him. List two or three areas in which you feel inadequate:

_____

_____

_____

_____

_____

_____

There are many great affirmations in the Word of God about His ability to enable us, in Christ, to recover the dominion for which man was created. Here is one to read and copy out.

Ephesians 2:10: _____

_____

_____

_____

Find and write the reference of at least two other biblical indications that God can and will help you to overcome your inadequacies.

_____

_____

- -

Discussion Guide   **LESSON 2**

GOD MADE ME
FOR HIMSELF

Genesis 1:1—2:3

This week help parents sense the *purposiveness* of their own creation.

1. Place Col. 1:16 on the chalkboard. Under it write: "I was made for Jesus, to . . ." (Go around the circle and ask each to complete the sentence). Record answers.
2. Discuss with your adults the idea of dominion (Gen. 1:26, 28), pointing out that God gave man all He created to care for (the key concept in dominion). Point out also that Jesus has ultimate dominion (Col. 1:16)—which means both *authority over* and *responsibility for* all in His care.

Because we are His, He has committed Himself to care for us.

3. Encourage discussion of:
   a. What special abilities and gifts has God given you? How can you use them to care for and enjoy His world?
   b. What childhood experiences helped you feel close to God or thankful for creation?
   c. What experiences might help our children see themselves as recipients of God's gifts?

SETTINGS

FIGURE 49

I'M SPECIAL STUDY 3

WEEK 3 **PERSONAL STUDY**

Was it usually hard (___) or easy (___) for you to obey your parents when you were a child? Write down *why* what you just checked was true in your case.

_____

_____

_____

_____

_____

_____

_____

_____

_____

_____

Which of the following words *best describe* the climate in your childhood home? Underline the one of each pair which is most accurate.

warm .... cold
loving .... unloving
accepting .... demanding
appreciating .... condemning
praiseful .... critical

What, if any, do you believe might be the relationship between the attitude toward obedience you checked above, and the "climate" terms you just circled?

_____

_____

_____

_____

_____

The Bible constantly connects *love* and *obedience*. Beside each of the following verses jot down a word or phrase which summarizes what it teaches about that relationship.

John 14:15
John 14:21
John 14:24
1 John 4:18
1 John 5:3

While we need to help our children learn to respond to us and to God because of love rather than fear, we also need to realize that *love* stimulates *love*.

.Our freedom to obey God is rooted in coming to know that He loves us—freely and fully.

So meditate for a time on 1 John 4:10–12. Respond to His wonderful love. And ask God to help your family experience that love through you.

- -

Discussion Guide **LESSON 3**

I WAS MADE TO OBEY GOD

Genesis 3

The obedience God wants is that which flows from love. It's the kind of obedience parents should strive to encourage and develop.

1. Divide into threes. Share one time as a child when obedience was particularly difficult, and why.

   Assemble. Talk about similarities or dissimilarities of experiences.

2. "Is God's desire that we obey Him from a motivation of love?"

   Give your adults nine minutes for private study of Gen. 3 to look for insights into this question.

   Discuss discoveries, listing all contributions on the chalkboard. (Also you may want to introduce John 14:15, 24, etc.)

3. a. How can we show that we love our children when we insist on obedience?
   b. Did our parents do anything that helped us want to obey? What?

FIGURE 50

I'M SPECIAL STUDY 4

WEEK 4   **PERSONAL STUDY**

Record here your responses to these two questions.

1. What is the most important thing I have learned this month?

2. How specifically have I tried to show my family members that I love them and that they are special to me, and to God?

- -

DISCUSSION GUIDE   **LESSON 4**

REVIEW

Genesis 1–3

This week both review key truths and help your parents evaluate what has been happening at home.

1. List the key truths of the past weeks on the chalkboard and ask each parent to share which seems most important to him or her . . . and why.
   - GOD MADE ME IN HIS IMAGE
   - GOD MADE ME FOR HIMSELF
   - GOD MADE ME TO OBEY HIM
2. Encourage parents to talk over what's happened in their home this month, sharing both "successes" and "problems."
3. Share prayer requests and pray together.

PART 2

SETTINGS

The Home

The Impact of Family
Intergenerational Models
Information Models
Intervention Models
Patterns in the Home

The Church

The Church as Organism and Institution
Sunday School as Faith Community
Sunday School Curriculums

The Christian School

The Christian School Ideal
Faith Community in the Classroom

Is there anything we can do in addition to linking parents with other adults in faith community relationships? And without restructuring our church or Sunday school into intergenerational groups? Is there any way we can attack the specific patterns of life within a family that hinder the development of

INTERVENTION MODELS

faith in children, and rebuild those patterns to become more of an expression of community?

Nothing can substitute for adult membership in faith community relationships with other adults. But given this, there are ways we can intervene to repattern the home.

"Intervention" is used in this chapter as a technical term, coined for a special use. An intervention is different from the broad approaches described in earlier chapters, which seek to touch each parent as a person and affect family lifestyle through a nurturing impact on the adult. Making use of intergenerational ministry and faith community groups as avenues through which to introduce information is nonspecific and assumes changes within the family system by changing the person of the parent.

Interventions, in contrast, are focused. They deal with specific, small units of behavior. Rather than dealing with the total patterns of a family's life, interventions use a series of tiny, apparently insignificant experiences to change patterns of lifestyle gradually over a long period of time.

Training events sponsored by a church for families are generally short term: they come in series of seminars or classes or films that last for six or eight weeks. Intervention approaches assume that the time span required is six or eight *years*.

Interventions expect no radical or immediate changes. Instead interventions are designed to provide a variety of simple, repeated family experiences that come in different forms time after time after time. Intervention expects to teach gradually through such experiences those new patterns of life for the family that facilitate the free flow of the processes related to faith communication.

CHAPTER **13**

It is important as we explore intervention techniques to remember that these are *ineffective when used in isolation.* As stated earlier in this section, effectiveness of *any* approach to ministering to children through the family requires adult participation in a faith community. It is only when parents are supported in their own faith development that we can expect interventions to have an impact on lifestyle.

There are many areas in which interventions can be helpful. These areas can be distinguished by the following characteristics. Intervention targets are areas (1) that are significant for faith development, (2) in which contemporary patterns of family life hinder the flow of one of the critical faith development processes, and (3) in which family experiences can be repatterned, to facilitate the flow of one of the processes. In this chapter we look at two of these target areas and illustrate what interventions can be designed to do.

Each of the interventions described in this chapter has been used in an experimental curriculum developed by the author. This curriculum linked children's Sunday school, an adult class in which parents explored on their level the same truth being explored by their children, and at-home materials for children and parents through which the Sunday teaching was carried into the home.

SHARING INNER STATES

One of the critical processes that facilitates the development of faith has been identified earlier as modeling. Modeling is that natural process through which one person identifies with another, and through imitation and other mechanisms not only learns patterns of the model's behavior but also takes on aspects of his or her personality. Jesus linked modeling with teaching when He said, "A disciple, when he is fully trained, will be like his teacher" (Luke 6:40). This helps us focus on the goal of all Christian ministry. Our goal is not to produce persons with an intellectual grasp of Christianity. Our goal is to produce persons who are growing to be more and more like Jesus. Transformation, not information, is the issue. And one of those ways in which transformation is facilitated is through modeling.

This leads us to two issues. First, children *will* model on their parents. For good or ill. Thus it is important that adults themselves be growing in their relationship with God. They need to be members of a vital faith community, and be undergoing themselves that transformation toward Christlikeness toward which they will guide their own children.

But there is more involved in modeling than the person of the parent and whether or not he or she is a good example of faith. There are factors within a family's lifestyle that either facilitate or hinder the children from modeling on their parents. We looked at seven of these factors earlier: things like close and loving relationship, opportunity to observe the model in a variety of life situations, etc. These factors affect both the ease with which the modeling takes place and, more significantly, the *accuracy of the modeling*. What the child models on will not necessarily be who the parent actually is, but who the child *perceives* the parent to be. It becomes very important then not only that a warm relationship grows between parent and child, but also that parents share what behavioral scientists call their "inner states," so the children can come to know accurately the parents' feelings, values, attitudes, and responses, as well as to hear the parents' beliefs and to observe their behaviors.

One problem is that in our culture free expression of feelings and talk about values is not encouraged. This is a particular problem with men, who typically grow up with a number of superficial relationships focused around activities (sports, hobbies, etc.), but who lack experience of more intimate relationships. In contrast women in our culture often have experiences with a girl friend or older woman in which close friendships develop and feelings and thoughts and experiences are freely shared. Yet even women do not share their inner states freely with children in the family setting. This cultural pattern, then, inhibits the free flow of a process that we have seen is important in faith development, and thus becomes a target for intervention.

What can we do as an intervention to encourage parents to communicate inner state information to their children? Especially where this kind of communication is not normal within the home, and thus may be threatening to the parents? Let's look at a number of interventions built into an experimental curriculum which was used in some five hundred churches over a period of years.

Figure 51 is an intervention designed to encourage simple sharing. It is taken from the *I'm Special* unit introduced in the previous chapter. In the first Sunday school session children were involved in a number of activities to help build an understanding of "image" as "like someone or something in some ways." Among the activities suggested for the home are two linked with pictures of parents. Each helps to broaden the understanding of "image," but more importantly, each is designed to stimulate sharing by parents about their personal feelings and experiences.

There are several things to note about this intervention. First, it is purposely nonthreatening. To simply demand that parents tell their "inner states" to their children is extremely frightening to adults, and raises all sorts of strange and fearful images. But to ask mom to tell what she remembers about the day some pictures of herself were taken is completely safe. In the same way, asking dad to tell something special that happened to him the year his picture was taken is also safe. Yet this simple intervention is significant. It does introduce into the family a king of communication that is quite lacking in many homes.

Second, note that the intervention by itself is seemingly powerless. It makes no major or long-lasting change in family lifestyle. But no great results are expected! Instead it is designed simply to be one of a number of interventions, each encouraging simple acts of sharing, that *together* and *over time*, will help build a new pattern and will actually in their use teach parents to share without ever having to explain that sharing is a goal. The unobtrusiveness as well as the simplicity and repetition of interventions are all part of their effectiveness in building into a family lifestyle those processes that facilitate faith.

God made me in His own image
GENESIS 1:26, 27

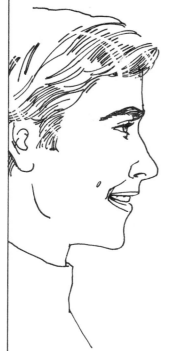

Find a picture of your father and a picture of yourself.

1. How is his picture like him?

2. How is his picture not like him today?

3. Tell your father how you two look alike.

4. Tell your father how you look different.

5. Ask your father to tell you something special that happened to him the year his picture was taken.

the quarter.

Put a quarter here

(FACE UP)

Look at yourself in a mirror.

You see an *image* of yourself.

To see if your image is exactly the same as you, write your name on a piece of paper. Hold the paper in front of a mirror.

What looks the same? What looks different?

Pictures are images. They are like you in some ways, but not like you in other ways. Only you can run. Only you can talk and think. Only you can be happy and love God and others. You are made in God's image. That means in some ways you are actually like God!

Wow! . . . Are You Ever Special!

¹*I'm Special*, Unit 1, Week 1. © 1978, Sunday School PLUS.

FIGURE 51
INTERVENTION MODEL: IMAGE[1]

I'm special because . . .

Find two pictures
of your mom.

1. How are the pictures like her?

2. How are they not like her today?

3. Ask her what she remembers about the day
they were taken.

4. Tell her how the two pictures look alike.

5. Talk about why she likes to keep pictures.

6. How is a picture an "image"?

Look at the dollar bill and

Both have the image of
the same man.

Are both images the same?
How are they different?

How can you tell they are images
of the same man when they are not
exactly alike?

Put a dollar bill here (FACE UP).

FIGURE 52
INTERVENTION MODEL: FEELINGS[2]

Family Feelings Fun

Tell your feelings!

Here's a game to play at home. Cut out the squares on page 7. On one side is an expression that "hides" a feeling.

To play the game, give each player an equal number of squares. Figure out on your own what you think the hidden feeling is and why the person feels that way. Then when it is your turn, read the "hidden feeling" statement on one of your squares. Any person in the game who can tell the feeling you thought of wins 2 points. Any person who can give the reason you thought of, why a person might have that feeling, wins 3 points.

HERE ARE SOME EXAMPLES:

Hidden Feeling Statement	Feeling	Possible Reason for the Feeling
• "Go away, I don't like you."	Hurt	Didn't ask me to the party.
• "Help! Help! Get away!"	Fear	A big dog is barking at me.
• "I don't wanna get up."	Tired	Stayed up too late last night.

[2]*God Made Me Able to Feel*, Unit 32, Week 3. © 1978, Sunday School PLUS.

"I won't go to bed. I hate you. I hate you!"	"I don't want to go to school."	"I'll never play with Joanie again. She's such a snob."	"You're really gross!"
"If you don't hurry, you'll be late."	"Don't you *ever* say that again!"	"You don't ever pick up your dirty socks!"	"Why do we have to move?"
"I don't know what to do. I just don't know what to do."	"Ooo! I just hate Miss Donaldson!"	"Our P.E. teacher plays favorites with her pet kids."	"But Chris gets 3.00 for his allowance!"
"It's no use. I'll just fail, anyway."	"I just got a 'Close Encounters' T-Shirt!"	"Turn off that television young lady!"	"I wish I could rub these freckles off!"
"O.K. But just this one time!"	"I took piano lessons, but my parents could only afford a few."	"Yech! That's gross!"	"Nobody likes me anymore."
"Go away and don't bother me!"	"I just want to curl up and die."	"Pick up your things, young man!"	"Aw, do I have to?"

There are many more illustrations of interventions designed to facilitate sharing. In the same lesson parent materials suggest the family conduct a brief Bible study at one mealtime. The study involves reading together Genesis 2:4–25, which both children and parents have already explored Sunday morning in their own classes. Family members identify what in the story helps us see that Adam was special to God. Then each member of the family is asked to share. "You are made in the image of God, too. How does knowing this make you feel?"

The key to this parent-directed intervention is that moms and dads will have had an opportunity in their adult group to interact with this passage and this truth. And they will have begun to work through its personal impact (see outline, Figure 47). With this preliminary experience, most will be prepared to make some self-revealing statement, and thus link with the Bible truth feelings on which their children can model.

Another series, on Abraham, suggested another type of intervention activity. Abraham left his home to go to a strange land. Families involved in this study were asked to pretend they, too, were called by God to move away from their home . . . that very day! Each family member was given a paper grocery sack, and five minutes. Each was to pretend he could take only whatever would fit into the sack when they moved: everything else must be left behind.

After the five-minute period, each member returns to the kitchen table with his or her sack. Each shows what was selected, and tells why each item was chosen. Then the family also talks about what was hardest to leave behind.

This process helps the family sense the faith of Abraham, who left his homeland on God's command. It also leads parents to share with their children, talking about what is important to them. In the process what is actually expressed are personal values, which apart from some such activity might never be clarified or expressed to the children.

Like the first illustration, this intervention is nonthreatening. Yet it is an effective way to stimulate the family members to express their inner states to one another.

Games provide another protected way to explore and talk about feelings. Figure 52 reproduces a game activity built into a unit of the experimental curriculum entitled *God Made Me Able to Feel*. This game is particularly helpful as a family intervention. It encourages parents as well as children to predict each other's feelings in various situations, and then to have the other person either confirm the guess or explain why he or she has a different feeling from what was expected. As one of a number of interventions focused on this aspect of the modeling target, it can make a real contribution to opening communication channels for sharing of inner states.

Interventions may be much more direct than the ones illustrated. Figure 53 is taken from a unit that explores "hard times," and uses the book and story of Job in an "associative" way. This at-home activity features a child interview of a parent or other adult: an interview technique already introduced and used during the Sunday hour. The questions the child asks do focus

FIGURE 53

INTERVENTION MODEL:
FEELINGS ABOUT CHILDHOOD[3]

An interview with

_____
(name)

by _____
(your name)

What is your name and when were you born?

_____

_____

What were some good things about your childhood?

_____

_____

_____

Do you remember any hard times when you were a child? What were they like?

_____

_____

_____

Was there ever a time when you felt God was mad at you and was punishing you?

_____

_____

_____

As a grown-up, have you ever had any tragedy or suffering? If so, what happened?

_____

_____

_____

How did you feel when the hard times came?

_____

_____

_____

Did you ever think maybe the hard times were punishment? Or your own fault?

_____

_____

_____

How did you feel about God when hard times came?

_____

_____

_____

Looking back now, can you see any reason God might have let you have the hard times? If so, what?

_____

_____

_____

[3]*UZ Gazette,* Unit 37, Week 3. © 1979, Sunday School PLUS.

quite directly on feelings. And they ask the adult to share a number of personal responses to situations in his or her childhood.

At the same time, the intervention "protects" the adult, in an interesting way. Note that the early questions focus on "when you were a child." Adults typically do not see themselves as the same person they were as a child. Thus they can talk about their child-self without it seeming to require a potentially threatening revelation of their adult-self. Interestingly, adults who are not threatened by sharing will shift from their childhood to present experiences when they reach question 4. Those who are threatened will continue to speak comfortably about their childhood. But in each case, this intervention does open the door to sharing inner states with children—information that would not normally be revealed.

Figure 54 adds one more illustration. This particular intervention is interesting because it encourages *mutual* sharing. This illustration is taken from a unit of study on the theme *God Is Victorious.* As a victor, God is able to help us and to use us, however weak we may feel. The unit uses the story of Gideon in an illustrative way as its Bible content.

Note that this intervention also uses prediction as a tool, as the child is asked to guess what mom or dad would draw to show a time one of them felt weak or uncertain. The predictive approach does more than focus the child's curiosity. It is also a technique that stimulates development of social role-taking ability. Usually well-designed interventions will perform more than one function.

Note too that in this intervention the initial sharing is to be followed by conversation. In it mom and dad and the children talk about how to deal with feelings of weakness and uncertainty, by thinking about what they will do when they feel this way.

It is relatively easy to multiply illustrations of interventions that focus on the communication of inner states. Once the basic principles underlying interventions and the nature of the processes they are designed to facilitate are understood, it is relatively easy to design interventions to link with whatever basic biblical concepts are being learned.

INSTRUCTION-AS-INTERPRETATION-OF-LIFE

This is another of the faith development processes we have identified. The key to instruction-as-interpretation-of-life is to link a Bible truth with many situations in which that truth will serve to guide our response.

FIGURE 54

INTERVENTION MODEL:
FEELINGS OF WEAKNESS
AND UNCERTAINTY[4]

Everyone feels weak and uncertain sometimes. You do. Your brothers or sisters do. Your mom and dad do.

Can you think of a time when you feel weak or uncertain? Maybe at school just before a test. Maybe in a game? Maybe meeting new people? Draw a picture of a time when you feel weak or uncertain. Then tell your parents about the picture.

What do you think your mom or dad would draw in a picture about a time one of *them* felt weak or uncertain?

Guess: _____

Then ask one of them to draw a picture of a time they felt weak or uncertain and tell you about it.

To Talk Over

1. How do people act when they feel weak or uncertain?
2. How can I be helped when I feel weak or uncertain? (Clue: Look at the binoculars on the back page!)

Ask your family to read this week's story of Gideon together (Judges 6:1–24).

    Why was Gideon threshing wheat in the winepress?
    What did God tell Gideon he was going to do?
    What did Gideon think of himself? (See verse 15.)
    What did God call Gideon? (Verse 12.)
    Why do you think God called Gideon a winner?

Now look at the way God sees you. Memorize one or both of these victory verses.

I win big through
Him who loved ME
Romans 8:37

I can do all I need to,
through Christ
who gives ME power
Philippians 4:13

How does it make you feel when
God says, "With Me, you're a winner!"

---

[4]*God Is Victorious*, Unit 31, Week 1. © 1978, Sunday School PLUS.

We have seen in earlier chapters that children lack the ability to conserve. That is, they do not adapt (respond in a situation) through the process of learning an abstract verbal concept and then applying that concept to interpret various situations and guide response. Much of children's learning is imitative, and their responses in situations are intuitive. They may make appropriate responses in a situation without ever linking their response to the concept that adults would see as guiding that response.

We've seen too that children are cognitive constructivists. This means that they often understand intuitively: that they build concepts through repeated experiences to which concept terms are linked. It becomes very important then that we try to teach children biblical concepts and realities in ways that are appropriate to how they think and how they learn.

As was pointed up in chapter 3, this is the genius of the instructional model provided in Deuteronomy 6 and 11. Teaching of God's Word was not a classroom kind of thing, where only words could be dealt with. Instead, teaching God's Word was to take place in the gettings up and lyings down and walkings along the way of family life. Simply put, the words of God were to be linked by parents with multiplied life situations, so that children's understanding of the concepts could develop in a constructivist fashion and appropriate faith-response behaviors would be linked to specific situations. God did not design this communication process to teach boys and girls abstract verbal concepts they could not comprehend or apply to changing circumstances.

Probably the concept of instruction-as-interpretation-of-life is one of the most difficult for parents. To most people in our culture, teaching and learning the Bible is a classroom/instructional kind of thing. Parents know how to conduct classes where they talk about Bible words. But it is much more difficult to see how to link Bible words with the shared experiences of family life.

How can this problem be dealt with through interventions? By recognizing the fact that one aspect of this kind of instruction is related closely to *cuing.*

The concept of cuing is quite simple. It is to arrange for a child to have a reminder—a cue—for desired actions *before* a behavior is expected. In instruction, the cue also is to be associated with the Bible truth (concept), so that the situation, the Bible truth, and the desired response will be linked for the child.

There are many ways to cue children. A parent can give verbal instructions ahead of time. A family can role-play situations they expect to come up, acting out what they will do and even predicting when such situations are most likely to occur. A particular location can be cued with a physical symbol. One can even cue by identifying a feeling that, when it comes, will bring to mind a Bible truth and appropriate response.

There are many advantages to cuing. First, cuing is a good way to link Bible truths with life. Second, cuing has the advantage of building positive behavior patterns. It helps a child do the right thing successfully, avoiding the need for correction afterward and the sense of guilt or failure this may bring. Because "discipline" means to train or disciple, *preventive* discipline that helps a child do right and avoid the wrong is always better than *punitive* discipline that punishes for doing wrong after the event.

A very helpful way to facilitate instruction-as-interpretation-of-life in a family is to use interventions that either cue children directly or involve the parents in cuing the children. By cuing effectively, we can help children identify situations in which a particular truth applies, and not only help them respond appropriately but also help them construct a more accurate intuitive concept of that truth.

One of my experimental studies focused on human nature as sinful. One of its sessions dealt with temptation and human susceptibility to do wrong. But temptations (times when we feel we want to do what we know is wrong) were not presented as wrong in themselves. In fact, our emphasis was to present temptation points as special opportunities to do right! A temptation point then can be a very good thing for us if we become stronger by choosing what is good instead of what is wrong.

Children, like adults, are familiar with temptations. Often these are linked for children with places or objects. The cookie jar in the kitchen or a brother or sister's tape collection may be a temptation point. So may the wash basin in the bathroom in a crowded home, when a child is tempted to dawdle in spite of the fact that others may need to get ready for school. So in this lesson the goal was to help children identify temptation points, and to cue them with a visible reminder of the Bible truth that points their way to right behavior. Figure 55 shows how this was done through a take-home paper.

In another unit, on *God Shows Me How to Give*, simple cues were included (see Figure 56). Time certificates were provided for children to cut out and to "spend" by giving of themselves to others. Cues may not always need to focus on behavior. Figure 57 cues by providing reminders of God's promise, "I am with you always."

FIGURE 55
CUING: TEMPTATION POINTS[5]

IN MY HOUSE

TEMPTATION PLACES

1. Connect the dots in a way that outlines the rooms in your house or apartment. Draw in furniture if you want.
2. Make a list of places you need to choose right or wrong in your house. We have started the list to give you a few ideas.

MY TEMPTATION PLACE LIST

Turn off T.V. when asked

Making my bed

Taking out the trash

3. Cut out the signs below and paste them at the places in your house where temptations are *likely* to come. Talk with your mom or dad about how you feel when you choose right.

TEMPTATION PLACE	TEMPTATION PLACE	TEMPTATION PLACE	TEMPTATION PLACE	TEMPTATION PLACE	TEMPTATION PLACE	TEMPTATION PLACE

[5]*Me, A Sinner?* Unit 35, Week 3. © 1978, Sunday School PLUS.

Interventions need not always be cues given to children. At times it is helpful to cue parents for life-linked instruction. This approach was taken in the first lesson of the "I'm Special" unit. Parents were encouraged to keep a "Special Diary," jotting down any special little things their children might say or do during the week. Friday night a dessert treat was suggested, with metal foil crowns for the children to wear while the diary entries were read, helping each child sense in a very intimate way that he or she truly is special, to mom and dad, and to God.

Parents can also be helped to cue their own children. In a unit that explored the Psalms and David's expression of his feelings to God, the activity in Figure 58 was suggested to parents for use in the family. This intervention activity cues both parents and children, and it stimulates healthy sharing.

INTRODUCING INTERVENTIONS

How can interventions be introduced into families today? In our experimental curriculum a system was used to link children's Sunday school classes, adult Sunday school classes, and take-home materials for both children and parents. Few churches have this kind of system in effect. But there are two avenues that each church *does* have through which interventions can be introduced to the home.

The first avenue is the Sunday school. Most publishers today are relatively sensitive to the significance of the home. Some even provide take-home activity suggestions. But it is more effective if someone in a department studies the children's lessons and designs an intervention that will focus, as have our illustrations, on one or more faith development processes.

It is also possible to use the Sunday morning service as an avenue through which to introduce interventions. Usually this is done through a bulletin insert, on which one or two activities like those illustrated in this chapter, are provided for all church families. The intervention activity should be linked with the topic of each Sunday's sermon, and should attempt to target that teaching on one or more of the faith development processes.

CONCLUSIONS

What can we expect from interventions like those described in this chapter? For one thing, a church that provides intervention activities regularly will itself communicate the importance of the family in ways that few churches today do. From my own research, even under the best of conditions, it seems unlikely that more than a few families will actually use the intervention ideas in their homes. Those who do will be helped significantly.

FIGURE 56
CUING: TIME CERTIFICATES[6]

These are time certificates. After you have read the Bible stories inside and thought of ways you can help people, cut out these time certificates. Put them in the wallet or checkbook you made in Sunday School.

One way we can give ourselves is by giving our time. You can "spend" these time certificates by giving them to your parents or your friends . . . along with your time.

10 MINUTES

First they gave themselves to the Lord and to us."
2 Cor. 8:5

My Time Is Yours

15 MINUTES

First they gave themselves to the Lord and to us."
2 Cor. 8:5

My Time Is Yours

20 MINUTES

First they gave themselves to the Lord and to us."
2 Cor. 8:5

My Time Is Yours

30 MINUTES

First they gave themselves to the Lord and to us."
2 Cor. 8:5

My Time Is Yours

FIGURE 57

CUING: REMINDER OF GOD'S PROMISE[7]

WHERE IS JESUS WITH ME?

Jesus is with me wherever I go.

To help you remember He's always there, cut out the figures of Jesus on page 8 and tape or glue them in the spaces below.

"I AM WITH YOU ALWAYS."

[7]*Jesus My Forever Friend*, Unit 34, Week 5. © 1978, Sunday School PLUS.

FIGURE 58
CUING: FAMILY FEELINGS INVENTORY[8]

TO DO TOGETHER

1. Let each family member share as you make a family feelings inventory.

- Things that happen at our house that we really feel good about.

- Things that happen at our house that bring feelings we don't like.

- "Don't like" feelings we can't do anything about.

- "Don't like" feelings that could be changed by doing right.

2. Feelings Map. On a large piece of paper or poster board draw the floor plan of your house or apartment. Let each child draw in the furniture in his or her own room.

Then talk together about where "don't like" feelings occur in your house (for example the kitchen counter, stocked with dirty dishes could be a family trouble spot; TV could be the place where arguments occur, etc.)

Cut out round paper circles and make faces just like the ones illustrated.

With a brad fastener or pin, attach the faces to your house-map where "don't like" feelings occur.

Next, decide together about which negative feelings cannot be helped. Which ones come because of doing wrong? How could doing right help change these feelings? Decide how you can do right in order to feel better at these trouble spots.

Put your house map in a conspicuous place. This week, as you remember to do what you think is right at each trouble spot, turn the face.

But interventions are only a part—and a relatively small part —of ministry through the home to children.

When interventions are provided along with opportunities for parents to be part of vital faith community groups, or along with intergenerational experiences, they can be a meaningful way to minister to the families who have primary responsibility for ministry to their own boys and girls.

---

[8]*Me, a Sinner?* Parent's Sharing Guide, Unit 35, p. 5. © 1979, Sunday School PLUS.

PROBE

▶ *case histories*
▶ *discussion questions*
▶ *thought provokers*
▶ *resources*

1. I have suggested in this chapter that *interventions* should focus on those processes that are vital in faith development, and should seek to pattern ways that family members relate in order to facilitate the free flow of these processes. The text gives examples of intervention, but focuses only on one aspect of the modeling process, and on the cuing dimension of instruction-as-interpretation-of-life. Interventions can and should focus also on salient features of each of the other processes, and on other aspects of the modeling and instruction processes.

   For this assignment, make a list of target areas on which you feel interventions should be focused to facilitate the five processes. Then choose one of the following projects.

   a. Select any three-lesson sequence from any primary or junior Sunday school curriculum from any publisher. Study each lesson carefully, and then design at least two intervention activities for each lesson. Hand in your activities, with a written explanation of what each is intended to do, and which process(es) each will strengthen.

   b. Develop three bulletin inserts for your church. Each insert should provide at least two intervention activities, linked with that Sunday morning's sermon. Develop one insert for three consecutive Sunday services. Hand in the inserts, along with a written outline of the sermon and an explanation of the process(es) each is intended to strengthen.

2. Figure 59 describes a proposed family resource library, each aspect of which is designed to pattern family interactions. Study the proposal and analyze each aspect of the product. Then write a paper explaining thoroughly how each product element might be most effectively used to shape faith development processes within the home.

3. In preparing the plans for the product outlined above for potential publishers, a questionnaire was given to several hundred parents from both conservative, evangelical churches and more liberal churches. Reread the description, in item 2 above, and then predict what percentage of parents from each of the two groups will check off each section of the scale beside each item on the questionnaire below. Use Figure 60.

FIGURE 59
FAMILY RESOURCE LIBRARY

A "family resource library" is available to you. It provides three 10–15 minutes "learning together" experiences each week for the whole family to participate in. Because audio tapes and special activity guides are provided, no preliminary preparation is required to lead the whole family into a fun, sharing time.

After "learning together" times there are a number of ways provided to help you build the truths taught into family life. There are projects the kids can do on their own. There are games, songs to learn, and many application ideas—ideas that fit naturally and spontaneously into the flow of family life, not in an artificial "class-like" setting. And there are full color teaching pictures, for family room and children's rooms.

The "resource library" includes monthly "learning together" units for three years, organized so you can choose the units your children need when they need them. Two keys are provided to help you choose—a Bible Truth key, showing what is taught; and a Life Need key, showing typical children's problems (fears, resisting peer pressure, etc.) that each unit deals with.

In addition to all this, there is also a special optional resource book with each unit for parents, which (1) gives complete background on the Bible truths taught in the unit, and (2) explains how each family activity helps build Christian personalities.

And, there is also an audio tape and workbook in each unit on a specific child-rearing problem, to show you how to help your child obey, to build a strong self-image, deal with public school problems, etc.

When you have completed your predictive scale, look at the actual results obtained on the author's survey (Figure 61, a and b).

What results are most surprising to you? What conclusions do you feel you could validly draw from this survey?

FIGURE 60
PREDICTIVE SCALE

PLEASE RATE each of the features described above on the continuum lines below, marking each between very attractive to me and not attractive to me.

not attractive   very attractive

1. 10-15 minute "learning together" times
2. no parental preparation
3. audio tapes and activity guides
4. "fun, sharing" times
5. projects for kids to do on their own
6. songs to learn
7. pictures for children's and family room
8. application that fits the flow of family life
9. monthly units you can choose
10. Bible Truth key to selecting units
11. Life Need key to selecting units
12. Optional Parents activity explanation
13. Optional How-to tape and workbook on child-rearing problems
14. OR Optional booklet on child-rearing problems

FIGURE 61a

CONSERVATIVE, EVANGELICAL RESPONSES

PLEASE RATE each of the features described above on the continuum lines below, marking each between very attractive to me and not attractive to me.

	not attractive				very attractive
1. 10-15 minute "learning together" times	—	2%	2%	15%	26% 55%
2. no parental preparation	12%	4%	24%	12%	24% 24%
3. audio tapes and activity guides	7%	3%	2%	13%	29% 46%
4. "fun, sharing" times	—	1%	1%	2%	32% 68%
5. projects for kids to do on their own	—	—	2%	18%	19% 61%
6. songs to learn	2%	2%	10%	24%	28% 34%
7. pictures for children's and family room	4%	4%	14%	25%	30% 23%
8. application that fits the flow of family life	—	—	—	40%	35% 61%
9. monthly units you can choose	—	—	—	13%	35% 62%
10. Bible Truth key to selecting units	—	—	—	7%	32% 61%
11. Life Need key to selecting units	—	—	2%	14%	40% 44%
12. Optional Parents activity explanation	—	2%	6%	18%	37% 31%
13. Optional How-to tape and workbook on child-rearing problems	2%	4%	2%	13%	43% 36%
14. OR Optional booklet on child-rearing problems	—	4%	4%	9%	36% 47%

FIGURE 61b
MORE LIBERAL RESPONSES

PLEASE RATE each of the features described above on the continuum lines below, marking each between very attractive to me and not attractive to me.

	not attractive				very attractive
1. 10-15 minute "learning together" times	—	2%	5%	18%	34%	41%
2. no parental preparation	10%	6%	23%	17%	23%	21%
3. audio tapes and activity guides	5%	6%	9%	19%	30%	31%
4. "fun, sharing" times	—	2%	1%	2%	40%	55%
5. projects for kids to do on their own	2%	4%	5%	17%	28%	44%
6. songs to learn	3%	8%	15%	28%	24%	22%
7. pictures for children's and family room	8%	13%	16%	24%	26%	13%
8. application that fits the flow of family life	—	3%	4%	9%	34%	50%
9. monthly units you can choose	1%	2%	8%	17%	33%	39%
10. Bible Truth key to selecting units	1%	7%	6%	22%	32%	32%
11. Life Need key to selecting units	3%	3%	6%	18%	35%	25%
12. Optional Parents activity explanation	—	4%	9%	26%	36%	25%
13. Optional How-to tape and workbook on child-rearing problems	3%	5%	16%	22%	37%	25%
14. OR Optional booklet on child-rearing problems	—	4%	10%	20%	30%	36%

262

PART 2

SETTINGS

The Home

The Impact of Family
Intergenerational Models
Information Models
Intervention Models
Patterns in the Home

The Church

The Church as Organism and Institution
Sunday School as Faith Community
Sunday School Curriculums

The Christian School

The Christian School Ideal
Faith Community in the Classroom

It's always difficult to think or to speak of an ideal. It's also dangerous. It is too easy for people to fall into the trap of visualizing some ideal standard . . . some "perfect family life" . . . and then feeling guilty when they fall short. Or angry when a mate fails to live up to expectations.

PATTERNS IN THE HOME

The fact is, no individual or family comes close to perfection. All of us, as imperfect human beings, struggle, fall short, constantly stand in need of grace, and must rely on forgiveness for our many failures. We trust in God's boundless goodness as the real ground of hope that our children will come to faith.

It's a dilemma. I want to be careful not to even suggest there is an ideal. Yet it would be inadequate to complete this section on ministry to the family without giving some picture of those patterns of family life that nurture faith. It is especially important because our examination of technologies—of intergenerational experiences, of information processing, and interventions—provides no clear images of the family lifestyle they are intended to encourage. We need some image of the goal: some impression of the flow of family life through which the growth of every family member in faith is effected.

Actually, talk of technologies is likely to subtly distort the real issues in nurture. We Americans are tragically susceptible as a people to projects: to "doing things" as the way to solve any problem. But in nurture of children in faith, the heart of the matter is the simple, spontaneous methods a family develops for loving and sharing as they grow, together, from a child's birth on toward maturity. So in this chapter I want to portray the simple things—to communicate a feeling for experiences that are so natural a part of living together that we seldom if ever identify them as "teaching" or as "nurturing."

In picturing patterns of life together in families I'm forced to draw on experiences with my own children, simply because these are the experiences that are available to me. And because those child-rearing years are now past, and I can look back with more understanding than I had then. At the time of this writing Paul is 25, the father of his own one year old. Joy, who was brain-damaged at birth, is 21 and the resident of a wonderful home in Kentucky, where she has lived for the last seven years. Tim, 19, is a freshman at Michigan State University in East Lansing, Michigan.

As I share recollections, I do not intend to suggest that our family life was ideal. In fact, as we lived through those years my wife and I were deeply aware of many failings. But looking back I can identify many positive things that, at the time, I did not really understand. Only now can I see the significance of some of the things we did spontaneously that were undoubtedly used by God to help our children grow, as persons and in their relationship with God.

COMMUNICATING BELONGING

I have many images of events I link with warmth and belonging. Most of them are associated with the children's bedtimes. As the children came along, each was given a special half hour time before going to bed. There were favorite songs we sang, sitting together on the bed as one child or the other lay wrapped in blankets. There were take-home pictures from Sunday school, changed weekly, slipped into a picture frame and hung on the wall beside the bed. Often we talked about the picture and the heroes of faith they portrayed. We talked too about the day: what had happened at school, unhappiness over a spat with a friend. When Paul was in first and second grade his favorite picture was an older classic, picturing Jesus watching over a sailor who struggled to hold the wheel in a stormy sea. We had a tiny night light that illuminated the picture. If it was turned so Paul couldn't see it, he'd call one of us. Nestled down under the covers, peering out from the pillow that half-covered his head, Paul wanted the picture placed where he could see it when the windows shuddered in the rain or the dark seemed to creep close.

In those days it was just a special time for us to share. Only later did I begin to realize how important it is to link the songs and symbols of faith with those moments in which love and belonging seem most strong.

Belonging was communicated in many other ways as well. There was something special about shared family vacations, spent traveling in the West. We sang then, too. And played twenty questions and license plate poker. One of our favorite games cast me in the role of story teller as I invented wild explanations for the names of the states and cities we passed through. And invented new Paul Bunyan tales to explain each geographical feature. We played together barefoot in the streams of Utah, and the children shrieked with laughter when the current pulled me, flopping, off my feet. We sat in the afternoon stillness of Zion national park. After reading one of the Old Testament's great nature psalms, we wrote a psalm of our own to record our experience and express our own feelings of awe. Each one contributed. We composed the psalm together.

Sports have always been a vital symbol of belonging in our family, particularly with the boys. When they were young we played Jarts in the back yard, tossing the oversized darts across the grass at plastic circles laid on the lawn. I remember noting how frustrated Paul became when he was unable to beat me at the game. Somehow beating dad, or at least not being beaten, seemed important to a first grader. So we changed the game. We still kept score. But our goal was to see how many points we could earn together, and whether we could beat our previous high.

When Paul was in third grade we began with football in the front yard. Through junior high school, fall afternoons were devoted to daily games of offense/defense (four downs to pass our way across the yard to a touchdown), with teams made up of neighborhood children. Dad had the enviable position of passer for both teams. Spring was baseball, with a wiffle ball and bat and an ugly hole in the front grass as testimony to the batter's box. Later basketball became our game. Through high school and college (and today) an hour or two pickup game at a nearby park or gym is part of the daily schedule.

Fishing trips were part of belonging, too, and were always timed to take the boys out of school for a spring and fall boat camping expedition. The links forged through all these times were never "worked at." They were forged because we liked to be together. Somehow, we just belonged.

INVOLVING PARTICIPATION

My strongest image of participation is of one painful night in Illinois. We'd just begun a family Bible time, which was a more or less frequent evening event. Paul was in eighth grade at the time. That night he was also in rebellion.

After a time of sullen noncommunication, he finally expressed his feelings about our times with the Bible. "You and mom are always taking aim at me," he complained. Somehow he had grown to feel that whatever we were reading and talking about was focused like some unanswerable criticism, demanding more than he was ready to give and piling up guilty frustration. It was true that usually Paul was the focus of our remarks. We assumed we knew more than he did, and therefore that he was the prime learner in our evening sessions.

That night, after apologizing for making him feel things I had never intended, I began to realize that my approach to family devotional times was theologically faulty. I had been building our family times on an unexpressed assumption: that as father, I was like the Old Testament priest, responsible for the instruction of the others. Somehow I had been selected out as a special individual, responsible to keep the door from God to my family open, and to keep the door to God ajar as well. The problem was I had not remembered that the priesthood underwent a dramatic change with the death and resurrection of Jesus. Rather than being the position of the few, a single strand of a single family (Aaron's line from Levi) all of God's people have been inducted into the priesthood! In Christ a kingdom of priests is established, and every individual is given with the Holy Spirit gifts that enable him or her to minister to others. My approach to family devotions had robbed my children of their heritage: participation in priestly ministry within the family.

After that event many things changed. We still had our times with the Bible and prayer. But instead of telling what I knew, I began to find ways to help the children look into the Bible themselves, and share what they found as ministry to the others. One of our first times after this event was with the Book of Proverbs. We would each read a chapter, and I simply gave a focus sentence for each chapter's search.

- Underline something in this chapter that dad needs to apply.
- Find something in this chapter that will encourage mom.
- Find something in this chapter that Tim is doing well.
- What in this chapter seems hardest for you to actually do?

After each of us had read, including Tim who was then a third grader, we had a chance to share our thoughts and discoveries with each other. Each person in the family functioned as a priest, ministering through correction, reproof, encouragement, exhortation, affirmation, and praise. The whole tone of our faith experiences was changed. Now each member of the family truly participated, as members who exercised priesthood, in those times in which we as a family expressed our faith.

Family experiences associated with holidays bring another image of participation. When Easter time came we planned such adventures as midnight sessions in an empty room of our house that we pretended was a catacomb. We read stories of the early Christians and talked about how important Jesus' resurrection must have seemed for them to be willing to suffer the threat of death and give up all they owned to hide in dark caverns rather than be untrue to the Lord. In the flickering light of a single candle, the faith of the early Christians seemed very real.

Christmas too was a special time. Each year when advent began we started a late night ritual, made special by being long after the children's regular bedtime. Each night we lit another candle placed around a manger scene we constructed each year from plaster of paris. One year we linked the candle lighting with Christmas music and ages old passages of Scripture promising the Savior's coming. The first nights were songs of longing, like the minor key "Oh Come, Oh Come, Emmanuel." And the passages were ancient, filled with longing and promise as well. As Christmas Eve approached the songs changed, and became more joyful, and the passages were taken from the prophets who sensed the joy God held in store. Then on Christmas Eve the celebration culminated with our youngest reading Luke's report of Jesus' birth. All the candles blazed, and we sang carols of unmixed joy.

FACILITATING MODELING

Everything I've already shared in these remembered images is intimately linked with modeling. The closeness, the sharing, the games together, the trips, the talk, the singing, and everything else that falls under the other categories to come, are linked with modeling. Time together. Caring. Sharing. Listening. All these are deeply rooted in the way we live our lives with, rather than around, our children.

My dominant image here is of an experiment I conducted at the Wheaton Christian Grammar School, which my son Paul attended through the eighth grade. I was exploring the children's attitude toward (sense of relationship with) God, and had established two hypotheses. First, that these children from Christian families and churches in a Christian school would have common beliefs and knowledge about God. And second, that these children would have widely different attitudes toward God. A corollary of the second hypothesis was that whatever sense of relationship was found in a given child, it could be traced to some factor in his or her family life.

A simple twenty-item test about God established that the thirty-five children in this class shared common beliefs about God. Several linked projective tests clearly indicated nine had a clear sense of close and personal relationship with God, and that five had a negative attitude toward God, feeling alienated and distant from him. A third set of tests analyzed such things as discipline and devotions and other things that, it's been suggested, are linked to the development of faith in children. Strikingly, none of these factors could be correlated with children's attitudes toward God. But just as strikingly, *one* factor did have a positive correlation to both positive and negative attitudes. Those children who believed that God was real to their parents had a sense of personal relationship with Him. Those children who sensed that God was not real to their parents saw Him as a person who was "a tradition," who "is hardly ever talked about," and who just "doesn't matter."

Somehow the parents' faith was caught, and even those who had all the right information about God and could score perfect papers on a test about what He is like did not feel they knew Him unless they sensed that somehow God was real to mom and dad.

I can't say how encouraging it was . . . and what a relief . . . to find Paul among the nine to whom God seemed both close and real.[1]

---

[1]For a complete discussion of this study, see Lawrence O. Richards, *Youth Ministry* (Grand Rapids: Zondervan, 1972), pp. 187–200.

PROVIDING INSTRUCTION-AS-INTERPRETATION-OF-LIFE

The images here blend. I think of the two daughters of a missionary family in a "Christian Home" course I taught at Wheaton College, and their memories of being reminded by a Bible verse every time they fell short of mom's or dad's standards. I remember how hard they said it was, even as graduate students, to overcome the feelings of condemnation that often came when they read the Bible. The parents had used instruction as a club. The Bible's words were associated with failure, and the damage inflicted robbed their children of the warmth and loving tone in which God speaks through His Word. In contrast, the images I remember from our family are not linked to any formal study or mention of the Word.

One of the first images is of driving with four-year-old Paul to church one Sunday morning in Dallas. Paul had been bad, and looking at him out of the corner of my eye I could see he was still troubled and unhappy about being a "bad boy." I remember on that ride talking with Paul about forgiveness. We had all been bad. But God loved us all, and Jesus loved us. Jesus loved us so much He even came to earth to die for our sins. It wasn't good to be bad. But when a person was bad, it was so good to know that Jesus still loved him. And, like dad, would love him always, no matter what. I'm sure that Paul never grasped the meaning of Christ's death or understood salvation then. But God did touch his life at that moment. The pain was washed away by the experience of my forgiveness that he sensed was real, and he trusted me enough to believe my promise that God loved him still.

Paul taught us too. A few months later Paul felt a sudden pain when he tried to go to the bathroom. His bladder filled, but some obstruction brought a piercing agony when he stood straining in the bathroom. After the third try, in tears, Paul asked us to pray it would go away. Both my wife and I hesitated, frightened of the prospect that this might be one of the times God would say, "No," and worried Paul wouldn't understand. But he begged again as the tears streamed down, and so we did pray, with a hint of desperation. We need not have feared. Paul had enough faith for both of us adults, and immediately his bladder emptied and relief came. It was a minor miracle to us. To Paul it was only what he had expected from God.

A few years later another project emerged from our practice of reading missionary stories together as a bedtime treat. We had read of an early missionary to Africa and Paul seemed intrigued. So we decided to develop a family "filmstrip" telling the story. We bought a long roll of white paper, and Paul listed the scenes that should be shown to tell the story well. Then he marked off the paper strip, and sketched the pictures, which he filled in with crayon. With the list of the pictures in his hand he walked up and down in front of my desk, dictating the story to go with each scene. I typed the script as he dictated it, and then he read his script into a tape recorder, while I marked each shift of pictures with a ringing bell. An opening was cut in a cardboard box, two long dowel sticks inserted in the paper roll, and the missionary tale was visualized . . . written, narrated, and illustrated by Paul.

I read with Tim too, up into his teen years. I remember his tears in sixth grade when he finished the Narnia series, that were quieted only when we talked about going back again, to relive the adventures with our fantasy friends. We read Johnny Cash's biography, *Man in Black,* and talked about the experiences he shared and the way God worked in his life. When Tim was in eighth grade he became curious about Revelation and could only be satisfied by a series of nights during which we read through the Bible book and a commentary on it by John Walvoord. And always reading generated talk and questions and the sharing of thoughts.

When my mother died I took young Paul, who had been close to his grandparents, to the funeral. He sat quiet through the day and night before the funeral, and wide eyed through my funeral message. It wasn't until that night he cried. And I sat beside him and hugged him and told him that I cried too, but that I had brought him along just so he could cry, and realize that in our sorrow we were also glad for grandma, who was now with the Lord she loved.

And I have an image of a dark night in Arizona. We'd gone up into the mountains to the upper Verde river, to ride down it on a raft and camp each night in its isolated canyon. Then on the third day we found no good place to camp, and pushed on until it was finally too dark. The canyon walls had finally fallen away, receding into the dark, and the river was turning sluggish. We came to one descending run of white water, and as Paul and I let the raft down by rope, Tim crouched in the twelve-foot rubber boat while clouds of bats flurried around his head. Then, somehow, we lost the channel and found ourselves in sullen backwaters, up to our knees in muck as we struggled to drag the raft back to find the current again. Finally the moon came out, and we could see! It was still dangerous there on the river. And we were still lost. But we thanked God for the moon, and for the light He'd given to help us on our way.

All these images blend with others. Like the Christmas ritual of counting the loose change that always found its way into jars, to be sent as our own birthday gift to Jesus to someone in need. Whenever I think of what God may have used to shape the faith of Paul and Joy and Tim, it is these things, not formal times or church sermons, that come to mind. It wasn't formal. And it wasn't regular, set aside as a daily duty of study and command. What it was was simply informal instruction, coming spontaneously and not as often as some would like, as an interpretation of the way we lived our life.

ENCOURAGING CHOICE

There are many images associated with choice, even though as a concept this process may be more difficult to describe. I remember Paul's first allowance. It was only a quarter. But it was enough to drive him excitedly to the corner store, to spend it all on penny candy and other perishables. So one morning as we drove to school I talked with him about what he might want to do with his money. We talked about presents he might want to buy when birthdays came, and about setting aside some of his money to give in church on Sundays.

Paul listened sullenly, clearly feeling that somehow I was about to rob him of the little he received. We sat for a moment in front of his school before I drove on the few blocks to my college. Finally he said, "Well, is a dime enough?"

It was then I explained that I had no amounts of money in mind, and that if he decided to spend it all and save or give nothing, that was all right with me. When I gave it to him it was his money, and I had no right to control it any more. My only reason for bringing it up was to help him think of some things he might not have thought of earlier. But he was free then to decide, and he never needed to worry that I would be unhappy or critical whatever decision he made.

Paul did think about it. And he decided he needed to save some for more important things than candy, and he needed some money for presents, and he needed some for the Lord. He also explained that since he had all these needs, twenty-five cents a week wasn't enough! Paul was right. He got a much larger allowance. And he set up a series of little boxes in his bedroom into which he divided his money when he received it each week.

Another image is of a sleazy green shirt that caught Paul's eye in grade school. He begged his mother for it, and she wisely bought it for him. The first time it was washed, it fell apart. Paul was crushed. Then Marla sat down and showed him the shoddy stitching and poor materials, and talked about what to look for when it was time to buy clothes. Before long Paul was choosing his own clothes. Wisely.

Even discipline was easily cast in the framework of choice. When we moved into our home in Illinois, before either of the incidents I've just mentioned took place, all three kids were wildly excited. They ran in and out of the house time after time, always forgetting to close the door. It wouldn't have mattered except that their mother has allergies, and our filtration system designed to remove pollens and dust did not work well with open doors. After many reminders I finally got out our ping pong paddle. That paddle had had little use, but when it was necessary to spank, the flat side made a maximum of noise with plenty of sting and yet no real damage. I got the kids together, and explained. "I know you don't want to harm your mother, and it's not on purpose you forget and leave the door open when you go out and in. But it does hurt her. So I want to help you remember. I'm going to put the ping pong paddle here by the door. The first time you forget, and leave it open, you get one spank. The second time, you get two. The third time, three.

"Now, I'm not doing this to punish you. I know you really want to remember, and do what's best for mom. This paddle is just to help you remember to do what I know you really want to." The paddle was placed by the door. And never used. It had helped them remember. And helped them choose to do what they really did want to do all the time.

I think the most gratifying image I have of choice is one that reminds me of Tim. He's the youngest, and is what we might call a vehement personality. He doesn't back down. He stands up loudly for his rights. Since his mom is also a vehement personality, there were times when battles erupted, and usually it wasn't a matter of one or the other being entirely to blame. Correction was always hard for Tim, and after a verbal battle he often retreated furiously to his room.

Time had to pass before anyone could talk about it with Tim. And then it was necessary to listen, sometimes for as much as an hour, to his own angry feelings and perception of how he had been mistreated. Then and only then could we talk about what he had said and done in his own heat. Of course it wasn't all his fault. Often he had just complaints. But he could face the part that had been his fault and accept responsibility for his actions.

I remember his angry promises, "I *won't* apologize." And I remember helping him think through what he might do. He might insist on his own rights, and stay hurt and angry inside. Or he could accept responsibility for his wrong actions, and apologize. It was hard for Tim. But never once can I remember a time when Tim failed to make the right choice, and take the first step toward reconciliation.

SUMMING UP

The images I've shared are positive ones. Not because there were no imperfections or weaknesses. But simply because these are images I have of life with the children. And these are images that I've come to see have meaning for nurture: a meaning I did not understand as we lived through those experiences together.

God graciously covers over our mistakes, and He works through us as we struggle to work out the meaning of faith in our own lives and in our families. Where there is a love that communicates belonging, a respect that invites participation, a sharing that facilitates modeling, common activities that demand Christian interpretation of life, and a trust that encourages responsible choice, *there* is a relational context in which faith can be born, and grow, and flower.

PROBE

▶ case histories
▶ discussion questions
▶ thought provokers
▶ resources

1. Write your own report of "images" from your childhood, organizing them into the five processes that communicate faith. These images may be positive or negative. It is only important that they be what actually comes to mind when you use the categories to stimulate recall.

   When you have finished writing up your images, do a thoughtful paragraph or two summing up what you learned in writing them.

   If this is a class study, try exchanging papers with another student, reading, and then sharing with each other your impressions of what you have each read.

2. In researching what behavioral scientists and educators have to say about the development of children, I've run across the following poem in at least seven different texts. What is your evaluation of its thesis? What does it suggest to you as a person concerned that children have faith?

   CHILDREN LEARN WHAT THEY LIVE

   If a child lives with criticism,
   He learns to condemn.
   If a child lives with hostility,
   He learns to fight.

274

If a child lives with ridicule,
   He learns to be shy.
If a child lives with shame,
   He learns to feel guilty.
If a child lives with tolerance,
   He learns to be pliable.
If a child lives with encouragement,
   He learns confidence.

If a child lives with praise,
   He learns to appreciate.
If a child lives with fairness,
   He learns justice.
If a child lives with security,
   He learns to have faith.
If a child lives with approval,
   He learns to like himself.
If a child lives with acceptance and friendship,
   He learns to find love in the world.

Dorothy Law Nolte

3. One of the most common assumptions of parents is that if one gives children household chores this will help them develop a sense of responsibility. Interestingly, research debunks this notion. In fact, "there is little evidence that the routine tasks, such as washing dishes, caring for pets, house cleaning, preparation of foods, repairing about the house, are associated with an attitude of responsibility."[2] How *would* you expect children to be helped to develop a sense of responsibility?

4. Many, many studies have been done, and books written, about the impact of different styles of discipline on children's development. Both permissive and harsh modes of discipline have been criticized for negative results. A number of Christian writers have also propounded various theories of child discipline, ranging from the use of natural consequences to strong action taken by parents to break children's sinful will.

    Look at three discipline studies in either behavioral science literature or books on discipline by Christian writers. Write a report on how the theories relate to the thesis of this book: that the critical issue in nurture is linked to the free flow of the five critical processes that have been identified here.

---

[2]William J. Meyer, ed., *Readings in the Psychology of Childhood and Adolescence* (Waltham, Mass.: Blaisdell, 1976), pp. 350ff.

PART 2

SETTINGS

The Home

The Impact of Family
Intergenerational Models
Information Models
Intervention Models
Patterns in the Home

The Church

The Church as Organism and Institution
Sunday School as Faith Community
Sunday School Curriculums

The Christian School

The Christian School Ideal
Faith Community in the Classroom

The contemporary church is both organism and institution. As organism, the body of Christ is people in relationship, loving and ministering. As institution, the congregation is people organized to accomplish tasks. Our problem in ministry with

THE CHURCH AS ORGANISM AND INSTITUTION

children arises when the patterns of one identity conflict with the other. All too often in children's ministry, the dynamics of the institution choke out faith community.

Reading the New Testament we meet the church as a living organism. We discover the body of Christ, the family of one Father. On page after page we come in touch with a ministering, loving people, who build intimate relationships with other members of the unique faith community formed by Jesus Christ.

Opening a contemporary book on organization and administration of the church—or on children's ministries—we confront the institution. We read there of boards and committees, of objectives and agencies, of recruitment and training and job descriptions and the proper use of buildings. Suddenly we're aware that something more than the simple organism of the first century is in view. So we must approach ministry to children within the structures and forms of the complex institution we know today as the local church.

It would be foolish to yearn for a return to the simplicity of the first century. For some, like the group that meets with the Wakefields, the house church of that era may be a valid option. But for most, unshakable traditions lock us into the church of today, which is institution as well as organism. Yet it would also be foolish to settle for institution. It would be foolish not to understand both organism and institution, and to guard ministry to children. Wherever a local congregation touches boys and girls, *there* a true and vital expression of faith community must exist. So we need to review what is involved in the church as organism, and in the congregation as institution.

THE CHURCH AS ORGANISM

Two dominant images are used in the New Testament to affirm basic truths about the nature of the church. God's faith community is said to be the body of Christ and the family of God. Each of these images examines the same reality from slightly different perspective. Each has a slightly different emphasis. The underlying reality is this: The church must be understood as people in relationship with God and one another. The two perspectives are that our relationship is with Christ and with the Father. The two emphases are that our relationship with one another is a ministering relationship, and a loving relationship.

The Body

As a body, the church is understood to be people in intimate relationship with Jesus Christ. He is the living head of the body, and we are member-cells of a living entity. We see the impact of

279

this image when we notice several significant features of each New Testament passage where the body is a dominating image (Romans 12, 1 Corinthians 12–14, Ephesians).

In each of these passages *spiritual gifts* are emphasized. The New Testament affirms that each believer is given a special endowment by the Holy Spirit. Because of this grace gift, he or she can minister to others and build others up. Thus each person in the body is spiritually significant. Each has his or her own God-given ability to help others grow in faith.

In each of these passages, *growth* is understood to be the goal of these personal ministries. Like the cells of any living body, each believer is vital in building up fellow members of the body of Christ. In fact, as a member of the body, each is to function "so that the body of Christ may be built up until we all reach unity in the faith and in the knowledge of the Son of God and become mature, attaining to the whole measure of the fullness of Christ" (Eph. 4:12–13).

In these passages, *love relationships* are emphasized. Hostility and alienation have been abolished in Christ, who unites us in the one body and brings the promise of peace (Eph. 2:14–18). Unity is now ours to experience as we are knit together by what Romans calls a "sincere" love, by being "devoted to one another in brotherly love" (12:10). Love is what 1 Corinthians identifies as the "most excellent way" (12:31).

The body is a reality. Because of Jesus we are united to Him and to one another. Because we are so linked, we have God-given ability to minister. But the link is experienced and the ministry free to flow only when mutual love creates a context within which spiritual service is rendered to one another.

The Family

As a family, the church is understood to be people in relationship with God the Father. This relationship with God is the basis for our brother-sister link with one another. Paul puts it clearly in Ephesians, writing of "the Father, from whom his whole family in heaven and on earth derives its name" (Eph. 3:14). In the first century, "name" was a most significant concept. Then "name" did not simply point out an individual or thing. "Name" made a statement about identity. To speak of the believing community deriving its name as family from the Father is a strong affirmation that we *are* family, that this identity of ours derives from God's own identity as Father.

Paul suggests that as family, "rooted and established in love," we are at last able to experience "together with all the saints" something that cannot be understood. In family we are able to "grasp how wide and long and high and deep is the love of Christ, and to know this love that surpasses knowledge—that you may be filled to the measure of all the fullness of God" (Eph. 3:17–19).

Here, as always, the image of family is linked with love. We are to experience love together. As we love, we are somehow enabled to experience what cannot be understood: the love of God. No wonder then the brothers and sisters who comprise this family are constantly challenged to love one another, fervently and from the heart. No wonder John cries out that "God is love," and "whoever lives in love lives in God" (1 John 4:16).

The passages where the image of family dominates do not stress ministry as such. But they do stress love. They make it clear that only love and intimacy and caring are appropriate when we understand the nature of the church as the family of the living God.

The Organic as a Context of Ministry

When the New Testament speaks of teaching and other ministries, it does so in the context of that organic relationship affirmed through images of the church as body and family. Always ministry is understood to be an interpersonal transaction. Always the relational climate of love is assumed.

There is no hint in the organic world of the New Testament of the formal classroom or of culturally defined "teacher" roles. Instead there is simply the warmth of closeness. There is the impact of life on life, as faith and the great truths of the faith are shared from person to person. In fact, for those of us who think only in institutional terms, the biblical descriptions of ministry in the organic context seem strangely emptied of the concerns that many find so important. We can gain insight into teaching in the organic context by exploring two passages of Scripture in which a teaching ministry is described. This is important, as we begin to focus particularly on that premier agency of the church's ministry to children, the Sunday school.

1 THESSALONIANS 2

In Paul's first letter to one dynamic young first-century church, he recalls teaching the believers in Thessalonica. Chapter 1 makes it clear that Paul's teaching was a ministry of the Word of God. He recalls how the word of the gospel came to pagans (1:5, 9), was welcomed (1:6), and then as faith grew "the Lord's message rang out" (1:8). Paul's ministry was a teaching ministry. And it was effective. Through the message the Apostle brought, a transforming faith was introduced into Thessalonica. Not only did individuals turn to Christ, but the new community became a living channel through whom the message of salvation was shared with others.

It seems important then to understand the dynamics of such an effective ministry. What does Paul himself emphasize as he remembers his ministry among them? And what does Paul seem to want them to remember? The answer is found in chapter 2, in which Paul focuses on the relational context of his ministry of the Word. To explain, Paul is driven to a common image: the image of family. His words, as he remembers his ministry with this faith community, are laden with warmth, glowing with remembered love.

"We were gentle among you," Paul recalls, "like a mother caring for her little children" (2:7). He then continues, "We loved you so much we were delighted to share with you not only the gospel of God but our lives as well, because you had become so dear to us" (2:8).

Paul refers to his readers as brothers (2:9), and then adds the image of a father with adolescents. "You know that we dealt with each of you as a father deals with his own children, encouraging, comforting, and urging you to live lives worthy of God" (2:11–12).

In this brief passage we catch a glimpse of the intimacy of apostolic ministry: an intimacy we may lose sight of when we envision Paul teaching, evangelizing, writing, traveling, zealously eager to bring the message of Jesus to the whole known world. Yet it is this busiest and most motivated of men who takes time to deal "with each of you." It is this man burning with the vision of a world waiting to be won who pauses to be gentle, and lingers to build ties through which a little congregation can "become so dear." How do we explain the phenomenon? Very simply. Paul understands the church as an organism. He knows that it is in the context and the climate of love that ministry flows. He sees the necessary harmony between loving people and building the kingdom of God. And he refuses to separate the teaching of God's Word from loving interpersonal relationships, knowing that only where both are present in a living way can a vital faith community be formed.

TITUS 2

This passage is distinctive for its unexpected picture of the teaching practiced in the context of the New Testament organic church. There are many words used in the passage that help us sense the breadth of meaning of "teaching" in the New Testament. It is not simply passing on information, as in the schooling/instructional sense, but instead integrating content into life, through involvement of the teacher with the taught. The passage is reproduced here (Figure 62) with boxes around the words and phrases describing New Testament teaching.

FIGURE 62
TITUS 2 (RSV)

But as for you, ⟨teach⟩ what befits sound doctrine. ²⟨Bid⟩ the older men be temperate, serious, sensible, sound in faith, in love, and in steadfastness. ³⟨Bid⟩ the older women likewise to be reverent in behavior, not to be slanderers of slaves or drink; they are to ⟨teach what is good,⟩ ⁴and so ⟨train⟩ the young women to love their husbands and children, ⁵to be sensible, chaste, domestic, kind, and submissive to their husbands, that the word of God may not be discredited. ⁶Likewise, ⟨urge⟩ the younger men to control themselves. ⟨⁷Show yourself in all respects a model⟩ of good deeds, and in your ⟨teaching⟩ show integrity, gravity, ⁸and sound speech that cannot be censured, so that an opponent may be put to shame, having nothing evil to say of us. ⁹⟨Bid⟩ slaves to be submissive to their masters and to give satisfaction in every respect; they are not to be refractory, ¹⁰nor to pilfer, but to show entire and true fidelity, so that in everything they may adorn the doctrine of God our Savior.

¹¹For the grace of God has appeared for the salvation of all men, ¹²⟨training⟩ us to renounce irreligion and worldly passions, and to live sober, upright, and godly lives in this world, ¹³awaiting our blessed hope, the appearing of the glory of our great God and Savior Jesus Christ, ¹⁴who gave himself for us to redeem us from all iniquity and to purify for himself a people of his own who are zealous for good deeds.

¹⁵⟨Declare⟩ these things; ⟨exhort⟩ and ⟨reprove⟩ with all authority. Let no one disregard you.

"Teach what befits sound doctrine": the Greek is *lalei ha prepei tē hygiainousē didaskalia.* "Teach" is *laleō,* "to speak, or to express oneself." In transitive uses it means "to assert, proclaim, communicate."

What is to be communicated here? Not "sound doctrine" itself, but what befits or is in harmony with sound doctrine. The teaching ministry of Titus involves holding up a lifestyle that is in harmony with the revealed truths that comprise the content of our faith.

"Bid the older men be. . . ." There is no separate word for "bid" in the Greek. The construction uses the verb *to be (einai)* both in verse 2 and in verse 10. This is a common usage, which here not only describes what Titus is to teach but also implies the imperative communication of the need to adopt the special lifestyle required.

"Teach what is good." The term *kalodidaskalous* is used only here in the New Testament. It is composed of two words, *kalos* ("good") and *didaskaleō* ("teach"). The older women are to be regularly involved in teaching or instructing the younger women.

"Train the young women." The Greek verb here is *sōphronizō*. It means "to encourage, advise, urge." In secular and classical Greek, it implied the teaching of morality, good judgment, and moderation. It was in effect advice focused on personal moral improvement.

"Urge the younger men." The Greek verb is *parakaleō* which means "to encourage or exhort." Close personal involvement with personal exhortation and encouragement to adopt a godly lifestyle is in view here.

283

"Show yourself in all respects a model" *(Seauton parechomenos typon)*. The teacher is to make himself visible to others as a model. "Model" is *typon*, which is not only a "visible impression," but "a pattern or example to follow."

"Teaching" in verse 7 is *didaskalia*, "the act of instruction."

"Training us" (v. 12) is *paideuousa*. This word is related to the bringing up and guidance or education of a child. We can view it as giving parental guidance and daily correction to bring a youth to maturity.

"Declare" in verse 15 is again *laleō*, "to speak."

"Exhort" is again *parakaleō*.

Finally, "reprove" in the last verse of the chapter is *elenchō*, which means "to bring to light, expose," and, in this context, "to point out, convince, reproving if necessary to convict."[1]

The picture of teaching that emerges is fascinating, for it turns our attention away from what we think of as "education" to the fashioning of a lifestyle of faith. Truth is a reality, to be experienced by God's people. So the "content" of the teaching enjoined here by Paul is not sound doctrine itself, but is the temperateness, soundness in faith, love, honesty, caring for husbands and children, self-control and submissiveness that "befit" sound doctrine. Teaching is not just a classroom affair that involves instruction, but is life-sharing interaction. It is love, guidance, encouragement, modeling an example of godliness that will help others live their lives in harmony with the divine revelation. As a process, the "teaching" of the New Testament is much closer to what is understood as socialization than to that schooling/instructional phenomenon, education. The significant differences between the two systems are illustrated in Figure 63.

Summing Up

In the New Testament we're taught to look at the church as an organism—as a living body, a loving family. In these images we find bold statement of our identity as a faith community formed by and around Jesus Christ. In these images we learn that we are one with many brothers and sisters, linked by our shared relationship with God the Father and called to live out that relationship in love.

When we adopt the perspective of the organic, we find relationships given the highest priorities. Ministry is understood to be an interpersonal transaction, taking place in a climate rich with love. Even "teaching" is an intimate venture, calling us to share our lives with others, motivated by a growing love for persons who, as we know them better, become very dear.

---

[1]Lawrence O. Richards and Clyde Hoeldtke, *A Theology of Church Leadership* (Grand Rapids: Zondervan, 1980), pp. 130–31.

FIGURE 63

CONTRASTS IN LEARNING
IN ARTIFICIAL AND IN REAL SITUATIONS[2]

ARTIFICIAL SITUATIONS (Schooling, Education)		REAL SITUATIONS (Socializaton)	
Psychological factors in schooling model		**Psychological factors in socialization model**	
atomic:	Response desired is to learn specific content (perception) and be able to restate it.	organic:	Response desired is integration of specific content (perception) into life pattern.
	Perception learned is not associated with motives and feelings.		Perception is learned in association with motives and feelings.
isolated:	Content learned is not integrated with present experience.	integral:	Content learned is immediately integrated with present experience.
	Content learned is not immediately useful.		Content learned is in useful and useable form.
	Content learned is not related to adequacy or competency of individual to live successfully in his culture.		Content learned is directly related to adequacy and competence of individual to live successfully in his culture.
Characteristics of schooling/ educational model		**Characteristics of socialization/ educational model**	
place:	special place and time, apart from the sphere of life in which the learner lives, set aside for learning	place:	in the normal processes and experiences of daily life (nonformal setting, close association with others in the social group)
teacher:	viewed as one who "knows" and passes on knowledge	teacher:	a person (or persons) who shares the situation and is viewed as a model who lives the content
content:	organized logically, with system imposed by the things being taught	content:	organized by applicability to the life situation in which it is taught
learning:	demonstrated by the ability of the learner to accurately repeat the content communicated	learning:	demonstrated by the ability of the learner to live a life appropriate to the content (beliefs) taught

---

[2]Ibid., p. 129. This material is a tabulation of material in Meyer Fortes, "Social and Psychological Aspects of Education in Tailand," in *From Child to Adult: Studies in the Anthropology of Education*, ed. John Middleton (Garden City, N.Y.: Natural History, 1970), p. 38.

The church as an organism is presented in Scripture as a dynamic entity. Here, in the relationships built within the faith community, we all grow, maturing toward Jesus' fullness together. Here we learn together to live lives that are worthy of God, in full harmony with sound doctrine. As we explore the church as organism, we come to the conviction that we will discover the heart and soul of ministry in a network of faith community relationships where love and acceptance meet.

To fashion effective ministry to children through the church, we must understand the nature of the church as an organism.

THE CHURCH AS INSTITUTION

We must understand the church as organism if we are to fashion an effective ministry with children. But it is just as true that we must live with the congregation as an institution. In the contemporary congregation we find boards and committees, objectives and agencies, recruitment and training and job descriptions. Here we find curriculums and departments and superintendents and secretaries, and all those structures that seem to be so important in carrying out a ministry with children.

We can best understand the church as an institution by looking at issues raised in what is probably the present standard work, *Childhood Education in the Church*, edited by Roy B. Zuck and Robert E. Clark.[3] In chapters covering the administration of children's work, Ruth C. Haycock looks at "Church Agencies for Children" and Robert E. Clark examines "Leadership and Materials." Their language and the issues they discuss orient us to the local church as an institution.

Agencies

Haycock points out that the institutional church tends to approach ministry by establishing agencies, through whose programs various needs will be met. There are a number of agencies created by the institutional church to serve children. Among them are the Sunday school ("to teach the Word of God in order that lives may be changed," p. 316), children's church ("to provide meaningful worship for children," p. 317), training hour (to learn "how to live the Christian life and gain . . . experience in carrying responsibility," p. 318), released time classes ("to highlight the significant nature of religion," p. 319), weekday clubs (to "reach many children and homes for the Lord," p. 320),

---

[3]Roy B. Zuck and Robert E. Clark, eds., *Childhood Education in the Church* (Chicago: Moody, 1975).

and Vacation Bible School (to provide "time for concentrated Bible study and varied activities," p. 321).

The activities of these agencies have to be coordinated. Generally a board or committee of Christian education is formed for this purpose. "Such a board usually includes the head of each educational agency, the pastor or director of Christian education, a representative from the church board, and sometimes a member elected from the church at large. It often meets monthly to recommend or set policy, approve personnel and curriculum, and coordinate the educational program in general" (p. 323).

The controlling nature of this supervisory board is illustrated in the following list of its specific responsibilities:

> Prepare a list of needs in the children's division.
> Write realistic goals which can be accomplished within specified times.
> Give guidance in organizing, administering, and supervising the departments.
> Correlate the work of the departments and agencies.
> Provide a balanced program in instruction, worship, fellowship, and expression-service.
> Seek to improve specific activities in music, worship, memorization, recreation, and teaching-learning.
> Publicize and promote the work of the children's division.
> Discover, enlist, and provide training for workers with children.
> Suggest and recommend curriculum for use in the children's division.
> Develop wholesome human relations and build a cooperative team spirit among the workers.
> Evaluate the work of the children's division periodically.

In addition Ruth C. Haycock suggests that the committee responsible for children's work should "study pupils' needs and then determine which agency should accept specific responsibility for which needs. Some overlapping is unavoidable and probably desirable, but a clear understanding of agency objectives provides for leaders a basis for selecting materials and activities and makes evaluation and progress possible" (p. 325).[4]

When a local congregation has a full set of agencies (see Figure 64), the task of staffing and coordinating is indeed a formidable one.

Leadership and Materials

In this context Robert E. Clark, a co-editor of the *Childhood Education in the Church* text, describes institutional leadership and materials for children's ministry. Leadership is essential, for "someone must be responsible for planning, organizing, di-

---

[4]Ruth C. Haycock, "Church Agencies for Children," from *Childhood Education in the Church* by Roy B. Zuck and Robert E. Clark. Copyright 1975. Moody Press, Moody Bible Institute of Chicago. Used by permission.

FIGURE 64
CHILDREN'S AGENCIES IN A
LOCAL CONGREGATION[5]

Level	Sunday School	Children's Church	Training Hour	Vacation Bible School	Weekday Bible Classes	Released-Time Classes	Activity Clubs
Birth to age 2	Cradle roll	Nursery (baby care)	Church nursery if adult training hour meets	Nursery for children of workers			
Ages 2 and 3	Nursery or two and threes	Nursery church	Church nursery if adult training hour meets	Nursery			
Ages 4 and 5	Four and fives	Kindergarten church	Kindergarten training hour	Kindergarten	Preschool classes	Kindergarten	
Grades 1, 2, 3	Primary	Primary church	Primary training hour	Primary	Grades 1 to 6 often together in one club in each neighborhood	Grade 1 / Grade 2 / Grade 3	Primary
Grades 4, 5, 6	Junior	Junior church	Junior training hour	Junior		Grade 4 / Grade 5 / Grade 6	Junior

[5]Ibid., p. 324.

recting, and making decisions" (pp. 335–36). In the same sense, organization provides the necessary framework for accomplishing the tasks or mission of those involved in children's ministry, and "involves the order or arrangement of people or activities and the relationships which exist between people or things" (p. 340). To accomplish the work, administration—planning, organizing, staffing, directing, coordinating, reporting, and budgeting—must be carried out. These activities will be most effectively achieved under the following circumstances:

1. Every worker needs a clear, written description of his position.
2. Lines of authority must be clearly established.
3. Responsibilities must be delegated and accountability should be expected.
4. Significant policies and procedures need to be written out.
5. Every problem must be solved at the level where it ought to be solved.
6. The plans of the workers and of the leaders must be integrated.
7. Lines of communication must be kept open in effective administration (p. 341).[6]

In following through, Clark provides the following job description for a teacher, first in the form of general responsibilities shared by all workers, and then listing the specific responsibility of a teacher in an agency like the Sunday school (see Figure 65).

Expectations

The material quoted in this section accurately reflects the issues dealt with in the Zuck and Clark text, and in most texts on children's work in the local church. The language is the language of the institution. And the issues are the issues that seem important from an institutional perspective.

It's clear from this text as from others that the writers and workers in our churches have praiseworthy goals. They want to see the children who participate in children's agencies reached for Christ. They want to see children grow toward Christian maturity. Yet as I look over their prescription for local church ministry, I'm troubled by a strange unease and forced to ask a number of disconcerting questions.

Is all this institutional machinery really necessary, when each of the agencies the machinery supports actually provides just *one hour of contact* between children and adults a week? Is all the energy and the time required to meet in committee, to develop job descriptions, to choose curriculums, to train and

---

[6]Robert E. Clark, "Leadership and Materials," from *Childhood Education in the Church* by Roy B. Zuck and Robert E. Clark. Copyright 1975. Moody Press, Moody Bible Institute of Chicago. Used by permission.

FIGURE 65
TEACHER JOB DESCRIPTION[7]

General Responsibilities of Personnel

Be regular in attendance and on time for presession activities.

Be well prepared and flexible to change plans if necessary.

Take care of routine matters efficiently.

Supervise and have control of their own area of responsibility.

Enroll in training opportunities provided by the church and other sources.

Follow up present and absent pupils.

Attend all workers' conferences and other meetings scheduled for workers.

Know how to lead pupils to Christ and guide them in Christian growth.

Provide social activities.

Participate actively in the program whether it is the opening worship, lesson, presession, or other activity.

Be alert for new ideas, be creative, and use variety.

Use teaching tools provided.

Correlate activities with other workers, agencies, and departments.

supervise and resolve problems, really going to make a difference in the lives of the children who gather in the church?

Another nagging question is whether the organizational and administrative energy expended is translated into what happens at the point of meeting. Does it make a difference in the quality of a single individual class? Or is most of the energy devoted to maintaining the institutional machinery itself, rather than enriching the learning environment?

Our dominant concern, however, is the fact that in all the lists and statements of responsibility, *the language of organism has been lost*! Where is the focus on a context of love? Where are the tender tones of family imagery: the wondering affirmation that you have "become so dear to us," and that "as a father deals with his own children" we reach out to touch, to encourage, to comfort and urge "each of you"? How is it that in the job description of a teacher we can read a phrase like "keeps his room and equipment in good order and reports needed repairs," yet never find a hint of shares "not only the gospel of God but our lives as well"?

This may seem like a minor complaint. It is, however, the very heart of the issue. *A failure to give clear stated priority to what has priority in Scripture is a symptom of our loss of understanding of the nature of the body of Christ and the*

---

[7]Ibid., pp. 349–51.

dynamic of a faith community. When job descriptions—those statements of just what is expected from a person who accepts a role in an agency—make no mention of the processes through which faith is formed and nurtured, and fail to reflect the warm tone of love ever present in the Scriptures, there is evidence that the institution has crowded out the organism. When this occurs, what happens at the point of ministry will be tragically distorted.

The church as we know it will continue to exist as organism and as institution. But in any given congregation, *one perspective or the other will dominate.* Either the institutional elements of congregational life will support the organic, and shape faith community experiences at the point of ministry, or institutional concerns will drain the local congregation of its vitality, while agencies become places where information about Christianity is provided, and faith ignored.

SUNDAY SCHOOL: ORGANISM OR INSTITUTION

When anyone speaks of the church's ministry to children, the first thought is always of Sunday school. This is the primary agency of ministry to children in all churches, the one agency in many. Because of the primacy of Sunday school, it's appropriate in this section to concentrate on this one agency and treat it as a model for other agency settings. What we learn about the Sunday school can be applied to any other agency.

The Sunday school is selected for study for another reason. This is the agency into which the most church energy is poured, for which the widest range of curriculum and resources are available, and for which the most organizational structures exist. It is appropriate then to focus on this agency, and to see what can be done to encourage development of the Sunday school as a place of faith community ministry.

Sunday School Today

As we begin an exploration of the Sunday school, several things need to be said. First, in many churches and in many Sunday school classes, the organic situation described in the New Testament does exist. There are teachers who love, and who build faith community relationships that nurture faith. Despite the many obvious disadvantages imposed by limited time, the Sunday school hour can be, and in many instances is, a significant time of ministry. We can thank God for the many loving teachers who share with and care for the boys and girls whose lives they touch in the Sunday schools of our churches.

Second, we need to face the fact that in many other churches

291

and in many more classes, the organic situation does not exist. Teachers adopt the cultural role rather than the biblical. The processes used in the classrooms transmit information, and actually work against the nurturance of faith. We need to be deeply concerned about such classes, and work in every way possible to build toward a faith community ministry.

Third, it is important to realize when we explore the Sunday school, the primary agency of ministry to children by the local church, we are *not* suggesting changes in a "successful" institution. The current state of the Sunday school is *not* healthy, by any criteria.

We can sense the problems by looking at statistics. Measured by numbers, the Sunday school is reaching fewer and fewer boys and girls. It shows a steady decline in enrollment over the past twenty years, a decline that cannot be linked with the decline in the number of children in the general population (see Figure 66). When we use the statistics provided by the 1970 and 1980 yearbooks of American and Canadian churches, we see a striking drop in Sunday school enrollment. Often Sunday school attendance has declined even when church membership has in-

FIGURE 66
SUNDAY SCHOOL ATTENDANCE

1950–1981

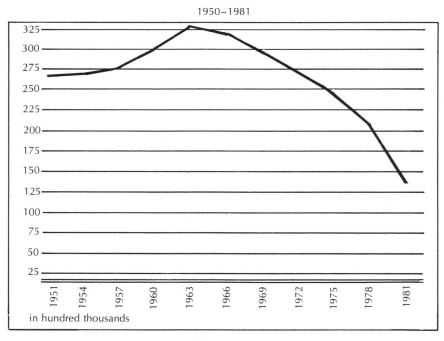

in hundred thousands

FIGURE 67
TEN YEARS OF GROWTH AND DECLINE[8]
Figures compiled from Yearbooks of American and Canadian Churches.

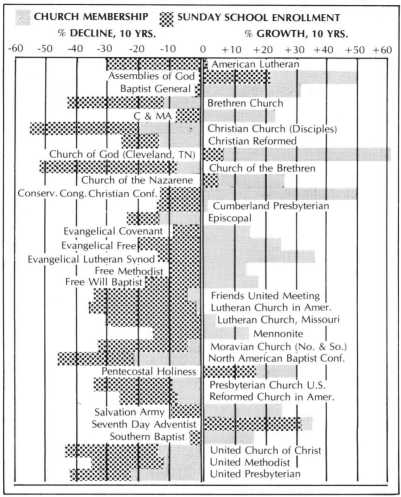

creased! Only among Seventh Day Adventists has Sunday school growth paralleled an over 40 percent growth in church membership. Whatever the statistics may mean, they make it clear that in taking a hard look at the Sunday school we are not in any way threatening a healthy, burgeoning institution, whose "success" sets it above criticism. Instead the statistics suggest we need to take a hard look at the Sunday school, for it is *not* successful.

---

[8]Figures compiled from Yearbooks of American and Canadian Churches.

A chart showing growth/decline by groups indicates just how serious the situation actually is (see Figure 67).

There are many other indicators that, in most churches, Sunday school is perceived in an institutional rather than organic way. I know of no one editing Sunday school materials who believes the prepared curriculum is used as intended. One young publishing house, which I recently served as a consultant in development of a new curriculum line, later reported they were not able to use the lesson designs they *knew* were best. The constituency rejected them and insisted on material patterned on paper-pencil, cognitive learning activities. Those processes that had been designed for faith community development were rejected as inappropriate to the church's images of the task of the "school."

There are other simple indicators. Ask children to name three friends. Almost never will those who go to Sunday school name others in their class, unless they are also known at home or in school. This is understandable. But it is still telling evidence that most classes are *not* relational settings like those described in the New Testament as ministry settings. Even fewer children will name their teachers as friends, although with training on how to function as a faith community, some 50 percent of a Sunday school class will identify a teacher as friend within six months!

Ask teachers to talk about teaching. Ask them to list their responsibilities as a teacher in Sunday school. Will they respond by listing such items as we noted in Figure 65, or will they use the New Testament language of the organism? Ask teachers to write down the names of each child in their class, and then to write beside each name three things they know about him or her. How many of the things they list will reflect that "each of you" kind of intimate knowledge reflected in Paul's letters to the Thessalonians and to Titus? Or ask teachers to describe what they remember of the last workers' meeting they attended: simply to list what was talked about or covered. Then read their paragraphs, and see if the thrust of the meeting was institutional or organic.

These, and many other things, are indicators of what is really happening in a Sunday school. In some schools a true faith community experience will be revealed. In all too many, what will be revealed is the sterile experience of an institutional Christianity that is orthodox in content, but powerless to communicate the reality of the love of God, or to provide a context for the growth of faith.

PROBE

▶ *case histories*
▶ *discussion questions*
▶ *thought provokers*
▶ *resources*

1. The orientation to institutionalism or organism is not only seen in the expectations of believers within a local congregation. It is also reflected in the training given by Bible Colleges and Seminaries. Below are course descriptions taken from two different schools that train Christian leaders for local church ministry (see Figure 68). In each case these are the *only* courses listed that specifically relate to children's ministry, and *all* the courses listed. Looking at these course descriptions, what conclusions can you validly draw? Think in terms of the graduates, the constituencies of the schools, as well as the school itself, the professors, and the students.

FIGURE 68
COURSE DESCRIPTIONS

SCHOOL 1	SCHOOL 2
Religious Education 133	**CE 510 Moral Development Through Christian Education**
One Semester, Three Credits	*Three hours*
Sunday School administration. Characteristics of various age groups and how to teach them. D.V.B.S. How to carry on a Sunday School census. Salvation for children—how to effect it. Study of Sunday School literature and how to write literature. Center of Interest projects.	Examination of evidences touching the development of moral sense and judgment in relation to cognitive and biological growth, with in-depth attention to Jean Piaget and Lawrence Kohlberg. Human development, conscience formation, and the theological concerns related to original sin, sinfulness, salvation, and nurture are brought to bear on the ministries essential to communicating distinctive Christian values from one generation to the next.
Storytelling, 349	
One Semester, Two Credits	**CE 622. The Church Ministry to Children.**
Purposes. How to select stories. Story plan. Selecting according to need and age group. Simple stories. The voice.	*Two hours*
Storytelling, 350	Understanding the nature and needs of early childhood with special attention given to ways of nurturing and enriching the moral and spiritual development of the child. Examination of the relationship of human development to the goals of Christian education for the child.
One Semester, Two Credits	
Use of word pictures. Active verbs. Facial animation. Jesus' use of stories. Active participation in storytelling.	

2. In this chapter I have suggested that the contemporary church is both organism and institution. Since dismantling the institution is not a live option, it becomes extremely important that institutional

machinery serve and enhance the organic dimension of the true church, which brings vitality to a faith community.

Look at the description of the organism given on pages 279–86. How might you revise the descriptions of the institutional machinery described in Zuck and Clark to support rather than distort the organic perspective?

Specifically, set out:
a. composition and duties of a board of Christian education (see p. 287)
b. role of leaders and administrators (see p. 289)
c. job descriptions for workers and teachers (see Figure 65)

3. The dual existence of the congregation as the church, the body of Christ, and as an institution in contemporary society puts many things in tension. It opens up the possibility that a given congregation may be functioning organically, as the church, or it may be functioning as a religious institution, with the dynamic of vital faith community crowded out and lost. A true faith community may have all the typical institutional machinery in place, and actually be functioning in a faith community way. How can we tell if a particular congregation functions as a faith community in the nurture of children, or not? Figure 69 is an evaluation guide, designed to help explore the perceptions of persons in children's ministry in the local church and to help identify observable behaviors that are indicators of institutional or organic orientation.

This evaluation guide is designed only to help you gather information. *It purposely does not tell you how to evaluate the information you gather.* It can be used in a class project for a thorough examination of a given congregation's ministry with children through the Sunday school. Or it can be used by leaders in a local church to explore the dynamics of their own children's ministry.

Here is how to use the guide.
a. Study each evaluation procedure and *decide beforehand* what kinds of responses will indicate organic/faith community qualities, and what kinds of responses will indicate institutional, schooling/instructional qualities.
b. Predict the kinds of responses you expect to get. Make your predictions as detailed as possible, and write a brief paragraph telling why you expect the results you project.
c. Follow through on as many of the following administration procedures as possible, and gather the data.
d. Work with others to check the data against your predictions. Pay particular attention to unexpected results.
e. Summarize the information gathered by each procedure, and in one paragraph interpret the relationship between the organic and institutional in this particular congregation.

FIGURE 69
EVALUATION PROCEDURES

Procedure One: Board/committee/council

1. In one paragraph, describe your board's responsibilities.
2. List the major contributions your own service on this board makes to ministry with children.
3. List as many things as you can recall that you have dealt with on this board in your last three meetings.
4. Complete the following:
   a. I feel competent to . . .
   b. My board role is most satisfying when . . .
   c. My board role is least satsifying when . . .
   d. My primary criticism of our ministry to children is . . .
   e. I think teachers in our Sunday school . . .
   f. I want the children in our Sunday school to . . .
   g. To improve our Sunday school we need to . . .
5. It may be that your function as a board member involves you with others at times other than board meetings. If so, write a one-paragraph description of the occasion and content of three such meetings with others, giving the approximate date of each contact.
6. List three words that you believe describe you, in your role as a member of this board.

Procedure Two: Teachers/department superintendents

1. In one paragraph, describe your responsibilities as a teacher.
2. List the major contribution you make as a teacher/superintendent.
3. List the names of the children you teach.
4. Write beside the name of each child you just listed three things that you know about him or her.
5. Complete the following:
   a. I feel good as a teacher about . . .
   b. I sometimes feel uncomfortable that . . .
   c. I think I am successful when . . .
   d. I wish I had time to . . .
   e. The children I teach are generally . . .
   f. The most important thing in teaching is . . .
   g. I want the children I teach to . . .
6. It may be that you sometimes meet with other teachers or staff besides Sunday morning. If this is so, write a one-paragraph description of the occasion and content of two such meetings, giving the approximate date of each.
7. What three words best describe your relationship with the children you teach?
8. What three words best describe your relationship with other teachers in your department/ Sunday school?

Procedure Three: Children who attend Sunday school (may be asked orally)

1. List the first names of three friends.
2. Tell me about the friends. Where do you meet them?
3. Draw a picture of what you like best about Sunday school.
4. Tell me about the picture.
5. Who is your Sunday school teacher most like?
   a. a parent
   b. a school teacher
   c. a friend
   d. a stranger
6. Tell me two things you know about your teacher.
7. Tell me two things you know about another person in your Sunday school class.
8. How do you feel when it's time to come to Sunday school?

PART 2

SETTINGS

The Home

The Impact of Family
Intergenerational Models
Information Models
Intervention Models
Patterns in the Home

The Church

The Church as Organism and Institution
Sunday School as Faith Community
Sunday School Curriculums

The Christian School

The Christian School Ideal
Faith Community in the Classroom

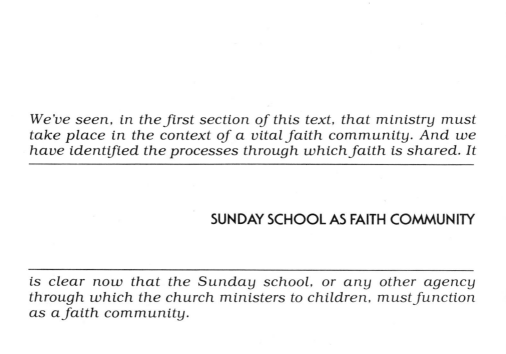

We've seen, in the first section of this text, that ministry must take place in the context of a vital faith community. And we have identified the processes through which faith is shared. It

SUNDAY SCHOOL AS FAITH COMMUNITY

is clear now that the Sunday school, or any other agency through which the church ministers to children, must function as a faith community.

Local congregations took on institutional characteristics for a very good reason. Congregations have a series of problems to solve if ministry to children is to be carried on through their agencies. To resolve these problems, leaders look within the culture for tools to use. It is only natural to adopt the tools of business management and organization that have proven so successful in America in resolving problems apparently similar to those in the church. Today the structure of a well-run congregation often can hardly be distinguished from the structure of a successful business.

There is only one problem. The church is different from other aggregations of human beings. The church is called by God to be body and family. The secret of the dynamic of Christ's church is not found in its organization, but in the transforming power of God operating through relationships within the faith community. Unlike a business, the mission of the church is not to produce a product, but to *be* the people of God!

Unfortunately, those institutional tools that work so well to produce products do not necessarily facilitate the development of a faith community. In fact, the priorities and relationships that are functional in running an institution will often push aside the priorities of the church as organism, and distort its functioning as a faith community.

The tensions that originally drove churches to institutional forms, however, still exist. There are problems that must be resolved. There are teachers to recruit and train. There are decisions to be made, and decisional processes to establish. So we must organize and administer. The challenge is *to do all these necessary things in ways that will promote the fullest possible expression of faith community at every level, and particularly at the point of ministry!*

In this chapter we want to look at how to approach the operation of a Sunday school so that the nature of the church is guarded, and so that ministry will take place in the context of faith community. Keys to building a ministering community will be discovered as we explore servanthood as an alternative to supervision, building of teaching teams, and forming learning groups.

SUPERVISION VERSUS SERVANTHOOD

Among every people there are leaders. This is just as true within the body of Christ as in any other group of human beings. What is important to understand, however, is that distinctive "body leadership" is different in a faith community from that in other organizations. The New Testament speaks of leadership in Christian community in a distinctive way, evoking the image of *servanthood.*

As servants, leaders in the body of Christ are called to equip others for their ministering work. They are not called to control the work of God, for Jesus is still living "head over everything for the church, which is his body" (Eph. 1:22–23). Leaders are to help others in the body learn how to solve their own problems under the headship of Jesus.

The servant leaders in Christ's body have authority. But it is not the right to command of the secular ruler. Instead the authority of servant leaders is rooted in relationship with Jesus, and involves a Spirit-given ability for building up rather than pulling down (2 Cor. 10:8). Rather than placing himself above others in the faith community, the servant leader in Jesus' church lifts others up, helping them accept that responsibility that is so significant a part of spiritual maturity.

The servanthood of the New Testament stands in contrast to the role given leaders in institutional structures. There, leaders are responsible for planning, organizing, directing, and making decisions. This control function of leaders is reflected in organizational charts, which typically show a pyramid structure meant to represent lines of authority and responsibility. Clearly here leaders are "over" other members of the body. In this structure too the leaders have ultimate responsibility for what happens in an agency, and all recognize the fact that they in effect "own" it. Control remains in the hand of leaders, and whether they exercise that control graciously or autocratically, all understand that it is their right and their role to control.

There are many implications hidden within each approach to leadership, which cannot be examined here.[1] It is enough now to make clear that in this chapter we look at leadership from the perspective of servanthood, convinced that the institutional role is denied to us by Christ Himself (Matt. 20:24–28). Only a servant approach to leadership can facilitate development of a vital faith community.

Adopting principles of servant leadership, how can we administer the Sunday school to build a vital faith community?

Charting Organic Organization

The institutional structure is typically charted as a pyramid. This form is appropriate. It accurately represents the relation-

---

[1]These implications, as well as how to lead as servants, are discussed at length in Lawrence O. Richards and Clyde Hoeldtke, *A Theology of Church Leadership* (Grand Rapids: Zondervan, 1981).

ships between people within that type of organization. It shows the lines of authority and responsibility, and implies all those functions ascribed by Clark to leaders. Everything that "over" and "under" suggest can be seen at a glance.

It is important that our charting of organic organization just as clearly imply what is intended by servant leadership. So our first step will be to *turn the normal structure upside down.* Our second step will be to represent relationships at the point of ministry in circular form. (See Figure 70.) This charting approach immediately indicates several significant changes in our concept of leadership and in the way we expect people to function. It also implies a new set of processes by which we expect decisions to be made and problems resolved.

FIGURE 70
TWO ORGANIZATIONAL CHARTS

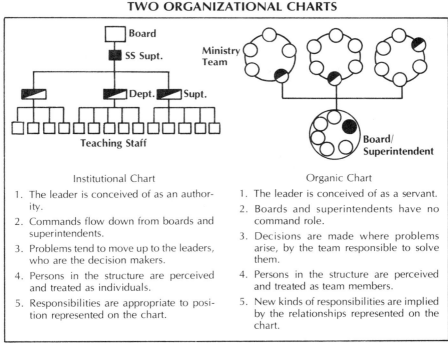

Institutional Chart	Organic Chart
1. The leader is conceived of as an authority.	1. The leader is conceived of as a servant.
2. Commands flow down from boards and superintendents.	2. Boards and superintendents have no command role.
3. Problems tend to move up to the leaders, who are the decision makers.	3. Decisions are made where problems arise, by the team responsible to solve them.
4. Persons in the structure are perceived and treated as individuals.	4. Persons in the structure are perceived and treated as team members.
5. Responsibilities are appropriate to position represented on the chart.	5. New kinds of responsibilities are implied by the relationships represented on the chart.

Responsibility and Ownership

Institutional structures make it clear that an agency is "owned" by the church, and that leaders bear ultimate responsibility for what happens within it. Those who fill teaching positions have only limited responsibility: the responsibility assigned by the institution.

In the organic structure, the team of persons who have been called by God to a particular ministry (say, to teach in the primary department) actually "own" that ministry. They are responsible for all that happens, as a team. When problems emerge—dissatisfaction with curriculum, difficulties with discipline, need for added teaching staff, etc.,—the team *as a team* must work out the solution. In this approach those who actually touch the lives of children at the point where ministry takes place, and who are best able to sense needs and work out solutions, have both the responsibility and authority to deal with problems.

Team Relationship

This is one of the most significant features of an organic organization. Its focus is on a team, not on individuals. In an institutional setting most teachers in practice operate as individuals, without significant support or sharing from others. The circular charting is meant to indicate that in an organic structure the team relationship has priority.

There are several reasons why this is vital. First, if the children are to be ministered to in a warm, loving faith community, it is basic that teachers in that department have a faith community relationship with each other! Second, to deal effectively with problems and to make wise decisions, team members need that open, sharing, and mutually supportive relationship with each other that grows only within true faith community. The ministering team, then, must *be* what it is so essential to provide for the nurturance of faith: a vital, living faith community.

Servant Leadership

The organic chart also helps us define the new set of functions for leaders. They are no longer "over" the ministry teams, with decision-making control. In fact, they have surrendered that kind of authority to the teams who are responsible to God for their shared ministry. Instead the leaders, as servants, are responsible *to enable and equip the ministering group to function as a team and to make wise decisions!* The leadership group may also serve in other ways. They may, for example, set up support structures (such as a single person through whom materials can be ordered), provide reports on expenditures to teams to measure against budget, or establish a library or visual aids resource room.

It is particularly important in the organic structure for leaders to maintain communication with the ministry teams, and to be available to provide "expert information" or advice when this is needed by a team in their decision making. In addition the leadership group will need to be sensitive to the climate of each ministry team, and to provide any help needed to enable them to function as a faith community with each other and with the children.

Because the leadership group is now a servant team rather than a decision-making body, the makeup of the group may also change. The institutional way of composing a Christian education board is to bring together a professional, a member of the church board, and heads of various departments. The assumption is that their task is primarily decision making, and so they function as an executive group made up of executives. This approach is no longer necessary or appropriate. Instead, different qualities will have higher importance.

The chief quality to look for in potential board members is now spiritual maturity, as reflected in leader qualifications listed in 2 Timothy and Titus. However, a wisdom and expertise gained through experience or training, which will make a leader a resource person for the ministry teams, is also important.

The shift to an organic organizational structure has one very striking impact. The new structure itself shifts the roles and responsibilities in such a way that, when we state "job descriptions," we find we have recaptured the language and the focus of the New Testament on vital faith community (see Figure 71). We have in effect revised our image of how the institutional church functions, to bring the institutional aspect of the local congregation into harmony with the nature of the church as body and family.

BUILDING TEACHING TEAMS

Research indicates that teachers in most Sunday schools have an image of the teaching role that is derived from our society. It is essentially an institutional role-image, in which the primary task is understood to be the schooling of children in Christian truths. The concepts so integral to the functioning of faith community and the nurture of faith simply are not major elements in Sunday school teachers' understanding of their roles. To build a team of teachers who will function as and create a faith community setting for ministry is a formidable task, which requires both training and support structures.

Training Teachers

In my own experimental work with the church/family-linked approach mentioned in chapters 10–14, it quickly became clear that Sunday school teachers needed to be retrained for a more biblical approach to their ministry. A training process was

FIGURE 71
ORGANIC ORGANIZATION/JOB DESCRIPTIONS

CHRISTIAN EDUCATION BOARD

1. Maintain close communication and relationship with leaders of ministry teams in Sunday school and other children's ministries.
2. Pray for, and communicate appreciation and support to all ministry teams.
3. Guard the health of each ministry team, helping to provide experiences or training needed to help team members fulfill their spiritual responsibility and their shared ministry.
4. Provide information, resources, and other support needed by ministry teams to enable them to perform their ministry effectively.

MINISTRY TEAMS

1. Meet together regularly to pray for one another and for the children.
2. Share with one another evidences of God's working as well as problems needing resolution.
3. Meet and resolve all problems as a team, seeking God's will through prayer and consensus decision making.
4. Call on the board and or superintendent for information, insights, resources, suggestions that may be helpful in making wise decisions.
5. Create a context of loving relationships within which to minister God's Word to boys and girls.
6. Communicate personal love and concern to each child, sharing themselves as well as the gospel.
7. Build a sense of love and concern in the classroom, helping the children minister to and care for one another as they are taught.

developed, refined, and used in some five hundred churches. It utilized taped mini-lectures, demonstration lessons, and a variety of workbook-guided activities focused to help teachers accept a new role-image of Sunday school teaching.

The process proved relatively successful and demonstrated that it is possible to help teachers move comfortably into a style of teaching appropriate to faith communication. Some 70 percent of the teachers trained accepted the new role-image, and the new understanding was reflected in their classrooms. About 30 percent of the teachers would not accept the new role. They persisted in seeing themselves as authorities (not friends), who were to tell (not share) truths with the children they taught. They also persisted in viewing the ministry of teaching as the transmission of information, so that the children would know what the Bible says. They expected that communicating truth on a cognitive level would somehow change the children's lives.

The training process can be outlined rather simply, and it can be initiated in a one day (Saturday) seminar.

First, teachers are involved in inductive Bible studies. They discover the *goal* of teaching is growth toward Christlikeness

(Luke 6:40; Col. 1:27–28), not simply transmitting information. They see that achieving this goal is related to developing a *friend* relationship with the learners (1 Thess. 2:7, 8, 11), and that the teacher is to *share truth* he or she is experiencing, not simply to "tell" others what the Bible says (1 Cor. 11:1; Phil. 4:9). After a summarizing mini-lecture, the teachers are led as learners through a demonstration lesson.

The demonstration lesson element in training is particularly important. It enables the teachers to literally *see* the role they will be fulfilling when they teach, and also to experience the process as a learner. This experience, participating and observing the behavior of a model, does more than anything else to help a trainee grasp the concepts that are taught during the training.

The third hour is devoted to defining the qualities that the teachers themselves identify as desirable or undesirable if they are to communicate faith rather than just information. Figure 72 reproduces one page from the training workbook. It guides the teachers to rank classroom qualities important to achieving the new teaching goals.

When individuals finish ranking, groups of three are formed and asked to agree on the three "most important" of the qualities. The whole group then reassembles to select a value that all have placed among the top three. [Note: In every training setting, the one value that every group placed among the top three was "love."]

At this point a mini-lecture explains that values must be translated into behavior. The whole group is asked to describe specifically what actions might be observed in a classroom that indicate a climate of love. The group members must be pressed, but are able to develop a list of some thirty to forty things that communicate love. This process is particularly important. It is designed to help each teacher build a picture of how he or she will act as a loving person in the classroom setting.

The teachers then return to their groups of three to go through this same process of describing how another of their top values will be expressed in the classroom.

This is followed by another demonstration lesson. Again the teachers are taught as they are themselves to teach. Afterward, the group focuses on three things that must exist within the classroom: involvement of the children in active learning, the development of personal meaning of the Bible truths studied, and the establishment of warm, close relationships. Together the teachers think through the demonstration lessons, trying to identify everything said and done that facilitated active learning,

307

FIGURE 72
VALUES IDENTIFICATION PROCESS
IN TRAINING[2]

In a moment you are going to come to a list of twenty (20) qualities that may seem desirable or undersirable to you in a Bible teaching setting. Looking for the "ideal" classroom, how would you rank these qualities? Place a 1 next to the quality you believe deserves the highest value, a 2 next to the second, and so on. The final quality, number 20, will have the lowest value of this group. When you have completed your ranking, wait until your trainer plays a tape segment before going on to the next page.

_____ boredom	_____ involvement
_____ chaos	_____ love
_____ disorder	_____ listening
_____ dogmatism	_____ openness
_____ friendliness	_____ quiet
_____ fear	_____ responsiveness
_____ freedom	_____ relevance
_____ flexibility	_____ respectfulness
_____ fun	_____ sharing
_____ interest	_____ warmth

developing the personal meaning of truth, and beginning warm relationships.

The training may then be concluded with a self-check quiz that restates and confirms the key learnings of the training. Or the session can be concluded with a third demonstration lesson. This relatively simple training approach did prove effective, and was a necessary first step in building ministry teams that would function in an organic way in children's ministry.[3]

---

[2]Larry Richards, *Communicating Likeness . . . a new way to teach.* Sunday School PLUS.

[3]A number of sets of training audio tapes (for mini-lectures), training booklets used by the teachers, and demonstration lessons that were used in the author's training seminars are still available. A complete set of materials can be obtained, while they last, from Dynamic Church Ministries, 1266 Woodingham Drive, E. Lansing, MI 48823, at a cost of $25 to cover postage, handling, and storage. Each set also includes three additional training sessions: on discipline, learning activities, and personal relationships.

Maintaining Supportive Relationships

Initial training is simply the beginning. It is a first step toward building a team. Two other elements have long-term, continuing impact.

The first element is a continuous training process that will facilitate building faith community. In our experimental work we have introduced each new study unit with a Serendipity.

The concept is simple. Sum up the thrust of the next unit of study, and teach it to the teachers as truth to enrich their own lives. On the other hand, the class process provides the teaching team with an opportunity to minister to one another and to build deeper personal relationships as they share in exploring the meaning of God's words for their own lives.

We noted in earlier chapters that a teacher who has first taken God's words to his or her own heart (Deut. 6) is a basic ingredient of sharing truth as reality. We noted too that the teacher's modeling is one of those vital processes through which faith is shared. The Serendipity is a vital part of the ongoing support given a teaching team and helps to keep the biblical priorities in clear focus. A Serendipity plan used to introduce one study unit is reproduced as Figure 73.[4]

The second factor in maintaining the team is deceptively simple. It is to set aside twenty to thirty minutes, as close to the end of class as possible, for the team members to simply talk about what has happened.

In one congregation this process was followed weekly, and the talk-it-over times were tape recorded. The length of these times varied from twenty minutes to thirty minutes, and the teachers were given no suggestions except to talk about what happened in class. The tapes were later analyzed, and several interesting things noted. Over time, the conversations focused more and more on the boys and girls in the class. When the behaviors the teachers described were listed next to the names of the children, a definite pattern of change could be documented. There was increasing responsiveness in the children, with growing expressions of concern for one another. Over time, the teachers used more and more warm and personal words. These brief minutes together had a definite impact on the relationships growing between members of the teaching team. Finally, over time the concerns of the teachers shifted. Initially they talked a lot about procedures and materials and other institutional details. Over a six-month period the conversations

---

[4]*I'm Special*, Teacher's Guide. Unit 1, pp. 4–5. © 1977, Sunday School PLUS.

shifted distinctly toward the language and the concerns of faith.

Through years of testing it has become clear that three primary motivating factors are linked with teacher enthusiasm and commitment. These factors are (1) a growing closeness to and love for the children being taught, (2) a sense of personal spiritual growth—the awareness that while teaching teachers are being taught, and (3) growing closeness to other teachers on the ministry team.

FIGURE 73

SERENDIPITY PLAN

Experience what your class will discover!

We communicate what is in our heart!
SERENDIPITY is a monthly adventure for the teaching staff. An adventure in discovering together the meaning of the Bible truths you'll be sharing with your class this week. And SERENDIPITY is learning in fellowship . . . learning with brothers and sisters who will love *you*, and support you in your teaching ministry and personal pilgrimage with God.
So don't miss SERENDIPITY!

SERENDIPITY: I'm Special!

I. Sharing (5 min.)
In a circle. Encourage each person to share "what I like best about teaching."

II. Going deeper (30-40 min.)
For larger staffs, divide into groups of four or five. Give each person paper and a dark crayon. Ask each to graph the peaks and valleys (up and downs) of his life. Each should have specific experiences in mind. Let each share his graph with the others in the smaller groups.

III. In the Word (20 min.)
Working in pairs, have everyone explore Genesis 1:26—2:25. The pairs should look for and record answers to these questions:
- Why is man special?
- How did God show Adam that he was special to Him? (Hint: Look in Genesis 2 for ways that God provided in Eden for man's needs—for beauty, creativity, accomplishment, etc.)
- How has God shown us, today, that *we* are special to Him?

IV. Expanding our awareness (20 min.)
Return to the larger group to first share discoveries in the passage. Then
- Discuss what difference it might make for a child or grown-up to see himself as "special" instead of worth-

less. (Perhaps some of the "lows" on the graphs of some of you were associated with a sense of inferiority or valuelessness? If so, sharing from personal experience here may give added insight into why it is important for us to see ourselves as God sees us.)

V. Worship and affirmation (until done)
Play a tape recording of Ps. 8, God's great affirmation of how important mankind is to Him. Then after a brief pause, add another voice reading Rom. 8:31–39.
Give time for silent prayer of thanks to God for each person's specialness to Him. Then lead the group to express agreement with God's great affirmation of themselves as special to Him. Let as many as want express praise in sentence prayers taking this form:

"God, because You have made me a special person, shaped in Your image, I am free to like (*have each fill in something he or she likes about himself*). Therefore I praise You."

VI. Dismiss . . .
after giving out *Teacher's Guides,* and telling your staff that this month they will help the children discover and experience their specialness to God.

In seeking to build a faith community setting for ministry with children, we do need to change the role-image of teachers and to help them see the ministry in a new light. But we must then provide for enrichment of the relationships in each teaching team, so that teachers themselves become a faith community group.

Staffing

One constant problem for most churches is staffing agencies like the Sunday school. Recruitment and training seem always to be critical concerns.

This issue is, if anything, even more important for those seeking to build faith community settings for ministry with children. Teachers in institutional and organic settings should have basic spiritual qualifications, being committed and growing Christians. But special traits are important for a team ministry. There must be a warm and loving personality and a willingness to care for the individuals being taught. There must be an openness to listening and sharing seldom found in an individual who thinks the business of teaching is transmitting information from mouth to mind. There must be an openness to working as a team member with the other teachers, and a recognition that it is important to support and be supported. As in the Timothy and Titus list of qualities for elders, we seek a matured or maturing Christian character for the ministry of teaching boys and girls.

The basic principles of the institutional solution to staffing are accurately described by Robert E. Clark. They include these suggestions: "Have a personnel committee who will contact and follow up prospective workers" and "keep the church informed as to personnel needs through bulletins, newsletters, sermons, and personal contact." All contacts are to be made in a "business like manner" stressing "the importance of the position" (p. 343.)[5]

Recruitment in the organic structure operates best through interpersonal networks. This is one good reason why a team that has ownership of its ministry is better able to solve problems. Whoever is recruited must be qualified on a very personal level: it is in fact personal qualities that qualify for ministry! Therefore knowing persons well is basic to recognizing their potential for ministering in the Sunday school. While it is certainly valuable

---

[5]Robert E. Clark, "Leadership and Materials," from *Childhood Education in the Church* by Roy B. Zuck and Robert E. Clark. Copyright 1975. Moody Press, Moody Bible Institute of Chicago. Used by permission.

to share requests for prayer with the congregation when a team needs new members, the most direct and effective approach is for team members to talk over persons they know who will fit into the team and into the ministry style. Individuals so identified can be invited to consider joining in the ministry, and encouraged to spend a few weeks at team meetings in the classrooms, to discover whether perhaps God is calling them to this ministry and if they would be comfortable in it.

Using the interpersonal network of relationships that each team member has developed within a congregation is more likely than the talent surveys and personnel committees of the institutional approach to identify and enlist the right persons for a faith community ministry.

BUILDING THE LEARNING GROUP

It's not only teachers who need to orient themselves to faith community relationships in the Sunday school. It's the boys and girls as well. Children as well as adults have an institutionalized view of Sunday school as schooling, and of their role as learners. Children can and will quickly learn new ways of relating, and enter in enthusiastically. But they must be taught how to learn together.

One important reason for the patterns that typically develop in a Sunday school is that children perceive the class as a place where adults retain the right of unilateral imposition. The adult, the person in control, is the only one whom the child must consider. This is shown in a number of ways. Visit a class. Notice how the children listen to a good teacher when he or she is interesting and maintains good eye contact. Then watch when a teacher bends forward to speak to just one child, or even worse to listen closely to what one child has to say. To the others this is a cue that they are free to follow their own concerns. Junior girls will giggle together. Junior boys may well push or begin to wrestle. The adult is no longer speaking to them; they are under no obligation to listen.

But we saw earlier that in a peer setting, where group members are coequals, different behavior is appropriate. When the perception of the group changes, then children will listen to each other and respond in reciprocal ways. This is one of the most significant findings of our research. Working with teachers and children together we *can* change the perception of the class setting. When the children see relationships in a reciprocal framework rather than as an adult dominated setting, then the children will begin to see each other as friends, show sensitivity to each other, pray spontaneously for others' needs, and even identify their teachers as friends.

It is important if we expect to build a faith community within the Sunday school to realize that we need to train the children as well as the teachers. This training primarily involves giving the children a new role-image, and a new set of expectations concerning what is appropriate in the Sunday school classroom. A special series of Sunday school lessons was developed to help the children work out together the new set of expectations. The lessons focused on listening, on identifying and expressing feelings, on expressing love, etc. Working through these lessons together in eight or nine consecutive Sundays, the children learned what to expect in Sunday school and how to relate to each other and the teacher. These lessons were extremely simple. But they were successful in changing the relationships within the classroom and in initiating a deeper level of sharing. Significant increases occurred in the children's sense of belonging and participation, in their greater identification with the teacher, and in appropriate application of Scripture to real incidents in their daily life.

While it is important that the relationships and ways of learning taught in the training lessons be supported in the regular class curriculum, working through a series of training lessons (which we called Launching Lessons) is important to establish for the children patterns of behavior that are appropriate in a faith community.

PROBE

▶ *case histories*
▶ *discussion questions*
▶ *thought provokers*
▶ *resources*

1. One of the Launching Lessons, designed to help children in a class learn what is appropriate to community Sunday school setting, is reproduced below (see Figure 74). It is a simple lesson, focusing on listening, and is designed to cue the children that the class is a setting for reciprocal relationships, not a setting in which an adult maintains the power of unilateral imposition.

   The Launching Lesson set is included with the Teacher Training tapes and workbooks mentioned earlier. They are available while they last with the $25 training package from Dynamic Church Ministries, 1266 Woodingham Drive, E. Lansing, MI, 48823.

FIGURE 74
LAUNCHING LESSON[6]

Lesson 2

FOCUS: Learning to Listen

1 Samuel 3:1–19

Background For You

Listening is an important part of communication. When someone listens attentively, He communicates concern and interest to the speaker. He expresses nonverbally, that the person he listens to is important to him and worthwhile.

Without real listening there can be no progress in developing understanding, or in building a love relationship between persons. Thus, *listening* is vitally important, both at home and during Sunday School. Listening *to* children and listening *by* children are important in building the context of love and sharing which is to characterize time spent together in Sunday School PLUS.

How listening builds relationships

Listening that builds relationships is listening that communicates love and concern. It is this kind of listening that will free your children to share their true feelings and emotions. Larry Richards, in his book, *How Do I Fit In?*, says of this kind of listening:

"Often we don't truly listen to others. You've seen people taking part in conversations like this. One person is talking, but no one else is listening. Everyone is just waiting for the person to stop talking so he can start in.

"At times like these, we're usually thinking more about what we plan to say next than about what the other person is saying. Our eyes wander, we open our mouths at the slightest pause in the other person's stream of words, we seem agitated and eager to have our turn to speak.

"When we're acting like this, our lack of concern for the other person is communicated— loud and clear. We don't really care about him; we simply have made a bargain with him. We'll let him talk at us if he'll let us talk at him. Neither of us has to communicate or come closer. Neither wants to, and neither does.

"No, listening that says, '*I'm interested* and *willing to come closer*' is the kind of listening that communicates caring. It's not worrying about what I plan to say next, but trying honestly to understand. I may miss the point. But if I'm really trying to understand, that other person will sense it and will recognize the fact I'm holding open the door of friendship."

Listening for feelings

Listening for feelings as well as for ideas is also important. When we listen, we can ask ourselves. "What is he saying about his feelings? How does he feel about this?" Then we can "reflect" what we think we hear: We can say, "You feel sad that . . . ?" Such reflecting lets the person know that we are trying to understand him . . . that we care about how he feels . . . that we care about *him*.

How do I fit in?

As the teacher, you are the model, the example. You help children learn to listen by the way *you* listen. Thus you can set the tone for this and other sessions, and open up communication lines which will free the children, and you, to share your real selves with each other.

But remember, you must show the children by the way you listen what is expected of them. They will over the weeks begin to identify with you and will soon be imitating you.

What will this listening do for my class?

● *Listening will help build good relationships between class members*. When a person realizes someone truly is interested in what he thinks and feels, he feels closer to that person.
● Listening will help build self-respect. Just to know that someone cares how I feel and is interested in what I say makes me feel warm and important. I begin to feel confident and worthwhile. I feel freer to share about myself. This kind of feeling about oneself is something we want to help children build.
● *Listening will help build group fellowship*. As the children begin to feel closer to you and each other, a sense of fellowship develops. This is important for every Christian group.

---

[6]*Teacher's Launching Handbook*, pp. 12–14. © 1977, Sunday School PLUS.

Bible exploration notes

To help children understand the importance of listening, we've chosen the Bible story, "Samuel, God's Good Listener" (1 Sam. 3:1–19). In this narrative we find an excellent example of a boy who listened well.

God had been conspicuously silent for some years in Israel (3:1). But the time was ripe for Him to speak again. A boy dedicated to God's service from birth, was now living and ministering with the priest, Eli. God would speak to Israel through him, and he would listen well and relay God's message clearly. Moreover, God's blessing would rest on him, and Israel would once again listen and respond to the Lord (3:19 ff.)

Sharing Love
Coming to know and love each other.

John 13:34

Have the green Sharing poster on display. Welcome each child warmly and personally; then gather them in class groups to talk about the following:

1. Have you ever tried to talk about something really important to you, and nobody listened? Tell about a time this happened to you.

2. How do you feel when someone does not listen when you are talking?

3. How do you know when someone is really listening to you?

Understanding God's Truth
Creative learning activities which give meaning to the Bible study.

Col. 1:9, 10

Put the blue Understanding poster on display. Through these activities, the children will come to realize that we can show love and concern for one another by listening. It will help your children learn that listening is expected in this new way of learning at church—listening to each other, as well as to the teacher.

1. Divide your class into pairs. Have each person tell his partner about the best Christmas he ever had. Tell your boys and girls to listen carefully, because each will later tell his partner's story to the class.
   Then let each person share the story his partner told. After each has shared, have the class talk about: "When you are listening to someone, how can you show that you really care about them and what they are saying?"

2. Have the partners change roles. One teacher can take all the children who *listened* in the activity above out in the hall. He should then ask them to "think of the most exciting thing you did last summer and tell your partner."
   Another teacher can talk privately for a moment with the other half of the group, and tell them:
   "You are called 'listeners,' but don't listen to your partner when he or she shares. Don't walk away or make noises. But act as if you don't care what he says. Ignore him; just pretend he isn't there."
   Then put the pairs together for two or three minutes. Come together and talk about the following questions.
   To the sharers: "What happened when you told your story? How did you feel? Why?"
   To the listeners: "Tell what you were told to do as a listener."
   For all: "How can we show someone we love and care about them when we listen to them?"

3. Or (for larger department groups) divide into teams of four, with two listeners and two sharers in each, and follow the same procedure as outlined in Activity #2.

Exploring God's Book
Seeing the truth in the Scriptures.

2 Tim 3:16

Place the red Exploring poster on display. Then move into today's Bible time.
FOR PRIMARIES

Samuel, God's Good Listener

An imaginative telling of 1 Sam. 3:1–19 to capture the interest of your first- to third-graders.

Samuel didn't know it, but it was a very special day. Something wonderful was about to happen to him! Let's see what it was.

"Samuel! Samuel!" called Eli, the priest of Israel.

"Here I am," answered Samuel, running to Eli.

"Samuel," said Eli, "it's getting late. Time to go to bed."

Samuel walked back to the tent-church where he lived and worked, and crawled into his bed. "I'm glad God chose me to live here with Eli," thought Samuel.

Eli was getting very old, and a strong eight-year-old like Samuel was able to help him in many ways. "Maybe," Samuel must have thought as he drifted off to sleep, "maybe God will want me to be a priest and help people worship Him. Wouldn't that be wonderful! I'll want to listen very carefully to all the things Eli teaches me."

Soon Samuel was drifting off to sleep. His eyes were closed, and he was almost asleep . . . when . . . suddenly, he heard a voice calling loudly, "Samuel! Samuel!"

Samuel sat up straight in bed. Then he jumped out and ran to Eli, and said, "Here I am, Eli. What do you want?"

But Eli looked toward Samuel and said, "Why, Samuel. I didn't call you. Go back to bed."

Samuel was sure he'd heard a voice, but shaking his head he went back to bed. He got snuggled down in, and pulled the blankets over his head. And then he heard that same voice calling again! "Samuel! Samuel!"

"Now I know that must be Eli," Samuel thought, and hurried to his room. "Here I am, Eli," he said. "What do you want?"

But again Eli said, "Samuel, I didn't call you. You'd better go back to bed and go to sleep."

Once again Samuel went back to bed. And sure enough, he heard the voice again! "Samuel!" And a third time Samuel got up and went to Eli. Eli started to send him back to bed again . . . but suddenly Eli stopped! "I wonder," Eli must have said to himself. "I wonder if maybe God could be talking to Samuel? I know he must have heard someone . . ."

Of course, Samuel hadn't known that it was God's voice. God hadn't spoken to Samuel before. For many, many years God had not spoken to anyone, because there was no one who would listen to Him, and do what He said! Instead, all the people of Israel did just what they wanted to do.

Now Eli said to Samuel, "Boy, I think it is God calling your name. I think God wants to speak with you. So if you hear the voice call you again, say this: 'Speak, Lord, for your servant is listening.' And if someone does speak to you, you will know it is the Lord. Now, hurry back to your room, and listen very carefully."

Samuel must have been very excited! He ran to his room, jumped into bed, and lay very quietly . . . listening. "Just think," Samuel must have thought, "God wants to speak to me!"

And then Samuel heard the voice again. "Samuel! Samuel!" And Samuel answered just as Eli had told him to: "Speak, Lord, for your servant is listening."

And so that day God began to talk with Samuel. Samuel listened very well, and God was pleased with Samuel. All Samuel's life he would listen to God, and Samuel would tell God's people what the Lord said.

Yes, that was a very special day for Samuel. God had spoken to him. God had found someone who would listen to Him.

Questions to discuss

1. Why do you suppose God had not spoken to people during Samuel's time?

2. If someone called to you as God did to Samuel, what would you have done?

3. How do you think you would have felt if you were Samuel and discovered the Lord was speaking to you?

4. Was Samuel a good listener? How do we know?

5. Today, God speaks to us through the Bible. What do you think it means for us to be "good listeners" to God today? How could you tell if a person has been really listening to God?

For Juniors

Reading and pantomiming 1 Sam. 3:1–19.

Read 1 Samuel 3:1–19 together. Then choose persons from the whole group to pantomime or role play the story for the others. Or in classes, do separate pantomimes or role plays. You will need a narrator, Samuel, Eli, and someone to be the voice of the Lord.

In preparing the pantomime or role play, talk through each part with the group, and talk about the feelings Eli and Samuel must have had.

When the pantomime or role play has been acted out one or more times (using different children), discuss the same questions listed under the story for Primaries.

Options: Class groups can do their pantomimes for each other. It might be fun to require everyone to be in the skit—as furniture, rocks, etc. Let the children be inventive!

Responding To God's Book
Applying truth to our life

Psalm 119:11

Put the purple Responding poster on display. Then with your children . . .

1. Review together what has been learned about listening and how it applies to times when you are together for Sunday School PLUS. You might let the children talk over these questions:

● Is listening important for us in class? Why?

● Why do you think it's important to listen to each other, as well as to a teacher?

● How can each of us be better listeners in Sunday school? What can we do during this week to become better listeners?

2. Work together to make posters on ways to be a good listener. Let each child explain the meaning of his or her poster to the group. Hang the posters around the room as reminders of good listening habits. (You may wish to continue this activity as a pre-session project for children who come early next week.)

---

2. Some children's ministries are so designed that they fit the organic model quite naturally, while others demonstrate no sensitivity to faith community issues. The two points below deal with such ministries.

   a. Pioneer Ministries, Inc., has for many years provided leadership and materials for girls' club programs in local churches. Recently the ministry has been expanded to add Pioneer Boys to Pioneer Girls. Correspondence with Sara Robertson, Ed.D., vice president for publications, included this very significant paragraph.

   Young people need and want models. One source is the family, but they also need other models as well. Since so many young people are in single parent families it is apparent that they need further adult contact if they are to have role models of both sexes. Spiritual growth occurs through the observation of Christian role models and through the relationships which can be developed in extended time spent together. These adult models should also be continuing to learn and grow through their experience as club leaders.

   One of the major goals of Pioneer Club ministries is the development of the relational climate. Study club materials (Box 788, Wheaton, IL 60187), and see if this goal is adequately translated through guidance given to teachers.

b. The letter on pages 319–20 (Figure 75) was received by the author from Christian Service Brigade, comparing its approach with that of another weekday "club" type ministry to children. Study the letter closely and evaluate each program described here as to its "fit" in the organic model. To get materials for evaluation from these two groups, write to:

Christian Service Brigade
Box 150
Wheaton, IL 60187

AWANA Youth Association
Rolling Meadows, IL 60008

FIGURE 75
COMPARISON OF CHRISTIAN SERVICE BRIGADE TO AWANA YOUTH ASSOCIATION

At the suggestion of our representative, Jack Corbett, I want to clarify the objectives of Christian Service Brigade and the differences from the AWANA program. There is often a good deal of confusion growing out of the similarities and differences of the two organizations.

First of all. I want to express my appreciation for the AWANA movement and its leadership. I have known the directors for many years and believe they are sincerely trying to fulfill the ministry which God has given them. While our philosophies differ, we are unified in a desire to bring children and youth into a personal relationship with Jesus Christ. There is no doubt that God is using the AWANA program in hundreds of churches today.

Thus, concerning differences with the AWANA organization, I do not want to be critical of a program which God is using. However, I would recommend Christian Service Brigade as the program for your church if your objectives agree with ours.

Keep in mind that both programs:
—are concerned about the spiritual needs of youth.
—have uniforms and awards related to a progressive achievement system.
—work within the structure of the local church.
—depend on the leadership of born-again individuals.
—utilize a weekly meeting as the center of activity.
—have a professional staff to provide counsel and training.

Here are some of the characteristics of the AWANA program:
1. AWANA emphasizes evangelism and outreach. Some programs seek to involve larger numbers of youth in order to "bring them under the sound of the Gospel."
2. There is heavy emphasis on Bible memorization. Much of the award system is linked to this. AWANA leaders stress the concept of influencing the subconscious through a rote memorization approach.
3. AWANA stresses competition through games as a basis for achievement. Various kinds of treats and prizes are awarded as part of the competition. The article, "Why Crafts Cannot Be Used Instead of Games," was written by an AWANA leader and presents this philosophy.
4. The median age of the AWANA program is about 10 or 11 years and often operates on a co-ed basis, involving boys and girls together under the leadership of men and women.
5. AWANA stresses the simplicity of its program, relying on large group activities such as games and Bible lessons which do not make heavy demands on leader preparation and supervision.

Now I want to present some of the distinctives of Christian Service Brigade.
1. CSB views itself as an agency of Christian education working within the local church. This involves an emphasis on both evangelism and training for Christian living. CSB has always been strongly evangelistic, but the weight of its programs is toward helping the church train its youth for Christian living and service.
2. CSB holds to the importance of a "total person" ministry. We cannot be content with "saving souls," but must go on to *develop lives*. Thus we believe it is important not to compartmentalize into "sacred" and "secular" distinctions. Luke 2:52 speaks clearly of the importance of growth in each area: mental, spiritual, social, physical. CSB is not a "weekday Sunday school," but a full activity and training program for boys.
3. The Brigade philosophy is based on the discipleship methods as taught and practiced by Christ Himself. While He ministered tirelessly to the multitudes, His greatest work was with individuals and small groups. When faced with the choice of a limited ministry to hundreds or an in-depth ministry to a smaller group, CSB chooses the latter. The program places emphasis on developing relationships with boys which become the basis for evangelism and discipleship training.

4. CSB stresses leadership quality and preparation. While the content of the Christian Gospel is supremely important, the human instrument of communication plays a vital part. Thus the Christian man must be a living example of what he wants boys to become. The man's character and example as a man, husband and father are vitally important to his leadership of boys. The Brigade program is so structured to allow these qualities to become evident, both in the variety and depth of contact.

5. While we admit the value of co-educational activities, CSB is a "boys only" program which is committed to developing and maintaining a strong masculine image for Christianity. This is further expressed in the reprint, "Why a Separate Program for Boys."

6. The CSB achievement program helps a boy integrate the Scriptures with all areas of his life. Bible memorization is an important part of this process with constant emphasis on comprehension of the Biblical truth, not just rote memorization.

There are many other distinctives which could be mentioned. Some are taken for granted like Brigade's strong commitment to a thoroughly evangelical doctrinal position. The CSB Standard of Faith has been the organization's "plumbline" for 40 years of ministry. CSB staff members base their lives and their activities upon a complete acceptance of the authority of the Scriptures.

I trust these contrasts are helpful to you without being unfair to fellow believers. In summary, I believe the most important consideration is not the difference between CSB and some other program but the objectives to which your church is committed. If you are building on the principles of Christian discipleship, Christian Service Brigade provides programs best suited to your needs. If, as a pastor said recently to one of our representatives, you "want the most for the least," then perhaps some other alternative is acceptable.

Regardless of the methods, materials or programs employed, the most important factor is the quality and commitment of the adult leadership. A man dedicating himself to God and serving faithfully as an AWANA leader will generally be more effective than a half-hearted Brigade leader. On the other hand, give a man the best tools available and he should do the best work.

If you have further questions or comments, I would be glad to hear from you. I trust that God will guide you in discerning your own objectives and those programs best suited to accomplishing them.

Sincerly,

C. Samuel Gray
Executive Director

PART 2

SETTINGS

The Home

The Impact of Family
Intergenerational Models
Information Models
Intervention Models
Patterns in the Home

The Church

The Church as Organism and Institution
Sunday School as Faith Community
Sunday School Curriculums

The Christian School

The Christian School Ideal
Faith Community in the Classroom

The Sunday school can and must be a faith community: an organic, relational setting in which processes that nurture faith operate. Maintaining faith community against the pressures of institutionalism is not easy. It calls for a distinctive

SUNDAY SCHOOL CURRICULUMS

approach to organization, and for the training of both teachers and children. It also calls for curriculums that support faith community relationships, rather than force teaching into the pattern of schooling.

Throughout this text, I've suggested that a tension exists between schooling and the organic learning of faith that takes place when children participate in a vital faith community. Several aspects of schooling, which contrast sharply with the framework for faith communication, were isolated in Figure 63. Schooling is concerned that the student learn content and skills, and be able to restate or explain concepts. Learning is essentially cognitive, and is not linked with experiences in which motives, feelings, and behavior are observed. Most strikingly, schooling is future-oriented. We teach the third grader so he or she is prepared for learning in the sixth, and the sixth grader so he is ready for high school, and the highschooler so he is prepared for college or for "real life." The future focus is fully understood intuitively by children and teacher alike, and a schooling context signals nonverbally, "What I learn here will be useful, but has no immediate impact on my life."

There are other characteristics of schooling. It takes place in a special place at special times, apart from where life is lived. The teacher is a person who knows and who has full control of the situation: a control exercised to make sure the children learn what they are expected to know. Content is organized logically, and step by step mastery is expected. Learning is demonstrated by the learner's appropriate use of words to recite or take written tests.

CHAPTER 17

Schooling has a valid place in society. When our goal is a verbal mastery of Christian or biblical ideas, schooling is valid within our churches. But the schooling approach is not in harmony with the framework unveiled in Scripture for the transmission of faith. In faith transmission, life itself is the context for learning. Truth is taught as interpretation of life as it happens, and instruction has immediate application. Teachers are those who have taken God's Word to heart, and thus model by their own lives—their actions, attitudes, values, and feelings—the reality that they interpret by God's words. Commitment, not knowledge, qualifies teachers. Relationships, not time and place, are the locus of learning. It is through belonging, participation, and modeling facilitated by warmth and loving closeness that a faith response to the Word of God is encouraged.

If the goals of schooling are the goals of our Sunday schools, then the patterns of the school are appropriate. But if we are concerned that our children have faith, then we must face the tension that exists between schooling and biblical models of teaching and learning. We must then, if our goal is to nurture faith, commit ourselves to build in Sunday school and other ministry settings a true faith community. And we must commit ourselves to patterns of teaching, in that setting, that are appropriate to the nurture of faith.

In a later chapter we'll look at ways the Bible can be used in the faith community Sunday school. In this chapter I want to look in a special way at Sunday school curriculums. Here we are not asking how they try to teach the Bible. Here we ask, Which curriculums incorporate processes that support faith community learning? Our question is, How can we tell in evaluating a curriculum whether it will support faith community processes, or whether it will force the Sunday morning experience into a schooling mold?

We do need this kind of analysis. We can train our teachers and build ministering teams. We can help boys and girls build a new perception of what is appropriate on Sunday mornings. But the curriculum we use will significantly shape the learning process, directing it into a schooling mold that stunts faith community, or enriching those processes that nurture faith.

EDUCATIONAL PROCESS

Two overall areas should be evaluated in determining whether a curriculum cues the teacher and students to a schooling or a faith community setting. The first area is that of educational process: the kind of learning experiences suggested and the way they are structured.

We can look at a number of things in a curriculum that serve as cues to teachers and tend to shape the class toward schooling or faith community experiences. Illustrations of cues in this chapter are taken from several currently published Sunday school curriculums. Because it is not my purpose either to recommend or to attack any particular publishing house, I simply note here that four fall 1981 curriculums were used. Two were major independent publishers, and two "shared approaches" materials produced jointly by a number of mainline denominations.

Aims as Cues

Stated goals or aims are the first cues to check. Do the aims orient the teacher to look at the class in schooling or faith community framework? Here are session aims taken from three different curriculums.

1. That we may try out ways to overcome get-even feelings.
2. That the student may trust God to help him when he feels inadequate.

3. That we may recognize some unfair situations and determine how to deal fairly.
4. This session will emphasize Jesus' teaching that God knows our needs and cares about each person.
5. This session will emphasize Jesus' teaching that each of us must forgive others and be forgiven by others and by God.

A glance at these aims shows immediately that 4 and 5 cue the teacher to concern about content. Information is highlighted, and a schooling setting is implied. On the other hand, aims 1–3 cue to things that are important in a faith community setting. For one thing, they suggest a relatively open process in which the children's feelings and experiences are important. References to "feeling inadequate" and "recognize some unfair situations" seem to suggest that both feelings and the children's "real life" experiences will be explored in the classroom. We've seen that the processes through which faith is nurtured do affirm the importance of exploring feelings ("inner states") and also the sharing of real life. Instruction-as-interpretation-of-life implies that a biblical truth/reality to be grasped must be linked with a number of personal experiences. While the Sunday school hour cannot reproduce the flow of weekday life, primary and junior age children are old enough to recall past experiences and to talk about what they expect to experience in the immediate future. These three lesson aims seem to suggest that on Sunday mornings the class will explore the real life experiences of the boys and girls and their feelings about them, seeking to interpret their life through the biblical revelation.

Convergent/Divergent Flow

Stated aims are not always carried out when a lesson is developed. So we want to move on and look at specific learning activities. Is there an open, divergent learning process, or a closed convergent process? A *divergent* process will flow toward an open exploration of a number of life settings, while a *convergent* process will tend to focus on certain specific settings. A *divergent* process will suggest activities that let the children generate their own illustrations of settings in which the truth explored applies. A *convergent* setting will control, by giving several illustrations of settings in which the children could apply the truth, but will not use these settings to encourage the children to talk about their own feelings and experiences. A divergent process will not, as a convergent process does, focus the attention of the teacher and children on giving "right answers" to the situations suggested. A *divergent* process will encourage the expression of the children's thoughts and feelings about their own experiences, while a convergent process will tend to focus in on the particular right answers provided by the curriculum writer. The divergent process is more characteristic of a faith community setting. The convergent process is characteristic of schooling.

In looking at the process in curriculums, it's important to survey an entire quarter of lessons rather than to judge by one or two. The place to focus evaluation is the final section of a lesson plan. Almost all curriculum materials have initial learning activities, followed by some interaction with Scripture, followed by one or more sections designed to relate what has been taught back to the lives of the boys and girls. It is this final section of the lesson plan that reveals the convergent (schooling) or divergent (faith community) orientation of the process.

In looking over the final learning activities specifically consider the following questions.

1. Do these activities carry out the stated lesson aim?
2. Do these activities have graphic priority? That is, do the number of column inches in the materials reflect the importance of activities designed to link back to life?
3. Do the activities encourage exploring several rather than only one or two life situations?
4. Do the activities involve the children in generating their own examples of life settings in which the truth studied might apply?
5. Do the activities encourage the children to talk together about their own experiences and feelings?
6. Do the activities encourage open exploration of the meaning of the truths studied for life situations, rather than direct them into "right answer" patterns of thought?

Figure 76 shows my charting of one of the fall 1981 curriculums studied in developing this chapter.

Lateral Versus Logical Thinking

In chapter 6 we noted that schooling focuses on logical thinking. Creativity, another name given to lateral thinking, is concerned with the ability to generate a number of associations and also unique associations. "How many times can we think of when children might be afraid?" calls for lateral thinking. But "When the big dog ran toward Joan, what do you think she remembered to help her not be afraid?" calls for logical thinking. The one process calls for many answers. The other seeks one answer. Brief quotes from two Sunday school lessons illustrate

FIGURE 76

ANALYSIS OF CONVERGENT/DIVERGENT PROCESS ELEMENTS IN CURRICULUM OF ONE PUBLISHER'S FALL '81 JUNIOR MATERIALS

Session Number	Does Process Carry Out Stated Goal?	Percent Space Given to "Application" Activities	Do Activities Encourage Exploring Several Life Situations?	Do Activities Engage Children in Generating Their Own Examples?	Do Activities Encourage Children to Talk of Their Own Experiences and Feelings?	Do Activities Explore Rather Than Direct to "Right Answer" Thinking?
1	Yes	25	Yes	No	No	No
2	Yes	20	Yes	Yes	No	No
3	Yes	16	No	No	No	No
4	No	16	No	No	No	Yes
5	No	20	No	No	No	
6	Yes	25	Yes	No	No	No
7	Yes	25	Yes	No	No	No
8	Yes	16	No	No	No	No
9	No	25	Yes	No	No	No
10	No	20	No	No	No	No
11	No	28	No	No	No	No
12	No	20	No	No	No	No
13	No	15	No	No	No	No

the two processes (see Figure 77). Sample A gives a teacher directions for a "discussion." But the pattern, with the "right answers" given in parenthesis, makes it clear that free association is not desired. Sample B, from the same curriculum, outlines an activity that stimulates true lateral thinking and gives enough freedom to motivate it.

Lateral thinking is particularly important in teaching children. Instruction-as-interpretation-of-life assumes that a particular biblical truth (reality) will be linked with a number of life situations. Children's thinking processes are constructivistic, meaning that a child builds understanding of a concept by linking it to many situations. Children do not *deduce* application from a principle, but rather understand the principle through seeing it linked to many situations. If our learning activities can help boys and girls actually generate a number of life-situation illustrations of a truth, children will be much more likely to build an intuitive grasp of that truth and sense its relationship to situations in which they find themselves.

In an earlier book, *Creative Bible Teaching*,[1] I suggested an

---

[1]Lawrence O. Richards, *Creative Bible Teaching* (Chicago: Moody, 1970).

FIGURE 77

FIGURE 77
LOGICAL VERSUS LATERAL THINKING ACTIVITIES

RECOGNIZING WAYS TO BE PHONY

Sample A	Sample B
Wearing a mask	Play the first part of the interview with the children on the *Teacher Cassette*. After they have answered the first question, turn off the cassette player and be ready to play the rest of the interview in a few minutes.
Hold up the mask from sheet 9, *Teaching Aid Packet*.	
Why do people put on masks? (To cover up who they really are. To try to be somebody else.) Even without a real mask some people pretend to be what they are not. Without a false face they give others a false impression.	How do *you* know when a friend doesn't like you anymore? How can you tell when he doesn't want to be friends anymore?
Can you think of ways people might create false impressions? (By the way they dress, bragging, spending a lot of money, being "two-faced.")	As students answer, write their ideas on the board. Older students may work in pairs and role play their ideas. Their answers may include: avoids me, gets angry quickly, picks on little things to disagree about, doesn't want to do things together, starts going around with other friends.
Why do people create false impressions? (To look good, feel important, get friends, get something they want, get attention)	
We call people who create false impressions "phonies." They are fakes, not true. How does God feel about people who make false impressions? Let's find out by looking at a member of King David's family.	Play the second part of the interview on the *Teacher Cassette*. Then ask your students if they agree with the students on the cassette.

application process that uses both logical and lateral thinking. Before the logical thinking activities were to be used, I suggested that teachers should involve their learners in lateral processes, to generate a number of life-situation illustrations in which a generalized truth might apply. *After* the lateral thinking generates multiple illustrations of application, *then* it is appropriate to focus on one or more specific situations to explore how a biblical truth interprets that situation and shows how to respond. The general process is outlined in Figure 78.

Because the logical thinking pattern is characteristic of schooling, a curriculum in which most activities call for logical thought will cue schooling/instructional relationships. However, predominance of activities calling for lateral thinking will encourage faith community relationships. If a Sunday school curriculum provides lessons in which most learning activities call for logical thinking, that curriculum will not support development of faith community.

In summary, then, we can describe the educational process elements of curriculums that will, on the one hand, push the class experience into the realm of schooling, and, on the other hand, facilitate the development of learning in faith community.

FIGURE 78

DIAGRAM OF CLASS PROCESS SHOWING PLACE OF LATERAL AND LOGICAL THINKING ACTIVITIES IN TEACHING CHILDREN

Generalized Truth	Varied Applications	Sensitive Area Determined	Person Response Encouraged
	Generated by the learners through lateral thinking.	Areas relevant to personal experience of *this* class determined by sharing.	How to respond in selected situations explored. Here logical thinking is appropriate.

SCHOOLING CUES

- Aims direct attention to concepts and content.
- Class processes converge on a few life situations as context for application.
- Activities call for logical thought, "right answer" solutions to problems posed by the curriculum writer.
- Logical thought predominates.

FAITH COMMUNITY CUES

- Aims direct attention to the children and their lives.
- Class processes diverge to deal with a variety of life situations.
- Activities call for lateral thinking, generation by the children of many situations from their own lives.
- Activities call for talk about typical situations and problems.
- Activities call for personal sharing of actual experiences and feelings.
- Lateral thinking predominates.

RELATIONAL PROCESSES

The second overall area to evaluate to determine if a curriculum cues the teacher and children to schooling or to faith community is what relational processes are built into the lessons. As we look at the instructions given to the teacher by the writer, we should consider what those instructions imply about personal relationships in the classroom.

Two excerpts from fall 1981 junior curriculums illustrate (see Figure 79).

A glance at these two columns shows immediately a sharp difference in teacher role and the relationships that following the lesson plan will encourage. Samples A and B both tell the

teacher what to say as well as what to do, very strongly patterning the class. But in Sample A the teacher is provided with questions designed to open up discussion, and is told to encourage
an interchange in which the "students think this through on
their own." Sample B uses the word "discuss," but the questions
put in the teacher's mouth call for specific answers, and the
"right answers" are given. The teacher thus is not seeking to
stimulate discussion, but rather to draw specific responses from
the boys and girls.

In Sample A the talk of general opinions moves directly to the
personal: the problems "you've been in." Thus personal sharing
is stimulated. Sample B attempts to move to various ways to
respond to others, but the children are to select ways from a list
provided in their materials. No sharing about how they have
shown love to those who hurt them, about how other people hurt
them, or who hurts them sometimes, or about how they will
show love, is stimulated. The whole process stays away from the
personal and is limited to the cognitive domain.

FIGURE 79
RELATIONAL PROCESSES
IN CURRICULUM

Sample A	Sample B
BIBLE APPLICATION	When students have finished playing the game, use these questions to discuss the concepts covered.
Objective: Students will tell what a modern junior should do to cooperate with God and do right.	Where does love for others come from? (God is love and the Source of all love.) How has God proved His love? (He came in the Person of Christ to die for our sins. God does not love us because we loved Him. He loved us even when we did not love Him.) What happens in us when we accept God's love and His sacrifice for our sins? (God in the Holy Spirit comes to live within us. We belong to God.) Where is God's love? (God is in us so His love is in us.)
Have students turn to page 23 in their books and follow as you read "In Between." **What do you think Eric should do?** Let students give their opinions. Encourage them to be specific and say why they think he should do a particular thing. Some may think their is no harm in Eric's going along with the rest of the gang. Others may think the right thing is for him to keep his promise to Jim, even if the others get mad at him. Encourage students to think this through on their own, rather than looking to you to give the final answer.	
What are some "stuck-in-the-middle" problems you've been in? What did you do? Give several students a chance to share. If they are hesitant, be ready to share an experience of your own—perhaps one where you felt you made the wrong decision.	Listen closely as I read 1 John 4:11. Why should we love others? (Because God loves us.) How can we love even those who hurt us? (God's love moves us to love them.) If we are not moved to love others, what do we know about our relation to God? (We do not belong to God.)
Have you learned anything since then that will help you face similar situations? Let those who wish to share do so.	Pick out ways from your response activity to show love to those who hurt us. How does Matthew 5:44 tell us to show love to those who hurt us? (Bless them with happiness. Do good to them. Pray for them.) As we let God's love shine out to those who hurt us, His love in us grows stronger.

In Sample A the teacher is given a specific instruction that moves him or her from the unilateral imposition to the coequal relationship. "If they are hesitant, be ready to share an experience of your own—perhaps one where you felt you made the wrong decision." This is a very significant teacher instruction. In sharing the teacher enhances his or her modeling impact by revealing inner states, as well as signaling to the children that despite being an adult, he or she is acting here as a friend. In Sample B the teacher never leaves the control role, never involves himself or herself in personal sharing, and instead maintains clear command of the situation by telling the children their responses are right or wrong.

The implications of patterns like these in a curriculum are clear. *If these two excerpts are typical of the whole series of lessons by the two publishers,* then use of curriculum A will support a growing faith community. And use of curriculum B will unquestionably force the Sunday school hour into a schooling/instructional mode, and make it impossible to build a faith community Sunday morning setting!

In some curriculums less clear guidance is given to teachers than in the two sampled above. With such curriculums, it's likely that training of teachers and children alone will have a lasting impact on the relational setting of the Sunday school. When detailed instructions are given to teachers, then it is extremely important to evaluate the relational impact of those directions. What are specific things to look for?

Taking another lesson from the two curriculums represented in Samples A and B, I counted the specific instructions given to teachers as to what to say and do during the lesson portion of the Sunday school hour. Curriculum A contained 24 such instructions; Curriculum B, 28. Teacher instructions are easy to distinguish. They may be in heavy black (indicating exactly what the teacher is to say) or indicated by such phrases as "Arrange for," "Let each plan," "Interview," "Have students write," "Tell," "Show the picture," etc. With the instructions to teachers identified in a given lesson, we can then go back and evaluate the nature and impact of those instructions. Here are several significant factors to look for. These categories have some overlap, but each pinpoints a significant area of schooling versus faith community relationships.

Interaction Pattern

What kind of interaction will be stimulated by the teacher's words and actions? Interaction that is *reactive* (designed to get the children to respond verbally to the teacher) is characteristic of schooling/instructional settings. Interaction that is *interactive* (designed to get the children to respond verbally to each other) is characteristic of faith community. When the teacher is instructed to share in the interactive *as a participant* the faith community aspect is particularly strong.

Control Dimensions

Instructions given to the teacher can pattern a closed system of interaction, in which the teacher never surrenders control, or a more open, noncontrol system. When what the teacher is to say or do constantly exercises that power of unilateral imposition, we have a high control setting. The high control setting is characteristic of the schooling/instructional setting. Instructions given to the teacher that suggest he stimulate open activities (such as free discussion, or letting the children decide, etc.) lessen control behavior, and may facilitate building faith community relationships.

Content Dimensions

Instructions given to the teacher may direct him or her to focus the class attention on content and on cognitive processes, or on experiences and feelings. There needs, of course, to be a balance here. But it is clear that a significant part of the class time needs to be devoted to exploring the experiences and feelings of the boys and girls in relation to the truth that is taught.

The relational importance here is obvious. In chapter 7 we noted the importance of peer relationships and peer modeling. One of our goals in the faith community setting is to build friendships, for friendships between children are vital for the sense of belonging, participation, modeling, and even for the generation of illustrations that makes possible a semblance of instruction-as-interpretation-of-life. For faith community, a significant number of instructions to the teacher must be focused on encouraging the children to express their own experiences and feelings.

Teacher Role

Do the instructions to the teacher cast him or her in the traditional role of the "teacher," qualified because he or she "knows" and can provide right answers? Or do instructions to the teacher encourage him or her to act in the role of a friend? The friend role is one in which true reciprocal behavior is stimulated. The teacher becomes one of the group, indicating this by personal sharing, listening, accepting, expressing appreciation, and those other behaviors identified in Figure 16.

332

Modeling

This is closely associated to several other categories, but deserves mention. Do instructions to teachers cast them in a modeling role? This requires the teachers to share their own experiences and feelings, both positive and negative, as they talk of personal beliefs and values. These modeling dimensions are not characteristic of schooling/instructional settings, but are characteristic of faith community.

We can, then, evaluate curriculum by examining the instructions given to the teachers, to note key factors that throw class relationships into either schooling/instructional or faith community modes. These are:

SCHOOLING	FAITH COMMUNITY
• Interaction as *reactive*, with children responding to teacher.	• Interaction is *interactive*, with children responding to each other.
• Teacher maintains tight control, seeking right/wrong responses.	• Teacher stimulates activities that are more open, less controlled.
• Teacher talk focuses on content and cognitive processes.	• Teacher talk often encourages sharing of experiences, feelings.
• Teacher in traditional role, as the "one who knows" in the class.	• Teacher in modeling role, as a participant who shares.
• Teacher statements withhold data related to inner states/modeling.	• Teacher statements express data related to inner states/modeling.

SUMMING UP

It is clear now, that the relational climate of the classroom is not the *only* factor to consider in selecting curriculum. There are a number of other concerns. What truths are being taught? What processes are used to link truth to life? How are the children helped to live the Word? All these are important issues.

But when we are dealing with a ministry to children designed to nurture faith, then we must pay particularly close attention to the relationships that a curriculum patterns. When our goals are the goals of schooling, to teach information about Christianity, then we will look at curriculum and class process from a different perspective. But when our goal is a ministry that builds faith, we must focus attention first of all on those things that facilitate or hurt the development of faith community within the agency structures of the church.

FIGURE 80
CRITERIA FOR EVALUATING CURRICULUM MATERIALS[2]

THEOLOGICAL CONSIDERATIONS

1. Are the materials based on the Scriptures as the major instructional source for Christian education?

2. Do they provide a faithful record of, and a friendly commentary on, biblical events and teachings, rather than an interpretation of events and teachings that is actually or potentially negative?

3. Do the materials speak with assurance of God's power and goodness in performing miracles, including the great miracles of Christ's virgin birth and His resurrection?

4. Do they uphold the Bible's validity in helping people solve problems today?

5. Do they emphasize the stable, dependable values that the Scriptures teach?

6. Do the materials encourage the learner to commit himself to Jesus Christ as his personal Saviour?

7. Do they make it clear that the learner's right relationship with God is a necessary precondition to his having right relationships with his fellowmen?

8. Do they help those learners who have given themselves to Christ to increase their faith and trust in Him?

SUBSTANCE AND ORGANIZATION

9. Do the materials state understandable and acceptable objectives?

10. Do they contain specific data, main ideas, and key concepts in balanced proportion and arrangement?

11. Do they achieve a focus on main ideas and key concepts to which all other content clearly contributes?

12. Are the materials appropriate to learner's abilities, needs, and interests?

13. Do they cause learners to repeat important experiences and review important ideas?

14. Do the materials increase in difficulty throughout the span of years they cover?

FEATURES HELPFUL IN LEARNING

15. Do the materials provide a variety of ways to stimulate learning?

16. Do they contain and suggest supplementary aids to learning?

17. Do they make thrifty use of the time available for learning?

FEATURES HELPFUL IN TEACHING

18. Are inexperienced teachers able to use the materials without difficulty or confusion?

19. Are teacher's guides or teachers' editions of the materials genuinely helpful, suggesting procedures that make teaching easier and more effective?

20. Do they contain suggestions for teacher planning and growth and for ways of evaluating teaching and learning?

---

[2]Ronald C. Doll, "Twenty Questions to Ask About Sunday School Materials," *Christianity Today,* 3 March 1972, pp. 503–4, as quoted in Robert E. Clark, "Leadership and Materials," in Roy B. Zuck and Robert E. Clark, eds., *Childhood Education in the Church* (Chicago: Moody, 1975), pp. 361–62.

PROBE

▶ *case histories*
▶ *discussion questions*
▶ *thought provokers*
▶ *resources*

1. Ronald C. Doll lists criteria for evaluating curriculum materials. Study his ideas listed in Figure 80 and write a one- to two-page thoughtful response.

2. A cooperative program joined by a number of larger denominations produces four curriculums, each with its distinctive approach: Knowing the Word, Interpreting the Word, Doing the Word, and Living the Word. The lesson below (Figure 81) is reproduced from a Living the Word winter unit. Its stated goal is to

    help students experience what it may have been like to belong to that early Christian fellowship. The small house-church communities contained real men, women, and children—real families who were small minorities fighting for human rights in a sea of secular paganism. To be a Christian was to be different. It took faith, courage, and a willingness to risk everything for the belief one held in a risen and living Lord and Saviour. This is the church and its people in the first century, A.D. By simulating a house church we hope the group will "walk in the sandals" of the early Christians and so learn something of what it means when one says: "I am a Christian, a follower of Jesus."[3]

    Looking through this lesson plan you will find no direct instructions to the teacher of what to say and do. Study the lesson however to define the relational style the curriculum supports, if any. Do you believe this lesson material tends toward a schooling or faith community setting? Be prepared to defend your conclusion.

3. There is no reason why the Bible study approach traditionally used by Evangelicals cannot incorporate faith community relational styles. A few curriculums do. Many do not. For your personal benefit select three curriculums *that would be acceptable in your home congregation.* Using criteria discussed in this chapter, evaluate whether they are likely to shape the Sunday school experience into a schooling/instructional mold, or into a faith community mold. Which is the best of the three? Which is the poorest? Which do you actually use?

---

[3]*Living the Word,* "A Story to Tell, Part 1," Leader's Guide, p. 2.

FIGURE 81
LIVING THE WORD LESSON PLAN[4]

SESSION 2: BELIEFS LEAD TO PERSECUTION

To help students experience vicariously the difference in life style that was part of being a Christian in a pagan society and the anxieties "being different" caused.

- Students will be able to list some of the injustices experienced by the early Christians.
- Students will be able to list several places where house churches were established and tell something of what these churches were like.

BIBLE PASSAGES

Acts 2:1—8:5 (Jerusalem church)
Acts 13:13—14:28, Galatians 5:1—6:10 (Galatian church)
Acts 18:1–17; 1 Corinthians 11:2—14:40; 16:1–4, 2 Corinthians 8:1–15 (Church in Corinth)
Acts 28:17–31; Romans 12:1—15:3 (Church in Rome)
Ephesians 4:6–20 (Church in Ephesus)

TO THINK ABOUT AS YOU PLAN

The believers were first persecuted by their own Jewish people. From about A.D. 30—60 Rome looked upon the Christians as merely a sect within the Jewish religion and gave them the same immunity from worshiping the emperor that the Jews received.

About A.D. 60 this attitude changed. Jewish leaders made sure that the Romans knew the Christians were *not* members of the Jewish faith. Roman officials became increasingly aware that these Christians were converting more and more gentiles to their way. These Christians were not influential; they were poor working persons. So Christianity was declared an illegal religion. This law put every Christian's life in jeopardy. If a Christian refused to worship the emperor, he was declared an atheist. This refusal to acknowledge the emperor as a god was the main cause of persecution. Soon Christains were hated, imprisoned, banished, cast in slavery, used in the public arena as food for the lions, and executed in a variety of ways. A Christian was always in danger.

Other charges against Christians included the charge that they were haters of humankind because they refused to attend public spectacles of the theater. They were charged with breaking up families and mocking the gods of other religions.

Enforcement of the law against Christianity varied from place to place. During the 300 years Christianity was illegal, the way in which the decrees were carried out depended on the local officials. Beyond this, however, there was constant persecution. Christians were discriminated against, were often deprived of justice, and deprived of social equality. We can recognize this same type of persecution of minorities in today's world.

Be sure all is ready for the centurion and the jailer to participate. Materials for the construction of the house church should be in the meeting area. Cloth for headdresses should be cut. See Student's Book, (page 40), for symbols in use for decorating the headdresses. The map showing the locations of house churches and the spread of the church should be posted where all can see it. Have supplies ready for those who will be working on a creed.

Read the section of Acts (11:19–26) that tells of the spread of the church. Read the Bible passages pertaining to the house church or churches formed by the leaders and students in your group.

- Construction resources for making house church such as cardboard, masking tape, felt pens, knives, string (page 29)
- Cloth for headdresses, felt pens (Student's Book, page 40)
- Poetry forms for creeds (page 30)
- "The Early Church Spreads Abroad" map (Resource Packet)
- Panel 1, "Christian Foundations," *Chart of Christian History and Culture* (if available)
- Resource persons to play role of centurion and jailer.

BIRD'S-EYE VIEW OF THE SESSION

- Work on house churches; write rules and creeds
- Arrest Christians
- Discuss experience
- Study the map
- Read story of Paul
- Share/Worship

---

[4]Ibid., Session 2, "Beliefs Lead to Persecution."

AS THE STUDENT'S ARRIVE

Students enter the house-church area by saying the password. New students will be briefed by one of the other students. The following work can be done in small groups.

1. Construction: Start building house church according to the plans made in previous session.

2. Rules: If these were not completed during Session 1, two or three students should complete these.

3. Creed: Create a creed for the house church. Use one of the poetry forms or the sentence "We believe in God as _____" (finish using at least three nouns to describe God). Two or three can work together on the creed.

4. Symbols or headdresses: Those not working in other groups can make these.

ARREST CHRISTIANS

The centurion can be in your meeting place as the students arrive. As the students work, the centurion will arrest one or two members of the house church. The prisoners are jailed without being given any reason. The jailer questions the prisoners about their beliefs. He then gives the prisoners an opportunity to sign a pledge that they will worship the emperor as God. If the prisoner signs, he or she is free but must take a copy of the pledge back to the house church. There the students must determine how to deal with the situation.

If the prisoners do not sign a pledge to worship the emperor, then they should write a letter to their house church asking for support. "If they hear that one of them is imprisoned or oppressed on account of the name of their Messiah, all of them care for his necessity, and if it is possible to redeem him [furnish bail], they set him free." (*Apology of Aristides* 125 A.D.) The jailer delivers the letter to the house church.

DISCUSSION

Gather as a total group. The house church should be nearly completed, the rules completed and the creed should be well underway. All members of a house church should vote on the rules and the creed. If there is disagreement, there will need to be a council of the house church and changes made.

Talk about the feelings of those arrested. How did those left in the house church react? Were there any replies to an appeal for help? The centurion and the jailer should join the discussion. They may add information from "To Think About As You Plan" (page 32).

STUDY THE MAP

Locate on the map cities where house churches were established. Use the Bible to discover the names of churches to which Paul wrote. Find these cities on the map. End the discussion with "The Story of Paul." Note from your reading of his story in the Bible the many ways in which he was persecuted (Acts 9—28).

ALTERNATE PLAN

If you do not use the house church simulation, students may write creeds and make symbols.

DISCUSS

What would the students, as Christians, do if arrested. How would they respond if one of their fellow Christians were arrested?

READ A STORY

Read together "The Story of Paul." Add to the story information about the many ways in which Paul was persecuted (Acts 9—28). Make this a research experience by having the students look up the Bible passages: Acts 9:23–25; 9:29; 13:50; 14:19; 16:22–24; 17:5–9; 18:12; 21:3–36.

STUDY THE MAP

Locate on the map the cities where house churches were established. Use the Bible to discover the cities with house churches to which Paul wrote.

SHARE/WORSHIP

• Share any finished creeds.
• Read Philippians 1:12–14, 27.
• Join hands in a circle. Each person give thanks for some one thing for which he or she would thank the early Christians.
• Sing "We Are the Church."

EVALUATE

Include students in the evaluating process. In what ways are we a community? Is there anything our community lacks? Where does the community need special attention. Are we a *Christian* community?

PLAN AHEAD

Is there someone from an official group in your church who will come for your next session? He or she may need background material explaining the duties of early church officers. A copy of the church constitution will help the official explain present day duties of individuals and groups.

PART 2

SETTINGS

The Home

The Impact of Family
Intergenerational Models
Information Models
Intervention Models
Patterns in the Home

The Church

The Church as Organism and Institution
Sunday School as Faith Community
Sunday School Curriculums

The Christian School

The Christian School Ideal
Faith Community in the Classroom

Twenty-five years ago a book like this one could have ignored the Christian school. Aside from Roman Catholic, Lutheran, Reformed, and Seventh Day Adventist school systems, there were possibly 350–450 Christian day schools in the United States. Today there are probably some 4,000. And two to three

THE CHRISTIAN SCHOOL IDEAL

new Christian schools are being established daily. Today some 20–25 percent of the population is being educated in private schools, most of them Christian. And so today any who minister with children must consider this new ministry setting in which multiplied thousands of children spend their days.

It's hard to trace the explosive growth of the Christian school movement. No contemporary history has been written. Only in the last decade have serious attempts been made to accredit schools, train administrators and teachers, and evaluate the colleges that want to train teachers specifically for the Christian school classroom. We can, however, sketch something of the process that may change the face of education in the United States. And we can sketch the weaknesses that leaders of the movement perceive, as well as understand their optimism for the next decade. In this context we can then go on to sketch the issues with which the Christian school movement must deal if Christian schools are to have an impact in communicating faith.

THE CHRISTIAN SCHOOL TODAY

Leaders in the Christian school movement see the Christian school as hesitating on the edge of fulfilled promise. But today they know that Christian schools are far from realizing the ideal.

Cultural Setting

Thirty years ago few Christian parents ever considered sending their children to a Christian school. The public schools offered a good education. The community was generally moral, and no sense of need for "a distinctive Christian education" was felt. Actually, the Christian schools that did exist outside the denominational framework were typically established for negative reasons. Parents wanted racially segregated education. They wanted to avoid sex education classes, to remove the temptations they felt came when modern dance was taught as physical education, and to avoid the corruption that might come with the teaching of evolution. There was no clear vision of a distinctive "Christian" education, simply a drive for separation from influences that were feared by very conservative Christians. Parents who valued Christian training, usually in a rigid and legalistic sense of that term, were the ones who sent their children to a Christian grammar or high school.

In the early 1960s and even into the 70s, parents who wanted their children to get a good education sent them to the public schools. The Christian school had low social acceptability, and the quality of the education provided was generally poor. Children in Christian schools tested six months to a year behind their age group.

Today that situation has changed. Today the Christian school is not only socially acceptable, but many parents view it as highly desirable. Thousands of Christian schools have come of age academically, and the public schools are widely perceived to offer inferior teaching. The view is attested by consistently falling test scores in the public schools, and by widely publicized scandals revealing multitudes of public high school graduates who can't even read the want ads with comprehension. Tests of children in the Association of Christian Schools, International (ACSI) have shown that academically the boys and girls are generally from one to three years ahead of those in public education. Only costs, which range up to $2,000 a year per child, keep thousands of families from adding to the flood of those leaving the public schools for the private.

Financial and Legal Considerations

The cost factor is a serious issue to the Christian school movement. Expenses are high, but salaries are generally only 70–90 percent of those in public schools. Yet many parents who are eager to send their children to Christian schools are unable to pay the necessary fees.

Even so the flood of children into the private school system has alarmed the public school establishment, and led to many legal attacks on the Christian school movement. One of the most serious is an attack by the Internal Revenue Service on the tax exempt status of Christian schools. The IRS argues that the Christian school is simply another private school (not a religious organization) and should not be considered tax exempt. Much of the energy of the Christian school movement is diverted into defending itself against such attacks, rather than being focused on growth toward its own ideal.

At the same time, other forces are being exerted that may open the movement to even more spectacular growth. Two concepts are currently being pressed in Washington. One argues that a tuition tax credit ought to be made available to parents who send their children to private schools. The other argues the radical but exciting notion that education ought to be offered competitively rather than through a public monopoly. This could be done, the proponents argue, if only parents were given vouchers for the amount of money the public spends on education per child, and these vouchers were used to pay the way of the children in whatever school the parents choose. The argument for the voucher system is not religious. Instead, the argument is that the only way to ensure quality education for America's children is to make the schools immediately responsible to the consumer. If a school fails to teach and provide an appropriate environment for learning, the parent would have the freedom to withdraw children and place them in another school that actually does the job.

It is stunning to realize that general dissatisfaction with public education has already led to some 20–25 percent of our children being educated today in private schools. There is no doubt that if the tuition tax credit law and especially the voucher law were passed, as many as 50 percent of the children in the United States might soon be enrolled in Christian schools! While the current political setting favors the public school lobby, continuing deterioration of public school education may well lead to a political perception that the tax credit or voucher systems are wanted by the public.

Curriculum

One of the most serious problems facing the Christian school movement is the lack of distinctive curriculum materials. Christian schools today have only limited and flawed curriculum options.

One option is to use textbooks provided by publishers for the public schools. This is a serious problem for many, because one of the arguments offered for the existence of Christian schools is the need for integration of faith and learning. To provide a truly Christian education, leaders realize, all that is taught in the public schools must be taught in the Christian school, but with a distinctive difference. There must be integration with and evaluation of the content by a biblical understanding of life. Children and youth need to be taught from the perspective of Christian commitment and a biblical world view. To have Christian teachers teach Christian boys and girls secular subjects in the same way these subjects are taught in the public schools falls short of a "Christian education."

Two approaches to integration have been taken. One involves the revision of older textbooks by "laundering" books that are ten to twenty years old to get rid of "objectionable" material and to add Bible verses. The books are then shifted down, making a sixth grade text a fifth grade text, etc., so the courses can be promoted as "advanced" materials. Aside from the deceptiveness of this approach, the laundering process adds only a thin veneer of Christianity. No real integration of the content is accomplished, and the ideal of a truly Christian education is violated.

The other approach to integration is also superficial. This approach has been taken by publishers who have created courses specifically for the Christian schools. A Beka Books offers detailed lesson plans, with the class process designed down to the minute. The rigid, authoritarian classroom structure it provides assumes that the teacher and the learning group need no training and no freedom for interaction. The Accelerated Christian Education (ACE) materials and the Alpha-Omega materials operate with self-guided learning packets, permitting individual students to operate at their own pace. Until forced by criticism to change, one group affirmed that "any housewife can be a Christian school teacher" with such materials. Examination of the materials shows that they are tragically superficial as they leave out critical thinking processes and opportunities for interaction with others. In fact they are little more than poor correspondence courses promoted as a school curriculum. And despite the sprinkling of Bible verses, significant integration of content and faith simply does not take place.

There are encouraging trends in the area of curriculum. The science material provided by Bob Jones University does make a serious attempt at integration. And new guides being developed at Fleming H. Revell publishing company focus on the integration issue. But the future of a distinctive curriculum for Christian schools that seeks to teach basic subject matter in such a way that faith and learning are integrated is still uncertain.

Associations

Today there are several associations and groups of Christian schools. These seem likely to coalesce into three broad groupings.

One group of schools will be oriented to Bob Jones University. It is likely that ACE schools will move in this direction. These schools will tend to be militant, legalistic, and rigidly separatistic in their approach to faith. Educationally they will be strongly traditional, with the teacher dominant and the children regimented. This group of schools will tend to treat the Bible cognitively, and it may or may not utilize materials that make a responsible attempt at integration of faith and learning.

The Reformed schools (CSI) have existed as a distinctive group for many years. In general they provide a good education, but have not seriously addressed the issue of integration. In many localities CSI schools are losing students at a time when other Christian schools are expanding dramatically.

The third group of schools are represented by ACSI (Association of Christian Schools, International). Some 1,600 schools in the United States are in the association, which is taking a number of steps to upgrade the quality of member schools. Schools in this group are most likely to make progress toward the ideal, as they have both a concern for integration and an openness to nontraditional classroom structures. While there is no guarantee that schools in this group will actually face and deal with the issues that must be faced, a number of positive steps have been taken. In 1981 regional training conferences hosted some 18,000 Christian school teachers. An intensive annual institute at Winona Lake, Indiana, reaches 400–500 administrators, and is expected soon to provide training for 1,000. It is possible that a distinctive school system, concerned with providing a context for faith development and intellectual integration of faith and life, may emerge through the ACSI.

Teachers and Administrators

Possibly the most serious problem facing the Christian school movement is the lack of qualified teachers. This is serious because, for those who dream of the ideal, a "qualified" teacher is not just someone who is a Christian and has a teacher's certificate. To be qualified for the ideal Christian school a teacher must have a vital personal Christian experience and must be a person who can build relationships with children that facilitate modeling. The teacher must not only be trained in the Scriptures but be able to integrate the subject matter he or she teaches with a biblical world view. While much of the effort of the ACSI focuses on training teachers how to integrate, the admitted fact is that teachers and administrators simply do not, and are not able to, integrate content and truth. Nor are they able to explain how to build a community in which faith will be nurtured in the classroom.

Much of the difficulty can be traced back to the colleges now preparing teachers for the Christian school movement. For many years Christian colleges had education departments that focused on preparation of teachers for the public schools. The dramatic decline in the number of teaching positions has left a glut of teachers on the market and has made education a less than attractive occupation. In response many Christian colleges have begun to advertise preparation of teachers for the Christian school, where jobs do exist. Unfortunately, in most schools there has been no change in the way education courses are taught. The critical question of integration is largely ignored, as are aspects of classroom process that are conducive to Christian nurture. Many Christian colleges supposedly preparing teachers and administrators for the Christian school require little or no biblical or theological training.

Thus while the quality of teaching in Christian schools as measured by traditional certification has dramatically improved in the past decade, there has been little improvement in those areas that might make Christian education distinctive. Tragically, most involved in the Christian school movement do not currently see discipling, faith development, or the building of a Christian lifestyle as significant goals for education.

Summing Up

We can sum up the current situation in the Christian school movement quite simply. Changes in our culture have stimulated stunning growth of Christian schools and have multiplied the number of children and young people educated in them. But Christian schools lack clear direction and distinctives. They have no source of adequate curriculum or of teachers and administrators trained for distinctive ministry. They face financial and political challenges that might conceivably stunt or destroy the movement. At the same time leadership is emerging in the critical areas. Steps are being taken to upgrade teachers, some new curriculum developments seem imminent, and a few colleges are beginning to train administrators to interact with those issues that are distinctive to the Christian school ideal.

TOWARD THE IDEAL

So far in this look at the Christian school the word "ideal" has been used often. But it has not been defined. How do people in the Christian school movement view the ideal? The tendency has been to focus on the question of integration.

Integration

The Christian school movement has been stimulated by those with strong conservative and evangelical convictions. These leaders, while stressing the importance of study of the Bible and the born-again experience, are not satisfied with a superficial evangelism or a programming of behavior. They see the school as a means through which mature, discipled believers, who understand their faith and their culture, can be trained. One influential leader in the Christian school movement is Ron Chadwick, a professor at the Grand Rapids Baptist Seminary in Grand Rapids, Michigan. In a brief statement of philosophy and purpose for the Christian day school, Chadwick writes,

> Much of education in the past has been secular education with a chocolate coating of Christianity. The morning devotions, prayer or Bible reading was to exert a hallowed influence upon school work of the day. But even the addition of a regular Bible course to the curriculum is only adding religion to an essentially secular content. In history, the word Christian has always referred to a Christian worldview based upon the Bible. To attempt Christian education by adding a Christian frosting to the cake of man-made and man-centered philosophy is neither consistent with Christianity nor is it distinctive. All four of the basic areas of curriculum content in the elemen-

346

tary and high school (Abstract Science, Social Science, Physical Science, Fine Arts) must be interpreted and integrated within the recognized world-view. Some still contend that secular education though non-sectarian is not Godless. But the aim of all education for the Christian should be the training of the child to glorify God. It is the purpose of education to restore man to his God-likeness in the world in which God places him.[1]

Few in the Christian schools have articulated objectives or goals. When these are articulated, however, a distinctive sense of religious purpose emerges. For instance, objectives developed by Roy Lowrie, president of the ACSI, reflect distinct evangelical concerns and concerns for development of the whole person. Lowrie lists the following objectives:

1. To teach that the Lord Jesus Christ is the Son of God who came to earth to die for our sins.
2. To teach the necessity of being born again by the Spirit of God by receiving the Lord Jesus Christ.
3. To teach that growth in the Christian life depends on fellowship with God through reading the Bible, prayer, and service.
4. To teach that each Christian should not, and need not, live his life under the dominion of sin.
5. To teach that a Christian should purpose to yield himself whole-heartedly to God, a sustained sacrifice, obeying all of his will.
6. To teach that the Bible is the Word of God and that it is practical and important.
7. To teach that all of life must be related to God if we are to comprehend the true meaning of life.

This initial statement of objectives by Lowrie can be characterized as the common doctrinal commitment of most of the schools in the Christian school movement. But Lowrie goes on to add a series of objectives that express a vision of Christian lifestyle to be developed through the ideal school. Reading them, we see that the ideal the leaders of the schooling movement have in mind implies distinctive personal and social development as well as commitment to basic Christian beliefs.

8. To integrate academic subjects with the Bible.
9. To show the way a Christian should live in this present evil world.
10. To teach the urgency of missions.
11. To promote the application of biblical principles to every part of daily life.
12. To teach the student to apply himself and to fulfill his responsibilities.
13. To teach the student to work independently and cooperatively.
14. To develop creative skill.
15. To develop critical thinking.
16. To develop effective skills for communication.

---

[1]From an ACSI statement of objectives.

17. To teach the knowledge and skills required for occupational competence.
18. To teach Christian social graces.
19. To teach our American heritage and the current problems facing our country and world.
20. To develop an appreciation of the fine arts.
21. To stimulate the desire for wholesome physical and mental recreation.
22. To show the student his present civic responsibilities and to prepare him for adult citizenship with the understanding that government is ordained of God.

Looking over the complete list it becomes clear that when leaders in the Christian school movement speak of integration they may focus on integration of content and faith, but they also envision an integration through the school of the whole person as a Christian within church and society. In effect, their goal is to do nothing less than was envisioned in the pattern outlined in the Old Testament law: to shape the child for a life of holiness in the context of a distinctive, godly community.

Community

While much attention has been given to the issue of how to integrate content and Bible in the Christian school, less has been given to the question of educational process and environment. Yet many leaders in the Christian school movement as represented by ACSI are not locked into traditional classroom structures. By and large, Christian school classrooms *are* traditional and in some branches of the Christian school movement are rigidly authoritarian. Yet other schools are open to flexible classroom processes, and while no Christian theory of classroom instruction has been attempted, leaders are at least beginning to think in these terms. Thus for the Christian school movement the questions raised in this text about the relational climate in which faith is communicated are particularly important. If the goals of the Christian school movement extend beyond the cognitive mastery of information and the development of skills, it is necessary to pay close attention to processes in the school setting that are related to achievement of the Christian school's nurture goals.

Aside from the financial problems facing the Christian school movement, there are probably three critical issues to be faced and resolved in the next decade if the ideal envisioned by those in the movement is to be reached.

The first critical issue is the ability of the Christian school to actually integrate academic content with a biblical world and life view. This will depend on the development of curriculum materials and resources, and on the ability of the leaders to train present and future teachers to do integration in the classroom. Because this issue is beyond the scope of this text, little more will be said of it here.

The second critical issue is the development of approaches to teaching the Bible so that effective integration with life is actually achieved. It is not enough to have Bible courses that drill in knowledge of Bible stories and biblical doctrines. Instead the Bible needs to be taught in such a way that truth is linked vitally with the immediate life and experiences of the students, so that truth can be experienced as well as verbalized. In a very real way, this is just the same issue as that faced by the home and by the Sunday school. Because the issue is so basic in every setting in which we attempt the nurture of children, part 3 of this text devotes four chapters to models of Bible teaching.

The third critical issue is the design of the classroom to function as a faith community. As long as Christian school leaders are satisfied to teach content and shape the beliefs of learners, a traditional schooling/instructional approach is sufficient. But as men like Chadwick and Lowrie flesh out the ideal, and call for a schooling that will "restore man to his God-likeness in the world," Christians will be forced to seek a unique school: a school that functions as a faith community to minister to children as whole persons, who must grow in every dimension of their personality. The next chapter of this text turns briefly to look at factors that need to be evaluated and explored if the Christian school is to approach the longed-for ideal. For the Christian school as for the family and Sunday school, the development of a faith community setting is not an option. It is a simple necessity if ministry to children is to be carried out in an effective, biblical way.

PROBE

▶ *case histories*
▶ *discussion questions*
▶ *thought provokers*
▶ *resources*

1. Visit a Christian school and observe. Talk with teachers and administrators. What are their goals? Can they clearly state their philosophy of Christian schooling? Talk especially about integration of faith and learning. Can the teachers give examples from recent teaching of how they attempt to relate content taught to a biblical world view? Can they give examples from their classroom of how distinctive Christian living is facilitated? Look at the textbooks and

other materials used. How near to or far from the "ideal" does this school seem to you to be?

2. For information on ACSI write to the organization headquarters on Malin Road, Newtown Square, PA 19073, Roy Lowrie, President. Some Christian schools have developed distinctive and outstanding ministries. One that has succeeded in building a strong link with the family and provides a model for integrating the family and school is the Norfolk Christian School, sponsored by Tabernacle Church, 255 Thole Street, Norfolk, VA 23505.

3. A first significant effort to provide a model for integrating a major subject area, grade by grade, is now being procuded by Dr. Ronald Chadwick. The guide suggests step by step plans for teaching social studies at each grade level in an integrative way. It is available by writing to:

Dr. Ronald Chadwick
Grand Rapids Baptist College and Seminary
1001 East Beltline N.E.
Grand Rapids, Michigan 49505

PART 2

SETTINGS

The Home

The Impact of Family
Intergenerational Models
Information Models
Intervention Models
Patterns in the Home

The Church

The Church as Organism and Institution
Sunday School as Faith Community
Sunday School Curriculums

The Christian School

The Christian School Ideal
Faith Community in the Classroom

Can the school classroom function as a place for ministry with children while still fulfilling its instructional mission? Many books and articles on education raise schooling issues that are closely linked with processes characteristic of the faith community. One day a textbook may be written on instruction in the Christian school, evaluating all these issues from the

FAITH COMMUNITY IN THE CLASSROOM

Christian's distinctive perspective. In this chapter we can note only a few of the issues raised by educators, and suggest that if we are to have truly "Christian" schools in which ministry to children takes place, our structure and approaches to instruction must be just as distinctive as our integration of faith and content.

There are many issues debated by educators today. Nearly all have direct relevance to the Christian elementary or secondary school. By sampling just four areas, we can see how a distinctive perspective on ministry with children calls for us to evaluate the issues educators raise, and find a unique direction for the Christian school. The four areas we will sample in this chapter deal with peer relationships, emotions, classroom structure, and moral development.

PEER RELATIONSHIPS IN THE CLASSROOM

Since the 1930s educators have debated the role of relationships between children in the classroom. Typically the debate has centered on criticism of the individualistic, competitive structure of classroom learning. The values clarification movement of the 1960s and the stress on cooperative learning of the early 70s criticized this characteristic of education. Today there is growing recognition that competitive, achievement-oriented learning processes are not "wrong." However, these styles of learning cannot by themselves prepare children adequately for a life that demands both individual initiative and collaboration with others. Both independence and interdependence are important.

19 This is particularly true in the context of Christian faith, which calls for the full development of believers as persons and also calls for them to live together in love as members in a body that depends on mutual ministry for its health. Awareness of a need for a variety of relationships in the classroom has encouraged definition of a number of issues closely linked with the kinds of relationships fostered in the school.

Cooperation/Competition

Emmy A. Pepitone has pointed out that while competition and cooperation are usually treated as opposites, it is better to view them as "different modes of interaction. Each involves very different behaviors, which need to be studied separately." Pepitone views the school as the most significant environment "for both independence and interdependence training."[1]

Both types of interaction are important if children are to learn to decenter (the process by which a person moves from "egocentrism," in which he or she can see the world only from his own viewpoint), and to live with a sensitivity to others around them. The potential to role-take, and the ability to make

---

[1]Emmy A. Pepitone, *Children in Cooperation and Competition* (Lexington, Mass.: Lexington Books, 1980), p. xxiv.

judgments about other children's inner states, increases at around six to eight years of age, even though children tend to hold their own view to be the correct one. By eight to ten greater skills for collaboration are available, and from ten to twelve complex evaluation of a number of persons' points of view is possible. During each of these periods additional kinds of cooperative relationships and learning activities become options.

Pepitone stresses the fact that role-taking and decentering are involved in both competitive and cooperative activities. But it seems intuitively as well as theoretically likely that there is much greater probability of developing a *concern* for others in cooperative activities. This is particularly true if the cooperative learning activities stress use of affective as well as cognitive data.

Friendships

In an earlier chapter we saw the importance of friendships in children's development. We also noted that the coequal relationships, so vital in certain kinds of social growth, do not develop when an adult exercises the right of unilateral imposition. So one question that needs to be raised in the Christian school is, How much of our classroom process needs to be designed to facilitate the building of friendship?

One study points out that evidence exists that children who fail to acquire age-appropriate concepts of social relationships and experience friendships are at a very serious disadvantage. Many personality inadequacies can be linked with inadequate friendship styles. At the same time, "the different skills that children need to acquire in order to become fully functioning members of society are very much left for them to pick up as best they may." The study goes on to suggest that "educators should, perhaps, devote more attention to the social patterns in the classroom and the ways in which these relate to educational development".[2]

Strikingly, most teachers can list behavioral cues that indicate social immaturity in children. They are thus aware of the boys and girls who most need help in learning to be friends. One list generated by twenty-five teachers in 1962 is shown as Figure 82. What is perhaps even more interesting is that research reported by Shirley Samuels found "that teachers could influence pupil acceptance by peers by overt reinforcement techniques."[3]

---

[2]Hugh C. Foot et al., *Friendship and Social Relations in Children* (New York: John Wiley & Sons, 1980), pp. 109–11.

[3]Shirley Samuels, *Enhancing Self-Concept in Early Childhood* (New York: Human Science Press, 1979), p. 102.

FIGURE 82

CHARACTERISTICS OF SOCIALLY IMMATURE CHILDREN IDENTIFIED BY ELEMENTARY AND JUNIOR HIGH TEACHERS[4]

Grade 1–3:
Does not play with peers in a controlled manner when not directly supervised.
Wants to be "It" all the time; jealousy when playing; will not take turns.
Will not share readily.
Withdraws from the group.
Inconsiderate—pushes shoves.
Lacks respect for others' property.
Does not cooperate in group activities; does not assume his share of the responsibility.
Interrupts; talks and bothers neighbors.
Plays with children younger than himself.

Grades 4–6:
Does not play or work well with others in his group:
(a) Picks fights; consistently employs pugilistic tactics rather than attempting to "talk it out."
(b) Uncooperative in planning games.
(c) Drops out of games when decisions are made against him (e.g., being called "out" in baseball).
(d) Wants his own way.
Tattles; tendency to report very slight infractions of rules and wrong behavior which is of little actual importance; judgment of wrong behavior corresponds to the evaluation of a younger child. Rapid changes in friendship loyalties—ie., a sudden turn against one's seemingly best friend. Extreme shyness with marked tendency to hand his head or cover the face when asked questions. Does not observe common courtesies:
(a) Walks in front of people.
(b) Interrupts when others are talking.
(c) Does not use "please" and "thank you."
Lacks respect for others.
Child feels that rules are made for everyone but him; consequently, makes own rules and does not follow the rules of the group.

Grades 7–9:
Plays with children younger than his group.
Interested in the opposite sex in the manner of a much young person (e.g., would rather play tag than do something socially with a person of the opposite sex).
Child often ignored by peers, which leads to: showing off, giggling, grimaces, pushing or poking, slapping or tripping; or to withdrawal.
Hesitancy in responding when addressed or questioned.
Has difficulty in participating in more highly organized games.
Takes no responsibility for own conduct (must be reminded to be quiet, sit down, etc.).

The point of these quotes is clear. Consideration of the pattern of relationships developed in the classroom and structuring the classroom to encourage development of friendships *is* significant if we are concerned with providing a truly Christian education that deals with the whole person.

If we return to our basic concept of faith community, we can

---

[4]Ronald C. Johnson and Gene R. Medinnus, *Child Psychology*, 3rd ed. (New York: John Wiley & Sons, 1974), p. 354.

see that relationships that facilitate belonging, significant participation, and peer modeling are important for the Christian day school. To work toward the ideal of the Christian school we need a distinctive educational theory that deals with the relational as well as conceptual in the classroom.

EMOTIONAL CONCERNS

As Alfred Binter and Sherman Fry point out in *The Psychology of the Elementary School Child,* "rational man has been, historically speaking, education's primary concern." Thus education has been defined in the easily measurable terms of "acquisition of knowledge and skills." Concern for the affective domain of feelings and emotion has lagged. Binter and Fry suggest several reasons for this particular lag. First, there is the difficulty in measuring emotional and affective growth. How do we know if what we are doing is effective, and how do we establish objectives? Secondly, there is the fact that emotional growth and affective change is long term, while academic understanding can be developed and measured in small, sequenced units. Thirdly, there is a more philosophical reason.

> There is no consensus among educators or parents, in particular, as to what emotions, values, beliefs, etc., children *should* hold about the events, institutions, and people that make up their world. The inability to come to grips with this problem, other than on very general terms, has inhibited educational development of meaningful curricula.[5]

The Christian school has a unique advantage when we turn our attention to the affective domain. The New Testament and the Old Testament provide a set of common values as well as beliefs, and they guide us to those attitudes and emotions appropriate for followers of Jesus. The Christian school is potentially an ideal context in which to deal with the emotional side of life.

However, resolution of the philosophical issue (that is, what values should we hold?) does not mean that the Christian school will effectively deal with feelings and affectivity. In an interesting book, Larry C. Jensen and M. Gawain Wells warn that

> no one experiences an emotion by being told cognitively to have the emotion. Many parents and teachers tell people they should have a feeling— they should love children, or they should respect someone, or they should relax. Such instruction does not produce the emotion. For many it produces a sense of guilt, inadequacy, or, at very best, an obligation for the individual to have the desired emotion. The teacher must structure an

---

[5]Alfred Binter and Sherman Fry, *The Psychology of the Elementary School Child* (Chicago: Rand McNally, 1972), pp. 183, 184.

experience to elicit the feeling desired and either refresh or build upon existing feelings, or provide the individual with a new experience.[6]

Jensen and Wells sketch emotional development broadly, and note a number of factors related to emotional and affective concerns. They suggest that

> a positive emotional climate in the home or school is the single most important factor in influencing stable emotional responding. Particularly important is the experience of being accepted by others, which produces an emotional feeling that "I belong" or "I'm worthwhile" or "I'm loved and a part of this group."[7]

The authors also discuss how empathy for others is developed, and how helping behaviors are encouraged. They suggest that empathy can be increased by means that are directly relevant to the structure of experiences in the classroom. Does the pattern of interaction in the school provide the factors noted in the following paragraph?

> First, allow the child to have the normal run of distress experiences; the child will develop a greater sensitivity to the needs and feelings of others. Shielding a child from distress experiences may narrow his base for empathic understanding in later years. Second, provide the child with opportunities to take the role of others and to give help. This care should foster the empathic awareness of the other's perspective. Third, encourage the child to put himself in the other's place—talking it through with him, including differences as well as similarities between himself and others. Also, of course, the opportunity to observe his parents and other persons behaving in altruistic manners will be important to developing altruistic motives. Models facilitate the process by communicating their thoughts and feelings as they help.[8]

Finally the authors provide model stories, illustrating how content can be used to help children experience, identify, and recognize emotions in themselves and others as a way of discovering how to respond.

When we look at the emotional aspect of the classroom, we must consider more than whether the classroom is a cheerful, happy place. We need to consider Christian perspectives on how persons should feel about themselves and others. We need to consider how to build a faith community in which children feel they belong and are important. We need to consider educational processes and ways of structuring learning to facilitate growth in the affective domain as well as the cognitive. We need to equip teachers to develop ways of teaching and relationships with

---

[6]Larry C. Jensen and M. Gawain Wells, *Feelings: Helping Children Understand Emotions* (Ogden, Utah: Brigham Young University Press, 1979), p. 20. Used by permission.

[7]Ibid., p. 11.

[8]Ibid., p. 19.

children so that emotions may be expressed. And we need to train teachers to use learning activities that link content with affective meaning.

The emotional aspect may be ignored in public education. But it must not be ignored in a Christian school that takes seriously the notions that it has been called into existence to *minister* to children and that it has a concern for growth of the whole person toward Christlikeness.

CLASSROOM STRUCTURE

Each of the two issues sketched so far has implications for the pivotal challenge for the Christian school classroom. Is there a particular classroom structure that will best promote values and kinds of learning to which Christians should be committed?

A number of viewpoints expressed by educators help us see the significance of classroom structure. For instance, Irwin Flescher believes that

> the real question of grouping [in schools] comes down to the basic philosophy of schooling. Children are placed in groups or classes to facilitate the learning process. Unfortunately, they are often distributed in groups for the purposes of academic competition and pressured learning. The educational process may be better served by a grouping arrangement which encourages cooperative relationships and the satisfaction of learning endeavors.[9]

This observation is significant when emphasis is placed on cooperative learning and on the emotional climate of the classroom. It is also significant when we consider creative thought processes, which are just as valid as and in some ways more valuable than the logical, vertical thinking processes associated with the academic. Strikingly, in *Modes of Thinking in Young Children* Wallach and Kogan demonstrated that "the presence in the associator of a playful, permissive task attitude" is vital in developing creativity.[10] The authors point out that a relaxed classroom setting freed from the pressure of short time limits and a lessening of stress on "correct" answers are also linked to creative thinking. They suggest that "there should be freedom from time pressure and there should be a playful, gamelike context rather than one implying that the person is under test."[11]

---

[9]Irwin Flescher, *Children in the Learning Factory* (Philadelphia: Chilton, 1972), p. 93.

[10]Michael A. Wallach and Nathan Kogan, *Modes of Thinking in Young Children* (New York: Holt, Rinehart, and Winston, 1965), p. 289.

[11]Ibid., p. 290.

The 1962 yearbook of the Association for Supervision and Curriculum Development reinforces this position, listing a number of classroom characteristics that can block openness and creativity. The list includes:

1. A preoccupation with order. Much of our practice seems to worship order, categorization, classifying, description and pigeonholing of one sort or another. Such a preoccupation is likely to discourage breaking loose and finding new solutions.
2. Overvaluing authority, support, evidence and the "scientific method." Such rigid, tight concepts often permit no question or exploration.
3. Exclusive emphasis on the historical point of view. This seems to imply that those things that have been discovered in the past are always good: change or the present is bad.
4. Various forms of "cookbook" approaches—the "filling in the blanks," "color the picture correctly" approach. This is an ever present danger of teaching machines, also, if they permit only the "given" answers.
5. The essentially solitary approach to learning often emphasized in some classrooms—creativity is very highly dependent on communication.
6. The elimination of self from the classroom.
7. The school which ruled almost entirely by adult concepts.
8. Emphasis upon force, threat and coercion. The use of "guilt" and "badness" as means of control; also severe forms of punishment, ridicule and humiliation. Anything which diminishes the self interferes with openness and creativity.
9. The idea that mistakes are sinful and that children are not to be trusted. Where mistakes are not permitted, there can be no experimentation. Teachers who fear youngsters and the possibilities that they may get out of hand cannot permit the kind of movement and freedom required by creativity.
10. School organizations which emphasize lock-step approaches, rules and regulations, managerial and administrative considerations, rather than human ones.[12]

It is important to realize that we're not speaking of a simple removal of certain negative practices. As Pepitone points out,

When restraints against comparing, communication, and helping each other are experimentally removed, children still do not naturally begin working well together. These restraints are theoretically removed in the open classroom, but providing a classroom climate conducive to cooperative interaction is not a sufficient requirement for collaboration. Elementary school children must be taught the social skills needed to be cooperative members of groups, and they must be taught to apply these skills to specific task groups.[13]

In addition, as Figure 83 indicates, the more "open" approach to schooling includes many complex factors that are strikingly different from the common "closed" approaches dominant in our society.

---

[12]Association for Supervision and Curriculum Development, 1962 Yearbook (Washington, D.C.: National Education Association, 1962), pp. 145–46.
[13]Pepitone, *Children in Cooperation and Competition*, p. 375.

FIGURE 83

OPEN/CLOSED SCHOOL SYSTEMS CONTRASTED[14]

Formal Controls
Orders
Instrumental

Mixing of categories		*Purity of categories*	
Teaching groups:	Heterogeneous —size and composition varied	Teaching groups:	Homogeneous - sizes and composition fixed
Pedagogy:	Problem setting or creating Emphasizes *ways* of *knowing*	Pedagogy:	Solution giving Emphasizes *contents* or states of *knowledge*
Teachers:	Teaching roles cooperative/interdependent Duties *achieved* Fluid points of reference and relation	Teachers:	Teaching roles insulated from each other Duties *assigned* Fixed points of reference and relation
Curriculum:	Subject boundaries blurred (interrelated) Progression: deep to surface structure of knowledge Common curriculum	Curriculum:	Subject boundaries sharp (less interrelation or integration) Progression: surface to deep structure of knowledge Curriculum graded for different ability groups
Pupils:	Varied social groups reducing *group* similiarity and difference—increased area of choice Aspiration of the *many* raised Fluid points of reference and relation	Pupils:	Fixed and stable social groups emphasizing *group* similarity and difference - reduced area of choice Aspirations of the *few* developed Fixed points of reference and relation

TYPE - OPEN

(1) Ritual order celebrates participation/cooperation
(2) Boundary relationships with outside blurred
(3) Internal organization:
   wide range of integrative sub-groups with active membership and success roles across ability ranges
   If prefect system - wide area of independence from staff, but limited exercise of power
   Range of opportunities for pupils to influence staff decisions, e.g. opportunities for self-government
(4) Teacher-pupil authority relationships:
   Reward and punishment less public and ritualized
   Teacher pupil relationship of control - inter-personal

TYPE - CLOSED

(1) Ritual order celebrates hierarchy/dominance
(2) Boundary relationships with outside sharply drawn
(3) Internal organization:
   narrower range of integrative sub-groups with active membership and success roles confined to high ability range
   If prefect system - under staff control and influence, but extensive exercise of power
   Limited opportunities of pupils to influence staff decisions, e.g. limited opportunities for self-government
(4) Teacher-pupil authority relationships:
   Reward and punishment public and ritualized
   Teacher-pupil relationships of control-positional

---

[14]B. Bernstein, *Class Codes and Control*, Vol. 1 (London: Routledge and Kegan Paul, 1974), p. 2.

Without describing that classroom structure exactly, we certainly can say that certain structures of classroom organization are more supportive of the values with which the Christian is concerned than are others, and that certain kinds of relationships support the development of faith community, while other relationship styles actually inhibit its development. It should be clear that if the Christian school movement is to fulfill its promise it will need to develop a distinctive approach to teaching and learning that is reflected in a classroom structure for which its teachers are trained, and for which curriculum is specifically designed.

MORAL DEVELOPMENT

Without buying into the theories of Kohlberg or others, it's clear that the Christian school must be especially concerned with moral development. As children mature, this will increasingly be expressed as a concern for *the content* that is the basis for reasoning, *the behaviors* appropriate to Christian moral commitment, and the development of *the capacity* of children to reason morally. Windmiller points out that "the development of a principled adult results from an interactive process of individuals with others in their environments. Accordingly, the teacher's concepts of morality should include not only developmental and social learning principles, but an understanding of the necessity of adult-pupil interactions in daily classroom events."[15]

Ted Ward, in *Values Begin at Home*, suggests ways that parents can help children deal with the conflicts that emerge as children grow, and ways they can interact that will encourage moral development. His principles are just as relevant to the classroom.

1. *Stimulate inquiry.* Moral conflicts cannot be resolved apart from understanding. What is the issue? What is at stake? What are the consequences? We need to stimulate each other's inquiry into these questions. Moral development absolutely depends on it.

2. *Stimulate verbalization.* Not everyone finds it easy to talk about important things. It's easier to talk about baseball and the weather. But we need to find ways to talk about the moral conflicts we face. This may mean enlarging the vocabulary, especially in dealing with children. Without the use of language to share and to discuss, moral development is slowed severely.

3. *Ask "why?"* Children should try to find their own answers to this question. Moral conflicts and moral development respond to the deeper look at *why*. "Never mind that we disagree," you might say, "just tell me why you see it that way." Seeking understanding comes first; seeking agreement should *follow.*

---

[15]Myra Windmiller, *Moral Development and Socialization* (Boston: Allyn and Bacon, 1980), p. 246.

4. *Provide experiences in which issues are examined.* People who are developing together, as in a family, need common experiences. In order to talk about moral aspects of life you need to share similar experiences. Acts of kindness shared together, such as visiting the sick or bereaved, taking flowers to a neighbor, or working together, make sense even to small children, *if* they are discussed and the moral issues are made clear. Experience and discussion of the good side of life provide the skills needed when the rough spots of conflict must be resolved.

5. *Dialogue (listen responsively).* Moral conflicts respond best to honest dialogue. Conflicts are rarely resolved by speech-making. Even if only one person is wrong, the process of communication demands that all involved have a chance to be heard. We all need to develop the skill of listening responsively. The secret is to *listen* instead of planning your reply. When you do say something, make sure you're responding to what the other person has said.

6. *Explore disequilibrium. Disequilibrium* means realizing that your basic beliefs seem inadequate. It occurs at several points in normal moral development. It sounds like this: "Dad, I've always believed that God made the world and that He is interested in me, but I'm really wondering now." The temptation is to hide such heresy under the rug. "But, Bill, you can't possibly mean that." Stop! Try this instead: "You've got some things to think through. Let's talk. Why don't you tell me how you're looking at it now?" Exploring *with* the person is far more helpful than trying to correct the person.

7. *Stand alongside.* When all is said and done, it's being there that counts the most. The Holy Spirit stands alongside as the presence of God with us. Even so, the major contribution we can make to others, especially within the family, is to stand alongside—even in times of conflict.[16]

Numerous experiments in "classroom democracy" and training in moral reasoning, which stress taking into account another's point of view, have been conducted. While no firm general results have emerged, a number of studies have shown suggestive results when the process included training the teacher in appropriate ways of interacting with the students, and specific training was given the children. For instance, Stuhr and Rundel present a twelve-week instructional design.

In the four introductory classes, hypothetical dilemmas were used to teach the children how to identify a moral issue and to participate in an informal moral discussion. The Selman filmstrips introduced role-playing skills.

The children next became involved in an examination and resolution of the natural moral dilemmas of the classroom. Classroom issues needed to be identified as proper for discussion and solution, whether their origin lay in teacher-student interactions, peer relations, or in the relationship of the group to other members of the school.[17]

---

[16]Reprinted by permission from *Values Begin at Home* by Ted Ward, published by Victor Books, Wheaton, IL, pp. 97–98. Copyright 1979 by Ted Ward.

[17]Stuhr and Rundel, "Moral Education in the Elementary School," in *Moral Education*, Ralph L. Mosher, ed. (New York: Praeger, 1980), pp. 242–43.

Using a "That's No Fair" list, the children were involved responsibly in determining what problems existed and how they should be resolved. The results: "The children who participated in the experimental class improved one-half a stage in moral reasoning, achieving a solid Stage 1 on the Kohlberg scale. In addition, they were able to demonstrate an improved ability to cooperate with others, as defined as the group's ability to work together to complete a task."[18]

The history of experiments with such groups as this fifth grade class indicate that providing isolated training experiences is relatively ineffective when the total classroom structure is untouched. But these experiments also suggest that children have the capacity to take more responsibility than they are given in most schools. It seems clear that if the Christian school is to achieve its stated mission of ministry to the whole child, including the development of Christian character and values, it *must* be concerned with the structure of the classroom and the kinds of interactions and learning that that structure facilitates.

SUMMING UP

There is in our society a strong movement toward the development of a separate Christian school system as an alternative to the public school. Leaders in the Christian school movement have stated objectives for the Christian school that go beyond the issue of "what" is taught, to issues linked intimately with the growth of children as Christian persons.

Currently the primary focus of concern in the Christian school movement is on integration of content and biblical world view. Curriculums that integrate content and the Christian world view are being developed, and institutes are being conducted to train current teachers and administrators in how to do integration in the classroom.

If the Christian school is ever to reach the objectives stated by its leaders, however, another area must also be given attention. This issue is not one of content, but one of process. How is the classroom going to be organized so that learning processes that embody distinctive Christian values are used, rather than processes that support other and often opposing values? This issue is certainly as important as if not more important than the integration issue, when we look at the Christian school as a context for nurturing faith. This issue must be resolved if our Christian schools are to become truly "Christian."

---

[18]Ibid.

PROBE

▶ *case histories*
▶ *discussion questions*
▶ *thought provokers*
▶ *resources*

1. Many issues linked with education have significance for Christians, to which Christians may bring a distinctive commitment. For instance, Ronald E. Bassett and Mary-Jeanette Smythe in *Communication and Instruction* discuss the effects of self-concept on success in school. First read the following excerpt, describing the views of two psychologists, and then respond to this resolution. "Resolved: it is not the responsibility of the Christian school or teacher to deal with children's self-concepts, but simply to provide the best opportunity possible to learn content understood from a Christian perspective."

   Purkey (1970) suggests this composite view of students who demonstrate high academic achievement:
   1. *They have a high regard for themselves.*
   2. *They are optimistic about their potential for success in the future.*
   3. *They possess confidence in their competence as persons and students.*
   4. *They believe they are hard workers.*
   5. *They believe other students like them.*

   Fitts (1972) is another psychologist who has reviewed the evidence of relationship between self-concept and school performance. He concludes that many important variables which affect academic performance are related to self-concept. Specifically, in Fitts' view, students with low self-esteem are likely to be characterized in the following way:
   1. *They have unfavorable attitudes toward school and teachers.*
   2. *They do not assume responsibility for learning.*
   3. *They have low motivation.*
   4. *They have low morale and are dissatisfied with school experiences.*
   5. *They have low class participation rates.*
   6. *They act in ways to create discipline problems.*
   7. *They have high dropout rates.*
   8. *They have poor personal and social adjustment.*[19]

---

[19]Ronald E. Bassett and Mary-Jeanette Smythe, *Communication and Instruction* (New York: Harper & Row, 1979), pp. 30–31.

2. A book by Robert E. Bills, *A System for Assessing Affectivity,* suggests a number of tools by which such issues as the kinds of relationships that exist in the classroom, and the locus of responsibility in the classroom, can be measured. Below are a few items from Bills' Locus of Responsibility Scale. How might such tools be used in a Christian school? What other kinds of scales and measurement tools might be helpful for a Christian grammar or high school?

> *How this class is run is decided:*
> 1. *almost entirely by us.*
> 2. *largely by us.*
> 3. *partly by us and partly by the teacher.*
> 4. *largely by the teacher.*
> 5. *almost entirely by the teacher.*
>
> *The teacher asks questions:*
> 1. *to see if we know the answers.*
> 2. *to see if we have studied.*
> 3. *to start a discussion.*
> 4. *seldom.*
> 5. *almost never.*
>
> *The teacher acts as if:*
> 1. *We can make up our minds ourselves.*
> 2. *We can usually make up our minds for ourselves.*
> 3. *He (she) should help when we need it or are having a problem in deciding and should leave us alone otherwise.*
> 4. *He should take the lead in deciding what we should think.*[20]

These items suggest various perceptions of who is responsible for what happens in the classroom. The amount of student responsibility will, and should, vary by grade levels. But there are theological implications in the question. For instance, if we apply the New Testament doctrine of priesthood of all believers to the classroom, what approach to responsibility is implied for the Christian school? Can you think of other doctrines that might also be relevant to the school?

3. It is likely that classroom organization and structure should vary according to developmental characteristics of children at different ages. For a major project, research classroom structure options, and in view of developmental characteristics briefly define appropriate classroom systems for 1st/2nd, 3rd/4th, and 5th/6th grades.

---

[20]Robert E. Bills, *A System for Assessing Affectivity* (University, Ala: University of Alabama Press, 1975), p. 114.

THE BIBLE
IN MINISTRY

PART 3

Christian educators are always concerned with the use of the *Bible in ministry*. We believe that Scripture is life-shaping; in it God communicates not only His Word but also Himself. In truth about God we meet the Person who is thus unveiled.

Traditionally ministry with children has been a Bible teaching ministry. In many churches however Bible teaching is understood in a narrow way, either as transmitting information and moral principles in a "telling" way (conservatives), or as providing experiences through which the experiences of Bible people can be shared (liberals). Each approach has developed a number of teaching methodologies and skills to enrich teaching. Without denying the validity of either approach or its methods as helpful in teaching the Bible, this section attempts to set forth additional approaches that can be used when teaching the Bible to children.

One thing gives focus to our exploration of the use of the Bible in ministry. The Scripture is understood as God's *revelation of reality*. The Bible is God's Word, unveiling that which man could never invent or even imagine, in order that we might by faith experience the reality unveiled. Bible teaching then must be designed to communicate Scripture as a reality that those who believe will seek, by faith, to experience.

The teaching of the Bible calls for educational designs and methods that will help children perceive Scripture as reality, and encourage them to experience the realities unveiled as much as is possible at their stage of development. The particular goal of this section is to illustrate how the principles first stated in chapter 3 can be applied in our design of curriculum, and in telling Bible stories in any of the ministry settings explored in part 2 of this text.

These chapters, as the rest of this book, are written in the conviction that it is important for children to know the great stories of the Bible and the truths they communicate . . . but that Bible content is learned best when it is taught in such a way as to nurture faith as well.

PART 3

THE BIBLE IN MINISTRY

Goals for Children's Ministry
Enriched Use of the Bible
Curriculum Redesign: The Next Generation
Varied Approaches in Teaching

When we get down to basics, we can say that two things are vital in ministry with children. The first vital component is the development of a faith community within which children can be nurtured. The second vital component is effective use of the Bible, building ways of teaching that are in harmony with the

GOALS FOR CHILDREN'S MINISTRY

biblical pattern of instruction-as-interpretation-of-life. So far we have focused on the first component. In this section of four final chapters, we look carefully at the use of the Bible with our boys and girls.

If you've read this text through to this point, one thing should be clear. One of our goals in planning ministry with children must be to shape a vital faith community, of which boys and girls are a part, as the essential setting for nurture. This stress on the setting and on processes that operate in faith community is meant to stand, balanced, against another goal. That is the goal of teaching the Bible to boys and girls, in ways that are in harmony both with what the Bible is, and how boys and girls learn. Bible teaching has been mentioned a number of times, but the "how" has not been stressed. In this final section we want to explore how we can teach the Bible to children effectively in the faith community setting. In a very real way these are the *only* goals we need to keep in mind as we plan for children's ministry. Other objectives are directly linked with them.

At the same time this stress on participation in faith community and on meaningful interaction with the Bible does raise an important question. How does conversion fit in? What about evangelization of children? In this chapter we want to review what should be involved in our understanding of the two goal areas and explore the question of child evangelism.

CHAPTER 20

NURTURE IN FAITH COMMUNITY

In our theological study in the first section of this book we saw that the nurture of children is to take place in a relational context. Boys and girls are to grow up, intimately linked in love relationship to one another and to adults. Our look at children's relationships with others pointed up that friendship relationships, in which children meet with others as coequals, are as necessary as relationships in which adults maintain a right of unilateral imposition. We also saw that friendships are important across the generations. Thus a complex set of interpersonal relationships, community, is appropriate for ministry with children.

But there is more to faith community than networks of relationships. Jesus Christ through His work in human lives shapes a *faith* community. This faith community is more than a group of people who have common beliefs, or who meet in ritualized patterns on Sundays. The faith community is composed of believers who share a common life, and who together experience the supernatural working of God. The marks of a faith community are recognized when a people of God find themselves fulfilling Jesus' commandment to love one another and discovering that as they grow closer each becomes very dear. The marks of faith community are recognized when a people of

371

God grow in love for the Lord, and find themselves increasing in their commitment to obedience. The marks of a faith community are recognized in worship, in compassion for others in society, and in the gradual transformation of values and attitudes and personality to reflect the concerns and the character of Jesus. Relationships are vital in faith community. But what sets the faith community apart is the supernatural action of the Spirit of God within a people who have come together to work out their commitment to Jesus Christ.

Not every congregation exists as a faith community. But every congregation of Jesus' people has the potential to become a faith community, whose members are intimately linked in love and are committed to live out together their obedience to the Lord. Even in those congregations in which most are not linked in faith community relationships, pockets of community do exist. What is stressed in this text is the utter necessity that, in whatever setting we minister to boys and girls, there faith community be formed.

But the existence of a faith community is only our first key to ministry. The second key is to realize that nurture within faith community takes place through five types of process as I have discussed earlier. Within the faith community we want to design our approaches to ministry to establish and enrich those processes that communicate the reality of the members' faith. Such faith nurturing processes are those that

- communicate a sense of acceptance and belonging
- draw the learner into the community as a participant in those activities through which Christian faith is experienced and expressed
- build modeling relationships between members of the community
- involve interacting with the Bible so that instruction becomes interpretation of life.
- involve the exercise of choice, so that personal commitments to the lifestyle of faith can be made

Understanding how faith is nurtured within a vital faith community sets before us our first goal in ministry with children. We must build a vital faith community, and establish those processes within that community through which faith can be nurtured in our boys and girls.

EVANGELIZATION OF CHILDREN

The April 1981 cover of *Moody Monthly* features a crayoned cover, showing a boy and a girl and affirming, "I am not too young to know Christ." Inside two articles pick up the theme. One quotes some twenty-three different authorities on various sides of the issue and concludes that "parents and teachers shouldn't avoid the salvation question out of fear of picking unripe fruit." The other briefer article points out that Jesus spoke of little ones who believe, and notes that the author received Jesus as a preschooler in Tulsa when he was three. Unfortunately, neither article raises or deals with the controversial and critical issues.

Part of the reason for the omission of such issues may be that in looking at child evangelism we must by the nature of the case raise questions that are unanswerable. What must a child understand? How old must a child be to be able to respond to Jesus? What is the relationship between faith and grasping what the Bible teaches about salvation? Is there such a thing as an "age of accountability"? While it may be impossible to answer such questions with any degree of confidence, we can affirm two aspects of the framework for thinking about conversion of children.

Framework for Thinking About Conversion of Children

Becoming a Christian involves a supernatural work by God. The Bible is clear in its portrait of human beings. Although loved by God, human beings are born in the grip of sin and are portrayed in the Bible as spiritually dead. It is only through God's work in Jesus that we are born again and, in the words of Ephesians, made "alive with Christ even when we were dead in transgressions" (Eph. 2:5). We understand that being born in a Christian family or participating in the life of a vital congregation does not and cannot make a person a Christian. There must be conversion, and conversion is a work by God always associated with personal trust in Jesus as Savior.

Becoming a Christian involves a faith response to God. The Old and New Testaments both give consistent testimony that it is faith that God accepts in place of a righteousness no human being possesses. This principle, stated so clearly in Genesis as Abraham believed God's promise and it was credited to him as righteousness (Gen. 15:6), remains consistent across every Old and New Testament age. But it is vitally important to make a distinction between the basis on which salvation is offered and the object of faith of believers across the ages.

For all time the basis of salvation has been the substitutionary death of Jesus for the sins of all humankind. The Old Testament sacrifices prefigured Jesus' work on the cross and prepared the Jewish people for the culminating sacrifice that would *cleanse* sins that were only *covered* by all earlier sacrifices. Paul explains to the Romans that it is on the basis of Jesus' sacrifice that God can "be just and the one who justifies the man who has faith in Jesus" (Rom. 3:26).

But throughout the ages the *object* of faith, that which called out a faith response in those being saved, has varied. The faith of Abraham was not fixed in the distant coming of the Son of God, but in the God who promised that "a son coming from your own body will be your heir" (Gen. 15:4). Abraham heard the promise of God about an impossible event, and disregarding the evidence of his and Sarah's age, he chose to put his trust in God.

This same God revealed Himself through the covenant promises to Abraham's children and offered forgiveness at the Old Testament altar. In every age God has spoken to human beings, as He now has spoken through His Son in the supreme revelation. Some have heard his Word and responded to Him in faith, passing from death to life. In every age, whatever the particular Word from God the believer heard, it was his or her *trusting response to the person who spoke that Word that constitutes faith.*

Thus in the New Testament James writes about two kinds of faith, one that believes that certain things are true about God, and another that is a personal trusting response to the one who unveils Himself when He speaks. Thus the writers of the New Testament were forced to invent a new grammatical construction when they tried to help us understand the nature of our relationship with Jesus. The Greek of that age spoke of "believing that" and "believing about." The writers of the New Testament joined the concept of belief with a new preposition *in*, and so coined what Greek scholars have come to call the "pneumatic (mystical) dative." Only by an entirely new expression could the writers of the New Testament communicate the fact that Christian faith is a spiritual relationship; that while we believe the words God has spoken to us, ultimately our faith is in *Him.* We may misunderstand or fail to grasp the meaning of what God says to us. But for the believer trust and confidence is reposed in the person of our God.

This theological distinction between the basis of the salvation we are offered in Christ and the object of faith is significant primarily when we struggle with the question of child evangelism. The early preaching of the apostles as recorded in Acts and the testimony of Old Testament prophecy as well as New Testament epistle is that the message that God speaks to us today is the message of our crucified and risen Savior. Abraham met God in the message of promise concerning the birth of a son in his old age. We meet God in the message of forgiveness won by the blood of Christ. Jesus is put forward by God as the place of meeting, where we come at last to see ourselves and God in saving perspective. When we understand sin and forgiveness as they are unveiled in Jesus, we respond in grateful amazement to the gracious God thus revealed, and joyfully rest ourselves in Him.

It is when we do understand this Good News of the gospel that we're forced to raise the question that troubles so many. How much of this can children understand? Understanding the limitations in children's ability to grasp the abstract, many draw back from even speaking about child evangelism. Perhaps, however, we ought to consider the possibility of children giving a true faith response to God *without* a formal understanding of what is involved in our formulations of the gospel. A child's simple response to Jesus may be analogous to the faith response of so many through history who have not understood the cross, but who have met God in the more simple Word He spoke to them, and who have believed.

The Significance of Growth

When all is said, it's not only difficult to point to a moment of conversion with children, it may well be unhelpful. Ultimately, our assurance of relationship with God does not come because we remember a date when we made a verbal commitment, but because we increasingly commit ourselves to live for Him, and discover a growing trust and love. It would be wrong to deny the possibility of childhood conversion. But it would also be wrong to treat response by a child to an evangelistic appeal as an end in itself. Instead we need to focus our attention on providing children with a place within a vital faith community in which they can come to know Jesus and be brought naturally to readiness to respond when God the Spirit does His work in their lives.

Looking back I remember well what I believe was probably the date of my oldest child's conversion. He was four at the time, and that Sunday morning he'd been bad. Riding to church I could see he was troubled and unhappy. I talked with him then about how much Jesus loved him. I told him I knew he'd done wrong, but that Jesus had died to pay for his sins, so they were gone now. He was forgiven, just as I was forgiven for the many things I'd done wrong.

The relief Paul felt was so obvious. Perhaps it was just that he sensed my forgiveness. I know he didn't understand in an adult way what I said. But I still suspect that that was the point in time when God's Spirit touched his tender heart, and he responded to the promise of forgiveness with a simple trust in God.

Later, in one of the churches we attended, Paul constituted five of the twenty-some "conversions" counted in our boys club program. He'd raised his hand and gone into the record books. It's possible that each time some fresh step of inner commitment was made. But whenever the point of conversion came in Paul's life, it was the first step in a life that has been marked by fresh challenges and fresh, deeper levels of commitment. The real challenge in ministry with boys and girls is to provide that context in which the first step can be taken . . . and then a whole lifetime of growth be supported.

The Role of Faith Community

There is one last principle that needs to be expressed. We can affirm the necessity of conversion. And, without understanding all that is involved, we can also affirm the reality of childhood conversions. What is important for us is to realize that both conversion and growth are intended to take place in the faith community context. Those processes that link a child or an adult to the faith community are the very same processes that God uses both to bring a person to the point of conversion and to nurture the new life that conversion brings.

If we take this concept seriously, we're forced to give priority to our own deep commitment to boys and girls! It's not enough to obtain an initial, overt response and then pass on. Those who care about children will make the deeper commitment and provide the long-term relationships and endless love that make faith community God's unique context for His kind of ministry with boys and girls.

THE PLACE OF SCRIPTURE

In the earlier chapters of this book we've touched on the role of the Bible in ministry with children. But until now we have not developed models for the use of Scripture or described patterns for teaching. However, the earlier chapters have introduced concepts that are foundational and must underlie our Bible teaching practice. It's helpful before we go on to look at the "how" of teaching the Bible with children to review the principles that shape our practices.

Scripture and the Faith Community

It is important first of all to realize that the faith community is itself committed to enflesh the living Word of God. In 2 Corinthians Paul picks up a common image, introduced in the

Old Testament and fulfilled in the New. The whole of that old revelation strained forward to a day when God would do a new work within the lives of His people. The law, chipped in stone in Moses' day, in this day of the Spirit is being retranslated, written "not with ink but with the Spirit of the living God, not on tablets of stone, but on tablets of human hearts" (2 Cor. 3:3). The call of God to the faith community is not simply to hear and agree with the Word of God. God's call to us is to put that Word into practice, and thus be Jesus' disciples (cf. John 8:31–32). This theme is often repeated in the New Testament letters. "Whatever you have learned or received or heard from me, or seen in me," Paul writes to the Philippians, "put it into practice." It is in doing God's Word that we draw close to Him, and find that "the God of peace" is with us (Phil. 4:9; cf. John 14:23–24).

The lifestyle of the faith community, then, is shaped as the members of the community seek to encourage each other to practice the Word of God. And the character of the Christian community is shaped as the Spirit of God works His transformation through the practiced Word, transforming God's people into Jesus' likeness with an ever-increasing splendor, which comes from the Lord (2 Cor. 3:18).

It is in fact in the commitment of the members of the faith community to enflesh God's Word and live lives under the authority of Scripture that the faith community becomes a context suited to teaching. Only when the written Word becomes part of the life of the communicator, and is thus modeled, can Scripture be taught in God's intended way. We need to be sure that we understand the faith community as a fellowship of believers who are committed to live out God's Word together if we are to grasp the real character of what it means to be the people of God.

Reality Unveiled

The people of God make their commitment to enflesh the Word because they are convinced that it is both reliable and relevant. We understand the Bible as truth: as a revelation from God, given in words, that strips away human illusions and unveils the basic issues of life as they really are. We come to understand God, ourselves, and our relationships with persons and things, and we are shown those values on which we can build our lives.

We approach Scripture not just as a collection of facts but as a revelation of reality, as a portrait of the life we are called to experience. We realize that each great expression that tells us more about who God is also points us to fresh experiences. Knowing God is faithful, we are invited to trust. Knowing God is just, we are called to do justice. Knowing God is love, we are affirmed as special, and we are taught to view every human being as a person of infinite worth and value. Each great unveiling reminds us that we are given a fresh insight into reality, and that God's words stand as signposts giving direction to our lives.

In chapter 3 we saw that the nature of Scripture as an unveiling of reality gives us a key for the teaching of children. Boys and girls may not be able to understand many biblical concepts. But since biblical concepts unveil reality, and reality can be experienced, it is possible to design learning experiences that appropriately link the Bible with what boys and girls can experience at a given stage of development. One key to teaching children the Bible is to do just this: to design the whole learning process to help boys and girls experience the meaning for them of truths they may not be intellectually able to comprehend.

Instruction-as-Interpretation-of-Life

The final principle is the biblical pattern for the teaching of children. The learning process does not flow in a vertical, logical way from concept to application. Instead of the classroom setting and cognitive process associated with education, Bible teaching with children was intended to be situational. In the situational pattern, Bible truths were introduced in the flow of daily life to explain to children what was happening, and to guide action. It was through the interpretation of many situations by the Scriptures that children's understanding of God's truth was constructed. Long before truths could be explained, they were intuitively understood.

It becomes important then in building our approach to teaching children to take the situational, instruction-as-interpretation-of-life pattern of Scripture as our basic model for the use of the Bible with boys and girls. We need to find ways to link the Scriptures with the life situations experienced by children, and ways to build their intuitive grasp of truths that will guide their response.

PROBE

▶ *case histories*
▶ *discussion questions*
▶ *thought provokers*
▶ *resources*

1. Thoroughly review the material contained in chapters 3 and 6 because it is foundational to the practices suggested in the final three chapters.

2. For many years Child Evangelism Fellowship (Warrenton, MO 63383), has focused on reaching boys and girls with the gospel. Today CEF has over six hundred missionaries and national workers in eighty-six countries, publishes a great variety of visualized lesson materials used by volunteer teachers in clubs and classrooms, and also publishes a bimonthly magazine *Evangelizing Today's Child*. In a letter Riedar M. Kalland, President of CEF, shared the following principles on which the organization's ministry to preschoolers/primaries/juniors is based. Study each of these principles and then write a brief paragraph evaluating each. What do you think each means in practice? If you have the opportunity, visit with a CEF worker and join him or her for a club meeting.

   A. *Children are lost and need to be saved.*
      1. *Children need to know the way of salvation.*

         God loves us.
         We are sinners.
         Jesus Christ, God's Son, died and rose again for our sins.
         We must receive Jesus as our Savior from sin.
         When we receive Christ we are saved from sin and have everlasting life.
      2. *Children must be given an opportunity to receive Christ and be counseled.*
   B. *The Christian child needs to be established in the Word of God and in a local church for Christian living.*
   C. *We must reach children with the Gospel where they are and direct them to the local church.*
   D. *Children can serve God and should be trained to do so.*
   E. *Teachers of boys and girls must have thorough and regular training.*

3. Reproduced in Figure 84 is a Child Evangelism Fellowship tract entitled "How to Lead a Child to Christ." It suggests six Bible verses to use with boys and girls, and suggests how the evangelist might explain each.

   Evaluate the tract. Then write your own paper telling another person how you believe children can be led to Christ.

FIGURE 84

CHILD EVANGELISM FELLOWSHIP TRACT[1]

1   HEAVEN . . . ONLY ONE WAY
Jesus said, " . . . I am the way, the truth, and the life: no man cometh unto the Father, but by me." John 14:6

2   I HAVE SINNED
For all have sinned, and come short of the glory of God. Romans 3:23

3   GOD LOVES ME
For God so loved the world, that he gave his only begotten Son, that whosoever believeth in him should not perish, but have everlasting life. John 3:16

4   CHRIST DIED FOR ME
. . . Christ died for our sins . . . he was buried, and . . . he rose again the third day according to the Scriptures. 1 Corinthians 15:3–4

5   GOD'S WONDERFUL GIFT
For by grace are ye saved through faith; and that not of yourselves: it is the gift of God. Ephesians 2:8

6   I RECEIVE THE GIFT
But as many as received him, to them gave he power to become the sons of God, even to them that believe on his name. John 1:12

(Reverse side . . . Instructions for Adults)

1   HEAVEN—ONLY ONE WAY
   Heaven is a wonderful place! The Bible, God's Word, tells us that there will NEVER be any tears, death, sorrow, crying, pain, or darkness in heaven. No sin can ever enter there. Heaven is a beautiful place. In the Bible we read that the city (heaven) is pure gold like as clear glass. Heaven is a prepared place. The Bible says that the Lord Jesus Christ, God's only begotten Son, is preparing (building) a place for all those who receive Him into their hearts—all who become members of God's family. Wouldn't YOU like to know that someday you will go to heaven to live with the Lord Jesus for ever and ever? Let me tell you how you can be sure of getting there.

2   I HAVE SINNED
   God's Word, the Bible, tells us there is just one thing that will keep us from going to heaven. A heart that is full of the darkness of sin will keep us from ever going to heaven. And everyone in the whole world has sinned. In Romans 3:23 we read: "All have sinned" and in Romans 3:10,

"There is none righteous, NO NOT ONE". Righteous means "right as GOD wants us to be right". Have you ever said anything, done anything, thought anything that wasn't right the way GOD wants it to be right? Have you ever lied, or cheated, or stolen or disobeyed? This is sin! God says, "the soul that sinneth it shall die" (Ezekiel 18:4).

Sin must be punished by death—spiritual death, which means separation from God. The Bible says no sin, or anyone who sins, can enter into heaven (Rev. 21:27).

3   GOD LOVES ME

I'm glad our story doesn't have to stop with that sad note. We read in John 3:16, "For God so loved the world that he gave His only begotten Son . . ." and in Romans 5:8, "God commendeth (showed) his love toward us, in that while we were YET sinners, Christ died for us." Only God could show such love. We are nice to our friends when they are nice to us, but when they aren't nice to us we find it very hard to be nice to them. This is not true of God. He loved us even though we did not love Him and had no thought of Him at all. God, the Father, loved us so much that He sent His only begotten Son, the Lord Jesus Christ, to die for us. And the Lord Jesus, who is God the Son, loved us so much that He was willing to come to earth to die for you and me.

4   CHRIST DIED FOR ME

Even though God loved us, He could not let our sin go unpunished. The Bible says in 1 Corinthians 15:3, "Christ died for our sins . . . was buried . . . and rose again . . . according to the Scriptures (Bible)." When the Lord Jesus, the sinless Son of God, died on the cross He died in your place and my place. He took our punishment so that we might go to heaven some day. Do you believe what God says in the Bible? Could you say this from your heart and really mean it, "Since God said it, then I believe it"? That is faith—taking God at His word.

5   GOD'S WONDERFUL GIFT

God has a gift for you! The Lord Jesus Christ, God's Son, died on the cross so that YOU could have this gift. Do you remember your last birthday? That gift you received? Did you pay for it? Work for it? Of course not! It was a GIFT! God wants to GIVE you everlasting life. You can't pay for it or work for it. You have to believe what God says in His Word—believe that this wonderful gift is for YOU! "For by grace are ye saved through faith; and that not of yourselves: it is the gift of God" (Ephesians 2:8).

6   I RECEIVE THE GIFT

There are lots of people who believe heaven is a wonderful place . . . they even believe that Christ Jesus died for sin on the cross . . . but they are not ready to go to heaven. Do you know why? Because they have never received Christ as their own personal Saviour.

In Revelation 3:20 we read, "Behold I stand at the door and knock: if any man (that means boy or girl too) hear my voice and open the door I will come in to him." The Lord Jesus is saying to you: "If you will open your heart's door by faith (believing) in Me, I will give you this wonderful gift of life—My life—and cleanse YOUR life from the darkness of sin." This is God's gift of salvation from sin. Will you receive Him now so that someday you can go to that beautiful place called heaven? All you have to do is open the door of your heart and receive Him.

Let's bow our heads and close our eyes while you thank the Lord Jesus for dying for you. You may ask Him to come into your heart and save you from your sins right now.

(Note: You may have to help in this prayer especially if you are dealing with a child.)

ASSURANCE

After the child (or adult) has received Christ into his heart be sure to show him from the Bible what God says about salvation. Ask something like this: "Now that you have received the Lord Jesus Christ in your heart will you ever have to die for your sin? No! In 1 Corinthians 15:3 we read that Christ died for our sins. Will you ever have to take the punishment for your sin? No! Why? Because the Lord Jesus took all your punishment for sin.

"But suppose we sin? (Read 1 John 1:9). The Lord Jesus will ALWAYS be with us to help us. We can call on Him at any time. Where is He? (Revelation 3:20). In my heart. We read in Hebrews 13:5 that He will never leave us or forsake us."

Show how one word of "I will never leave thee" may be "worn" on each finger of one hand. Urge him to read his Bible, to pray, and to witness.

PART 3

THE BIBLE IN MINISTRY

Goals for Children's Ministry
Enriched Use of the Bible
Curriculum Redesign: The Next Generation
Varied Approaches in Teaching

The Bible portrays the teaching of children as situational. As life is shared within the community of faith, biblical truths are introduced to explain and to guide as one walks along the way, lies down, and rises up. But in our schools and churches we also concentrate teaching in special time periods and in special places. Often too we share the Bible at home outside of

ENRICHED USE OF THE BIBLE

specific situations calling for instruction. And so the question must be raised, How are we to use the Bible in teaching children so that our teaching is in harmony with the nature of Scripture, the processes of the faith community, and the abilities of boys and girls to learn and to respond?

Generations of boys and girls have been brought up in the United States with their lives enriched by the Bible they have been taught in our Sunday schools and in the home. Of course some have heard the Bible simply as information and filed that information away. Later some may have turned away from Jesus and His claims on their lives. But others have responded in faith to God as a Person. The pictures of Jesus and the tales of the Bible have taken root and early experiences with the Bible have flowered into mature faith.

Some children have heard Bible stories in cold, impersonal settings, with none of the dynamics of the faith community. And some of these boys and girls have been awakened to faith anyway. In many Sunday schools and homes others have learned the Bible from adults who truly loved them, and have grown up feeling that wonderful sense of belonging and of being surrounded by a caring, faith community.

It is important as we evaluate our present efforts in ministry with children not to become critical or to deny the value of what has been done. This emphasis on the need for vital faith community relationships in the settings in which we minister to children is intended to lead to an enriched ministry with boys and girls, not to attack efforts that may fall short of that ideal. In the same spirit, to point up the weakness of schooling/instructional approaches to teaching the Bible is not to attack others, but to struggle toward ways of teaching that may enrich our teaching of the Bible.

And it is important to go on! I've had the privilege of studying ancient files of Sunday school lessons from some of our well-known publishing houses. Tracing teaching across the decades, I've found that the tools we have now are unbelievably better and more sensitive to critical teaching issues. As we saw in chapter 17, some curriculums today are supportive of faith community processes. And some also handle the Scriptures in creative, effective ways. Our goal in looking at enriched use of the Bible and later at curriculum construction is not to suggest that there is a great gap fixed between the concepts suggested here and what is being done at present. Instead my goal is to suggest that we need to go on. We need to continue to evaluate how the Bible is best used with children, and how curriculums can be constructed to fit theologically defined guidelines, and how specific teaching processes can best fit the way children learn.

PRINCIPLES REVIEWED

A number of concepts introduced earlier lead to principles that guide us in an enriched use of the Bible with children.

The Piagetan dilemma suggests that children cannot grasp the concepts and information communicated in the Bible. Why are the cognitive limitations of the young not an insurmountable obstacle to the use of the Bible with boys and girls? There are serious difficulties when we use a schooling/instructional model of teaching with children. But there is more to Scripture than information to be communicated in schooling modes. And boys and girls are more than minds.

So we begin our thinking about how to teach the Bible to children with a special set of assumptions.

1. *The Bible is God's revelation of reality.* Bible truths are not just abstract concepts. They are intimately related to and are an unveiling of reality. Because of this link with reality, Bible truths are intended to shape our perceptions and to guide our experience of life. While Bible truths can be "known" cognitively, they are intended to be "known" experientially and to be linked with life.

2. *Children as persons can experience reality.* Children may not be able to adequately conceptualize Bible truths, but they can experience them. "Forgiveness" may not be understood, but it can be received and extended. God's omnipresence may be beyond comprehension, but "Jesus always sees me" can be linked with children's experiences and so become part of a child's perception of reality.

3. *"Experienced reality" provides common ground between the Bible and children.* The Piagetan dilemma is resolved if we shift our focus in Bible teaching from trying to school children in biblical concepts to trying to help them link simplified truths with their own experience.

These assumptions lead to a simple yet important principle. Our view of Scripture as truth (reality unveiled) helps us see that *the issue in teaching children is not the communication of biblical concepts and their mastery on the formal (adult thinking) level. Instead the issue in teaching children is to translate the great truths of faith into units that can be experienced by boys and girls.*

This understanding of teaching helps us see another important thing. "Teaching the Bible" is *not* simply telling the Bible story and then using workbooks and other tools to drill for mastery of story content or application. Teaching the Bible calls for the design of a variety of learning experiences in the teaching setting through which children will directly or vicariously experience, on their own level, the reality to be communicated. The entire classroom process needs to be designed to translate *what* is being taught into experienceable reality, which can then be linked with or interpreted by biblical terms.

How then should we go about planning learning experiences for boys and girls in the various settings in which we teach them the Bible?

DETERMINING WHAT WE SHOULD TEACH

A number of approaches have been taken historically in selecting Bible content to be taught to children. Many curriculums simply build lesson series around such themes as "Stories of Baby Moses" or "Creation." The stories are told, a moral ("take care of your little brothers and sisters like Miriam took care of Baby Moses") is tacked on, and because the lesson includes biblical material it has been viewed as teaching the Bible.

Other curriculums have reflected more thoughtful approaches. Some editors have catalogued all the stories in the Bible and attempted to grade them to fit the characteristics of children of different ages. Other editors have felt that the Bible must be taught chronologically to children at every age, and so moved in each curriculum cycle from Genesis to Revelation. Other editors have selected story material according to character, or moral categories, or by life needs. Each approach, however, seems to assume that *what is being taught* (the key truth, the moral, etc.) *is to be derived from the story.* And so the construction of curriculum has generally involved selection of stories on the basis of what can be deduced from them.

When we approach the Bible from the standpoint of truth and see it as a revelation of reality, we begin our curriculum construction at a different point. We do not study stories to see what can be taught from them. Instead we look at the whole of Scripture's revelation and seek to determine those great, basic affirmations about reality that are central to a biblical understanding of life. In essence we ask what core truths presented in God's Word should shape the believer's world view and lifestyle.

There are several characteristics that help us recognize such core, or foundational, Bible truths. For one thing, they make an affirmation of identity. By this I mean they place things in distinctive perspective. To say "God is a Heavenly Father" makes an affirmation about the kind of Person God is and provides us in that affirmation with a perspective from which we can sense something of God's attitude toward us.

Another characteristic of core truths is that they suggest

appropriate responses that lead us to experience the reality portrayed. For instance, the Bible's affirmation of God as Father is directly related by Jesus to the believer's experience in prayer (cf. Matt. 6:5–15). We need not babble vain repetitions like pagans, who desperately hope to attract the attention of indifferent gods. When we know God as Father, and approach Him with confidence in His parental love, both our readiness to pray and our confidence in prayer are transformed.

The first step in planning for the teaching of Scripture then is not to go to the Bible's stories but to turn to the whole unveiling, and select those core truths that shape the Christian world view and guide our responses in life. We thus learn to live in the reality that the Scriptures reveal. *What* we should teach children is not Bible stories, but *basic Bible* truths that are relevant to the world view and experience of God's people whatever their age (see PROBE #1, Figure 85).

Later we'll look more carefully at learning activities in the class process. For now, however, it's important to note that when we build our teaching approach on the assumption that our goal is to translate core Bible truths into thoughts and activities that will help children experience the realities Scripture teaches, every part of the class becomes "Bible teaching." It is totally wrong to think of the story told children as the "Bible" part of a lesson. When we understand our teaching of the Bible as translating truths into experienceable reality, every learning activity can be and should be directly related to that task.

DEFINING USES OF BIBLE STORIES

As long as we are teaching children, there will continue to be a need for using story material from the Bible. What we gain by beginning the construction of lessons or units with theology— with core truths that shape the Christian's understanding of reality and of how to live in this world—is a new freedom in the selection of stories and a new creativity in telling them.

As long as stories were the starting point in planning a curriculum, whether those stories were selected by supposed appropriateness for an age group or were clustered historically ("stories of David"), the stories were treated as if they were the *source* of the lesson. The Bible stories were thus treated deductively. The story was told, and then the meaning was explained. In the history of the Sunday school, much of the Bible was treated as a source of moral exhortations rather than a revelation of reality. It may be appropriate for Christians to be kind as Dorcas was, to be brave like David in the face of the "giants" in our own life, and to imitate Samuel's willingness to listen to the

Lord. But it is extremely important that the life responses of believers be responses to God: that how we choose to live be directly linked to the great truths about reality that God has shared in Jesus and in His Word.

As long as those who teach the Bible to children feel that what they want to teach must be logically derived from a Bible story, many foundational truths will not be touched. And many Bible stories will be warped away from the meaning they have in the context of Scripture, so that they are taken to "teach" concepts or actions that are not intended by the writer.

What happens when we affirm that what we teach is not necessarily derived from the stories we used, but rather comes from the whole testimony of Scripture? What happens when we see every learning activity as directly related to teaching and interpreting a core truth, rather than believing that only the Bible story "teaches" a truth? We are freed to use the Bible stories in different and in creative ways, as an element in teaching, and not as the whole of teaching.

Before I'm misunderstood, I do believe that Bible content (stories, memory verses, etc.) should be central in children's classes. After all, the source of all we teach is Scripture. And we want children to grow up with an awareness that it is God's Book, through which He speaks to us, and through which He guides us in our daily life. But to accomplish this we do not have to attempt to deduce what we teach *from* our stories.

Earlier I suggested several ways in which Bible stories can be used in classes nondeductively. I summarized those uses under three headings: enactive, associative, and imitative. Let's look at each of these uses more closely.

Enactive Uses

Children play out the Bible story, participating imaginatively in the events, and to some extent experiencing what happened then as real to them.

It's easy to generate illustrations of enactive uses of Bible stories or material. A unit on grace (the theological core) picks up a story Jesus told in Matthew 18 to communicate something of its meaning to children. The story is of sheep who go astray but who are brought back by the Good Shepherd with joy. Children are given roles as good sheep, curious sheep, and "independent" sheep who want to do what they want to do when they want to do it. Others are given roles as shepherds, with the task of bringing their flock to places where they can rest and find cool waters. As the sheep act out their roles, emotions swirl; frustration and anger develop as the "independent" sheep go astray.

389

Talking about the feelings afterward helps the children sense something of the amazing grace of a God who continues to treat us with such patience and love even when we do wrong.

Associative Uses

Children are introduced to a biblical concept translated in experienceable form. The Bible story is told not as the source of the concept, but to illustrate it, and in order that the concept might be associated with the Bible. An example is the preschool lesson mentioned on page 126 in which the abstract concept of God's omniscience was translated to "Jesus always sees me." Here the Bible story (that of Nathanaiel, John 1:43–51) is selected because it illustrates rather than "teaches" what is being communicated.

The New Testament often uses the Old in just this way. Looking back at the experiences of Israel in the wilderness Paul affirms in 1 Corinthians that "these things happened to them as examples and were written down as warnings for us" (10:11). In Romans Paul affirms that God is both free and sovereign, and illustrates his point by showing how the principles of freedom and sovereignty operated in the lives of Old Testament personalities (Rom. 11). A similar kind of argument is used in Galatians, in which the commanded rejection of Hagar and Ishmael illustrates the impossibility of mixing covenants of law and promise. In none of these cases is the basic theological truth taught in the incident. But in each case history illustrates and the events can be rightly associated with the core truth.

We must *first* establish what core truth we intend to teach, and develop ways of formulating that truth for children as well as learning activities that link it with their experiences. *Then* we can go to Scripture and find illustrative stories to associate with the basic truth just as stories are used by the New Testament writers.

Imitative Uses

Children may also be introduced through Bible stories to models who demonstrate how we can respond to God. Daniel chapter 1 is an illustration of a passage that can be used with juniors in this way. Daniel's response, based on his commitment to his God makes him a beautiful example. Many of David's experiences can be used in the same way.

Hebrews 11 is filled with this kind of illustration from the lives of Old Testament saints whose response to God was based on *faith.* James directs attention to Job both as a model of *patience* in the face of suffering and an illustration of *God's mercy.* Peter points us to Jesus as a model of *submission* when we suffer for doing good (1 Peter 2:18–25).

The Bible itself thus uses Old Testament stories in each of the ways that I'm suggesting we should use the Bible with children. In general neither Old Testament nor New Testament "teaches" basic theological concepts or core truths through events. Instead the basic truths are affirmed propositionally, as events are explained and interpreted or as a prophet speaks authoritatively of God. But the basic truths that *are* taught are all illustrated in historic events and in the experiences of the people of God. We are much more in harmony with the way the Bible itself uses stories if we turn away from approaches to story telling that pretend to derive what is taught from the stories. We are much more in harmony with the way the Bible itself uses stories if we instead build our lessons for children by (1) starting with a core truth, which shapes the Christian's perspective of reality and his life in the world, (2) then translating that core truth into simple terms and into learning activities that will enable its lived meaning to be experienced by children, and (3) selecting Bible stories to use in the class process in enactive, associative, or imitative ways.

Much work must be done with the concepts introduced in this chapter before their significance is grasped. Rather than to go on and discuss the concepts in great detail, it seems better to suggest projects in the PROBE section of this and other chapters through which an individual or a class group can build understanding and skills. Each of the following PROBE projects is designed to build on the concepts introduced here and to show how a mastery of the uses of the Bible with children can be developed.

PROBE

▶ *case histories*
▶ *discussion questions*
▶ *thought provokers*
▶ *resources*

1. How would you complete Figure 85, with appropriate responses to encourage to the realities each truth orients Christians to? What Bible stories or material might you select for use in a lesson or series of lessons designed to help boys and girls build the appropriate understandings and lifestyle?

FIGURE 85
ILLUSTRATIONS OF CORE TRUTHS SUITABLE FOR TEACHING

CORE TRUTH	APPROPRIATE RESPONSES(S)	BIBLE CONTENT
God is a heavenly Father		
God is forgiving		
God is faithful		
God is just		
God hears prayer		
God is creative		
Jesus loves me		
Jesus is coming again		
God is merciful		
God gives good gifts		
God is all powerful		
God is a peace maker		
God is patient		
I am special		
I am a sinner		
God made me able to feel		
I can serve others		
God guides me		
God speaks to me		
I can praise God		
I can obey God		
I can love others		

2. Work up a list of biblical core truths, according to the criteria stated on pages 387 and 388. The list in Figure 85 is suggestive, not complete. If possible work with a group of others to develop as complete a list as you can of truths you believe children between four and eleven should be taught as they are nurtured in Christian faith.

3. When you have identified your list of core truths, list each on a separate sheet of paper. On each sheet of paper,
    a. Jot down a number of ways that the truth might be stated in simplified terms.
    b. Jot down as many ways as you can think of that this truth might be experienced by boys and girls. How will it affect their feelings? Their attitudes? Their actions?
    c. Begin making a list of ideas for learning activities you might use.

4. Begin to build an understanding of enactive, associative, and imitative uses of Bible stories. Here are several projects that can help.
    a. Read through the New Testament and make a list of every Old Testament story used. Study how the writer uses the story and the function it has in his teaching.
    b. Select any Old Testament historical book or one of the Gospels and list every story told in it. Determine first what core truths on your list from (2) above are illuminated by each story in its context. Then note whether the story seems to you to be most adaptive to enactive, associative, or imitative uses.
    c. Two lessons reproduced in this text feature enactive uses of the Bible. They are found in Figure 42 (pp. 214–17) and Figure 81 (pp. 336–38). Study each carefully.

5. Another project is to select at least three primary or junior lessons from four different Sunday school curriculums. Study the function the Bible story has in each lesson and in each curriculum. Could you develop a series of curriculum evaluation criteria that would help a person select the *best* lessons on the market (not considering the faith community criterion developed in chapter 17)?

6. The lesson below (see Figure 86) is taken from a unit entitled *God Made Me Able to Feel*. It uses the Psalms in an associative way, to help children place their emotions in biblical perspective and learn how to deal with them. This lesson focuses on negative feelings, suggesting that even these feelings can be expressed to God. The Bible story is in the form of a play and to illustrate an imitative use of the story with children.

   The lesson also illustrates a number of learning activities designed to teach the core truth and response to it. Included are activities to be done at home during the week and a song to be taught to the boys and girls.

THE BIBLE IN MINISTRY

FIGURE 86[1]
SAMPLE LESSON: GOD MADE ME ABLE TO FEEL

[1]*God Made Me Able to Feel,* Teacher's Guide, Unit 32, 12–16; "Discover Together," Unit 32, Week 2. © 1978, Sunday School PLUS.

Directions:

You can make your own personal Feelings Clock. Start by drawing twelve feeling faces. Arrange these faces, with pictures or names of each family member in twelve spaces around a paper plate. Attach two hands (equal size) to the middle of the plate with a brad fastener. One hand can point out how you're feeling and the other hand to the person who has stimulated that feeling. Put positive as well as negative feeling faces on your clock. At the bottom of the clock leave a space for a note, explaining the "why" of your feelings.

PART 3

THE BIBLE IN MINISTRY

Goals for Children's Ministry
Enriched Use of the Bible
Curriculum Redesign: The Next Generation
Varied Approaches in Teaching

In the last chapter I suggested that when we think of teaching the Bible to children we not try to begin with Bible stories. Instead we need to begin with core theological truths, translate them into words and activities that boys and girls can experience, and thus understand "teaching the Bible" as the total process. Bible stories become a part of this process of teaching

CURRICULUM REDESIGN: THE NEXT GENERATION

basic Bible truths, but are not used as the source *of the truth taught. Instead they are to be selected and used in enactive, associative, and imitative ways. Now we need to turn to those elements of the class that do not involve the Bible story, but that we must still understand are true Bible teaching.*

We approach curriculum with the conviction that every activity is Bible teaching and should be designed to communicate core truth in forms that enable children to experience the reality unveiled in the Scriptures. With this conviction, it's clear that we need to establish some principles to help us plan our lesson process.

FAITH COMMUNITY RELATIONSHIPS

This principle is not directly related to our subject, but as we saw in chapter 17 is a vital part of lesson design. Whatever learning activities we plan, we must be sensitive to the way they encourage those processes that build faith community relationships between teachers and children, and between the boys and girls and each other. Generally most learning activities will be designed to facilitate the flow of relational processes we've seen earlier.

MULTIPLE LEARNING ACTIVITIES

We have seen earlier that the genius of instruction-as-interpretation-of-life is its unique "fit" with the way children think and the way they learn. The pattern laid out in Deuteronomy 6 features a situational approach to teaching. Rather than introduce an abstract verbal concept in a schooling/instructional setting, parents and others in the faith community use the words of Scripture to explain situations as they occur. Children's experiences then as now were relatively limited. And so teaching took the form of multiplied repetitions, linked with the daily doing of boys and girls. The things children were taught in this way would not be understood in a formal, adult thinking, way. But the children would grow to have an increasingly accurate intuitive grasp of Bible truths that would shape their perception of life situations. And children would also have an increased grasp of how to respond appropriately.

We've seen earlier that this situational approach to teaching laid out in the Scriptures fits what we today recognize as the constructivistic nature of children's thinking. Boys and girls build their impressions of the world, and adapt not by learning some abstract idea and applying it. Instead they meet a concept in multiplied situations, and from those experiences build an intuitive grasp or perception that helps them interpret situations and respond in them. Later, as children grow cognitively, their understanding undergoes progressive transformations. Ultimately, as adults, they will be capable of the fullest kind of understanding available to human beings and will be able to think about biblical truths in formal ways. But as children they need help to build intuitive understandings and encouragement to make faith responses in their daily lives.

This overview helps us face the critical problem for those who intend to teach in more structured settings. Whether we are planning "lessons" for the home, or the Sunday school or other church agency, or for the Christian school, our problem is to design learning processes that fit constructivistic rather than formal thinking, and communicate Bible truths in ways best fitted to the way children learn. How, in group settings where we work with limited time and space, can we teach the Bible in a way that reflects Deuteronomy 6?

Several things need to be said in answer. First, no classroom processes can ever *take the place of* the informal curriculum provided by life itself. This of course forces us back to an affirmation of the importance of the home. Boys and girls need others to talk and share and teach them as the different situations of their life occur.

Second, the classroom process needs to provide a variety of learning activities that are linked with the recurring incidents of children's lives. One goal of using a number of learning activities is to help the children build an impression of the meaning of the core truth being taught from a number of perspectives. The greater number of situations that illustrate the meaning or operation of the truth being taught, the more likely boys and girls will build an understanding of that truth on the intuitive level.

Several principles are immediately suggested by this concept of using multiple situations. We should never rely on *single* illustrations either to demonstrate the meaning of a Bible truth or to demonstrate how a truth might be applied in a child's life. We should always work toward multiple illustrations. We should also tend to avoid vertical thinking processes, and in children's classes place stress on lateral (creative) thinking. As you recall, vertical thinking tends to move toward one "right" answer. Lateral or creative thinking seeks to generate a number of associations. This also suggests a way we can test the learning of children. We can test the intuitive grasp of children of the meaning of a Bible truth not when they say back the words we have given them as an answer on tests or quizzes, but when they are able to generate a number of examples of appropriate situations when encouraged to explain the meaning of a truth they have been taught.

Finally, the classroom process needs to utilize the kinds of learning activities that will *cue* boys and girls to recognize out-of-class situations where their choices will be guided by the Bible core truth that the lesson is designed to teach. Two types of cuing are discussed later in this chapter. Both however are concerned with the same issue: that the boys and girls be helped to recognize those situations in daily life that can be interpreted and in which responses can be guided by basic Bible truths.

CUING BY EMOTION

Emotional Map

To understand the importance of cuing by emotions we need to introduce the idea of an emotional map and how it functions in human experience.

We can begin with the more common concept of a *cognitive map.* This is one way of picturing how the mind is supposed to work and how learning takes place. This concept envisions the mind as analogous to a road map. On the map of any state, for instance, all the cities and towns are points, and the roads and highways are drawn as lines that link towns together. Building on this analogy, concepts or facts are envisioned as the towns, and associations between ideas are envisioned as the roads that link them together. Education becomes a process that adds new concepts and facts to the cognitive map and is also concerned with creating more associative links (roads) between ideas. The notion is helpful, because it reminds us that it is never enough just to provide information. We must also stimulate thinking, and thus encourage learners to link information together in significant ways.

Most education in the schooling/instructional model deals with adding new information and attempting to help persons link what they know in significant and meaningful ways. Much of our traditional teaching of the Bible, in Sunday schools and seminaries alike, focuses on building a conceptual map in which Bible truths are taught and appropriately linked with one another, thus shaping a biblical belief system. We teach so that learners will have a cognitive mastery of the Word of God.

But the challenge faced by Christian educators and ministers alike has not been to build a biblical belief system, but to help believers develop a Christian lifestyle shaped by a distinctive biblical perception of the meaning of life in the world. We have all had to consider how to help people who *know* what the Bible says translate that information into an appropriate lifestyle, infused by living faith. Simply put, knowledge does not automatically transfer into values, attitudes, and behavior. In fact, many believers are unable to see the relevance of many truths that they "believe" for the situations of their daily life!

There seems to be little doubt that the construction of a cognitive map that is distinctively "Christian" will not, in itself, necessarily lead to any transformation of life or even appropriate responses of faith in daily life. The mental linkage of idea to idea does not provide the kinds of associations that will make what is known intellectually available for use in daily situations.

It's here that taking into account the fact that human beings are more important than disembodied minds becomes critically important. We need not even go so far as some who suggest that the affective is the critical element. We need only admit that thoughts and experiences and likes and dislikes are all associated with the emotional world to begin to build a paradigm of Bible teaching that offers much promise for teaching all age groups.

The basic assumptions are these. The experiences that you and I and other human beings have in the world are not only linked with our thought processes but also with our emotions and feelings. It is in fact our emotional responses to situations that trigger our thoughts and shape our perceptions, rather than our analysis of a situation triggering our emotions. *As long as our understanding of the Bible and its teachings are not linked to our emotions, it is unlikely that we will remember and apply appropriate Bible truths.* Later we may wonder, Why didn't I think of it *then*? But truths located only on the cognitive map are not likely to be called to mind in an existential situation.

This is another aspect of the genius of the Deuteronomy 6 pattern that casts instruction-as-interpretation-of-life. When God's words are spoken of *in situations,* where the emotional and affective components of the experience are immediately associated with the concepts, a linkage of concept and affect is immediately achieved! But in the classroom, where concepts are typically divorced from emotion and affect, the Bible is learned in a way that tends to make its truths *unavailable* for those very life situations they are intended by God to help us interpret!

What then can we do in the classroom setting to teach the Bible so that what we teach *is* available and thus more easily transferred to real life? *What we can do is to design learning activities that link the truth being taught to appropriate locations on the learner's emotional map.*

At this point we need to explain a little more the nature of what we're calling here an emotional map and specify several assumptions. The first assumption is that human beings experience a range of emotions *in common.* We see this suggested in

1 Corinthians 10:13, where Paul says "no temptation has seized you expect what is common to man." We see it also in the reminder in Hebrews that Jesus is able to sympathize with our weaknesses because He "has been tempted in every way, just as we are" (4:15). The argument is that all human beings share a common nature and are subject to the same kinds of testing. At their roots, the human experience and the full range of emotions to which we are subject are common to all humankind.

A second assumption is that our common emotional life is *not* related to common *experiences*. One individual may suffer the death of a loved one, another may be deserted by a spouse, yet another may have business that takes him away from home. The specific experiences are different, but the sense of loss and alienation may be the same. The common location on the emotional map of three such individuals is directly related to how they feel about what has happened to them, not to whether or not their situations are the same.

With this said, we now have some helpful guidelines for designing in-class learning experiences that can be cued to the actual daily experiences of the learners outside of class. In fact, we have a tool to link the real-life experience and the Bible truths we teach in such a way that truths are more likely to be recalled and applied in assessing a situation and guiding response to it. That tool is, *whenever we teach a core truth we must attempt to link that core truth to emotions associated with situations in which it is to be applied.* When a person is in the situation and feels a particular emotion, that emotion with other situational data will then trigger the recall of truth and shape perception of the situation.

Emotions and Children

The use of the emotional map in teaching is actually most significant for adolescents and adults. They experience a wider, more differentiated range of emotions and are able to link up with emotions through recall and through projecting into the future.

A number of things make it more difficult to use emotions as cues with children. For instance, children's emotions differ from those of adults in that they are more intense, are typically brief, are often immediately expressed, and are typically undifferentiated. That is, the younger children are, the less they are able to identify their feelings except in general terms. The common unpleasant emotions of children are fear, shyness, anxiety, anger, jealousy, and unhappiness. The common pleasant emotions are affection, pleasure, and happiness. It is often impossible to guide a preschooler beyond "sad" as a way of identifying his or her unhappy feelings, or to help boys and girls make distinctions about the situations that cause different feelings.

Another problem in using emotional cues with boys and girls is linked with an issue we explored earlier: their capacity to social role-take. Often in teaching we want to link what we are encouraging in terms of response with sensitivity to how others feel. This too is almost impossible for many younger children.

While it is difficult to design feeling-linked learning activities for younger boys and girls, we should begin to build such learning activities into lessons for older primaries and for juniors. The PROBE at the end of this chapter and the next reproduces lessons that illustrate various kinds of learning activities that are feeling linked. We can, and must, build links between concepts and feelings in our classes if we are to help children perceive truths, and experience them, as realities.

CUING BEHAVIOR

We've noted earlier that because the Bible as truth is an unveiling of reality, what we teach to children can be experienced by them even when they are unable to comprehend the concepts involved on a formal level. To help children construct intuitive understandings of the truths we teach, we want to (1) utilize a variety of learning activities that will provide many settings in which the truth taught can be perceived. In the same way we want to encourage creative thought processes, in which we help the children generate many associations of the truth taught with the things they experience in daily life. Also, we want to (2) use learning activities that help children tie a truth being taught to what we've called their "emotional map." We want to be as sure as we can that affective components are associated with truths, so that feelings will cue recall of a truth that will guide response. There is one additional principle that helps us as we design in-class learning activities for children. We want to (3) use learning activities that will help to "frame," and thus cue, behavioral response.

There is again a theological rationale for this emphasis. Again and again the Old and New Testament writers remind us that we are not just to be hearers of the Word, but we are to be doers. The very nature of Scripture, as an unveiling of reality, calls for us to respond in faith and act on what Scripture says. If we are in a room and see a door in one wall, when it's time to leave we'll choose to exit through the door. Seeing the door guides our actions when we are ready to leave. In one sense, Scripture provides the "eyes" with which we recognize the "doors" in every situation. When we look at our life situations with our eyes enlightened by the Word of God, we then perceive the doorways through which faith calls us to walk. Always the one who trusts God will respond, for faith is always linked in Scripture with a response to God that is translated into inner or overt behavior. The Word unmixed with faith will not produce obedience, and faith without such works is dead and meaningless. Thus there is always an appropriate stress on behavior when we communicate God's Word.

In essence then we want to teach the Bible to children in such a way that they will recognize and make appropriate responses in their daily lives.

Again we sense the genius of Deuteronomy 6. Not only were adults present in children's daily lives to help them interpret their situations by God's Word, but they were also present to guide the children's behavior in those situations. Thus instruction-as-interpretation-of-life linked life situations, the Word, all the feelings that were generated and modeled in the situation, and behavioral response, which again might be verbally guided and modeled by the adult. *In no other pattern of teaching can all these elements be so effectively linked.* But there are things that we can do in classroom situations not only to work toward a feeling-linked and intuitive grasp of Bible core truths, but also to encourage appropriate faith (behavioral) responses!

The principle we want to use is that of cuing to specific frames of children's lives.

Cuing involves a very simple idea. *To teach a child to act a particular way at a specific time, we want to arrange for him or her to receive a cue for correct action before the action is expected.*

Frames are an equally simple concept. *Frames are recurrent situations in a child's life, marked by settings, particular activities, particular people, etc.* For example, special places such as rooms in a child's house may provide a frame. Or special times, such as bed time, when Mr. Rogers comes on television, lunch, recess. Frames can also be marked by people in settings. Mom coming to my room to say goodnight. My little brother when I'm trying to play with my blocks. Two older boys when I'm on my way to school.

Such frames in children's lives are significant. They are recurrent. They are in fact the very stuff of life for children: they are the realities of the lives of boys and girls. And it is these realities we want to link with responses that are in harmony with what God has revealed.

How can we link behaviors with cues that will be recognized by children before the desired actions are to be taken? In a variety of ways. We can place visible reminders in locations where they can stimulate response. The picture of Jesus in Paul's bedroom when he was a child was a cue for times when he felt afraid of the dark. He would look at the picture standing in the light entering from the gap where his door was ajar, and remember he was not alone. The symbols placed in locations where boys and girls were likely to feel temptations, described earlier, were placed there as cues.

Talking over situations before they happen and planning what to do can also serve as frame-linked cues. Older children can role-play problems, linking the role-play to the persons in particular frames or to such things as, "When Johnny wants me to stay even though mom said to come home by five." A chiming of the clock fifteen minutes before bedtime can serve as a cue. And boys and girls who are quite young can act out situations with cut-out paper people, with the action practiced associated with any number of situations or persons that will constitute recognizable frames. Through such learning activities the frames themselves can cue children for actions that put truths they are being taught into practice.

In general, while learning activities that utilize emotional and frame cuing can be used with all children, we will tend to rely more on emotional cuing with older children, and more on cuing specific behaviors within frames with younger children.

SUMMING UP

We can summarize principles that will guide us in developing Bible teaching lessons for use in school-like settings. We recall that our goal is to build even into classroom groups as many of the dynamics of learning associated with the Deuteronomy 6 pattern as possible. To accomplish this we plan learning activities based on the following principles:

1. Build the relational climate and processes appropriate to faith community.
2. Use a number of learning activities that place the Bible truth being taught in a number of settings. And use lateral (creative) thinking processes to stimulate the children to develop a number of associations of the truth with their life situations.
3. Develop learning activities that directly relate the Bible truth being taught with the emotions and feelings of the learners, thus cuing both recall of the truth and response in life situations by the emotion they generate.

4. Develop learning activities that focus on specific frames in children's lives, linking truths and particularly actions to those frames. Thus the frame itself, or something within the frame, can cue appropriate behavior.

Utilizing these principles we will not be able to duplicate the ideal kind of teaching in which truths are linked with life situations as they occur. But we can bring Bible teaching into much closer harmony with the Deuteronomy 6 pattern, and effectively link the Bible we teach with the experiences of boys and girls.

PROBE

▶ *case histories*
▶ *discussion questions*
▶ *thought provokers*
▶ *resources*

1. Figure 87 duplicates a Sunday School lesson for primary and junior boys and girls. It is the third in a series of four built around the core truth, *God Is Merciful*. The concept of mercy is broken down in this series into the simpler formulation, "I care . . . so I help." Bible stories show Jesus performing acts of mercy in which He helps those whose needs He is sensitive to. And children are helped to see that one appropriate response to this truth is that we, His people, can also care about and help others.

   The figure also duplicates the teacher's lesson and a take-home page from the same lesson.

   Look over both this lesson and the one in the previous chapter. Examine the learning activities they use. Then write out *ten additional* learning activities for each lesson. Five of the activities for each should involve linkages of what is taught with children's emotional maps. Five of the activities for each should involve ways of cuing children's behavior within specific frames.

2. Begin now to develop a lesson plan of your own. Select one of the core truths you have identified earlier, and go back over your worksheet for that truth. Select a Bible story or stories you will use, and outline a lesson process step by step. At this point you need only to list activity ideas, not to write them out as a finalized lesson plan.

FIGURE 87

SAMPLE LESSON:
GOD IS MERCIFUL[1]

LESSON 3
FOCUS:

The Gentle Touch

To discover how to let people know we care about them when we do mercy.

Much "charity" and too often official "welfare" is given with a degrading and impersonal brusqueness. Standing at arm's length, money or food are given, and the giver hurries back to more comfortable surroundings with more comfortable friends.

"Mercy" however, involves "I *cared* . . . so I helped." Somehow there is to be a gentle touch that accompanies doing mercy. A gentle touch that communicates care, and makes the person helped feel valued.

sharing LOVE

Coming to know and love each other. John 13:34

Begin this week with a simple sharing activity. Sit together in smaller class groups. Ask the boys and girls to talk about which of two things they would rather have someone do "IF" . . . Talk about *why*.

- If you had broken you leg and had to stay home, would you rather that someone send you a get-well card or someone visit you?
- If you were lonely, would you rather that someone gave you a game, or gave you the game and came over to play it with you?
- If you were low on food, would you rather someone brought to your door a box of groceries they had picked out, or invited you to their home for your favorite meals?
- If you had a broken ankle would you rather someone asked you to come out and watch them play basketball, or asked you to go outside and sit in a chair to play catch or a table game with them?
- If you were having a long boring weekend, would you rather have your friends come by to tell you about the neat movie they just saw or have your friends invite you to go with them to see the movie?

There may be some differences of choice. But in most cases the boys and girls will probably choose the second option.

After these have been talked about, point out that the second choice in each is *personal* . . . the person showing mercy is doing something *with* the other person, not just *to* or *for* them. Doing something *with* other people is one way to let them know we really care when we help.

understanding
GOD'S TRUTH

Creative learning activities which give meaning to the Bible study· Col. 1:9, 10

1. Poster Making. Have the boys and girls make a poster or poster area for today's learning activities. For Primaries have the letters cut out, ready to be taped to the wall or a large cardboard poster. Juniors can cut their own letters from construction paper. The poster words should look like this:

CARE

AND HELP

After the poster has been completed and prominently displayed, let the children revisit several of the Interest Centers they worked on last week. This time the purpose will be to see how real *caring* is communicated for the mercy-needs listed or displayed.

---

[1]*God Is Merciful*, Teacher's Guide, Unit 39, pp. 21–26; "Discover Together," Unit 39, Week 3. © 1979, Sunday School PLUS.

You won't want to spend too much time at these Understanding projects this week. But do help your boys and girls see that some mercy-needs can be met best with in-person contact.

2. Art Center. In which of the pictures on the wall is the person helped feeling really *cared* for?

3. News Center. Is there any way people might help meet some of these mercy-needs that would let the person(s) helped know you really care?

4. Mercy-At-Home Center. How could we let people in places listed on the map know we care for them as people? How can we *care* as well as help?

Again, do not expect deep or great suggestions at this stage. This week's *Understanding* activities are simply to help your boys and girls become more aware of the need to communicate caring with helping. And to prepare them for the Bible stories which illustrate how Jesus communicated to others that He cared for them as He helped.

exploring
GOD'S BOOK

Seeing the truth in the Scripture. 2 Tim. 3:16

HE TOUCHED ME!
Luke 5:12–13

An imaginative and dramatic telling of the Bible story.

"Oh, He's just showing off!" That's what one of the men sitting in the shade said. "Yes," said another. "He just does those miracles and heals people to get a crowd to listen to Him."

Who do you suppose they were talking about? Yes, they were talking about Jesus. They didn't understand that He really *cared* about the people He helped. Jesus cared . . . so He helped.

But how could the people who thought Jesus was showing off ever find out that He really did care?

"I don't believe He really cares" one of the men sitting there said again.

"Oh, yes He does!"

The loud firm voice came from behind a tree. And then a man who said those words came from behind the tree so everyone could see him. "My name is Able, and I know Jesus really cares!"

"How do you know," someone said? "Yes," another spoke up. "How do *you* know?"

"I'll tell you," Able said. "But first, look at my hands." The men looked. Able's hands were strong and tan. "Look at my face," Able said. Everyone looked. Able's face was smooth and tan. "Just a few days ago," Able began his story, "I couldn't use my hands at all. They were crippled, and wearing away with the disease of leprosy. Just a few months ago no one could stand to look at my face. It was wrinkled and covered with sores and ugly scabs.

"Yes, I was a leper, and had suffered from that terrible disease for many years! People couldn't stand to look at my face. For years no one would come near me because they were afraid they'd catch my sickness. For years no one would touch me.

"My father wouldn't touch me. My mother wouldn't touch me. No one would come near me.

"Then one day I was begging in the street in the city. Everyone went way around on the other side of the street when they saw me. No one would come near. Sometimes a person would throw some money to me, or some food . . . but they would never come near. Well, that day Jesus came into the city where I was. I was so excited! I'd heard that Jesus had power to heal people, so I shouted to Him, and fell to my knees right there on the street. I begged Jesus to cure me of my terrible disease.

"At first Jesus didn't answer. He just walked toward me.

"I could hardly believe it! Usually everyone ran away when I got near them. But Jesus was walking toward me. And He came closer! And closer! And closer! Finally, He was standing right beside me! I didn't even dare look up at Him. But I did beg, Lord, if you want to, you can make me well.

"For a moment Jesus was quiet. Then . . . then He stooped over and reached down. He touched me! For the first time in many years another person had touched me! And He spoke softly. 'I do want to help you. You are well.'

"And I looked at my hands. They were strong and tan again! I put my hands up to my face. All the sores were gone! Jesus had made me well!"

"Just a minute!" said one of the men sitting by the tree. "I believe Jesus made you well all right. He had healed a lot of people. But you were in a city. You said yourself. Don't you realize Jesus just wanted to show off to the crowds in that city? Jesus didn't *care* about you at all!"

Able just smiled. "No, you weren't listening very well to my story if you think that."

"What do you mean?" the man asked.

"Jesus touched me *before* He made me well! No one had touched me for years. I was so terribly lonely. When Jesus *touched me* in spite of how awful I looked with my leprosy, I *knew He really cared about me.* Jesus cared . . . and *then* He helped."

Questions to Discuss:

1. How do you think you would feel if no one had touched you for many years? No one ever hugged you or took your hand or sat close to you?

2. Before Jesus came, do you think the leper had any friends? How could you show mercy to a lonely person?

3. Why do you think Jesus touched the man with leprosy? He could have made him well without touching him.

4. How important do you think it is to know that people who help us really care about us?

5. Look at the picture on the front page of DISCOVER. Can you tell the Bible story in your own words from just looking at this picture?

FOR JUNIORS:

This week the imaginative Bible story is printed in DISCOVER. Have the Juniors read the story and talk about the discussion questions. Then, if you wish, have them turn to the STUDY CENTER in the DISCOVER. This week's study activities feature four short incidents that show more ways Jesus actions showed that He *cared* as well as helped.

You may want to do the study activities in class. Or, leave them for at-home learning.

responding
TO GOD'S BOOK
Applying truth to our life. Psalm 119:11

For the last two weeks your group has been exploring possible mercy needs. Now it's time to plan and prepare for mercy missions!

For the "Around the World" emphasis, choose the activities that focus on communicating with church missionaries and or planning gifts to special needs mentioned in DISCOVER.

For the "neighborhood" emphasis, there are a number of "personal touch" projects that might be done, songs to be learned in preparation, etc.

One Special Note:

You may want to take a "mercy mission" trip during next week's Sunday morning time. If so, check next week's lesson now to see if there are activities suggested there you would like to use this week.

1. Choosing Missions Projects. If your children are focusing on the "Around the World" mercy emphasis, now would be a good time to choose a project to give to. Help the boys and girls set a goal on how much they want to earn to send by the end of the month.

2. Letters. To show *care* as well as help, plan with your boys and girls and write a class letter each one can sign. This letter can tell *why* they want to help with the "Around the World" project. It can ask questions if they wish to. It can include a report of ways they are earning money or gathering goods. And, of course, each member of the class will want to sign the letter.

Or, older children may want to each write their own individual letter, sharing why they want to share mercy.

Preparing these letters this week will also help make the money earning projects the children undertake more vital and real.

3. Audiocassette. This is another personalized possibility. Make a cassette recording to send with the gift. Plan with the children what to say. You may also want to have them practice and then record songs such as "I Will Sing of the Mercies of the Lord" (back page of DISCOVER 4).

4. CARE Visit Preparation. Pick one of the mercy need locations you discovered last week and prepare to visit it with your class. This may be an institutional setting, a hospital, a shut-in from your church or neighborhood or any of a number of possibilities. Last week's activities were designed to help you and your children learn of the many mercy opportunities that exist in your area.

Here are some of the things that can be done in preparing to make a CARE visit—a visit that will let people know your boys and girls care as well as help.

● **Singing.**

Singing is welcome in many settings. Use music your children know, or teach new songs. Practice for singing on a mercy mission can take much of the rest of your hour.

● **Picture Album.**

Many residents of nursing homes and other institutions have few if any visitors. Some have no living relatives. Children as a class or with their families can "adopt" such a lonely senior citizen. Institutionalized people who are without family and friends have rooms that are conspicuously barren of family photos and momentos. Your boys and girls can help these lonely people feel more like part of a family by sharing mounted pictures of themselves along with other communications of caring. Use colored poster board or construction paper to make a freestanding background for the picture and other items might include a personal note from the child to the institutionalized person. A note might read something like this:

Dear _____ ,

My name is Kevin. I am nine. I have two dogs, Puff and Ivan. And I liked Star Wars. Did you see Star Wars? If not, I'll tell you all about it.

I am glad I could get to visit you. I care a lot about you. I hope you like me, too. I want to come and visit you again. My phone number is _____ . Call me sometime, okay?

Do you like to play checkers? When I come again, I'll be with my mom or dad or brother, Kenny. Kenny is real good at checkers. Maybe you could beat him. I never can.

Your friend,
Kevin

One of this month's mercy memory verses could be printed on the outside or next to the child's picture

● **"I Care For You" Bookmarks.**

Have the boys and girls clip off the corners of envelopes. (Old ones will do.) They can attach their picture to the bookmark and decorate as they want to. The envelope corner can be slipped over book pages to serve as a book mark. Young Primaries may enjoy preparing simple bookmarks like these for institutionalized people.

● **Mounting a Picture.**

Colorful pictures of flowers or outdoor scenes can be cut from magazines and mounted on construction paper. These simple picture gifts, signed with a child's name, can be another personal kind of "I Care" gift. Again, Primaries will enjoy this most.

- **Yarn Plaque.**

  Cardboard such as on the back of tablets can be covered with a bright paper or painted. To complete the plaque punch holes spelling out "God loves you" or "I Care for You." Link the holes colored yarn. (See illustration.)

For Primaries: Use an awl or old ballpoint pen to punch out the holes in advance of class time.

For Juniors: simply make an outline of the words and let them punch their own holes.

The boys and girls can personalize the plaques by giving them with a card with their name, picture, phone number or address.

- **Mercy Outing.**

  Groups from rest homes or retirement care centers are usually homogenous when on field trips or outings. So often we've seen clusters of institutionalized senior citizens sitting, isolated from the mainstream of society, in shopping centers, parks, and at civic events. How neat it would be for a group of families or your teaching staff to plan with your boys and girls an outing for institutionalized people - an outing in which you communicate caring by "being with" those you're trying to help.

  You'll need to work closely with institutional authorities as to how you will coordinate with their staff, plans, liability, control, etc. But most institutions will welcome your classes' desire to show mercy in fresh creative ways. For example, you might like to take a group of lonely senior citizens to a ball game. Ball games are always more fun when kids are around! Or, you might want to visit a park where children can put on a "show" of their skills. (i.e., frisbee throwing, tumbling, punt-pass and kick, etc) and the golden agers can teach the kids a few old tricks like shuffle board, championship checkers, tiddly-winks and "old time" story-telling.

  There are many ways that you and your boys and girls can say "I care" to someone or to a whole group who receive a mercy visit. Plan ways that are best for the particular visit you are planning together.

  And, if you wish, remember that next Sunday morning . . . when all your children are most likely to be able to take part . . . may be the ideal time to go together.

AFTER CLASS CHECK

It can be frightening yet exciting to plan to meet an individual or group you feel led to care for and to help. Most importantly, it can be a truly moving experience God can use to open hearts of the boys and girls to the real meaning of mercy. A meaning that we learn first of all in Jesus Christ . . . and that your boys and girls will learn as they see His attitude toward others in you.

Here's a true story about Jodie, a college teacher. When Jodie was a child, she felt hurt. People who gave things to her family didn't "feel" mercy and compassion.

KENTUCKY STORY

When I was a little girl growing up in rural Kentucky, my family was very poor. Once a year church people from town would drive up to our little house in their big, shiny cars. They always brought used clothing and shoes for my six brothers and sisters and I. But the rest of the year these "rich folks" would have nothing to do with our family. They wouldn't even let their children play with us.

Every year, when the people came with their shoes and clothes, I felt *ashamed*. Our parents made us all smile politely and say sweet "thank yous" for the town folks' leftovers, but inside we didn't really feel thankful.

We didn't usually think of ourselves as poor. But on those days when the clothes were delivered, we were made to feel poor! We felt the church people really didn't care about us. They never stayed to visit. I don't think they ever bothered to even learn our first names. All they seemed to care about was their own feelings of having "done their duty." They helped us, I guess, but it didn't *feel* like help.

Signed:

Jodie Coulter

TALK OVER:

With your mom or dad talk over how you think the church people from town could have helped Jodie's family in a way that wouldn't make them feel "poor." How would you show mercy to Jodie's family in ways that show you really cared about them?

PART 3

THE BIBLE IN MINISTRY

Goals for Children's Ministry
Enriched Use of the Bible
Curriculum Redesign: The Next Generation
Varied Approaches in Teaching

In teaching the Bible we seek to communicate God's Word in a way that touches the total child, shaping his or her perception of life, his attitudes, values, and behavior within the context of

VARIED APPROACHES IN TEACHING

the shared commitments of a vital faith community. It's exciting to realize that we have many tools that enable us to make our Bible teaching varied, stimulating, and exciting.

In this text two major themes have been stressed again and again. The first theme is that Christian teaching and learning is not "schooling," but instead is the transmission of faith within the context of a vital faith community, requiring enrichment of five vital nurture processes. The second theme, made explicit in this last section, is that the Christian faith community is formed around the person of Jesus, and is marked by a commitment to His revealed Word. It is our common commitment to live out God's Word and experience the realities faithfully portrayed in Scripture, which gives the Christian community its structure and form.

Thus it's particularly important to explore how we are to teach the Bible to children within the faith community.

What I've suggested in these final chapters is that the schooling/instructional model of teaching the Bible is not the best way. Yet there are ways to design our teaching processes even in formal settings that involve elements of the biblical pattern, instruction-as-interpretation-of-life.

We've seen in the last two chapters several characteristics of

C H A P T E R

23

such teaching. We begin our construction of lessons and units by determining core theological truths that we will teach, recognizing that the whole of Scripture rather than stories is the source of these truths. We design a variety of learning activities through which the concept can be communicated as experienceable reality.

We use Bible stories in the teaching process not as the source of the truth being taught, but enactively, associatively, or imitatively. We try to help boys and girls build an intuitive grasp of truths that may be beyond their formal understanding by placing the truth in the context of a number of life settings. And we encourage response to the truths taught by the use of learning activities that cue by emotions or by the frames of children's lives.

In this chapter I want to introduce one additional dimension. This dimension is found in our patterns of talk in the classroom. Teaching never means the provision of raw experiences. Always we must talk about and think about learning activities. The quality of our teaching and our learning will be directly linked with both the quality of our learning activities and how we talk together about them. While the patterns of talk that we identify as teaching may be linked with any learning activities, in this chapter we look at how they can be used with Bible stories. We want to look then at six different approaches to "teaching" a Bible story: feeling-linked, role-taking, generative, modeling, values clarification, and moral dilemma.

Each of the approaches will be used with a familiar Bible story, that of the dilemma faced by young Daniel in Babylon in the king's court, reported in Daniel 1. In the context of the unit, we can take the core truth as "God strengthens us." The story itself can be used either associatively or imitatively in the context of a lesson that will include a variety of learning activities. The story as reported in the New International Version follows.

> In the third year of the reign of Jehoiakim king of Judah, Nebuchadnezzar king of Babylon came to Jerusalem and besieged it. And the Lord delivered Jehoiakim king of Judah into his hand, along with some of the articles from the temple of God. These he carried off to the temple of his god in Babylonia and put in the treasure house of his god.
>
> Then the king ordered Ashpenaz, chief of his court officials, to bring in some of the Israelites from the royal family and the nobility—young men without any physical defect, handsome, showing aptitude for every kind of learning, well informed, quick to understand, and qualified to serve in the king's palace. He was to teach them the language and literature of the Babylonians. The king assigned them a daily amount of food and wine from the king's table. They were to be trained for three years, and after that they were to enter the king's service.
>
> Among these were some from Judah: Daniel, Hananiah, Mishael and Azariah. The chief official gave them new names: to Daniel, the name Belteshazzar; to Hananiah, Shadrach; to Mishael, Meshach; and to Azariah, Abednego.
>
> But Daniel resolved not to defile himself with the royal food and wine, and he asked the chief official for permission not to defile himself this way. Now God had caused the official to show favor and sympathy to Daniel, but the official told Daniel, "I am afraid of my lord the king, who has assigned your food and drink. Why should he see you looking worse than the other young men your age? The king would then have my head because of you."
>
> Daniel then said to the guard whom the chief official had appointed over Daniel, Hananiah, Mishael and Azariah, "Please test your servants for ten days: Give us nothing but vegetables to eat and water to drink. Then compare our appearance with that of the young men who eat the royal food, and treat your servants in accordance with what you see." So he agreed to this and tested them for ten days.
>
> At the end of the ten days they looked healthier and better nourished than any of the young men who ate the royal food. So the guard took away their choice food and the wine they were to drink and gave them vegetables instead.
>
> To these four young men God gave knowledge and understanding of all kinds of literature and learning. And Daniel could understand visions and dreams of all kinds.

FEELING-LINKED APPROACH

One way that we can use Bible stories with children helps them become sensitive to the feelings and emotions implicit in the biblical record. At times, as with David's psalms, the Bible makes the feelings associated with specific events explicit. In other situations the emotional impact on Bible characters is not explicitly stated, but can be deduced from the context.

In a feeling-linked approach these emotions are included when telling the Bible story, so that the storytelling is not a bare recitation of facts.

Several things can be accomplished through the feeling-linked approach to Bible teaching. For one thing, it will help the children become aware of their own emotions, and help them to learn words that correctly label various feelings. This is an important process, for it helps children begin to understand and develop the ability to express what their own emotions are. Also children will become more sensitive to the feelings of others, and better able to recognize emotions in others. Finally we can also help children learn ways to act when feelings are strong; they will do right instead of wrong and will be helpful instead of harmful.

How might the Bible story be told if we were to take a feeling-linked approach in our lesson? Something like this, with the italicized material representing a pause in the story telling to talk over feelings.

Daniel and three of his friends were in Babylon, a great city far away from their home. They were there to go to school, and study hard for three whole years. For those three years they wouldn't see their mothers or fathers or their other friends. They couldn't even keep their own names! They were given strange new names: Belteshazzar, and Shadrach, and Meshach, and Abednego. How alone they must have felt, and maybe even afraid. *Can you think of some other words that tell how they might have felt? Which of these pictures of faces show how Daniel might have felt?*

But then a terrible thing happened. Daniel and his friends were given food that God had told His people not to eat! What should Daniel do? If he refused to eat the food, the people in Babylon might be angry. Maybe they wouldn't let him have anything to eat! But Daniel didn't want to disobey God. "Be strong," he must have told himself. And Daniel decided he just would not do wrong and eat the Babylonians' food or drink their drinks.

So Daniel went to the man in charge of all the students in Babylon and asked permission to have different food. And the man in charge was terrified! His face got white, and his hands began to shake. His eyes were wide open, and his face began to sweat. He told Daniel, in a quivering voice, "You don't know what you're asking! Why, the king himself decided what you should eat and drink. If I let you eat other food—and you got sick or something—why, the king would kill me! You don't know how terrible our king is, or how afraid of him I am! *How do you think people look when they're really afraid? What do you think the man in charge will do now? What do you think Daniel will do?*

Daniel knew the king might be angry. He knew the king was a terrible man. Daniel knew the king might even hurt him and his three friends if they refused to eat the food of Babylon. But Daniel also knew that God would give him the strength he needed to do right. God is greater than the king. God would help Daniel to do right. So Daniel thought about God, and the fear wasn't as strong. It wasn't easy. But Daniel bravely spoke up anyway.

"Just let us eat our food for ten days. Then see if we look weak. I know God will keep us well and strong on the food He wants us to eat." And you know what! Daniel was right! Ten days later, Daniel and his friends looked stronger and better than all the others who had eaten the king's special food.

How thankful and happy Daniel and his friends must have felt. They were so thankful that God had taken care of them. How glad they were they had been strong and had done the right thing! *How do you think Daniel felt about God then? What do you think he did to show God how he felt? How do you think Daniel felt about himself? Did Daniel feel strong? Brave? What might Daniel have felt about himself if he had forgotten God and done the wrong thing?*

If we want them to move on to linkage, we might continue with a question pattern something like this.

- What are some times when boys and girls today might feel afraid to do what they know is right?
- How will they feel if they remember that God is able to take care of them and make them strong enough to do what is right?
- How will they feel if they forget God and do what is wrong?
- How will they feel if they let God help them do right?

ROLE-TAKING APPROACH

The role-taking approach is closely linked with those which focus on feelings. The distinction is more one of stress than of kind. In the feeling-linked approach we try to help children understand and identify emotions and to gain insights into the kinds of actions associated with emotions. In the process we enrich Bible teaching by highlighting the emotional aspects of the stories, helping to bring them more to life for boys and girls. In a role-taking approach we want to stress not the feelings themselves, but the perspective of the persons in the story. We are trying to help children look at the events in the biblical narrative from the point of view of the Bible characters.

It's clear that role-taking approaches in teaching will need to be coordinated with children's ability to decenter, as discussed in chapters 6 and 7. But as children are able, we want them to learn to approach the Bible with a sensitivity to the people who are actors in its stories, so that what God was teaching them through their experiences can be better understood.

Here is the same Bible story from Daniel 1, retold with a role-taking approach. Notice both the similarities and the differences between this and the first approach.

Daniel and three of his friends were in Babylon, a great city far away from their home. They were there to go to school and to study hard for three whole years. For three years they wouldn't see their mothers. For three years they wouldn't see their fathers. For three years they wouldn't see any of their other friends. Why, they couldn't even keep their own names! They were given strange new names: Belteshazzar, and Shadrach, and Meshach, and Abednego. *How do you think Daniel and his friends must have felt? What do you think would be hardest for them? Why is it so hard to be away from family and friends?*

Then a terrible thing happened! Daniel and his friends were given food that God told His people not to eat! What should Daniel do? If he refused to eat the food, the people in Babylon might be angry. Maybe they wouldn't let him have anything to eat! But then, Daniel didn't want to disobey God either. And God had told Daniel's people the kinds of food they should eat and what they were not to eat. *What would make this a hard thing for Daniel? Why wouldn't he want to displease the Babylonians? Why wouldn't he have wanted to disobey God?*

Daniel decided he would not disobey God. "Be strong," Daniel must have told himself. How good to know that God was able to make him strong and help him do what was right.

So Daniel went to the man in charge of all the students in Babylon and asked permission to have a different food. And the man in charge was terrified! He liked Daniel, but he was afraid of the king. He told Daniel he was afraid. "The king himself decided what you should eat and drink. If you didn't eat his food, and got sick or something, the king would kill me!" *What do you think the man in charge will do? Will he let Daniel eat what God wants? Why, or why not? What do you think might change the man's mind?*

Daniel knew how afraid the man in charge of all the students was, and he knew the king might be angry. So Daniel asked for a test. Let Daniel and his friends eat the food God wants for just ten days and see if they are still healthy. It was a good idea! So Daniel and his friends got to eat the food they knew they should for ten days. And at the end of those ten days they looked healthier than any of the other students! God had taken care of Daniel and his friends when they obeyed Him. *What might Daniel have known about God that helped him suggest this test? How do you think Daniel and his friends felt when they were waiting for the ten days to pass? What do you think they said to God then? How do you think they felt after God had helped them stay strong and well? What do you think they said to God then?*

GENERATIVE APPROACH

When we use a generative approach in Bible teaching we try to help the boys and girls link the experiences of the Bible characters to experiences of children like themselves. In essence we try to help them relate the Bible events to life by encouraging them to do lateral thinking about the Bible events, building a number of associations between what happened then and what happens today. Here is the same story, told in such a way that the boys and girls are asked to link its salient features with children's experiences.

Daniel and three of his friends were in Babylon, a strange city far away from their home. They were there to go to school and to study hard for three whole years. For three years they wouldn't see their mothers. For three years they wouldn't see their fathers. For three years they wouldn't see any of their other friends. Why, they couldn't even keep their own names! They were given strange new names: Belteshazzar, and Shadrach, and Meshach, and Abednego.

And just when they were feeling so alone, a terrible thing happened! Daniel and his friends were given food that God told His people not to eat! How hard that must have been for Daniel. He wanted to please God. But the people in Babylon told him he had to do what they said! *Do you think boys and girls today ever have hard choices to make? What are some of the hard choices children have to make, when someone wants them to do things that may not be right? Tell us some of the things. How do children feel when they have a hard decision to make?*

It must have been hard for Daniel and his friends, but they decided they would please God. So Daniel went to the man in charge of all the students in Babylon and asked permission to have different food. But the man in charge was very afraid. He liked Daniel, but he was afraid of the king. He told Daniel he was afraid. "The king himself decided what you should eat and drink. If you don't eat his food, and you get sick or something, the king will kill me!"

Daniel understood why the man wanted him to eat the king's food. But Daniel knew he must obey God. Somehow God would work it out. So Daniel asked for a test. "Just let us eat our kind of food for ten days, and see if we're healthy." It was a good idea! So Daniel and his friends got to eat the food they knew they should for ten days. And at the end of the ten days, they looked healthier than any of the other students! God did take care of Daniel and his friends. God made them strong and brave to do what was right, and He took care of them when they obeyed. *Let's think about some of the hard things children have to do that you told us about.* (Show cardboard figures of children and adults.) *Let's take turns showing what we will do if we remember God can make us strong and help us when we obey Him.* (Children and teacher take turns acting out "hard" situations they have described, showing that God can help others just as He helped Daniel do right.)

MODELING APPROACH

A modeling approach to telling the Bible story is similar to the generative, with one important difference. Rather than seeking to move from features of the story to a number of general associations—to a list of a number of things that "boys and girls today" experience—the story events are linked with the real experiences of the teacher and the children in the class. In this approach a number of different illustrations are suggested. But more importantly, because these are the real experiences of people in the classroom group, their sharing and their experiences provide for both adult and peer modeling. We might tell the Daniel story this way if we were using a modeling approach with this Bible story.

Daniel and three of his friends were in Babylon, a strange city far away from their home. They were there to go to school and to study hard for three whole years. For three years they would not see their mothers. For three years they would not see their fathers. For three years they would not see any of their other friends. Why, they couldn't even keep their own names! They were given strange new names: Belteshazzar, and Shadrach, and Meshach, and Abednego.

And just when they were feeling so alone, a terrible thing happened! Daniel and his friends were given food that God told His people not to eat! How hard that must have been for Daniel. He wanted to please God and obey Him. But the people in Babylon told Daniel he had to do what *they* said! *Have you ever felt God wanted you to do something that was very hard for you to do? Tell us about it, Jimmy? Why was it so hard for you? How did you feel? (Share about a time when you felt God wanted you to do something hard, and tell how you felt at that time too.)*

It was hard for Daniel and his friends. But Daniel decided he would do what God wants. So Daniel went to the man in charge of all the students in Babylon and asked for different food. But the man was very afraid. He liked Daniel, but he was afraid of the king. He told Daniel he was afraid. "The king himself decided what you should eat and drink. If you don't eat his food, and you get sick or something, the king will kill me!"

Daniel understood. But Daniel knew he must obey God. God would help Daniel obey, and God would take care of Daniel and his friends. So Daniel asked for a test. "Just let us eat our kind of food for ten days, and see if we're healthy."

So God did take care of Daniel and his friends. God made them strong and brave to do what was right, and God took care of them when they obeyed!

Did God help you do right that time it was hard for you? What happened when you did right? (Also tell about how God helped you, and how you felt about your decision afterward. It may be helpful to tell about a time when you forgot to trust God to help you obey too. And how much better you feel when you do remember God, and let Him help you do right.

VALUES CLARIFICATION APPROACH

In the 70s a values clarification approach was widely used in teaching in the public schools and in Christian education. There are in fact a range of teaching strategies available for use within the values arena, and study of them will stimulate a number of ideas for use with Bible stories and other in-class activities. Three good sources for theory-rooted practices are worth studying:

Hennessy, Thomas C. s.j., ed., *Value/Moral Education: The Schools and the Teachers.* New York: Paulist Press, 1979.

Superka, D. et al. *Values Education Sourcebook.* Boulder, Col.: Social Science Education Consortium, Inc., 1976.

Values Concepts and Techniques. Washington, D.C.: National Education Association, 1976.

Here we are taking the simplest approach to clarification: simply describing a value-laden situation, presenting alternatives from which choices must be made, helping the students weigh the alternatives, encouraging the making of and affirming of choices. In values settings in real life the choice is then acted on and life is lived by acting repeatedly on the value chosen.

In using this model with Bible stories we structure the story to show how this process must have gone on in the Bible characters' minds, and let the children enter into the process with them. The Bible story thus is worked through by the children, and in the process they learn how to approach their own choices and consider the alternatives that led God's people to respond in faith to Him. How might the Daniel 1 story be told using this approach? Perhaps something like this.

Daniel and three of his friends were in Babylon, a strange city far away from their home. They were there to go to school and to study hard for three long years. For three years, they wouldn't see their families or their friends, but would live with the Babylonians. Why, they were even given Babylonian names to show they were Babylonians now: they were called Belteshazzar, and Shadrach, and Meshach, and Abednego.

But then a terrible thing happened. Daniel and his friends were given Babylonian foods to eat. And some of those foods were things God had told His people they shouldn't eat. What should they do? Obey God, or live like the Babylonians?

Daniel decided to obey God. So he went to the man in charge of the school in Babylon and asked permission to have different food. But the man in charge was terrified! He liked Daniel. But he was afraid of the king. He told Daniel, "The king himself decided what you should eat and drink. If you don't eat his food, and get sick or something, why, the king will kill *me!*"

Let's think about what Daniel might do now. Here are some things he might do. Can you think of others? (Write the following on the chalkboard, and add any ideas the boys and girls suggest.)

- Refuse to eat the food of the king
- Eat the Babylonian food
- Tell the man in charge he would eat the Babylonian food but not do it

(When the alternatives list is completed, build a list of what might have been important to Daniel in deciding. Again let the children add their ideas to the list. But focus their thoughts on what Daniel's evaluation of the situation must have involved.) *Here are some things Daniel may have*

424

been thinking about. Which do you think seemed important to him? Which were most important to Daniel?

- I don't want the king to hurt me and my friends.
- I don't want the king to hurt the man in charge of the students.
- I don't want to be like the Babylonians.
- I don't want to disobey God.
- I want to trust God and let Him help me do right.

(After talking over these and other thoughts the children may suggest, tell the rest of the story.)

Daniel knew he could trust God to help him if he did the right thing. So Daniel asked for a test. "Let me and my friends eat our kind of food for just ten days, and see if we're still healthy." It was a good idea! Daniel and his friends did obey God, and did eat the food they knew they should. And God did take care of them! At the end of the ten days Daniel and his friends looked healthier than any of the other students! God had taken care of Daniel and his friends when they obeyed Him. How glad Daniel must have been that he trusted God and did what was right.

When this approach is used in a Bible story, a natural and important follow-up activity will help the children identify some difficult thing they know they should do to please God. Help them work through the same process of looking at alternatives and thinking about motives for the choice they may make. Trusting God and letting Him help them do what is right will be one of the key factors in choosing, just as it was for Daniel.

MORAL DILEMMA APPROACH

A final approach is one that will seldom be used with children. Its purpose is not really to communicate the Scriptures or to build understanding, but instead has a technical goal. That goal is essentially to create cognitive dissonance and force moral reasoning to a more significant level. The difficulty in using this approach is that children's capacity for moral reasoning is limited. It might be used, however to cause older children to pause rather than to give the all too glib verbal answers . . . "obey" . . . that sometimes come from our Sunday school teaching. Moral reasoning questions have been used with elementary school children, and there may be times when a moral dilemma approach is appropriate in Bible teaching with boys and girls.

In this approach the story might be told as in the other approaches, with the story again interrupted at the point at which the man in charge of the students expresses his fear. At that point, moral reasoning questions like these might be introduced.

1. Should Daniel eat the food God wants, or disobey the man in charge of the students? What is the right thing for him to do? Why?
2. Is it fair for Daniel to risk the lives of his friends and the man in charge of the students? Is it fair for the king to get angry if people don't eat what he selects?
3. Suppose Daniel eats his own kind of food, and the king asks what he has been eating? What should he say? Why?

VARIED APPROACHES

These illustrations are not meant to show the "right" way to teach Bible stories to children. The way the Bible story is used in a particular lesson will depend on the core truth being taught, and the enactive, illustrative, or imitative use of the story within that total context. What these are intended to illustrate, however, is that there are many ways that the stories of the Bible can be used to teach and apply the great realities of the Word of God to our lives and to the lives of children. We can enrich our teaching of children, and enrich our uses of the Bible, if we are aware of some of the many options that are ours and commit ourselves to designing class processes that communicate the message of the Scriptures in living, vital ways.

PROBE

▶ *case histories*
▶ *discussion questions*
▶ *thought provokers*
▶ *resources*

1. The culminating activity for a person using this text in a class is obvious. It is the writing of a unit of at least three lessons, designed to communicate a core Bible truth to children of a specified age. Each lesson should build in guidance to encourage the building of the faith community, and a variety of learning activities linked with Bible stories that will help children grasp and experience the truths taught. If this text is being used in a course, I recommend that this project replace the final exam. The lesson may be designed for a formal setting like the Sunday school, a children's club, or a Christian school classroom.

2. However, before beginning the difficult task outlined above, here is one more children's lesson to study (see Figure 88). It takes a most difficult core truth as its theme: *God Is just.* Two things are notable. First, the initial activities are designed to help the children feel in-

tensely the impact of justice/injustice, locating the concept on boys' and girls' emotional map. Second, the biblical material is not taken from a story told in the Old or New Testament. Instead it is a "made up" story that provides the context for introducing material from the prophet Amos. It shares what might have happened if a poorer family in Israel in the days of Jeroboam II had actually heard the prophet Amos speak and had experienced the injustices against which he so boldly spoke. The lesson is included to suggest the possibility that more options exist for us in teaching the Bible with children than we are aware of, and to provide a sharper example of linking concepts to the emotional map as well as placing them on the cognitive map.

FIGURE 88

LESSON 1
FOCUS
SOMEBODY CARES[1]

Amos 2:3–16; 3:9–11; 8:1–8

God's anger at injustice shows that He cares about doing right by people.

UNDERSTANDING GOD'S TRUTH

Creative learning activities which give meaning to the Bible study.

Col. 1:9, 10

A. EXPLORING TRUTH THROUGH ACTIVITIES

As the boys and girls come in, give them today's DISCOVER TOGETHER. Have them look at the three cartoons. 9 Juniors can write down what they think the observer in each is thinking or saying. Primaries can talk with a teacher about what is happening and what they think the observer may be thinking or saying.

When class begins, let the boys and girls volunteer to act out (role play) a number of different responses an observer might make to each situation.

* Cartoon 1: dropped books "Observer" might laugh, stomp on dropped papers, help pick them up, offer sympathy, etc.

* Cartoon 2: apple thief "Observer" might say "what a shame," call the police, warn the blind man, say "someone ought to do something," etc.

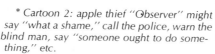

* Cartoon 3: hungry outcast "Observer" might criticize, punish, ask the children to share with the outcast, ask how they think the boy feels, etc.

B. PRESENTING THE TRUTH

Write Amos 3:10, "They do not know how to do right," on the chalkboard. Tell them that once God sent a man named Amos to His people with a special message. God wanted them to know that He was angry because they were not doing right.

Introduce here the word "justice." Write it and the word "just" on a large sheet of paper.

---

[1]*God Is Just.* Teacher's Guide. Unit 7 © 1976, Sunday School PLUS.

Explain: God is just means what is best for people. God cares about people. God wants us to care about people too. It is right to care about others.

Exploring God's Book

Seeing the Bible truth in the Scripture

2 Tim. 3:16

BIBLE BACKGROUND (Amos 2, 3, 8)

In the days of Amos the northern kingdom of Israel (See SERENDIPITY, III, p. 5), experienced great prosperity. Spiritually and morally however there was a deep decline. The worship of God had become a formal, empty ritual, conducted at cities other than Jerusalem, where God had said He was to be worshipped. There was a great gulf between rich and poor, and the wealthy systematically defrauded and profited from the misery of the poor.

Against this background the words of Amos, a poor man himself who was chosen by God to carry words of warning to the rich, reveal clearly how far the lifestyle of Israel had departed from the Divine ideal.

The Old Testament tells us that if Israel had kept God's Law, doing right by the Lord and one another, there would be no poor in the land (Deut. 15:4, 5). God's Law defined a lifestyle which is both loving and just. But the Hebrew people had departed from God's ways. They forgot that love for God and for others underlies the commandments. Now Amos strode into the cities of the rich . . . dusty, dressed in his poor rags . . . to announce the anger of God and His coming judgment.

Through words of Amos Israel was given a fresh vision of God, whose deep concern for all people is expressed in His justice.

Bible Story

You may want to use a tape recorder for the prophet's words in this unit. If so, have someone with a deep voice speak the paraphrased verses of the messages.

ANGRY WORDS

An imaginative telling of the Bible story for Primaries.

Inside the big house, the rich people of the big city of Bethel were having a party. The women had beautiful dresses. They had beautiful furniture made of ivory and gold. They had the best of food on tables piled high with plenty. The men made a lot of money every day.

Outside the big house was a family of poor people. The boys and girls smelled the good smells of the food inside—but they didn't have enough to eat. They were hungry. The man didn't even have a coat to wear. And it was cold. One of the rich men inside the house had taken his coat away because he owed the rich man money.

Inside the house people were laughing and happy: outside the house the poor family was hungry and sad.

(Talk with the children about where they would rather be—inside, or outside? It is not bad to have good things. But sometimes it is better *not* to have plenty. When might that be?)

Suddenly a man marched up outside the house, and called out loudly to the people having the party, Let's listen to what he said.

Prophet's first speech

The Lord says, I will punish you. You have not listened to God's word. You care more about money than about people. You make people give you their coat when they borrow money—they get cold, and you have a party! I will punish you for this, God says (Amos 2:4–16).

(Let the children talk about how the people in the house might feel about the message. How might the poor family feel about these angry words.)

"The people came out from inside the house to listen to the loud voice shouting outside. They saw a man named Amos, a poor farmer. Amos told them God had sent him with a message. A message of warning! God was becoming angry.

Prophet's second speech

God is angry with you. You are His people, but you are not acting as God acts.

You do not know how to do right. You rob others for money. You hurt them. And I will punish you! (Amos 3)

429

(Talk about how the people inside the house might feel now? Would they be afraid? Or laugh at Amos? Why?)

The rich people from inside the house didn't want to listen to Amos. They told him to go away! But Amos was God's messenger. Amos had to tell these uncaring men and women that God does care.

Prophet's third speech

You trample on the needy. You cheat the poor. You sell them rotten fruit to make more money. You would trade a man for a pair of new shoes! I will not forget your actions. I will punish you (Amos 8).

(Talk now about the things that made God angry. How many of them can the children remember? Do they understand what each means? Point out that the bad people did not care about what was best for other people. They only wanted what they thought was best for *them*. But God wants us to care about others and to do what is best for them.)

Questions to Discuss

For Primaries: Rather than ask the usual sequence of questions and talking about the Bible story, let the children draw pictures about the story. Give each crayons and a large sheet of paper. Ask each to "draw the Bible story." When the boys and girls are done, sit in a circle and have each show and tell about his picture.

This approach will help you tell how much your Primaries have grasped of this difficult story and its teaching. Don't expect too much this first class—the concept will be developed in the next weeks.

FOR JUNIORS: This unit involves your Juniors in direct Bible study. Give them an introduction to Amos as God's Angry Man. Let them read verses from the key passages (You may want to ditto selected verses so each child can have his own "focused" text to read and study.)

Give each junior these questions to guide his reading:

Who is God angry with?

What has made God angry?

What is the life of the rich like?

What is the life of the poor like?

What pictures might we draw to show the teaching of this Bible book?

Then begin a mural to show Amos' teaching about God as a Just Person. The mural can be crayoned on a roll of paper table-cloth. Use the second quarter (2nd 6 feet of a 24 foot roll of paper) for this week's portrayal.

The value in doing a mural is in planning the pictures. So get your Junior's together to plan the drawing project. Talk with them about God's anger, what His anger is caused by, the two contrasting groups (wealthy, poor), the relationships between the two, and God's concern for the poor whom the wealthy of Israel did not care about at all.

You may wish also to title the mural portrayal. Perhaps a title from Amos, such as "let justice flow" (5:24), would be good.

Responding to God's Truth

Applying truth to our life. Ps. 119:11

1. Read to the children the first part of Ann Hilliard's story. Talk with them about how Ann felt when she thought no one cared.
2. Then either ask them to think of other people who may feel as Ann felt. (Let them suggest orphans, people overseas in wars or famine, etc. But also help them think of children who are "different" in their school or neighborhood.)
3. Or let them talk about whether they have ever felt this way themselves. Share how other people help them, or make them feel worse. Etc.
4. Or let the children look through a number of clippings from newspapers or news magazines. Let them pick out pictures showing things they believe God would be angry about today. Talk about why they made each selection.
5. Or ask each child to draw a cartoon like those found in the DISCOVER TOGETHER for this week to show "injustice." (Keep relating the concept of justice to God's character, as in the definition presented earlier.)
6. Or look over the DISCOVER TOGETHER cartoons again and decide the best thing for an observer who cares about what is best for people to do.

7. OR take this time to teach the two new songs correlated with this unit: Who Cares? (on page 7) and The Justice Song (on the back cover).

Conclude class this week by pointing out that because God is just, He does care about what happens to each of us. God will do what is best for us, and wants us to think about what is best for others to do.

Close (for the Juniors) with sentence prayers, thanking God that He is righteous and just.

AFTER CLASS CHECK

This week your boys and girls will have learned enough to identify times when they have felt unjustly treated, or to identify examples of unjust treatment of others by drawing cartoons or selecting illustrations from newspaper headings.

INDEXES

Index of Persons

Index of Subjects

A Beka Books, 343
Abstract concepts, 101, 112, 123, 124, 126, 127, 154, 159, 161, 162, 399
Accelerated Christian Education, 344
Acceptance: nonjudgmental, 41
Activities: competitive and cooperative, 354; cuing, 404; feeling-linked learning, 404; learning, 307, 388, 389, 400; multiple learning, 399–401
Adolescence: cognitive development, 115; and identity crisis, 93
Allowances, 272
Alpha-Omega, 344
Altruism: adult, 173; impulses, 135; teaching, 133
Association of Christian Schools, International (ACSI), 342, 344, 350
Awana Youth Association, 318–20

Behavior: and knowledge, 401
Behavioral science, 102–5
Behaviorism, 169
Belonging: communication of, 265–67
Bible: associative uses, 390; communication of, 55, 405; conservatives and, 55, 61; contextual teaching, 389; deductive uses, 388; and emotions, 402, 403, 418; enactive uses, 389; and faith community, 376–77; imitative uses, 390; inductive studies, 306–7; intuitive understanding, 400; as knowledge, 61–62; and knowledge of God, 61; memorization, 389; necessity of data, 121–24; New Testament use of Old Testament, 390; as propositional revelation, 122; reality of, 377–78; reliability of, 64; response to, 323, 377; as revealed truth, 61–62; revelation of reality, 63–64, 122, 386; stories, 387, 388–91; teaching, 62, 122, 125–26, 378 386, 388; and theological issues about children, 73; and truth, 64, 65, 67; truths, 386, 387, 388, 391, use of, 58, 270
Bible Colleges, 295

Bob Jones University, 344
Body of Christ. *See* Church: as a body
Broadway Church of Christ, 221

Catechisms, 178
Character: building of, 56–57
Child evangelism, 372–76
Children's church: definition, 286
Choice: freedom of, 80, 158; responsibility in, 80
Christian education board, 287, 305, 306
Christian schools: associations, 354–55; and beliefs about God, 269; classroom structure, 358–61; cooperation/competition in, 353–54; cultural setting, 341–42; curriculum, 343–44; as a faith community, 349; financial and legal considerations, 342–43; friendships in, 354–55; integration of content and faith, 348–49; and the Internal Revenue Service, 342; method of Bible teaching, 349; and moral development, 361–63; philosophy and purpose, 346–47; teachers and administrators, 345–46
Christian Service Brigade, 318–20
Christlikeness, 240, 306, 358, 377
Chruch: authority in, 302; as a body, 279–80; children in early, 44–45; counterculture movement in early, 136; dynamics of, 301; education in early, 40; expectations of, 289–90; as a family, 280–81, 282; homesize groups in early, 39; institutional, 286–91, 305; intergenerational, 201–3; mutual ministry in early, 39–40; as organism, 279–86
Chruch library, 223–225
Classroom: processes, 400
Cognition: potential for, 117; social, 98, 140–41, 143, 157–59; structural theorists on, 99
Cognitive development: classification level, 109; concrete level, 109; concrete period (7–11 years), 114–15; and conservation, 114; definition, 108; and distancing strategies, 116–17; and faith con-

437

Index of Scripture